MAKING THE GRADE

MAKING THE GRADE

Strategies for Reading in the Social Sciences, Sciences, and Humanities

W. Royce Adams
Santa Barbara City College

D. C. Heath and Company
Lexington, Massachusetts   Toronto

Address editorial correspondence to:

D. C. Heath
125 Spring Street
Lexington, MA 02173

Text Design: Greg Johnson
Cover: Terrence M. Fehr

Published simultaneously in Canada.

Printed in the United States of America.

International Standard Book Number: 0-669-21379-9 (Student Edition)

International Standard Book Number: 0-669-28157-3 (Instructor's Edition)

10 9 8 7 6 5 4 3 2 1

Preface

Upon entering college, many students are confronted with reading tasks that greatly exceed those expected of most students in secondary school. Studies have shown that students' failure to adjust their reading styles to the materials they encounter in college and their purpose in reading them can result in low academic achievement or dropping out. Unfortunately, most content-area instructors neither are trained to help nor accept their responsibility for helping students study-read for their courses. Showing college students how to adjust their reading styles to the various academic disciplines is the main objective of *Making the Grade: Strategies for Reading in the Social Sciences, Sciences, and Humanities.*

Certain general study-reading skills are required in nearly all subjects. Yet each major area of the curriculum has a logic, a body of data, a vocabulary, and a concept load that seeks the form and expression most compatible to it. Discovering the thought patterns and underlying structures particular to a given subject area can greatly improve reading efficiency, for this knowledge enables readers to adapt their reading styles more readily to the materials. The writing patterns found in the social sciences, sciences, and humanities should be treated separately, allowing students to understand the similarities and the differences among the three major academic disciplines.

Most reading–study skills textbooks are structured around the skills themselves, usually with a chapter devoted to each, leaving students with the feeling that the skills are more important than their use in unlocking meaning. In effect, these skills are falsely presented as a content of their own. This is not to deny the importance of these skills. *Making the Grade* does present study skills, but more emphasis is placed on their application to the three major content areas and the reading adjustments needed in each.

Making the Grade begins with an Overview. The rest of the text is divided into three parts. Part I deals briefly with the four basic study-reading strategies: preparing to read, comprehending what you read, processing what you read, and proving you understand what you have read. Here students are introduced to general strategies for study-reading that apply to all disciplines: skills such as attitude, time management, concentration, exploring before reading, marking and note taking, mapping techniques, summarizing, and test taking.

Part II deals with specific strategies for study-reading in the social sciences, sciences, and humanities. The vocabulary and distinct writing patterns most frequently used in each of these areas are presented through actual textbook examples, to which the general skills discussed in Part I can be applied (and for which they can be modified if necessary). The inclusion of imaginative language in the humanities section is an attempt to counter the many reading skills texts that give little or no attention to literature. To believe that students who struggle to read can't handle poetry or fiction is simply not to know them. To teach reading at any level without exposing students to the power of literature is a disservice. As Louise Rosenblatt says in her book *Literature as Exploration,* "Whatever the form—poem, novel, drama, biography, essay—literature makes comprehensible the myriad ways in which human beings meet the infinite possibilities that life offers."[1]

Part III contains practice exercises with actual materials from each of the subject areas. The practices are structured so that students will be required to apply what they are taught in both Part I and Part II. Teachers looking for only objective comprehension checks and quizzes for ease of scoring and grading will be disappointed. While some objective tests and quizzes are used throughout the book—indeed, a section on how to take objective tests is included in Chapter 4—many of the comprehension checks for the practices require longer written responses. Some questions don't have ready answers and are designed to stimulate class discussion

1. *Source:* Noble, 1986, 6.

and debate. In some cases, essay answers are required, despite the unfortunate pressure brought on some institutions to "objectify learning."

Each chapter begins with an overview of its content and a statement of objectives. At the end of the chapter are a summary and page references to the practices in Part III that can be used to develop the skills taught in that chapter. Some written form of student interaction for processing learning is required intermittently after each skill or theory is presented, usually in the form of a reading journal entry. Students are shown how to maintain a reading journal and told why doing so is a requirement for using this book. The journal thus becomes a tool instructors may use to make certain that students are learning correctly. A supplement to this book, which serves as a type of lab manual, the *Student's Reading Journal*, is available for instructors who wish to have their students maintain a ready-made journal. In addition, the *Students' Reading Journal* contains pre- and post-tests in each of the three academic areas.

Answers to the practices in Part III appear in the Instructor's Guide. In addition, resources used in developing this text and suggestions for teaching with the text and the *Student's Reading Journal* are included in the Instructor's Guide.

To help students develop listening-notetaking skills, a video tape containing three twenty-minute lectures will be made available to those instructors adopting *Making the Grade*. All of the three taped segments—one on social science, one on science, and one on the humanities—are from unrehearsed classroom situations. A set of model lecture notes provided by each instructor appears in the Instructor's Guide and can be reproduced for students so they can compare their notes with the instructor's after viewing the video. For a copy of the videocassette, write to the English Editor, D. C. Heath and Company, 125 Spring Street, Lexington, MA 02173 or your local representative.

Making the Grade can be used in various ways, in the classroom or in a laboratory situation. The book does not have to be read in a linear fashion once Part I has been covered. Instructors are free to assign any of the three content areas of Part II in any order. Not all the practices in Part III have to be assigned. In fact, there is more material than can be covered in one term, allowing instructors to select those sections and practices their students need most.

I have tried not to pull any punches in this text. Reading selections are not "watered down" or chosen for their ease of reading; rather, they represent textbooks actually being used in numerous colleges across the country as recommended to me by content-area instructors. The contents of this book are based on the research I have done in content reading and on my thirty years of teaching students that they *can* learn if they want to learn.

Many people deserve acknowledgment for their help in completing this book. Among them are editors Paul Smith, Margaret Roll, and Carolyn Ingalls at D. C. Heath and Company, and the reviewers who shared their expertise: Clare Hite, University of South Florida; Barbara Risser, Onondaga Community College; Bonnie Mercer, Rochester Community College; Gloria de Blasio, Santa Rosa Jr. College; Joseph Thweatt, State Technical Institute at Memphis; and Mary Ludwig, Tacoma Community College.

W. Royce Adams

Contents

Chapter 12: *Expository Writing Patterns in the Humanities* 187

Isn't example an easy writing pattern to spot? **187** What about the use of comparison and contrast in humanities books? **190** What about the cause-and-effect writing pattern? **192** How is definition used as a humanities writing pattern? **195** Don't art and music textbooks frequently use description? **196**

Chapter 13: *Strategies for Study-Reading Fiction* 200

What's the point of studying fiction? **200** OK, so what are some strategies for study-reading fiction? **201** How is reading a novel different from reading a short story? **209** Doesn't reading a novel take lots of time? **209**

Chapter 14: *Strategies for Study-Reading Poetry* 212

Why do people read and write poetry? **212** How should you read a poem? **214** What exactly is overinterpretation? **216** Are there some questions to help with reading poetry? **218**

Chapter 15: *Strategies for Study-Reading Drama* 223

Why do people read plays if they are meant to be seen? **223** How is reading a play different from reading fiction? **224** Do the five drama study-reading guidelines work? **225** Are there literal, interpretive, and affective questions that apply to drama? **231**

Chapter 16: *Research Sources in the Humanities* 238

Isn't doing library research just a lot of busywork? **238** What's the best way to begin? **238** What's the difference between primary and secondary sources? **239** What are some useful reference works in the humanities? **239** What else is available? **243** What happens when you find a good source? **244**

PART III: PRACTICES 249

Overview of the Four General Study-Reading Strategies

PREPARING TO READ

This overview discusses (1) the purpose of this book, (2) the reasons that study-reading books and courses exist, and (3) four general study-reading strategies: for *preparing* to read, *comprehending* what you read, *processing* what you read, and *proving* that you understand what you read. The four strategies and the skills involved in each are defined and explained more fully here and throughout the text. **Your objective in reading this overview is to learn what the four strategies are and how learning to apply them to your textbooks will benefit you.**

Why read this book?

So, here you are reading a book that cost good money and that was written by someone you don't even know. Who is the author, anyway? Why should you trust what he has to say? Will you learn anything worthwhile from reading this book? Why has reading this book been required or recommended? What are you supposed to get from the book? Are you going to enjoy it? Is the price worth it? You may be asking yourself questions like these. If not, you should be.

I can answer some of these questions, at least the ones about the author, by getting personal for a moment. A while back, during my last two academically unproductive years of high school, I worked after school and on weekends for a supermarket chain. When I graduated, I was quite prepared to continue lugging lettuce crates and hauling hundred-pound sacks of potatoes around in the produce department. On busy days, I was elevated to a checkout position or sent behind a false wall to peep through little holes at possible light-fingered souls. At the time, I might have aspired to become the store manager someday. But reflecting back now, I realize I had few thoughts about my future, let alone any thoughts of real consequence. I was just doing what I was doing. Making money seemed more important than going to school. I had a girlfriend. College? Who needed it?

Fortunately, my parents felt otherwise. Although my mother had graduated from high school, my father had been forced to drop out after the tenth grade to go to work. My parents wanted me to have what they felt they had missed. It was my dad who took the time and effort to check into my high-school records, to talk with the school principal, and to get college application forms for me to submit. So, like a dutiful son, I reluctantly did as my parents asked. Somewhat surprised and totally unprepared, I found myself attending Southern Illinois University.

It must have been easy to get into college in those days, because I was no "hotshot" student. In today's educational jargon, I would have been called an "underprepared" student, a student "at risk." My test scores placed me in that ego-deflating course traditionally called "dumbbell English," which immediately threw a blanket of inferiority and self-doubt over me. The textbook and instructor in an economics course I was taking convinced me that I had a serious language deficit. In my philosophy class, those old Greeks—Plato, Aristotle, and Socrates—had trouble communicating to me. And, being used to a fixed schedule in high school and at work, I naively thought that I had time on my hands because I had to attend classes only 15 hours a week. I gave real meaning to the term *freshman*.

College life began for me as an oblong blur. Some students seemed to have a knack for college and to be quite prepared for and familiar with the academic life and community. Not me. Before the end of the first quarter, I had to drop two classes when probation beckoned like a crooked finger. Sweeping up the old supermarket produce department was starting to look better than ever.

I began "studying hard." Or so it seemed. I put in the hours trying, but, compared with other students, I just didn't seem to have the hang of studying. Concentration was often evasive. At times my brain felt wrapped in gauze, filtering out things that should be coming in. Somehow I managed to limp through a second quarter and to start a third. By this time, however, the Korean War was at its peak, and I knew that because of my poor grades, the draft board was about to close in on me. To avoid the army and to get relief from an academic struggle, I exchanged college for four years in the navy.

My navy experience is another story, but the class system in the service, based on who has a college education and who doesn't have, was enough to make me see the advantage of an education. After my "tour of duty," I went back to college, this time at Washington University in St. Louis, with no particular major in mind. Even though the GI Bill provided some financial help, I had to work almost 40 hours a week while taking a full semester course load, because I had a family to support (I told you my navy experience was another story). Now I was classified as a "returning student," meaning that I was older than most and out of academic shape. The first semester that I was back, I went on probation. My advisor told me that I couldn't possibly sustain good grades for graduate school and get through the university curriculum while working 40 hours a week.

He was wrong. With a schedule that allowed virtually no social life but many hours of learning how to study, with no reading or study-skills courses available, no tutors or learning centers, I fortunately learned on my own how to survive in college. Many times I felt that the academic world wanted to be rid of me, that maybe I didn't belong, that I wasn't "a member of the club." Yet I learned how to juggle my limited time and how to win at what in some cases seemed to me nothing more than pedantic hide-and-seek knowledge games played by smug, unsympathetic instructors. But I also had many excellent teachers who introduced ideas, knowledge, and values unknown to me, instructors who taught me to think for myself by challenging beliefs I held out of habit and to see that I was in a privileged educational environment.

The words *psychology, anthropology, philosophy, science, humanities,* and *literature* all took on new meanings. Learning was anything but easy. Life became a routine of work, classes, studying. My family saw little of me. Sleep became a stranger. I turned into a social hermit, with no time to hang around campus for discussions and arguments with other students. It was not an ideal situation. Still, I was older, motivated, and having a love affair with learning.

Gradually and ironically, this "dumbbell" English student found himself leaning toward a major in English. I began writing "acceptable" essays. Some were even praised and read in class as models, although they often had mechanical flaws (I'm still learning to write!). I developed shortcuts for reading long assignments in boring books. I learned to take useful notes that served as study aids for tests. I learned to use the library resources to find out things I should have known already but didn't know. A world of information and interests continued to open up to me.

My attitude toward myself, my life, and the world started changing in a challenging direction. I struggled well enough over the next few years to be admitted to graduate school, where, to my amazement, I decided to become, of all things, an English teacher. No one was more surprised than I. Although I might have become a great checkout clerk, maybe even a grocery-store manager, I'm happy I went in the direction I did.

I share this personal information because I want you to know that we probably have a lot in common. I want you to know that if you want to succeed badly enough in the academic world, you probably can. I have spent much of my professional career trying to convince students like me that college has much to offer and can indeed enrich one's life. I know what it means to feel inferior as a student, to feel lost in courses that assume I know more than I do, to feel sometimes that I don't belong, to be embarrassed by a lack of knowledge. I also know what it's like to give up college for a while, to experience life some, then to come back.

Now what about you? Chances are that this book is being used in some type of reading or study-skills course. Maybe you've chosen to take the course, maybe you've been advised to take it, or maybe you've been told you *have* to take it because of test scores. Maybe you *know* you need the course, maybe you're not sure. Maybe you are getting credit for the course, maybe not. Maybe you're excited about taking the class, maybe not. Maybe you'll enjoy the class, maybe you're not sure. Maybe this book will teach you something worthwhile, maybe not. Certainly, there are plenty of "maybe's" involved at this point. Still, there are "four knowns" I think you should consider.

What are the "four knowns"?

You may hear teachers, counselors, and even parents telling you that reading is the most important subject in school. Well, it's not. Even though you are enrolled in a course that treats reading and study skills as content subjects, they aren't. Reading and study skills are just that—*skills*, not subjects. That's the *first* known. As you read through this book, you will discover that reading selections from various content courses are used in all the drills. This is done so the strategies taught are revealed as merely techniques, guides, or advice on ways to get meaning from content-course textbooks.

Ideally, I should not be writing this book for use in a college reading "course." As an English major, my focus in college was American literature, not the social sciences, sciences, or the humanities. To write this book, I had to read many social science, science, and humanities textbooks to see what, if anything, they had in common. I had to analyze the vocabulary and language usage in the various subjects of each area, the writing patterns used, the organization of the chapters, and the content. I had to read in educational research journals about methods that have been proved to help the student learn and then to develop practices that will help the student acquire those skills. Although I gained a liberal education doing all this, I don't believe that it is necessarily the English teacher's responsibility to teach reading and study skills for courses other than English.

Instead, all subject-matter teachers who require you to buy a textbook—whether in social science, science, or the humanities—should know enough about reading and study skills to help you with any problems you encounter in reading their assigned textbooks. They are the best ones to teach the vocabulary of their subject. They should show you how best to read and use the book they have selected for the course, explain the writing patterns used by the author, help you take notes on their lectures. They should be the ones to teach you the best ways to test your understanding of the course content they teach. They are the experts in their field, best equipped to help you read their subject matter. Unfortunately, though, this seldom happens, leaving *you*—and me—with the task of learning how to learn.

However, there is a fortunate side to all this. Educators have found that many students fail in college because they don't know how to read the assigned textbooks adequately; therefore, special courses have been designed to teach the skills of reading and studying. With the educational system the way it is, you should be happy that courses teaching you how to learn better even exist. I wish they had existed when I began college.

My many years of teaching both content and skills courses force me to agree with Neil Postman, a well-known educator, when he says the following:

> If there is one thing that most teachers in America are *not* concerned with, it is the process of learning. This can be verified by spending a few days visiting representative classrooms . . . [and] evidence from textbooks on methods of teaching, which have as much relevance to what is actually happening in classrooms as campaign speeches have to do with the actual running of government. As any teacher who is concerned with the process can tell you, it is scarcely possible to teach how something is done without also teaching content. How can you teach how a poem might be read without also teaching the poem? How can you teach how a scientific theory is developed without reference to the great theories that the great scientists have constructed?[1]

The answer to Postman's questions is that you can't. That is why much of this book contains excerpts from social science, science, and humanities textbooks, some of which you may actually use in those courses. All the study-reading strategies taught in this book are designed around content subjects with the hope that you will learn how to apply these strategies on your own.

If you select your classes and instructors carefully, you will find that there are subject matter instructors who are concerned with the learning process; they select textbooks designed to help the learning process and teach their courses with an awareness of proper learning techniques. They will do everything they can to help you succeed. Until all teachers at all levels do this, though, books like this one will be necessary.

A *second* known is that many college textbooks are difficult to read. Some seem written more for the approval of other teachers in their field than for a student audience. The fact that you may have trouble reading a particular textbook does not necessarily mean that you are a poor reader. You may simply lack the linguistic background or general knowledge that the author of the text assumes you have. If you are given another book, in a subject for which you do have the background knowledge and language, you may have little or no difficulty with that book. Don't be too quick to condemn yourself if you have trouble with some textbooks.

Recently a research study checked the reading difficulty of a typical chapter in a selected chemistry textbook. The analysis revealed that 67 ideas, plus additional concepts in the margins, appeared in a 9-page chapter.[2] How does a student who has never had chemistry before select the key elements of the chapter? Which of these ideas and concepts are the most important? Ideally, an instructor who chooses to use such a book will be prepared to show you how to distinguish scientific main ideas from scientific details and how best to approach reading each chapter assigned. In most cases, though, you are left to sort things out on your own.

Students coming to college who have read widely and taken college preparatory courses generally have less difficulty, because they have developed their

1. *Source:* Neil Postman, "Learning by Story," *The Atlantic.* December 1989, 120.

2. *Source:* Carol V. Lloyd and Judy Nichols Mitchell, "Coping with Too Many Concepts in Science Texts," *Journal of Reading.* March 1989, 542–45.

reading and vocabulary skills more than those who have not read much. The more you read and increase your vocabulary, the more success you will have in study-reading textbooks.

A *third* known is that many first-year college students have not read much and do not read much. When tested, these students score below the level needed to pass college courses. Then, when these students are told they must take a college reading course because of low test scores, they resent it. Yet studies show that although some students with low reading scores manage to stay in college and get passing grades without enrolling in reading courses, "the type of textbook reading experiences, vocabulary, and comprehension development offered should benefit those students in their quest for educational excellence."[3] So be happy for the opportunity to learn.

When you encounter a difficult textbook or reading selection, don't be too quick to give up. Some of the passages from other textbooks used in this book gave me trouble. I often reread sentences and paragraphs just to make sense of them. I had to look up words I didn't know. I had to *study* the content. Just accept the fact that some reading materials are more difficult to get through than others. Remember that the more you read in a particular field, the easier the reading will become. Give yourself the time and space to improve.

A *fourth* known is that there are certain basic learning skills that can be applied to all reading materials: the four general study-reading strategies explained in the next few pages. In addition, each subject area—the social sciences, the sciences, the humanities—has its own writing patterns and specialized vocabulary. This book, after presenting the four general strategies, focuses on specialized patterns and vocabularies used by writers in various academic disciplines. Then the book provides practice in study-reading strategies, using selections from actual textbooks so that you can become a more independent learner.

Aren't all textbooks alike?

While there are some similarities in textbook writing patterns, there are also some distinct differences in vocabulary and language use. To see these differences, read the following three distinctly different treatments of a bear.

Description 1:

bear, large mammal of the family Ursidae in the order Carnivora, found almost exclusively in the Northern Hemisphere. Bears have large heads, bulky bodies, massive hindquarters, short powerful limbs, very short tails, and coarse thick fur. They walk on the entire sole of the foot and normally move with a slow, ambling gait. However, they are capable of moving with great speed when necessary and some can obtain bursts of 35 mi (56 km) per hr. Most bears can climb trees and swim well. They stand on their hind feet to reach objects with their paws. Nearly all species are omnivorous, feeding on fruits, roots and other plant matter, honey, carrion, insects, fish, and small mammals. A bear is a formidable adversary and may attack a human if it is injured or startled. . . . North American brown bears, including the Kodiak bear and GRIZZLY BEAR, are regarded by many authorities as varieties of *U. arctos*.[4]

---

3. Keflyn X. Reed, "Expectation vs. Ability: Junior College Reading Skills," *Journal of Reading*. March 1989, 537–41.

4. *Source: The New Columbia Encyclopedia,* ed. William H. Harris and Judith S. Levy. Columbia University Press, 1975, 252.

Description 2:

Although grizzlies could be eaten, they were not so palatable as the black bear. They tasted like "coarse pork." The oil, however, was valuable in cooking, better than lard. Bear fat soon came to be preferred to butter or lard in New Orleans, and hunters learned to boil it "upon sweet-bay leaves" which improved its keeping qualities. It kept sweet and good in any season. One big bear when fat in the fall, in preparation for his winter's sleep, might provide thirty gallons of bear oil.[5]

Description 3:

"I shot a bear!" the boy on the dock was calling. "I shot a whole bear!" He was a boy in dungaree coveralls and a soft flannel shirt; both knees were gone out of the coveralls and his carrot-colored hair was stiff and shiny from salt spray. . . .

Earl lay on the dock with his big head on a coil of tarred rope, his hind paws crumpled under him, and one heavy forepaw only inches from a bucket of baitfish. The bear's eyes had been so bad for so long, he must have mistaken the boy with the rifle for Father with a fishing pole. He might even, dimly, have remembered eating lots of pollack off that dock. And when he wandered down there, and got close to the boy, the old bear's *nose* was still good enough to smell the bait. The boy, watching out to sea — for seals — had no doubt been frightened by the way the bear had greeted him. He was a good shot, although at that range even a poor shot would have hit Earl; the boy shot the bear twice in the heart.

"Gosh, I didn't know he *belonged* to anybody," the boy with the rifle told my mother, "I didn't know he was a *pet.*"

"Of course you didn't," my mother soothed him.

"I'm sorry, mister," the boy told Father, but Father didn't hear him. He sat beside Earl on the dock and raised the dead bear's head into his lap; he hugged Earl's old face to his stomach and cried and cried.[6]

The first description is a scientific attempt to classify, to describe a bear's appearance, activities, food habits, and environment. It is a general description that doesn't consider the characteristics of any individual bear. The writer presents mostly facts and uses a scientific vocabulary, such as *Ursidae*, *Carnivora*, and *U. arctos*. Based on observation and measurement, the facts presented would be accepted by anyone who knows about bears.

The second description comes from a social science text. While somewhat scientific in not exploring anyone's feelings about bears, the author of this passage is a historian, more interested in telling us how hunters and explorers used the bear. The language conveys information and does not attempt to affect our emotions or imaginations in any way.

The third description doesn't try to classify the bear or tell how people used it in the past. Instead, the author describes the death of an old pet bear named Earl. To me, this fictional bear seems more real than the bears in the other two passages because it touches our emotions. The boy who shot the bear, at first elated that he had downed the animal, learned that the old bear, someone's pet, was only after his fishing bait. The author creates a vivid picture of the grieved owner holding the dead bear's head in his lap. Whereas the first two passages convey general information, the third passage creates a personal, visual, and emotional experience.

5. *Source:* Kathryn and John Bakeless, *They Saw America First.* Lippincott, 1975.

6. *Source:* John Irving, *The Hotel New Hampshire.* Dutton, 1981, 40.

Different kinds of writing, then, call for different types of reading and thought. When you approach a particular kind of writing, you need to realize that it has its own viewpoint, its own vocabulary, its own purpose. Part II of this book provides more examples and information relative to these differences. Part III provides practices in developing the skills involved in each subject area.

If we put all these "knowns" together, the bottom line is this: You—and you alone—are in charge of your education. This book and the course using it can help you develop the study-reading strategies necessary to read better and more independently. You are being provided an opportunity to learn strategies that will make your reading assignments in academic courses more productive and meaningful. Take advantage of this book, this class, and the support systems your college offers. How well you "make the grade" will depend on your attitude toward learning and how successfully you apply the study-reading strategies presented in this book.

What are the four study-reading strategies?

Whether they know it or not, good students often apply four general study-reading strategies to their textbook assignments. These strategies will be shown in more detail throughout the book. For now, here is an overview of them.

The first strategy is *preparing to study-read*. Before reading a textbook assignment, establish a proper attitude toward learning. Make certain that you are in a quiet place and have enough time to cover the assigned material. Have at hand all materials needed to do the assignment, such as a dictionary, class notebook, supplemental texts, study guides, pens or pencils, and so on. Check over the assignment sheet or notes provided by the instructor. Before reading, survey or preview the assigned pages to see what topics will be discussed and how the assignment connects with what you have already studied. Have in mind the scope of information you will be covering during your reading.

The second strategy is *comprehending what you read*. Good readers separate main ideas from details, draw inferences, recognize the author's biases as well as their own, adjust their reading rate according to the type of passage being read, and add new words to their vocabulary. How well you comprehend depends on your own background knowledge, your vocabulary, and your interest in the subject. Don't worry about speed of reading. Your goal in reading textbooks is to become efficient. Reading rates vary, depending on interest, background information, vocabulary level, and purpose for reading. Speed is not important at this point. When you have finished with this book, though, it will be surprising if you aren't a faster reader than you are now, just by having developed the skills presented here.

The third strategy, *processing what you read*, involves taking notes, keeping a journal, knowing where to do research in a particular field for further knowledge, and connecting what you learn to real-life experiences. This strategy helps you internalize or make what you learn into something useful in the discovery of new interests and unknown potential. College may be the last chance you have to explore a variety of topics, to read from broad areas, to meet people from other cultures who think and act differently than you do, and to discover your own talents, interests, needs, and biases.

The fourth strategy is *proving you understand what you've read*. Once you have completed reading assignments, a quiz, test, essay, or written report usually follows. No matter how well you studied, if you can't perform on these follow-up activities, you'll get little credit for what you know. You ultimately have to show in some way that you understand what you read. More important, you don't want to learn something just so you can pass a test. You should want to learn for life.

All these strategies are explored in detail and explained in the following pages. Your goal should be to learn the skills involved in these strategies and to apply them to your reading assignments in both this class and your other classes.

FINAL THOUGHTS   At this point, you should know that I understand what many of you are likely to be feeling as you begin this book and this school term. The book has been written with you in mind. As you work through it, you will learn to master—a step at a time—the skills that make up the four general study-reading strategies. How well these strategies work for you depends on how willing you are to learn, practice, apply, and modify them to fit your other courses. Learn from any mistakes you may make in the practice exercises in Part III. This book and this course provide an opportunity for you to make the grade if you truly want to.

PROCESSING WHAT YOU JUST READ

✍ As you work through this book, you will periodically be asked to process or synthesize what you have read by summarizing information or writing answers to questions in a reading journal. Keeping a reading journal is an important part of using this textbook because it requires that you stop at key places to make certain you understand what you are reading.

If you are using the *Student's Reading Journal* that accompanies this text, go to page 30 in it and follow the directions given.

If you are not using the *Student's Reading Journal*, I suggest that you buy a regular 8½-by-11-inch spiral notebook to use only with this text. Make certain you have it with you every time you read an assignment here. When you get to a subheading that says "Processing What You Just Read," open your journal and put at the top of your entry the date, the title of the chapter you are reading, and the page number. Then write whatever you are asked to do.

Write with a pen. Pencil tends to smear after a time. Don't write on the backs of pages; doing so can make your writing difficult to read over time. When you are asked to make an entry, don't be too quick to write. Think through what you have to say. Feel free to write anything you want to say in addition to the requested response. Jot down questions you need to ask the instructor; note anything that surprises you or that you want to learn more about. The reading journal is ultimately yours and will help you learn to process what you read (Strategy 3) as well as provide you with a record of what you learned during this course. Your instructor will probably ask to see your reading journal periodically, so write neatly.

Keeping a well-maintained, thoughtful reading journal is important if you are to get the maximum from this book. Recent research has shown that journal keeping has many learning benefits. Believe me, it's not just busywork but an important comprehension activity.

If you don't have a notebook you can use as your reading journal right now, write your answers to the following questions somewhere from which you can later copy into your reading journal.

In your reading journal, answer the following questions. Feel free to look back for the answers, but use your own words as much as possible. Use the example in Figure 0.1 on page 10 as a model.

1. What are the "four knowns"?
2. How can they affect you as a student?
3. Explain in your own words the four general study-reading strategies you are going to learn more about.
4. What is your reaction to what you just read?

When you are finished, you will be ready to begin reading about **Strategy 1: Preparing to Read.**

WHAT DO YOU THINK?

Thinking back on it, I couldn't imagine a more crucial skill than summarizing; we can't manage information, make crisp connections, or rebut arguments without it. The great syntheses and refutations are built on it.

Mike Rose, *Lives on the Boundary*.

FIGURE 0.1   Example of a reading journal page

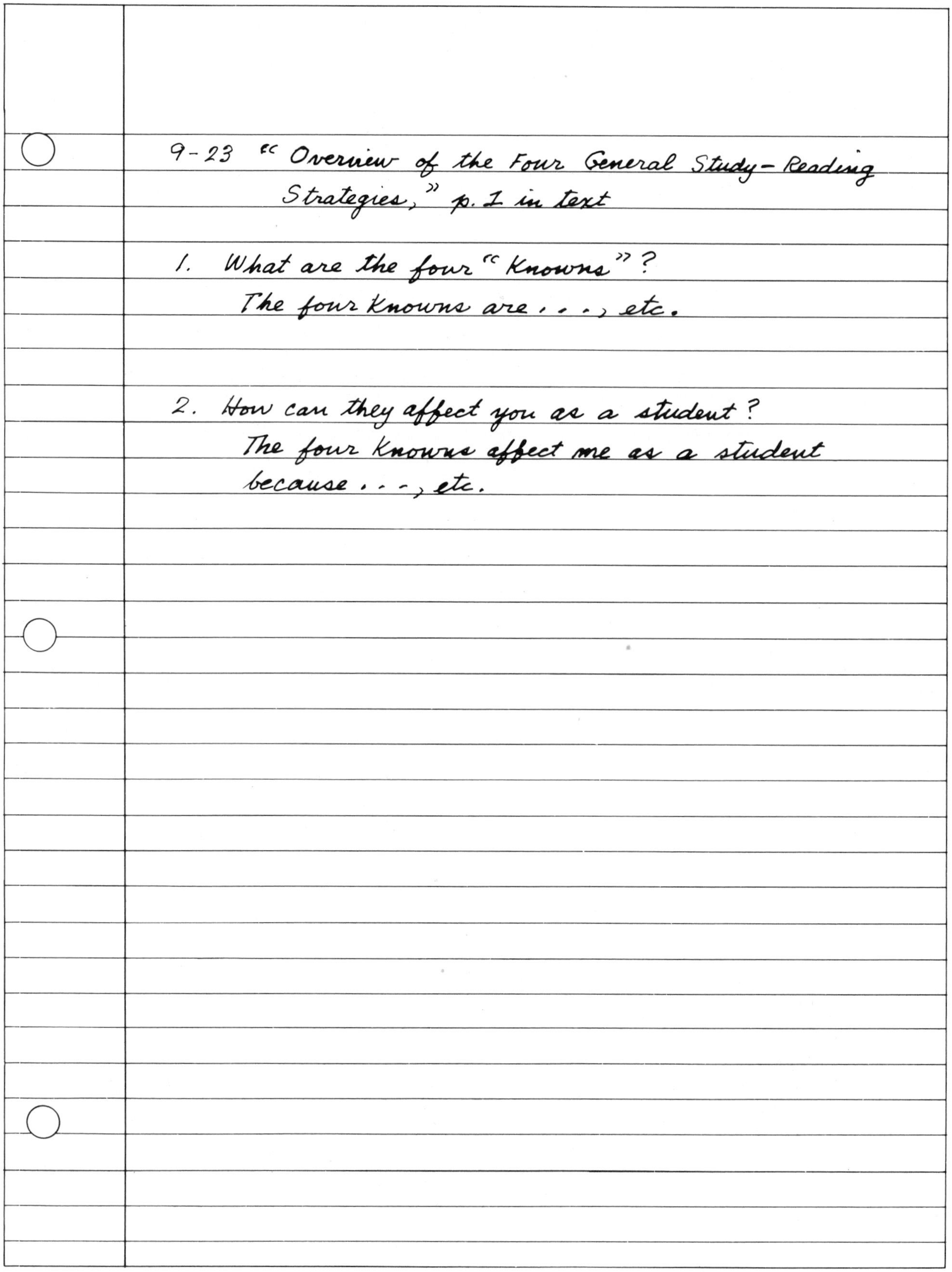

9-23 " Overview of the Four General Study-Reading
         Strategies," p. 1 in text

1. What are the four "Knowns"?
    The four Knowns are . . ., etc.

2. How can they affect you as a student?
    The four Knowns affect me as a student
    because . . ., etc.

PART I

THE FOUR GENERAL STUDY-READING STRATEGIES

CHAPTER 1

Strategy 1: Preparing to Read

PREPARING TO READ

Preparing to read an assignment means more than having the textbook in front of you. Preparedness involves (1) establishing the proper attitude toward learning, (2) selecting a quiet place for studying, (3) allotting time to complete the assignment, (4) having the materials necessary for marking and note taking on hand, (5) understanding the assignment, and (6) knowing the structure and organization of your textbook. These points are explained in more detail in this chapter. **Your objective in reading this chapter is to understand and learn to apply the skills necessary for *Strategy 1: Preparing to Read.***

What's attitude got to do with it?

Whether you succeed in college depends in part on your attitude toward yourself and learning. Doing well in college requires a motivation to learn, an interest in acquiring knowledge, and a willingness to learn from mistakes. Motivation, your reasons for attending college, is very important. If you enrolled in college simply because everyone else did, or because it's what your parents want, or because you've heard it will lead to a better job, you may be starting off on the wrong foot. You should be attending college because it's what *you* want, or because you want to find out if it's what you want.

Part of your motivation for attending college may be that you've heard it's the best way to get a better-paying job. That may be true; many people do go to college for that reason. However, the true purpose of attending college is to read, hear, and think about people, places, and ideas you never knew existed. College provides a chance to learn about nations, cultures, religions, and historic events that have brought the world to where it is today. It offers an opportunity to meet and talk with people from all parts of the globe. Above all, it allows you to pursue a wide variety of interests and to learn who you are and where your talents lie. A proper college education will challenge your present beliefs and either strengthen them or expand your limited awareness. A proper college education will help you make sense of the world and your responsibility to it as an educated person. A degree obtained without the addition of these benefits doesn't contain much value for you or society.

Is it difficult to learn how to study?

Studying and learning require hard work, more than most first-year college students realize. You need determination and a willingness to put time and effort into educating yourself. Contrary to what many students think, most learning does *not* take place in the classroom. An instructor may introduce you to information about a course, or help clarify certain points, but the real learning takes place when you are on your own, going over and rewriting class notes, reading and taking notes from textbook assignments, doing extracurricular reading in the library, researching and writing reports and essays, and having study sessions with classmates. These activities require time, energy, and a determination to succeed. They take you beyond just passing a course. If you are not prepared for such a commitment, then you may not be ready for college. Come back when you can commit yourself.

The independence that college offers can trip you up if you're not aware. The first few weeks of college may offer a false sense of freedom from past routines. Because most classes only meet two or three days a week, it appears that you have more free time than you do. In some classes it doesn't seem to matter if you're late, because they are too large for anyone to notice or the instructor doesn't say anything about tardy arrival. Some instructors don't even take attendance. No one checks to see if you brought your textbooks or if you are keeping up with the assignments. But taking advantage of these "freedoms" can create a dangerous, immature attitude that reflects an inability to manage your time properly.

At times, some classes may seem too difficult. That's when you really test your attitude and motivation. Do you drop out, blaming the teacher or the textbooks? Do you blame your high-school teachers for not preparing you? Do you blame your parents for not making you study more? Do you blame yourself, convinced that you lack learning ability? Or do you assume the responsibility for learning, by working harder, and seek help if you need it?

College isn't meant to be easy. If it turns out to be, then in all likelihood the classwork is below your ability. Some courses demand more of you than others. If the work seems too difficult, causing you anxiety, talk to your instructors about your problems. Instructors maintain office hours so they can discuss your work with you. Most instructors welcome the chance to get to know you better, to answer your questions, and to exchange ideas. They will respect you for your concern and interest.

If you don't want to talk with your instructor, see a counselor. Take advantage of any resources your college has, such as counseling centers, learning centers, tutorial services, your adviser, school nurse, or dorm resident. You won't be the first student or the last who needs to ask for help and guidance. Colleges are well aware of the problems students face, and most of them are equipped to help or direct you to someone who can.

Learn from your abilities, and improve in your areas of weakness. If you plan to stay in college for an A.A. (associate of arts) degree, a B.A. (bachelor of arts) degree, or beyond, it's important to learn about yourself at every opportunity. The time you spend in college may be your only chance in life to concentrate so much on learning what there is to learn, who you are, and what your many possibilities may be.

PROCESSING WHAT YOU JUST READ

✍ If you are using the *Student's Reading Journal* that accompanies this text, go to page 32 in it and follow the directions given.

If you are using your own notebook as a journal, answer the following questions as you were directed on page 8.

1. Why are you reading this book, and what do you hope to gain from it?
2. What is your attitude about taking a reading or study-skills class?
3. What kind of student are you? Are you committed to learning? Are you motivated and responsible? Do you want to be a student?
4. Why are you in college? What do you hope to gain from attending?

Where is the best place to study?

Obviously the best place to study is a quiet area without a lot of distractions. Try to establish a place where you can study on a regular basis, a place that's used for nothing but studying. Set up an area of your own, in some quiet room where you live, with a desk or table and all your books at hand. Many study specialists recommend that your desk face a blank wall. Don't try to study around a television or radio. Some students claim they work better with music in the background. Studies show, however, that once you become aware of the background music you are no longer concentrating on your studies. Train yourself to study without it. If you must have music playing, keep the volume low and the music mellow.

WHAT DO YOU THINK?

America's young have become literally attached to the TV, the stereo, and the radio. And if you take those away, they go through more loss and despair than if you took away their parents.

David Klimek, psychologist

If you don't have a study room at home or where you are living, use the library. Many college libraries have study rooms you can reserve if the main room is too distracting for you. If you must leave your home to study, make certain that you take what you need with you: the correct textbooks, assignment sheets, course syllabus, pens or pencils, class notebook, and so forth. The library provides a study support system with access to reference books, specialized dictionaries for various subjects, and librarians who can help you find what you need.

Although it has been shown in studies that students of comparable intelligence who study in the library get 0.4 grade point higher than those who study elsewhere, the library is not without distractions, either. Here, from another study, are the types and frequency of distractions that interrupt the library study of college men and women:[1]

Distraction	Men	Women	Both
Conversation	32%	26%	29%
Aimless looking around	15	15	15
Leafing through books	14	10	12
Students walking by	12	7	10
Applying makeup	0	16	8
Attraction to others	9	5	7
Daydreaming	7	5	6
Reading and writing letters	4	7	5
Arranging hair and clothes	2	7	4
Miscellaneous	5	2	4

1. *Source:* D. C. Troth, "A Ten-minute Observation in the Library." *School and Society,* 29, 1979, 336–38.

You can see from this table the importance of finding an environment even in the library that maximizes your chances of developing good study habits.

Is there a best time to study?

The best time to study, even if it's only for 20 to 30 minutes, is before and after each class. Allow time before each class meeting to review any assignments you already have read for the course and go over any notes you made from the previous class meeting. Review any notations or markings you made in your textbook when you read the assignment. After class, review your lecture notes and immediately rewrite them, connecting lecture notes with textbook notes. If you have any questions about part of the lecture, write them down. Then talk them over with the instructor during his or her office hours before the next class meeting.

If you must study for long periods of time, take frequent short breaks. Always take time out between chapters or when you switch to a different textbook. Stretch, relax, rest your eyes; just don't fall asleep! Also, it is better to study the same subject at the same time each day, developing a habit that helps you settle down to work.

Everyone's biological clock varies. Some people study better in the morning, others at night. The most important point is to study when you are not tired. Each study period should be about an hour long, with a ten-minute break. Don't schedule your classes back to back; doing so robs you of time in between to digest what you've learned by reviewing before and after class meetings. Some students take all their classes in the morning, one right after the other, so that they will have a "free" afternoon. But unless you are very disciplined, such a schedule usually results in a great deal of wasted time and poor grades.

What's a good way to manage study time?

The structure of your college schedule, unlike your high-school schedule, can appear to leave you with lots of time. But in reality it doesn't. For instance, if you take 15 units of coursework during a term, that means you will spend at least 15 hours a week in the classroom. Instructors expect you to devote *at least* 2 hours of study time for each class period. That comes to *at least* 30 hours a week. Together with class time, that totals a minimum 45-hour study week. Unfortunately, too many beginning students don't use the time between their classes wisely; they put off their studying until nighttime, when they are either too tired or too involved in social activities.

How well you do in college will have a great deal to do with how well you manage your time. Never miss the first day of classes. That's when instructors usually give you handouts that provide information on their office location, office hours, telephone extension, an overview of the course, assignments, and grading policies. They explain what the course will cover, what textbooks you will need, and any long-term assignments, such as term-paper projects. If an instructor doesn't provide this information, don't be timid, ask for it. Use this information to plan your schedule.

Look at your class schedule on a full-term basis as well as on a weekly basis. One efficient way to plan a schedule is to buy a calendar with room to write in notations for each day of the week. After going through all your class handouts, write in all long-term-assignment due dates for all your classes. Then, as a reminder, make a notation on the calendar for each of those same assignments on a date two weeks before it is due. Next, for each class you are taking, write down the time and room number on each day the class meets during the term, noting any holidays. Do this in pencil in case you need to change your schedule later. Now you have a visual reminder of the times during the term you will be in class and the days projects are due.

Most time management experts also advise that you buy or make up a weekly time chart divided into one-hour segments. Once your class schedule has been finalized, fill in each day of the week with all your activities indicated from 7:00 A.M. to midnight. During the first two weeks of class, write down how you spend your time each day. By the third week of classes, you should make a final schedule that eliminates any spots where you have wasted time. Then follow this schedule through the term. Figure 1.1 shows how such a schedule might look. Notice how study times are arranged according to class days and times. For example, this student studies English last on Mondays and Wednesdays because it's her first class to meet on Tuesdays and Thursdays. She has also scheduled time to review material in a class right before the class meets and right after. Take a minute to notice how this student utilizes her time.

Why bother with all this scheduling stuff?

When I was preparing this book for publication, one teacher who reviewed the manuscript recommended that I not include all this information about scheduling. Why bother? she asked. Most students never trouble to make out schedules anyway. That may be true. Still, the fact that students don't often make schedules does not mean they shouldn't. If you tend to waste time or procrastinate, or if you just feel that you want to get the most out of your time, then make a schedule. At least try it for the first few weeks of class. Many students feel a schedule truly helps them.

With each term, you have to reprogram yourself for new courses, times, and classrooms. Usually, after a week or two, you go from one class to another without much thought. If, right from the beginning, you establish times of the day when you study for a particular class, you will build a routine that you follow almost automatically. Studying will then become a habit, not something you try to fit in here and there when it suits you.

If you have trouble organizing your time, here are three steps you can follow to develop proper time management. *First*, make a study plan like the one in Figure 1.1. It may take a week or so of modifications based on class changes, class conflicts, and general orientation to a new term. *Second*, follow your schedule until the routine has become a habit. This is the difficult part, because, until the habit has been formed, you often have to force yourself to stick with the schedule. Habit forming takes practice; you can't wait until you are in the mood to study. *Last*, you have to make a conscious effort to establish good study conditions and to apply the study skills that help you avoid being distracted. Forcing yourself to concentrate on studying is not easy. Sometimes distractions from outside sources interfere; sometimes inner distractions, like daydreaming, lead you astray. That's why establishing a proper atmosphere is part of preparing to study-read.

What about students who have to work?

If you have to work attending college, it is better not to take a full course load. I did, and in retrospect I'm sorry. Too busy to meet many other students I would like to have known better, I had no opportunity to share or study information. I suffered from lack of sleep, often studying inefficiently when I was too tired. Frequently, both my job and my college work suffered. I was in too big a rush to get through and realize now that I tried to do too much. "Too old too soon, too wise too late."

Working and attending college can be mixed, but few students can work more than 15 to 20 hours per week and still find enough time and energy to attend classes

FIGURE 1.1 Study plan

	MON.	TUES.	WED.	THURS.	FRI.	SAT.	SUN.
7:00 – 8:00 A.M.							
8:00 – 9:00	Study speech	English class	Study speech	English class	Study speech		
9:00 – 10:00	Speech class	↓ Review English	Speech class	↓ Review English	Speech class	WORK	
10:00 – 11:00	Review speech / study math	BREAK / study psych	Review speech / study math	BREAK / study psych	Review speech / study math	WORK	
11:00 – 12:00	Math class	Psychology class	Math class	Psychology class	Math class	WORK	
12:00 – 1:00 P.M.	Review math / LUNCH	↓ Review psych	Review math / LUNCH	↓ Review psych	Review math / LUNCH	WORK	
1:00 – 2:00	Study history	LUNCH	Study history	LUNCH	Study history	WORK	
2:00 – 3:00	History class	COMMUTE	History class	COMMUTE	History class	WORK	
3:00 – 4:00	Review history / BREAK	WORK	Review history / BREAK	WORK	Review history / BREAK	WORK	
4:00 – 5:00	Study psych	WORK	Study psych	WORK	Study psych	WORK	
5:00 – 6:00	BREAK	WORK	BREAK	WORK	BREAK		
6:00 – 7:00	DINNER	DINNER	DINNER	DINNER	DINNER		
7:00 – 8:00	Study English	Study math	Study English	Study math	Study English		Review math & psych
8:00 – 9:00	↓	↓	↓	↓	↓		Study speech
9:00 – 10:00							
10:00 – 11:00							
11:00 – 12:00							

and do the assignments. Many students try, only to have to drop classes later in the term. This wastes more time than starting out with a lighter class load. You need to evaluate how many hours of work and how many hours of coursework you can handle. If you must work many hours, then take fewer classes, even if doing so means taking a longer time to get a degree. Statistics show that more and more students are taking longer to complete their college work. And that's OK.

Don't be in a hurry to get through college. A tendency exists for students to rush through school. Why? Attending college is not just accumulating credits for a degree. College is, or should be, a unique intellectual and social environment. Give yourself time to take advantage of its opportunities.

WHAT DO YOU THINK?

Students today limit learning to the classroom and the fast-trackers are setting the pace. They're defining themselves according to external things — money, power, status — and choosing courses that will get them these things. They're terribly preoccupied with their bodies but they've lost touch with mental disciplines. What this means is that fewer students are using higher education to find out who they are, the sort of human beings they ought to be, or even the kinds of careers that are worthy of pursuit.

Alexander Astin, UCLA Higher Education Research Institute

What does all this have to do with preparing to study-read?

Everything I have said so far pertains to study-reading preparation. Without the right attitude, motivation, setting, and enough time to think about and react to what you read, little will come from reading your textbook assignments. Nothing in this book will work for you without the proper approach to the college environment, the courses you take, the books you read, and yourself as a student. In his book, *This Is Reading*, Frank Jennings states:

> Meaning and understanding are necessary to thought. They are not sufficient. To think . . . requires that we do something to ourselves and our surroundings with what we have learned. We have to make judgments about these matters and act upon them too. Unless we change our attitudes and behaviors, we are not thinking.[2]

Properly done, reading is a thinking act, provided that thought goes into what is read. Too many students open a textbook to an assigned page and begin reading with no preparation, little concentration, and no thought. Their false goal is simply to get the assignment done rather than to think about its validity and significance. Such an approach treats learning as a chore, not an opportunity. If that is how you work, then perhaps you aren't ready for college activities.

Yes, there will be times when you feel like you're fighting a textbook assignment, when you don't think you can concentrate, when the material isn't making sense, when the content bores you, when things in your personal life overwhelm your ability to study. Such times are part of the college package. Expect them. But if you are prepared for those times, you will be able to apply the skills and strategies presented in this book to help you through them.

2. *Source:* Delta, 1965, 141.

PROCESSING WHAT YOU JUST READ

✍ If you are using the *Student's Reading Journal* that accompanies this text, go to page 32 in it and follow the directions given.

If you are using your own notebook as a journal, answer the following questions as you were directed on page 8.

1. Make a study plan similar to the one in Figure 1.1, establishing how you will spend your time during the coming week. Stick to it as best you can.
2. Explain why you don't need a study plan.

What's the best way to prepare to read a textbook?

Let's back up a minute. Before you read your first textbook assignment for any course, take a few minutes to explore the textbook itself. Have you, for instance, already explored this book? Are you aware of its purpose, its organization, the way chapters are structured, the total scope of the book? How does what you are reading now fit in with the rest of the text?

✍ If you don't already know the answers to the following questions, look through this text and answer them.

1. What is the full title of this book? (This is found on the *title page* at the beginning of the book.)

   _____

2. When was it published? (Look at the *copyright date* on the back of the title page.)

   _____

3. What is the purpose of this book, and for whom was it written? (Read the *Preface* for this.)

   _____

   _____

   _____

4. How is this book divided and organized? (Look over the *Table of Contents.*)

   _____

   _____

   _____

5. How does the information in this section fit in with the next section and the last one?

   _____

   _____

6. Which of the following does this book have? (Circle all letters that apply.)
    a. index
    b. glossary of terms
    c. appendix

You should apply these questions to each of your textbooks. The helpfulness of this information varies from textbook to textbook. However, the more you know about the contents of your books, the more useful they can be.

But how do you prepare to read an assigned chapter?

You should prepare to read an assigned chapter by first surveying or previewing it. By taking a few minutes to look over an assigned chapter, you force your mind to settle down and concentrate on the content you are going to be learning. There have probably been times when you've started reading an assignment, only to find that your mind has drifted and you aren't aware of what you're reading anymore. That generally happens when you haven't prepared yourself for the task at hand.

Here are some methods for preparing to study-read taken from dozens of studying techniques:

1. Read the title of the chapter carefully. Think about what it means. Connect it with the title of the textbook. Ask yourself what you may already know about the subject. Turn the title into a question that can serve as a reading guide, a purpose for reading. For instance, if the title of a chapter is "Newton's Laws of Motion," turn it into these questions: What are Newton's laws of motion? Who was Newton? What's important about Newton's laws? Then do the same thing with any chapter headings and subheadings. Read looking for answers to your questions.

2. Many textbook chapters provide an overview at the beginning, some provide a list of objectives for you to accomplish while reading, and some include a summary of the chapter's contents at the end. Look for these elements, especially a chapter summary, and read them carefully. Textbooks aren't mystery novels, so there is no reason you can't look ahead to see how the chapter ends. Reading an overview or summary before you read the entire chapter gives you the key points to look for and helps focus your mind on the subject. If there are no such aids, try to predict or anticipate what the chapter will cover. You don't have to be right; just having some speculations will help you concentrate better when you read.

3. Look for any reading aids the author has supplied, such as pictures, cartoons, graphs, tables, and charts. Read their captions. These may not make total sense when you are previewing, but they make a connection with the chapter content. Notice boldfaced or italicized words. They are usually key words that you will need to learn when you read the chapter in detail.

4. Look over the chapter for any questions or objectives that may be spaced throughout or at the end. Think about them as you read, looking for answers when you start study-reading carefully. Many instructors base their class tests on the objectives and questions in the chapter.

5. Check the length of the assignment. If you can't read it all during the time you have for study-reading, divide it into logical parts. Make a check mark at the point where you plan to stop.

All this doesn't take as long as you may think. Giving a few minutes to these steps aids concentration and helps you think about what you are reading.

PROCESSING WHAT YOU JUST READ

✍ If you are using the *Student's Reading Journal* that accompanies this text, go to page 34 in it and follow the directions given.

If you are using your own notebook as a journal, answer the following questions as you were directed on page 8.

1. Compare the way you generally prepare to study-read with the way you just learned.
2. Explain what you need to do in order to be better prepared to study a particular course you are taking now.

Does all this preparing stuff really work?

Whether the strategies for preparing to study-read really work for you depends on how well you understand and apply them. Studies have shown that they definitely have worked for many students.

✍ Beginning on page 23 is part of a chapter from a textbook[3] used in college business courses. Suppose you are taking a business class and this is your first reading assignment. Practice what you've been learning about surveying or previewing by looking for answers to the following questions and writing the answers in the spaces provided.

1. Read only the chapter title and headings within the chapter. In the space provided, make up three questions about the content that you could use as reading concentration guides.

_____

_____

_____

2. What are the major parts into which the chapter is divided?

_____

_____

_____

3. What do you predict the chapter will say about business communication today?

_____

_____

_____

4. Based on the summary at the end of the chapter, what are the main points that will be made in the chapter?

3. *Source:* Ruth G. Newman, *Communicating in Business Today.* Heath, 1987, 2–13.

---

5. What kinds of questions does the author ask at the end of the chapter?

---

6. What do you already know about this subject, and how long would it take you to read this chapter?

BUSINESS COMMUNICATION TODAY

1

Business Writing: How Is It Different?
The Spoken Word at Work: Changes and Choices
Summary
Discussion Problems

ompany X is a large manufacturer of computer software products. If today you were to stroll through its lengthy corridors, you would see employees at every level—from technicians to senior executives—putting their thoughts down on paper. Systems analysts are writing instructions to programmers, who are laboring to distill their thoughts into neat, compact phrases. Marketing people are presenting surveys to product managers. People in technical communications are compiling information for a new product brochure. The company president and the chief financial officer are tearing apart a ten-page rundown of company finances. A network of communication, much of it written, extends from employee to employee, upwards, downwards, and sideways. This network also reaches beyond headquarters to Company X's West Coast subsidiary, to customers and potential customers, to suppliers, the media, and government agencies, and to many other people who this day are the audience for the ideas, messages, and explanations important to the company's operations.

Company Y does not manufacture a product, but it does have something to sell. It is a successful service organization, and its business is employment. On this day, counselors and recruiters are spending a great deal of time on the phone contacting potential employers and setting up interviews to screen job candidates. They are also participating in interviews and conferences. Nevertheless, in offices up and down the halls, at any odd minute when people are alone, you will probably spot them writing— jotting memos to each other about new clients and rumors of job opportunities, corresponding with employers, and drafting reports to senior members of the firm about potential growth markets, new ideas for attracting clients, and the many other subjects that preoccupy them.

Company Z is not a large firm. It is a family-owned enterprise that rents and sells uniforms to hospitals, laboratories, and other medical facilities. Its office and management staff includes about 30 people, and virtually half of them are "jacks-of-all-trades." Today Carol Taylor is out of the office, visiting a new bio-tech facility where she believes many new kinds of protective uniforms will be required. When Carol returns to the office, she will file a trip report to be read by her co-workers and retained in the company's active file. Her regular officemate, Peter Jones, is at his desk putting the finishing touches on a lengthy report about the company's current public relations and advertising tactics. This report is important to

Peter because he knows that Bob and Joan Green, the firm's owners, will be reviewing his ideas about how to get the company's name mentioned in the newsletters of several of the city's larger hospitals.

In these three settings we catch a glimpse of some of the activities that in our system of free enterprise we call *business*. But if we ourselves are not part of the daily business scene (and often even if we are) business may be only an abstraction. Economics textbooks tell us: "Business is the production of goods and services to be sold for a profit." And, of course, business is precisely that. But it is also the daily reality of the people who produce those goods and services, men and women who get up in the morning with specific ideas and tasks on their minds and head out their doors bent on "making a living"—exchanging time, energy, skill, and insights for wages or salaries. To perform effectively throughout their workday, they must share information, ideas, and opinions with one another. In short, they must communicate.

If anything is obvious about today's business environment, it's that words have more importance and power than ever before. If we had started with A and described a different firm for each letter of the alphabet, we still would not have exhausted the almost limitless number of verbal interactions that businesses require of their employees during a single day of normal operations. Business people communicate to describe ideas, processes, products, and services.

The size and intricacy of our business organizations have made communication more essential than ever before, and our technology has made it more abundant. Even a simple instrument like the telephone offers communications options that once would have seemed astonishing—messages relayed to new locations, conference calls across great distances, and many other possibilities. Today, when a manager has something to say, the means to say it quickly are almost always at hand.

Even though spoken communication has increased, today's technological revolution has diminished neither the volume nor the frequency of written communication. The written word, whether typed onto paper or entered onto a terminal screen, continues to lie at the heart of business communication. As in the past, the operation of a business continues to demand that people express their ideas in words and transmit those words in a form that can be retained if necessary, usually with some degree of permanence. For most employees, this requirement makes writing a critical skill.

Rather than decreasing the amount of writing and reading that employees face, modern technology has added to its abundance by increasing the ease and speed with which we can collect, store, and transmit data. The copying machine alone has revolutionized the way business communication is handled—not just the author of a document but anyone with access to a copier can easily retain or transmit the information that document contains. And the computer has, of course, made information management a whole new business discipline. Even small companies are likely to have memory typewriters and word-processing equipment, and large establishments commonly make use of terminal-to-terminal electronic mail and desktop computers that allow managers and employees to access enormous pools of information.

No wonder that effective communication (and especially effective writing) is given such a high priority in today's business environment. Brevity and clarity are watchwords, and the favorite edict of programmers—"garbage in, garbage out"—can be taken as an admonition to all business people. Mangled ideas, snarled sentences, and muddy verbiage are wasted effort. Moreover, if sent to the wrong person or badly timed or tactless, even a clear and succinct message can be counted as waste.

■ Business Writing: How Is It Different?

As human beings, we think with words, and our thoughts move so swiftly that it is difficult to be conscious of the words that contain them. But writing alters this state. As we write, we make our thoughts visible and accessible; we can refine, revise, or expunge them. All writers, whether business writers or poets, are engaged in this process of capturing thoughts by carving them into words. Nevertheless, people put their thoughts into writing for very different reasons, and these differences are rooted in the writers' feelings about potential readers.

For instance, people who write in their diaries are capturing memories and impressions, perhaps to savor them later but rarely to share them. Poets and novelists normally hope for an audience, but with or without one, they generally feel compelled to write. Two groups of writers, however, write exclusively to be read: journalists and business writers. For both of these, the effect their words have on an audience is critical. This similarity can provide some provocative insights into the pressures and challenges that confront business writers. Because they write for an audience, both reporters and business writers are greatly concerned about clarity; they know that their readers have limited time and many distractions. Furthermore, as writers, both reporters and business people are working under severe time constraints; they know the importance of deadlines. And finally, despite the pressures on them, both groups are highly accountable for their accuracy.

It is interesting to compare the *lead* of a news story to the tightly constructed opening of a well-written business memo. Both are digests of critical information that cater to the reader's need to know what will follow. And, in a sense, both are contracts between the writer and reader—

promises that the indicated information will be the writer's primary focus. The lead can, for the same reasons, also be compared to the *executive summary*, which introduces a long report and provides a capsule of its contents for executives who must set priorities concerning what documents to read, how thoroughly, and in which order.

Despite such similarities, there is an important difference in the outlooks of reporters and business writers. For reporters, events and their own reactions to those events provide the primary motive for writing. But for business writers, concern for the reader's response is usually paramount. If you ask business people why they write, nine times out of ten the answers you receive will focus on the reactions of prospective readers. The reason for writing will be described in words such as these:

"Because I want to persuade *them* to . . . "
"Because I need to ask *them* to . . . "
"Because I want to sell *them* a . . . "
"Because we want *them* to understand our . . . "
"Because we would like *them* to explain their . . . "
"Because we would like *them* to attend our . . . "

More than any other kind of writers, business people try to know as much as possible about their readers. A simple profile generally will not suffice; they must have information about their readers' particular situations, interests, and needs. And since they write to people inside and outside their own organizations, to people they supervise, to peers, and to superiors, business writers do not always have easy access to this information. For instance, to plan an ad campaign or design a sales letter for a specific audience, a marketing specialist will spend time and resources learning about that audience's concerns. Similarly, almost any business writer will usually need to appraise his or her intended reader before writing.

■ The Spoken Word at Work: Changes and Choices

Just as the importance of writing has increased in today's business environment, so has the importance of speaking. In a typical workday, business people use speaking and listening skills in a wide spectrum of activities. A list of the most obvious and important might include interviews and conferences (face-to-face and by phone), meetings (work sessions and formal gatherings), speeches, and formal presentations. It's also true that in the compressed schedule of a busy workday even casual conversations can contain nuggets of important ideas or signals concerning the way people feel

about projects or problems. Therefore, although our primary focus in this text is on written communication, we will not disregard the spoken word.

Today, selecting the right medium for sending a message can be an extremely important decision. The age-old practice of dictating a letter to a secretary who transcribes it and sends it off to the mailroom is losing ground. First of all, the cost of this traditional method of communicating has skyrocketed. In 1930, the cost of preparing such a letter was approximately 30¢; ten years ago, it was $3.31; in 1984, it had reached $7.60.* Making a long-distance phone call today will therefore often be less expensive than writing a letter. Moreover, new technologies are now available that make oral communication especially attractive. Conference calls are regular events in most companies, and in large companies teleconferences that provide not only audio but also video reception are frequently used to disseminate information among large numbers of employees, sometimes over great distances.

Writing and speaking in a business setting have much in common: both are audience-centered, task-related, and purposeful. But they are not equally effective in all situations. Sometimes written communication serves best, and at other times a form of oral communication is more appropriate; frequently both must be used in tandem.

The two primary factors that business people consider when deciding whether to write or to speak are *spontaneity* and *permanence*. At times, business communication needs to be spontaneous and immediate; at other times, it should be carefully considered and controlled. On some occasions, a permanent record of the transaction is essential; on others, permanence may be undesirable.

*Reported in *The Boston Sunday Globe Magazine*, January 1, 1984, this cost survey was done by the Darnell Institute of Business, a Chicago-based publishing and subscription service founded in 1917.

THE SPOKEN WORD AT WORK: CHANGES AND CHOICES

7

Compare, for instance, the relative benefits of a letter and a phone call. If expressing yourself powerfully is your main concern and you need to choose your words with great care, a letter will certainly serve you better. On the other hand, if your main concern is to see how the other person will react or to draw a prompt response, a phone call can provide immediate feedback and allow you to revise on the spot. It is important to remember, however, that any benefits are available to both parties. Although a copy of a letter provides the writer with a permanent record, the letter itself is a permanent record for the recipient. Therefore, to offer a preliminary idea or a tentative conclusion, a phone call (or face-to-face conference) is often the best option.

Let's see how you might choose to handle some specific situations.

1. You want to recommend a new piece of office equipment to your manager. Do you write an explanatory note outlining your rationale and giving cost estimates before meeting with her to propose the purchase? Or do you call first to see if she shows any initial interest before taking the time to research costs?

2. Harry Black from marketing is late with his report on a new ad campaign for your group's product, and your manager has asked you to see why marketing has been giving the group such poor support. Do you phone Harry or go see him in person? Do you drop him a line first to let him know what's on your mind? Are there other people you should contact before getting in touch with Harry?

In the first instance, if you have a close working relationship with your manager and if you feel that she is likely to share your belief that the equipment is needed, then you probably can simply phone her for a quick okay before preparing your cost estimates. On the other hand, if you feel that your suggestion is likely to surprise her, you might want to document your rationale and the likely costs in a written report, giving her a chance to consider it before you request a meeting.

In the second instance, your course of action depends a great deal on your assessment of Harry and what you know about his current behavior. Has he been really busy—or is he simply stalling? If the report is late because he has been busy, a friendly memo may be enough of a push. If he ignores the memo, you might have to try to arrange a face-to-face meeting. And if he refuses to meet with you, a formal memo on which you copy your own manager might be the best strategy—and you certainly would keep a permanent copy of that memo on file.

There is no absolutely right procedure in either of these cases. The lesson to be learned is that one does have alternatives and it is important to consider them carefully.

The issues of spontaneity and permanence are significant even when selecting among the available modes of oral communication. One might, for instance, prefer a face-to-face conference to a phone conversation because the conference will allow the audience to be monitored more closely. Not only voice signals but also facial expressions and body language (posture, gestures, etc.) will suggest feelings and attitudes, thereby helping the speaker to know precisely when to clarify ideas or revise an approach. As a further illustration, suppose that you have the choice of disseminating information through either an informal meeting or a videotape presentation. The meeting would provide a freewheeling forum for communication, but the presentation would allow you to choose your words carefully and to retain a clear record of how you stand on the issue examined.

Although strategic considerations should be given the most weight, time and cost factors must also influence decisions about the most appropriate mode of communication. These two factors depend heavily on available technology. As we have already pointed out, given today's wage scale, the time-consuming process of dictating and transcribing a letter can be extremely costly; on the other hand, in many large companies an employee can compose a memo on a terminal, press the "send" key, and distribute the message throughout the firm or even across the country. Also, companies of all sizes use the Postal Service's Express Mail or overnight delivery by private couriers to expedite written correspondence. All of this suggests that if time or cost is an important issue, it is best to do some investigation and make comparisons. The results are often surprising.

For most business people, writing and speaking tasks intersect throughout the day. To carry out a single project often requires phone calls, correspondence, and meetings. At the beginning of this chapter, we looked through a wide-angle lens at a panorama of communications at several different firms. Now we will zoom in on two other companies to follow two employees as each moves through a fairly typical workday.

Tod Andrews

At a large, well-known financial service and investment house, Tod Andrews, a recently hired marketing researcher, arrives at work to hear the phone ringing in his cubicle. The person on the other end is his boss, Frieda Barrymore, who manages the marketing research function. "I have a new project for you, Tod, " she says.

Frieda explains to Tod that she had a long meeting the previous afternoon with several of the company's senior officers. A large part of the discussion centered on a tax-exempt bond fund that the company is currently offering in 13 states. The issue was whether or not to distribute the fund nationally, as proposed by the fund manager. "Tod, you will have to do some solid research on this one. We need to know how the fund is doing and to examine the pluses and minuses of offering it nationally. You'll want to talk to Herb Zolski, the fund manager; but, of course, keep in mind that he's really eager to see its distribution expanded. And maybe there are some tax wrinkles here—I'm wondering why we originally limited this one to only 13 states."

Tod takes some notes as he talks with Frieda and then suggests that he can have his preliminary report ready in about a week. She feels that he ought to be able to get back to her sooner on this, but when he explains that he feels he needs to talk with all the district managers who currently handle the fund, she agrees that a week is an appropriate amount of time.

Tod heads for a centrally located terminal and logs on; in a matter of minutes he has the names, addresses, and telephone numbers of all the district managers. Next, he drafts a letter to them explaining that he will be contacting them by phone for pertinent information about the bond fund. In addition, he contacts the fund manager to set up an appointment at the earliest opportunity, which turns out to be later the same day. Tod also takes one more step. He's heard through the grapevine that Herb Zolski, an old-timer in the company, can be somewhat of a dragon to deal with and is especially impatient with younger employees who don't appear to know the lay of the land. Tod therefore telephones David Ames, a senior researcher with whom he frequently works, and arranges a business lunch. He hopes to be briefed on some of the ins and outs of managing tax-exempt funds.

For the remainder of the morning, Tod holes up in his cubicle with a copy of the bond fund's prospectus, a legal document that describes the features and mechanics of a fund to customers.

Analysis	Let's list some of the communication tasks that fill up Tod's workday:

- He talks to his boss on the phone and takes notes on the conversation.
- He studies the prospectus, takes notes on the main features of the fund, and lists points to discuss with the district managers and fund manager.
- He has a lunch meeting with David Ames to help prepare himself for the conference with the fund manager.
- He participates in that conference, takes notes, and later dictates a quick review of the meeting into his personal tape recorder.
- He writes a memo to the district managers to let them know he will be calling them in a few days. (The memo is transmitted by electronic mail and is received at the outlying offices the same day.)

By the time Tod leaves the office at the end of the day, he has spent more than 75 percent of his time in tasks that require communication skills. And this proportion is not due solely to the nature of his job. As we look over the shoulder of Joan Fisk, an employee who holds an entirely different kind of position in a very dissimilar company, we will see that communication plays an equally crucial role in her workday.

At 8:30 in the morning Joan Fisk is driving down the highway heading for her office. She is a quality control supervisor at a large Midwestern manufacturing company whose major product is plastic sheeting.

Joan Fisk

As Joan's car heads toward the plant, she is thinking about the presentation that she will be giving at 2:30 that afternoon to her boss, several other members of the department, and three of the division's senior executives. She has been preparing this talk on "the costs and benefits of quality assurance" for a full week. Yesterday she made the final corrections on the graphic displays she will be using, and now she is bothered by the thought of one more detail she wishes she had added.

On the way to her office, before crossing the plant floor to the east wing, she stops at the cafeteria for a cup of coffee. With the Styrofoam cup in her hand, she enters her office, and before she can put the cup down, sees a pink slip taped to her phone: "Call Rudy in Baltimore. Urgent!" She wriggles out of her coat and reaches for the phone.

Rudy Denby is a wholesaler who distributes the sheeting manufactured by Joan's company. He tells her that one of his largest customers, Bondex, has notified him that an entire shipment is defective and that it will be returned to the plant. Rudy says Bondex has enough sheeting to last until the replacement order is received, but if that order is defective, then "goodbye customer." Furthermore, Rudy feels that a letter of explanation should be sent immediately to Hugh Morley, Bondex's purchasing manager, to assure him that there will be no further problems with the product.

Joan promptly makes two more phone calls. First, she telephones Seth Ordway, the product manager in charge of the particular kind of sheeting that was shipped to Bondex. This is the second complaint that she has received about a shipment of this product. She knows the news she has to impart will not be happily received, but the problem has to be handled promptly. She believes an informal talk over lunch might be a good way to open the discussion, so she sets up an appointment to lunch with Seth at noon. Her second phone call is to her boss, Ted Stein, manager of quality control; he listens to her story and (as she expected) asks to see the preliminary draft of the letter going to Bondex. In the time remaining before lunch, Joan puts the finishing touches on her afternoon presentation and starts drafting the letter.

When Joan's workday comes to an end, she has engaged in the following communication tasks:

Analysis

- She has talked to Rudy Denby regarding the Bondex fiasco.
- She has also talked to her boss, Ted Stein, about the same situation.
- She has had a lunch meeting with the product manager, Seth Ordway.

- She has polished her costs/benefits presentation and checked the order of the graphics.
- She has drafted a letter to Hugh Morley, the Bondex purchasing manager, reviewed it with her boss, and begun a new draft.
- She has delivered her presentation, and then returned to her office to take notes on the follow-up discussion and to sketch out an action plan based on the suggestions she received.

Like Tod Andrews, Joan Fisk has spent most of her day communicating. Although they work in different parts of the country, in very different companies, and at very different jobs, these two people cannot carry out their responsibilities with any degree of success unless they are proficient communicators. Few business people today can.

■ Summary

In today's business environment words have more importance and power than ever before. Modern technology, rather than decreasing the amount of writing and reading required of employees, has added to it. Whether writing or speaking, most business people cannot carry out their job responsibilities successfully without the ability to communicate effectively.

Two groups of writers—business writers and journalists—write exclusively to be read. Both groups strive for the utmost clarity. Both are also held accountable for their accuracy. Both must meet deadlines imposed by others. But while reporters deal with their own reactions to events, business writers are primarily concerned with the response of their readers. They need to know as much as possible about their intended audience.

In the business arena, the importance of the spoken word may equal that of the written. Business people use speaking and listening skills in a wide spectrum of activities throughout the workday. Speaking, like writing, should be audience-centered, task-related, and purposeful. In determining whether a message is to be spoken, written, or both, communicators weigh the advantages of spontaneity versus the need for permanence. Time and cost considerations may also influence the choice of medium.

■ Discussion Problems

1.1 Consider an actual job that you or someone you know well holds or has held. (It could be a summer job or a college internship.) Describe the kinds of communication most frequently needed and the methods used. Describe ongoing kinds of communication that are important to running the business.

1.2 John McClintock supervises Lewis Bantam. In the last few months John has observed that Lewis's performance on the job has been slipping. Lewis's projects are frequently behind schedule, and he is often late arriving at work. If you were John, would you arrange a conference with Lewis or send him a carefully written memo? Would you do both? Explain.

1.3   Barbara Whitman has to tell the five employees she supervises about several new and fairly complex procedures that will change the department's method of doing inventory. How should she handle this responsibility? Explain.

1.4   Would Tod Andrews be wiser to prepare a questionnaire for the district managers rather than attempting to confer with them by phone? Explain your answer. Can you think of alternative procedures that Tod might use?

1.5   Do you think that Joan Fisk's plan to discuss a difficult problem at lunch is a good strategy? Explain your answer. If you feel that another option would be better, describe it.

Your wording will probably vary, but compare your responses to these:

1. Three very basic questions could be made from the title and headings, such as these: What is business communication like today? How is business writing different from other kinds of writing? What are the changes and choices of the spoken word at work? Study-reading for answers to those questions would give you good comprehension.

2. There are four major parts indicated right under the chapter title, based on the chapter headings: "Business Writing: How Is It Different?" "The Spoken Word at Work: Changes and Choices," "Summary," and "Discussion Problems."

3. There is no right or wrong answer here, but, based on the title, chances are you predicted the chapter would explain what business communication is like today.

4. The importance of the written and the spoken word in business today is stressed, with technology increasing the amount of reading and writing employees must do.

5. The questions are for discussion rather than for written responses and seem to be based on people and events described in the chapter.

6. Responses are too varied here for any model. Everyone's background and reading abilities determine the answer, but you now know how much of your time and effort will be needed to read and understand this chapter, something you didn't know before you explored the chapter.

Generally, you would apply these methods for preparing to study-read in your head, an approach that would take far less time than it did to answer these questions. But if you can get into the habit of using these methods, you'll develop your own best way for using previewing to make certain you get the maximum from your study-reading time.

FINAL THOUGHTS You have learned that being prepared to study-read involves (a) your attitude toward learning, (b) the place you have chosen to study, (c) the time you have allotted to reading the assignment, (d) having the materials necessary for marking and note taking on hand, (e) a clear understanding of the assignment, and (f) an awareness of the structure and organization of the textbook. You can modify the six guide questions on pages 21–22 to help you preview or survey a chapter before reading it. Doing so helps you focus on the content, aids your concentration, and results in better comprehension of what you read. The next chapter will deal with developing your comprehension skills as you study-read.

Source: Reprinted by permission of UFS, INC.

PROCESSING WHAT YOU JUST READ

✍ If you are using the *Student's Reading Journal* that accompanies this text, go to page 35 in it and follow the directions given.

If you are using your own notebook as a journal, answer the following questions as you were directed on page 8.

1. Summarize the main points of this chapter.
2. Discuss how committed you are to becoming a student. How much time can you devote to studying? If you have to work, will you adjust your schedule accordingly?
3. Explain this statement by Robert Fulghum: "There is no one way to learn anything—learn how you learn."

For more practice on **Strategy 1: Preparing to Read**, go to Part III, page 250.

CHAPTER *2*

Strategy 2: Comprehending What You Read

PREPARING TO READ   The second general study-reading strategy, comprehending what you read, requires an ability to (1) identify topics and distinguish main ideas from supporting details, (2) make inferences, (3) recognize bias, and (4) mark textbooks. **Your objective in reading this chapter is to learn what *Strategy 2: Comprehending What You Read* includes and how to use it in connection with *Strategy 1*.**

Why is reading comprehension so important?

Although listening to lectures and participating in class activities involve learning, you will probably be required to spend more time in college reading than undertaking any other learning activity. If you are truly going to take advantage of your college experience, you will also want to read as much as you can on your own. Reading, as already mentioned, is a skill. As a skill, it requires continual development and flexibility based on purpose, need, and interest.

Skills have to be learned and once learned have to be maintained. Otherwise, like muscles, they weaken and get out of shape. For college students who lack reading skill flexibility, the going is rough. They are confronted with a reading load that exceeds by far anything they have encountered before. If they approach all their reading assignments in different classes with the same style, they are likely to find themselves hopelessly behind, no matter how hard they work. The lack of study-reading skills is a serious problem and a major cause of college dropouts.

But the study-reading techniques you learn now can also take you beyond college. Unless you plan to stop reading and learning once you have obtained your degree, you will need reading skills for the rest of your life. More information appears in print now than ever before. Almost every trade and profession demands that you keep up with constant changes and innovations. When you are on the job, you will again be on your own and required to be aware of advancements in your field. The skills you master now can become lifelong habits that will keep you well informed, keep you from being manipulated by incorrect information, help you see through false political promises and campaign rhetoric, and help you resist biased, lazy, or stagnant thinking. College is merely a starting place, not the end to learning.

What's the difference between topics and main ideas?

The key to all good reading is recognizing (1) what an author is writing about, (2) the main idea being expressed, and (3) the details or evidence used to support the main idea. A **topic** is the subject being written about. The **main idea** is the primary point the author wants to make about the topic. To prove or argue the main idea, a writer must supply **support** by using details, facts, examples, reasons, events, or comparisons.

37

✍ The following passage comes from the chapter on business communications that you read in Chapter 1. Read it, and then answer the questions that follow. Have your dictionary handy in case you need it.

> Just as the importance of writing has increased in today's business environment, so has the importance of speaking. In a typical workday, business people use speaking and listening skills in a wide spectrum of activities. A list of the most obvious and important might include interviews and conferences (face-to-face and by phone), meetings (work sessions and formal gatherings), speeches, and formal presentations. It's also true that in the compressed schedule of a busy workday even casual conversations can contain nuggets of important ideas or signals concerning the way people feel about projects or problems.

1. What is the *topic* of the paragraph?

    _____

2. What is the *main idea* regarding the topic?

    _____

    _____

In this case the topic of the passage is the importance of speaking in today's business world. The author's main idea is that the importance of speaking in today's business environment has increased just as much as the importance of writing has. Both the topic and the main idea are revealed in the first sentence. Sentences that reveal the topic and the main idea are called **topic sentences**, as you probably already know. The rest of the paragraph provides support for the main idea by giving examples of the place and importance of speaking in the business world.

✍ The following paragraph, in its original source, comes right after the sample paragraph you just read. Read it, then answer the questions that follow.

> Today, selecting the right medium for sending a message can be an extremely important decision. The age-old practice of dictating a letter to a secretary who transcribes it and sends it off to the mailroom is losing ground. First of all, the cost of this traditional method of communicating has skyrocketed. In 1930, the cost of preparing such a letter was approximately 30¢; ten years ago, it was $3.31; in 1984, it had reached $7.60. Making a long-distance phone call today will therefore often be less expensive than writing a letter. Moreover, new technologies are now available that make oral communication especially attractive. Conference calls are regular events in most companies, and in large companies teleconferences that provide not only audio but also video reception are frequently used to disseminate information among large numbers of employees, sometimes over great distances.

1. What is the *topic* of the paragraph?

    _____

2. What is the *main idea* regarding the topic?

    _____

3.   What *support* for the main idea is provided?

_____

_____

_____

_____

Again, the topic and main idea appear in the first sentence. The topic is selecting the right medium for sending a message in the business world. The main idea is that proper selection of the medium is extremely important. Two major supporting examples are provided: (1) a comparison of the cost of sending a letter and making a phone call, and (2) the attractiveness of new technologies, such as conference calls and teleconferencing. This paragraph is actually supporting the main idea of the first sample paragraph you read, about the increasing importance of speaking in today's business world.

✍ Here is the next paragraph from our sample. Look for the topic, main idea, and support as you read it so you can answer the questions that follow.

> Writing and speaking in a business setting have much in common: both are audience-centered, task-related, and purposeful. But they are not equally effective in all situations. Sometimes written communication serves best, and at other times a form of oral communication is more appropriate; frequently both must be used in tandem.

1.   What is the *topic* of the paragraph?

_____

2.   What is the *main idea* regarding the topic?

_____

_____

3.   What *support* for the main idea is provided?

_____

_____

_____

_____

In this case the topic is both writing and speaking in a business setting. The main idea is that the two have much in common but are not equally well suited to all circumstances. Notice that the first sentence does not contain all of the main idea; it is continued in the second sentence. Support is provided by comparing and contrasting writing and speaking: Both are audience centered, task related, and purposeful. But sometimes written communication is better; at other times speech or oral communication is better; and at times it is necessary to use both. The word *but* is important here, indicating a shift in the point being made.

✍ Here is the next paragraph from our sample. Read it, looking for the topic, main idea, and support so you can answer the questions that follow.

> The two primary factors that business people consider when deciding whether to write or to speak are *spontaneity* and *permanence*. At times, business communication needs to be spontaneous and immediate; at other times, it should be carefully considered and controlled. On some occasions, a permanent record of the transaction is essential; on others, permanence may be undesirable.

1. What is the *topic* of the paragraph?

   _____

   _____

2. What is the *main idea* regarding the topic?

   _____

   _____

3. What *support* for the main idea is provided?

   _____

   _____

   _____

   _____

The topic here is the two basic factors, spontaneity and permanence, that business people have to consider when deciding whether to use written or oral communication. The main idea is that there is a need for both. The support, which is not very specific, simply says that sometimes communication should be spontaneous, at other times controlled; on some occasions, a permanent record should be kept; at other times, it is not desirable. Notice the use of the phrases *at times, at other times*, and *on some occasions* to help distinguish the supporting examples.

✍ Now read the last paragraph in the series on business communication. Again, look for the topic, main idea, and support so you can answer the questions that follow.

> Compare, for instance, the relative benefits of a letter and a phone call. If expressing yourself powerfully is your main concern and you need to choose your words with great care, a letter will certainly serve you better. On the other hand, if your main concern is to see how the other person will react or to draw a prompt response, a phone call can provide immediate feedback and allow you to revise on the spot. It is important to remember, however, that any benefits are available to both parties. Although a copy of a letter provides the writer with a permanent record, the letter itself is a permanent record for the recipient. Therefore, to offer a preliminary idea or a tentative conclusion, a phone call (or face-to-face conference) is often the best option.

1. What is the *topic* of the paragraph?

    _____

2. What is the *main idea* regarding the topic?

    _____

    _____

3. What *support* for the main idea is provided?

    _____

    _____

    _____

    _____

In this paragraph there is no one topic sentence. While it is easy enough to pick out the topic, it's not that easy to identify the entire main idea. The topic is the relative benefits of a letter and a phone call. The main idea is that there are times when one is better than the other and that any benefits are accessible to both parties. The support is a series of comparisons and contrasts: If powerful expression is the main concern, a letter is better. If it's important to get someone's reaction or a quick response, a phone call is better. This example supports the first part of the main idea. The second part is supported with the example of a letter being a permanent record for both parties; thus, it may be best to offer an untested idea by phone with no record. Notice the placement and use of the transitional expressions *on the other hand, however,* and *therefore* as reading aids.

It is important to be able to recognize main ideas and support in paragraphs, but we generally read passages longer than one paragraph at a time. A main idea in one paragraph may in fact be a supporting detail for a larger main idea. Here, for instance, are the sample paragraphs you've already read as they appear together:

main idea

support

Just as the importance of writing has increased in today's business environment, so has the importance of speaking. In a typical workday, business people use speaking and listening skills in a wide spectrum of activities. A list of the most obvious and important might include interviews and conferences (face-to-face and by phone), meetings (work sessions and formal gatherings), speeches, and formal presentations. It's also true that in the compressed schedule of a busy workday even casual conversations can contain nuggets of important ideas or signals concerning the way people feel about projects or problems.

main idea

support

Today, selecting the right medium for sending a message can be an extremely important decision. The age-old practice of dictating a letter to a secretary who transcribes it and sends it off to the mailroom is losing ground. First of all, the cost of this traditional method of communicating has skyrocketed. In 1930, the cost of preparing such a letter was approximately 30¢; ten years ago, it was $3.31; in 1984, it had reached $7.60. Making a long-distance phone call today will therefore often be less expensive than writing a letter. Moreover, new technologies are now available that make oral communication espe-

support { cially attractive. Conference calls are regular events in most companies, and in large companies teleconferences that provide not only audio but also video reception are frequently used to disseminate information among large numbers of employees, sometimes over great distances.

point 1 { Writing and speaking in a business setting have much in common: both are audience-centered, task-related, and purposeful. But they are not equally effective in all situations. Sometimes written communica-

Point 2 { tion serves best, and at other times a form of oral communication is more appropriate; frequently both must be used in tandem.

main idea { The two primary factors that business people consider when deciding whether to write or to speak are *spontaneity* and *permanence*.

support { At times, business communication needs to be spontaneous and immediate; at other times, it should be carefully considered and controlled. On some occasions, a permanent record of the transaction is essential; on others, permanence may be undesirable.

support for previous paragraph { Compare, for instance, the relative benefits of a letter and a phone call. If expressing yourself powerfully is your main concern and you need to choose your words with great care, a letter will certainly serve you better. On the other hand, if your main concern is to see how the other person will react or to draw a prompt response, a phone call can provide immediate feedback and allow you to revise on the spot. It is important to remember, however, that any benefits are available to both parties. Although a copy of a letter provides the writer with a permanent record, the letter itself is a permanent record for the recipient. Therefore, to offer a preliminary idea or a tentative conclusion, a phone call (or face-to-face conference) is often the best option.

Notice how the last paragraph is really support for the main idea of the fourth paragraph: Sometimes business communication needs to be spontaneous and at other times permanent. Then notice how both the fourth and fifth paragraphs are really support for the main idea of the third paragraph: Written and oral communication have much in common, but they are not equally well suited to all circumstances. If we continue to work backward, we see that the progression of main ideas goes from rather specific to more general. Notice how the main ideas fit together:

Paragraph 1	The *importance of speaking* in today's business environment has increased just as much as the *importance of writing* has.
Paragraph 2	Proper *selection of the medium* (speaking or writing) is extremely important.
Paragraph 3	Written and oral communication have *much in common, but they are not equally well suited to* all circumstances.
Paragraph 4	Sometimes communication *should be spontaneous*, at other times *controlled*.
Paragraph 5	There are *times when one form of communication is better than the other*, and any *benefits are accessible to both parties*.

Notice that the main ideas of the last four paragraphs together support the larger main point of the first paragraph.

When you read your assignments, you need not only to detect main ideas in individual paragraphs but also to see how the ideas fit together as a whole.

PROCESSING WHAT YOU JUST READ

✍ If you are using the *Student's Reading Journal* that accompanies this text, go to page 37 in it and follow the directions given.

If you are using your own notebook as a journal, answer the following questions as you were directed on page 8.

1. Explain in your own words the difference between a topic and a main idea.
2. Why is knowing the difference between the two important for good comprehension?

Is it true that marking up a textbook while reading really helps distinguish topics from main ideas and support?

Properly marking your textbook and making notations in the margins can help you visually separate topics from main ideas and support. But, more important, marking assists reading concentration and provides a great aid for test review. True, books are costly, and you might get a good resale price for an unmarked textbook at the end of the semester. But the money you will get for a used book is far less than what you will gain by marking up your book so that it is useless to anyone but yourself. The basic tools for learning in college are books. Marking them effectively is one of the most intelligent ways to use your tools.

Let's face it. Most textbooks are not exciting reading. Unless you are vitally interested in the subject, the reading can seem boring or too difficult. Sometimes personal matters interfere with your ability to concentrate on reading assignments. In these cases, reading closely can be a real problem. That's another way marking up a book can help.

Marking up a book—as long as it is your own—is not sacrilegious. Many textbooks are even designed for that purpose, providing large margins on the pages and space for your own notes. Just the act of underlining certain phrases, writing about points of agreement and disagreement, noting something you want to look into further, brings the content more sharply into focus and preserves those points in your memory.

Reading may look like a passive activity, but it isn't. Although you can't have a face-to-face conversation with the author of a book, you can have a type of dialogue through marking. You can respond to an author by writing down any questions you have in the margins, jotting down a "yes" or "no" as your reaction to a statement, circling words you need to look up, and underlining main ideas in order to find them quickly when you review. Marking your reactions and questions in your book forces you to deal more closely with what you are reading.

Good textbook marking is a skill. There is no one way to mark up reading passages, but you should be careful to select only the main ideas and important details. Doing so provides you with a visible outline of the material. Don't accept everything you read. Ask questions, disagree, rephrase key ideas, connect your experience to what you are reading. If you don't already have your own workable marking techniques, try these:

1. Underline major points.
2. Draw a vertical line in the margin to emphasize a point already underlined.
3. Put a star or asterisk in the margin by an important statement.
4. Place a question mark in the margin by a statement you don't understand.
5. Use numbers to indicate a sequence of ideas or parts of a concept.
6. Circle words that you need to look up or that might be on a test.
7. Write your reactions and comments in the margins.

Notice the way in which one student marked the following passage while reading.

writing / speaking
import.

Just as the importance of writing has increased in today's business environment, so has the importance of speaking. In a typical workday, business people use speaking and listening skills in a wide spectrum of activities. A list of the most obvious and important might include interviews and conferences (face-to-face and by phone), meetings (work sessions and formal gatherings), speeches, and formal presentations. It's also true that in the compressed schedule of a busy workday even casual conversations can contain nuggets of important ideas or signals concerning the way people feel about projects or problems.

6 examples
of need
for speaking
skills

Today, selecting the right medium for sending a message can be an extremely important decision. The age-old practice of dictating a letter to a secretary who transcribes it and sends it off to the mailroom is losing ground. First of all, the cost of this traditional method of communicating has skyrocketed. In 1930, the cost of preparing such a letter was approximately 30¢; ten years ago, it was $3.31; in 1984, it had reached $7.60. Making a long-distance phone call today will therefore often be less expensive than writing a letter. Moreover, new technologies are now available that make oral communication especially attractive. Conference calls are regular events in most companies, and in large companies teleconferences that provide not only audio but also video reception are frequently used to disseminate information among large numbers of employees, sometimes over great distances.

what effect have
computers had?

cost
factor

new
technology
factors

Writing and speaking in a business setting have much in common: both are audience-centered, task-related, and purposeful. But they are not equally effective in all situations. Sometimes written communication serves best, and at other times a form of oral communication is more appropriate; frequently both must be used in tandem.

same >

difference >

The two primary factors that business people consider when deciding whether to write or to speak are spontaneity and permanence. At times, business communication needs to be spontaneous and immediate; at other times, it should be carefully considered and controlled. On some occasions, a permanent record of the transaction is essential; on others, permanence may be undesirable.

2 important
factors for
decision

Compare, for instance, the relative benefits of a letter and a phone call. If expressing yourself powerfully is your main concern and you

Example
letter vs. phone

need to choose your words with great care, a letter will certainly serve you better. On the other hand, if your main concern is to see how the other person will react or to draw a prompt response, a phone call can provide immediate feedback and allow you to revise on the spot. It is important to remember, however, that any benefits are available to both parties. Although a copy of a letter provides the writer with a permanent record, the letter itself is a permanent record for the recipient. Therefore, to offer a preliminary idea or a tentative conclusion, a phone call (or face-to-face conference) is often the best option.[1]

Notice that the passage is not overmarked. Only key ideas, questions that need answers, and reactions are noted. The student has now made a permanent record of reactions to and involvement with the passage. These markings will be helpful come review time.

PROCESSING WHAT YOU JUST READ

✍ If you are using the *Student's Reading Journal* that accompanies this text, go to page 37 in it and follow the directions given.

If you are using your own notebook as a journal, answer the following questions as you were directed on page 8.

1. Write a paragraph that begins "There are at least three good reasons for marking your textbooks when you study-read." Then provide three reasons.
2. Explain why you probably will or will not mark in your textbooks.

What does it mean to make inferences?

Sometimes authors don't come out and say exactly what they mean; instead, they suggest, hint, or imply a particular meaning. As a reader, you can't expect an author always to use a direct statement, so you need to make inferences about the author's meaning. An **inference** is an educated guess, a guess based on some known fact or reliable clues.

Read the following paragraph from Joseph Campbell's *Myths to Live By*. As you do, see if you can begin to make an inference about the way Campbell feels about his subject.

> In relation to the first books and chapters of the Bible, it used to be the custom of both Jews and Christians to take the narrative literally, as though they were dependable accounts of the origin of the universe and of actual prehistoric events. It was supposed and taught that there had been, quite concretely, a creation of the world in seven days by a god known only to the Jews; that somewhere on this broad new earth there had been a Garden of Eden containing a serpent that could talk; that the woman, Eve, formed from the first man's rib, and that the wicked serpent told her of the marvelous properties of the fruits of a certain tree of which God had forbidden the couple to eat; and that, as a consequence of their having eaten of that fruit, there followed a "Fall"

1. *Source:* Ruth G. Newman, *Communicating in Business Today.* Heath, 1987, 6–8.

of all mankind, death came into the world, and the couple was driven forth from the garden.[2]

The topic is the biblical account of the creation of the earth and the first humans. But, as you were reading, did you get the impression that the author believes the story he is summarizing?

Based on the way Campbell retells the biblical account of the origin of the universe and the creation of the first man and woman, we can make an educated guess that he doesn't literally believe the story. His phrase in the first sentence "*as though* they were dependable accounts" hints at his skepticism. In the second sentence, beginning "It was *supposed* and taught," there is also a hint at disbelief. Although he hasn't come out and said, "I don't believe these stories are factual," we can infer that Campbell probably doesn't.

In a later paragraph, Campbell has this to say:

> It seems impossible today, but people actually believed all that until as recently as half a century or so ago; clergymen, philosophers, government officers, and all. Today we know—and know right well—that there was never anything of the kind: no Garden of Eden anywhere on this earth, no time when the serpent could talk, no prehistoric "Fall," no exclusion from the garden, no universal Flood, no Noah's Ark.[3]

When we read this passage, our inferences are proved correct.

Isn't this a biased interpretation?

Some people, particularly those raised to interpret the Bible on a literal level, might take offense at Campbell's comments here. He is challenging, even ignoring, their strong beliefs by stating "Today we know—and know right well—that there was never anything of the kind." For such readers, Campbell is wrong and expressing a bias contrary to their own. Good readers will not shut down when this happens but open up even more in order to put their beliefs to a test.

If we read on in Campbell's book *Myths to Live By*, he has this to say about the stories of creation found in *all* religions:

> They [stories of creation] speak, therefore, not of outside events but of themes of the imagination. They are telling us of matters fundamental to ourselves, enduring essential principles about which it would be good for us to know; about which, in fact, it will be necessary for us to know if our conscious minds are to be kept in touch with our own most secret, motivating depths. . . .
>
> Taken as referring not to any geographical scene, but to a landscape of the soul, that Garden of Eden would have to be within us. Yet our conscious minds are unable to enter it and enjoy there the taste of eternal life, since we have already tasted of the knowledge of good and evil. That, in fact, must then be the knowledge that has thrown us out of the garden, pitched us away from our own center, so that we now judge things in those terms and experience only good and evil instead of eternal life—which, since the enclosed garden is within us, must already be ours, even though unknown to our conscious personalities. That would seem to be the meaning of the myth when read, not as prehistory, but as referring to man's inward spiritual state.[4]

2. *Source:* Joseph Campbell, *Myths to Live By.* Bantam, 1972, 23.
3. *Source:* Campbell, 24.
4. *Source:* Campbell, 24–25.

Here Campbell tries to explain his interpretation of the Bible story, which we can accept or reject. But if we let our biases interfere with understanding the beliefs of others, then we won't be receptive to new ideas or broader viewpoints. We will merely be holding on to our beliefs because we are expected or told to believe them, not because we have carefully thought them through.

A misconception about textbooks is that they are full of factual knowledge. While textbooks certainly do present many facts that can be readily accepted, their authors are only human, with biases and preferences that often come out in their writing. A **bias** is a type of prejudice or leaning toward a particular belief or viewpoint. For instance, most introductory psychology books contain much of the same information, but how much emphasis is placed on a particular theory, or which famous psychologist gets more space depends on the author's biases. All American history books will provide the same dates for Franklin D. Roosevelt's presidential terms, but they will differ regarding his proper place in American history or the amount of coverage he is given. One historian may write of him as one of the greatest presidents, whereas another may dwell on his faults.

In order to read beyond the literal level of a textbook, you will often need to make inferences and be aware of an author's biases. But you, too, have biases and preferences. When you find you are in conflict with the ideas of an author or teacher, be open-minded; listen carefully to what someone else has to say. You have to examine and understand the opposite viewpoint before you can reject or accept it.

You wouldn't be getting much of a college education if you weren't exposed to teachers and authors who disagree with your beliefs. Don't be too quick to let your biases keep you from trying to understand viewpoints of people who differ from you. One of the exciting things about attending college is your ability to come to terms with new ideas. You may fortify your beliefs in some things and change them altogether in others. That's called education.

PROCESSING WHAT YOU JUST READ

✍ If you are using the *Student's Reading Journal* that accompanies this text, go to page 38 in it and follow the directions given.

If you are using your own notebook as a journal, discuss at least two areas in which you have grown up having strong beliefs but have never really been challenged by yourself or others (*examples:* political or religious beliefs, opinions about abortion, gun control, drug legalization, etc.). Remember to date your journal entry and provide the questions and this page number.

How do all these skills in Strategy 2 connect with those in Strategy 1?

In applying *Strategy 1*, remember, you prepare yourself for reading by surveying the reading assignment. After previewing the assigned pages, you are ready to read closely for comprehension. Your mind is on the subject; you've raised some questions you want to answer; you have readied yourself to study-read for comprehension.

An important part of applying the skills in *Strategy 2* is to avoid reading the entire chapter at once. Instead, try this:

1. Read from one heading to the next and stop. If there are no headings, read only a few paragraphs or so, a passage that seems to make up a unit of thought.

2. After you have read a section, mark it, identifying main ideas, supporting points, inferences, and author biases.

3. When you are satisfied that you understand what you have read, or if you have written down any questions you need answered by the instructor, read until you get to the next heading and stop, marking your text and writing down any questions.

4. Continue going from heading to heading until you have completed the assignment. If you don't have time to read the entire assignment in one session, you will find that your previous markings and questions will help you when you come back to finish.

When you have read an entire chapter, look back over your markings and try writing a summary of the main points. If there are questions at the end of the chapter, see how many of them you can answer. Look back for answers to those you don't know how to respond to.

I will say more in Part II about comprehension skills, but these pointers should help you in the meantime.

FINAL THOUGHTS   You now know the skills involved in *preparing* to study-read (*Strategy 1*) and those for *comprehending* what you read (*Strategy 2*): identifying topics and distinguishing main ideas from supporting details, (2) making inferences, (3) recognizing an author's biases and your own, and (4) marking textbooks. Part II will help you develop more specific comprehension skills for reading the social sciences, the sciences, and the humanities.

Now you are ready to apply Strategy 3: Processing What You Read, the subject of the next chapter. Make certain, however, that you understand the first two strategies before going on to Strategy 3.

Thelma Washburn becomes the first on her
block to separate her garbage.

Source: Renault, *Sacramento Bee.*

PROCESSING WHAT YOU JUST READ

✍ If you are using the *Student's Reading Journal* that accompanies this text, go to page 38 in it and follow the directions given.

If you are using your own notebook as a journal, answer the following questions as you were directed on page 8.

1. Summarize Strategy 2.
2. Define *bias*. Then discuss two biases you have and whether you feel they are good biases to hold.

For more practice on **Strategy 2: Comprehending What You Read**, go to Part III, page 270.

CHAPTER 3

Strategy 3: Processing What You Read

Building on Strategies 1 and 2, this chapter explains the skills involved in the third general study-reading strategy, the ability to process and synthesize what you read in order to remember it. Four specific skills are discussed: (1) how to take notes, (2) how to map and outline chapters, (3) how to write summaries, and (4) how to make personal connections to what you study. **Your objective in reading this chapter is to learn the skills of *Strategy 3: Processing What You Read* and how to apply them.**

What is meant by "processing what you read"?

After surveying reading assignments, as described in Strategy 1, and reading closely, as explained in Strategy 2, you need to make certain you process the information so that you can make sense of it, connect it to what you know and need to know, and synthesize it for quizzes, tests, and later use. *To synthesize* means to take parts and put them into a whole. Strategy 3, Processing What You Read, offers you some practical approaches for taking reading notes, an outlining method called *mapping*, and tips on writing summaries so that you can put pieces of information together to form a complete picture.

Unless we process or synthesize what we study, we forget it rather quickly. A study by Hermann Ebbinghaus, frequently mentioned in introductory psychology books, shows just how quickly we forget if we don't do something to help us recall what we learn. Figure 3.1 shows how rapidly forgetting occurs according to the Ebbinghaus curve of forgetting.

Notice how quickly we forget within the first hour of learning. Then there is a slow decline. This means that the more time you let pass before reviewing what you learned in a class or after reading an assignment, the more you will forget.

Another study on forgetting textbook material, involving 3,605 students, was done by H. F. Spitzer. You can see the results in Figure 3.2.

According to Spitzer's study, the most forgetting occurs quickly on the first day. During the next fourteen days, forgetting remains great. By the time forgetting slows down, there's not much left to remember. To counteract forgetting of textbook material, process what you learn as quickly as possible, then review frequently. A well-marked textbook and good reading notes help synthesize what you read and become useful aids when you review for a test.

Why take reading notes if you have marked your textbook?

Although marking your textbook as you read requires concentration on the subject and the notation of main ideas, questions, and problems, it does not guarantee that you have learned the material or processed it for later use. By writing up notes or

FIGURE 3.1   Ebbinghaus curve of forgetting

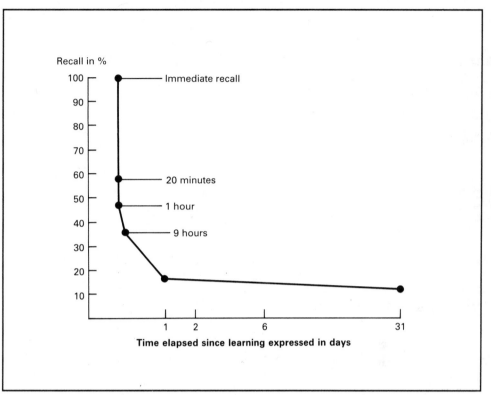

Source: Hermann Ebbinghaus, *Memory*. Columbia Univ. Press, 1913. First published in German in 1885.

summarizing what you study-read, you synthesize the information and create a study file for frequent review so that you won't forget as time goes by.

If the Ebbinghaus and Spitzer studies teach you anything, it should be the need to review frequently. A regular review of good reading notes prevents the need to reread pages and pages of assignments. Review your notes from previously assigned chapters *before* reading each new assignment. That way you can recall what you've already studied and see how it fits in with the new material. This kind of review consistently reinforces what you have already learned and prohibits new information from pushing your previous learning out of your mind.

While you may be able to skip the review process and get a passing grade by cramming, that's all you will get. You won't have learned or synthesized what you have studied. Of course, if all you want is to pass the course tests, to "get by" with no real learning, then you might as well stop reading this book right now and go your own way.

What's the best way to take reading notes?

No "best" way to take reading notes exists. I'll show you several methods, and you can select what works best for you.

One simple method for taking reading notes is to write a full-sentence or outline summary of each of the major headings of a chapter. If an instructor's class lectures differ from what you read in the text, you might want to use what's known as a mapping technique. Or, if you discover that class lectures are often connected with the textbook, you may want to use the split-page method.

FIGURE 3.2   Spitzer's curve of forgetting

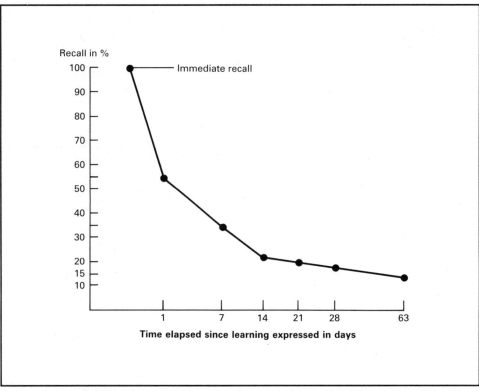

Source: From H. F. Spitzer, "Studies in Retention," *Journal of Educational Psychology.* 30 (1939), 641-56.

The summary method

Once you have marked your text properly, you can use those markings to write a summary of the chapter's main divisions. Writing a good **summary** or **paraphrase** (restating the information in your own words) requires understanding the main idea, organizing the supporting information, and stating that information in your own words. Include in your summary only the major points, leaving out details that aren't important or that are used only as examples to clarify the main point. Where possible, condense or compress information, using key phrases that will trigger your memory. Write in complete sentences, using your own words as much as possible.

Writing a summary requires that you truly process what you read. For example, Figure 3.3 shows a sentence outline summary of the portion of a chapter from a business communications text that you read in Chapter 1. The student has placed the chapter title at the top of the page along with the page numbers for future reference and drawn boxes around the titles of the major headings that are being summarized. Look over the notes and see if they help you remember the selection.

Notice that the page has been divided into two areas. The space on the left is used for key terms or concepts. The space on the right is used to write complete sentence summaries about those key points. By working this way, the student has processed what was read and now has reading notes for review.

If you don't want to write full-sentence summaries, you might prefer a type of outline summary which places the key points in a form similar to that in Figure 3.4. Compare Figure 3.3 and Figure 3.4. Notice that Figure 3.4 does not use complete sentences. Instead, it is a list of key points and subpoints. The summary method used in Figure 3.3 requires more time but could ensure longer and better retention. Try both styles to see which one provides the best results for you.

FIGURE 3.3   Sentence outline summary

Key Terms	Chapter 1: Business Communication Today pp. 6-11
	I. Business Writing: How Is It Different?
lead of news story = opening of well-written memo	People put their thoughts into writing for different reasons. The differences depend on the way writers feel about their readers. For instance, people writing diaries don't plan to share, but journalists and business writers must consider their audiences. Both are under the pressure of time constraints. Both open their
"tightly constructed openings"	writing with "tightly" written or condensed information that lets the reader know what is coming in more detail.
audience important	The difference, however, is that journalists are reporting events, whereas business writers generally try to persuade, sell, or convince their audience of something.
wide spectrum of choices	II. The Spoken Word at Work: Changes and Choices
	The importance of speaking in today's business world has increased, just as it has for reading. Which medium to use for communicating a message is very important, since new technologies often
teleconferencing	make phone calls or teleconferences cheaper than sending letters. Whether to use writing or speaking
2 main factors: −spontaneity −permanence	depends on two main factors: spontaneity and permanence. When a record of a transaction is needed, writing is better. When speed is important, oral communication is better.

FIGURE 3.4   List outline summary

Key Terms	Chapter 1: Business Communication Today pp. 6-11
	I. Business Writing: How Is It Different?
lead of news story	— Different purposes
	* diary
tightly constructed openings	* newspaper article
	* business memo
	* business report
audience and purpose	— Different audiences
	* newspaper lead and business memo both are tightly constructed
	* different purpose — one to inform, the other to persuade, sell, or ask
	II. The Spoken Word at Work: Changes and Choices
	— Speaking as important as reading
teleconferencing	— New technologies offer choices in communication
	* phone: cheaper than letters and faster
	* teleconferencing: audio and video
selection factors	— Two main factors in selecting form
— spontaneity	* spontaneity: quick, no record
— permanence	* permanence: careful, record of transaction provided

FIGURE 3.5   Map of chapter with five major headings

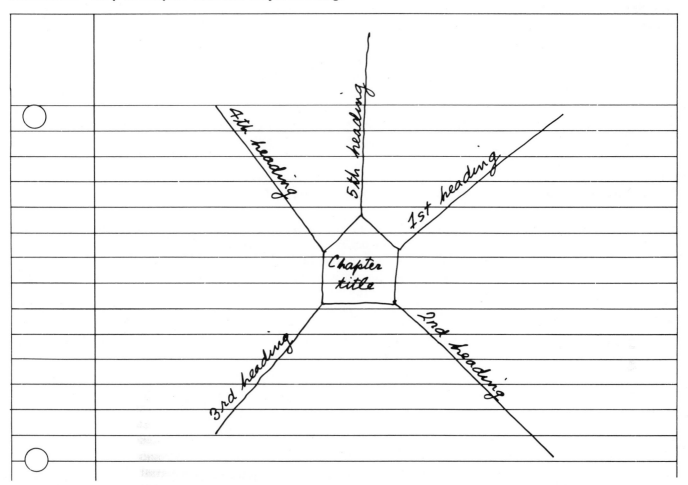

The mapping technique

Mapping is a note-taking system that allows you to organize visually the key points and subpoints of a chapter on one or two pages. A well-done "map" of a chapter allows you to look quickly at the material you have read and remember its content. If a chapter is too long for you to get all its information on one page, simply divide the chapter into two or more manageable parts.

For instance, if in previewing a chapter you notice that it has five major headings, you might take a page from a notebook and draw a design like the one in Figure 3.5.

A chapter with three major headings might be mapped out like Figure 3.6 on page 57. As you read from one heading to the next, stop to fill in the important points under each heading on your map. The map of the entire chapter might resemble Figure 3.7 on page 58.

When you have finished, all the major points and key details for the chapter or section you are reading will appear on one page. Make certain that you design your map so that you can read everything you've written without having to turn the paper around. Notice how easy it is to review from the map in Figure 3.7. Items were written so that you need only look at the map to get an overview of the entire chapter. In addition, the student has highlighted key terms and written a brief summary.

Naturally, the patterns for maps depend on the organization of the chapters read. Use any pattern that helps you understand and see the chapter as a whole. Be neat, and include only the main ideas and key words that will help you remember what the chapter was about.

The split-page method

The **split-page method** keeps notes on reading and lectures together and works best when lectures closely follow the textbook assignments. This system requires dividing the page from a loose-leaf notebook into three parts. The left part is for reading notes, the right part for lecture notes, and the bottom for a summary that connects the reading and lecture material.

Notice how the split-page method is used in Figure 3.8. The notebook page was divided into two parts nearly to the bottom. Then a line was drawn across the page, leaving space to write a summary. When you take lecture notes, avoid writing information you already have in your reading notes. Use the lecture-notes space to put down what was not in the textbook.

Isn't this a lot of work just to take reading notes?

Many students I've known don't want to bother with this extra step of taking reading notes. They believe that marking or highlighting their textbooks is enough. They delude themselves into thinking that they will remember what they have read, because they feel they are learning as they mark. But their grades and class retention don't prove them correct.

Try all these methods or others you may have learned. You will find that different courses require different types of reading notes. Adapt these methods in any way that works best for you and the particular course you are taking.

PROCESSING WHAT YOU JUST READ

✍ If you are using the *Student's Reading Journal* that accompanies this text, go to page 39 in it and follow the directions given.

If you are using your own notebook as a journal, answer the following questions as you were directed on page 8.

1. Explain the three methods for taking reading notes and the advantages of each.
2. What have you learned so far from this chapter that might help you with your study-reading?
3. What is meant by "processing what you read"?

Is there any good advice on taking lecture notes?

Even though this book focuses on strategies for reading textbooks, taking lecture notes is equally important for college success. Taking good lecture notes is a skill, and in many ways it is similar to taking good reading notes. Here are seven pointers:

1. The first step in taking good lecture notes is learning how to listen. Just as you need to prepare to read, you need to *prepare to listen*. Make certain you have read the assignment before coming to class. Frequently, class lectures are based on information in the textbook. If you have read the assignment, then you will be familiar with terms, dates, places, names, or incidents the lecturer may discuss. Review your reading and previous lecture notes just before class to "tune in" to the upcoming lecture.

2. Research shows that we listen better when we are actively involved in listening, but that we are easily distracted and often hear only what we want to hear. So it is important that you learn to *overcome distractions*. Don't approach a lecture thinking that it will be dull. Such an attitude defeats listening and implies your lack of knowledge or interest rather than the lecture's dullness. If you expect to be bored, think of yourself as the dull one who needs to broaden your perception of the world.

FIGURE 3.6 Map of chapter with three major headings

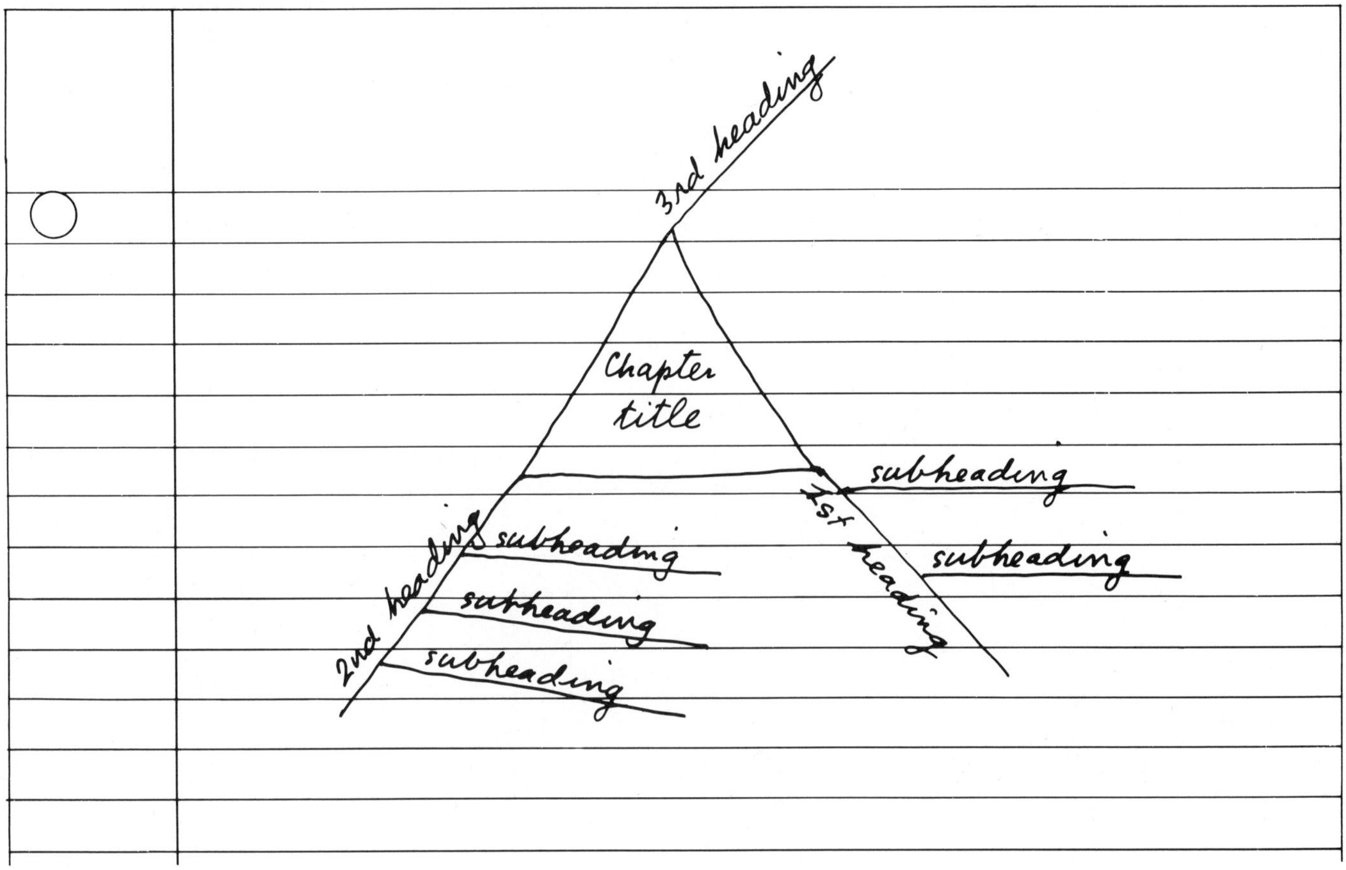

Don't let the lecturer's appearance or mannerisms distract you from the content of the lecture. A lecture is not meant to be entertaining; it's meant to inform.

3. *Don't be passive* during a lecture. Don't just sit back and wait for the instructor to say something you think should be written down. You have to find the main ideas and supporting details in a lecture just as you do in a textbook. Listen for clue words that signal important points or changes in topic. If a lecturer says, "There were four major causes of the Civil War," then get ready to catch what those four causes were. If you hear the instructor say, "Second," and you missed the first point, make a note to see him or her later to get what you missed. When you hear the words "On the other hand" or "For example," perk up. The lecturer is preparing you for especially important information. Signal words and phrases in a lecture are the same as in a reading: *the reasons for, on the contrary, furthermore, similarly, therefore,*

WHAT DO YOU THINK?

Know your strength. The most important thing is to know what you're good at. Very few people know that. All of us know what we're not good at. But the reason why so few of us know what we're good at is that it comes so easy. You sweat over what is hard to do.

Peter Drucker, management professor

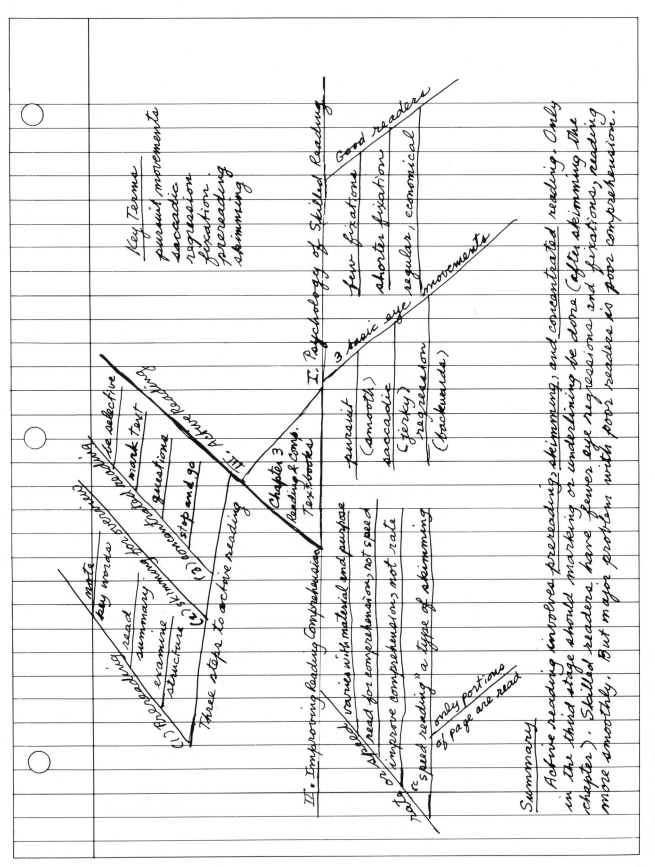

FIGURE 3.7   Map of entire chapter

FIGURE 3.8 Split-page method for keeping notes

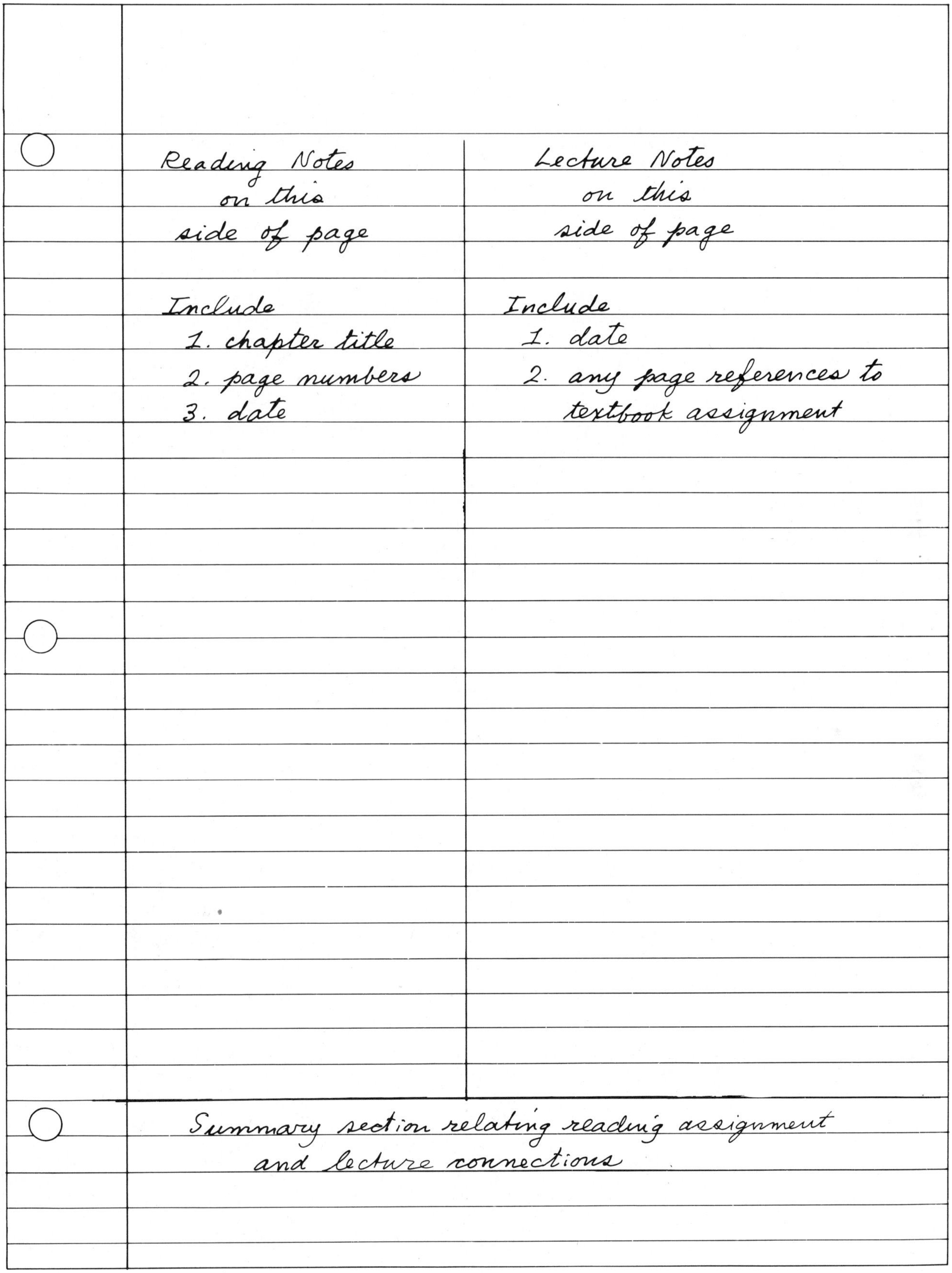

Reading Notes on this side of page	Lecture Notes on this side of page
Include 1. chapter title 2. page numbers 3. date	Include 1. date 2. any page references to textbook assignment

Summary section relating reading assignment and lecture connections *in conclusion, as a result, remember that, the basic concept is.* You know their meanings; use them to help you listen. If the lecture situation permits, don't be afraid to ask questions. I tell my students that no question is stupid if you don't know the answer. What's stupid is not to ask.

   4. *Don't try to write down everything.* When a lecturer is providing you with a story or an illustration of a main idea, write down the main point, not the details. A few key words jotted under the main idea are all you need. Be selective, and use some type of shorthand. It's impossible to get down every word, so write in a "Me-Tarzan-you-Jane" style. For example, if in an American history class, the lecturer is saying,

> Of course there were numerous reasons for the conflict between the North and the South, but I want to discuss four major causes for the outbreak of the Civil War. One, of course, was tied to the growing body of Southern extremists, like Jefferson Davis of Mississippi, who had been demanding that Congress pass laws protecting slavery in the territories.

your notes might read like the ones in Figure 3.9.

   Use parts of words, numbers, symbols, or underlining to call attention to important words or ideas. Whatever will trigger your memory later is all you need.

   You might want to tape lectures, but doing so requires that you sit through the lecture again! Of course, if you want to tape a lecture and still attempt to listen carefully and take notes, that's up to you. You can then use your tape as a backup to replay parts of the lecture that you may have missed or for practice in taking notes. But never use it as a substitute for listening to the original lecture.

   5. *Take neat notes.* Even though your notes may not be in complete sentences and full of symbols, don't be messy. Don't doodle or draw pictures. These are signs that you are not really paying attention. Leave space for things you miss that may be mentioned again later or come up in a question-and-answer period after class. You may want to rewrite your notes more neatly as a way to reinforce what you heard and make a more permanent record of the lectures.

   6. Unless you plan to recopy your notes, don't use a spiral notebook. *Use an 8½-by-11-inch loose-leaf notebook.* Use one side of the sheet only so that you can spread your notes out when you look them over. If you don't want to lug a notebook around, take enough blank paper to each lecture, then place your notes in your notebook afterward. Number the pages for future reference.

   7. *Review your notes frequently.* After class, go over your notes as soon as possible. (Remember the Ebbinghaus curve of forgetting?) Check with another classmate on anything that wasn't clear to you. Or, even better, go see your instructor. Rewrite your notes if there's a need, using the split-page method already described. And look over your previous notes just before the next class lecture.

FIGURE 3.9   Key words in notes

4 main causes of Civ War :
    1 – So extremists demand Congr pass slave laws in terr.
       (Jeff Davis of Miss)

Source: Reprinted by permission of UFS, INC.

How do you make "personal connections" when studying?

Over the years I have encountered many types of students from diverse backgrounds. Some have treated college as a game that could only be won by seeing how little they could do to "get by." At the opposite extreme, some have assumed their responsibility and discovered values, a sense of worth, and an answer to the questions "Who am I? What are my interests? What do I want my life to be?" Those who have found satisfactory answers to those questions are the ones who can be classified as "educated."

There may be times in college when you feel that some courses, the textbooks, the lectures, the studying are all irrelevant, boring, too tough. I know I felt that way periodically. That's when you must ask yourself why you are in college, what you want in the long run, not the short run. You have to weigh your answers based on your own values. Sometimes to reach your goal you have to put up with rotten teachers and so-called required courses. All I can say is that some of the courses I took in college became and continue to become "relevant" years later.

FINAL THOUGHTS

In her book *On Becoming an Educated Person*, Virginia Voeks says,

> A fund of information and ideas is a set of tools. Using them, you can do wondrous things: You can solve more reasonably the problems you meet; you can interpret more fully the events about you; you can predict more adequately and even partially control the events to come. Using them, you also can acquire more easily further facts and ideas. Facts, concepts, principles, and ideas can be extraordinarily useful tools.
>
> However, if you merely collect and store them, facts and ideas are pointless. They are of no more value than a basement full of hammers, saws, and lathes, whose owner proudly displays them to visitors, but leaves them to rust the remainder of the time. Similarly, the mere possession of information is almost worthless.[1]

In order to keep what you learn from rusting in the basement, you need to make personal connections, to keep in mind your long-range goals. What sort of person you become will be based on your ability to take charge of your learning. Everything you have read so far helps you make personal connections with what you study. But you have to make these strategies work for you. No one else will or can do it for you.

You now know what skills are required for three of the four general study-reading strategies: *preparing* to read and *comprehending* and processing what you read. This chapter dealt with the skills required to master the third strategy,

---

1. *Source:* 2nd ed. W. B. Saunders, 1964, 6.

processing what you read: (1) how to take reading and lecture notes, (2) how to write complete sentence summaries, (3) how to outline and map chapters, and (4) how to make personal connections to what you study. In the next chapter, you will learn about the fourth strategy: proving you understand.

PROCESSING WHAT YOU JUST READ

✍ If you are using the *Student's Reading Journal* that accompanies this text, go to page 39 in it and follow the directions given.

If you are using your own notebook as a journal, answer the following questions as you were directed on page 8.

1. Summarize the seven points for taking good lecture notes.
2. What is the connection between the Ebbinghaus curve of forgetting and taking reading and lecture notes?
3. What is the most important thing you learned in this chapter that will help you study better?

For more practice on **Strategy 3: Processing What You Read**, go to Part III, page 285.

Hiller A. Spires and P. Diane Stone, both at North Carolina State University, have developed an approach called the DNA (Directed Notetaking Activity). It is a self-questioning approach for taking better lecture notes. Here are some of the questions they encourage students to ask themselves before, during, and after a lecture. You might want to use them yourself.

BEFORE THE LECTURE

How interested am I in this topic?

If my interest is low, how do I plan to increase interest?

Do I feel motivated to pay attention?

What is my purpose for listening to this lecture?

DURING THE LECTURE

Am I maintaining a satisfactory level of concentration?

Am I taking advantage of the fact that thought is faster than speech?

Am I separating main concepts from supporting details?

What am I doing when comprehension fails?

What strategies am I using for comprehension failure?

EVALUATING AFTER THE LECTURE

Did I achieve my purpose?

Was I able to maintain satisfactory levels of concentration and motivation?

Did I deal with comprehension failures adequately?

Overall, do I feel that I processed the lecture at a satisfactory level?

From Hiller A. Spires and P. Diane Stone, "The Directed Notetaking Activity: A Self-Questioning Approach," *Journal of Reading*. October 1989, 37.

CHAPTER 4

Strategy 4: Proving You Understand

Source: Reprinted by permission of UFS, INC.

PREPARING TO READ

Once you have prepared to study-read, comprehended, and then processed what you have read, you generally have to prove you understand by taking quizzes and exams, or by writing essays or reports. This chapter shows you how to prepare for and take exams. **Your objective in reading this chapter is to learn strategies for test taking so that you can prove to your instructors that you understand what you have studied.**

How do you prepare for an exam?

If you have applied the first three strategies for study-reading, you have already started to prepare for exams. Marking your textbooks, taking reading notes from them, and reviewing those notes frequently is the best way to prepare for a test or quiz. Remember the Ebbinghaus curve and Spitzer's study of forgetting? (If you've forgotten, review pages 50–52 and take notes this time!) Those studies reveal how quickly we forget about 80 percent of what we learn. However, if you have been reviewing your reading and lecture notes as advised in Strategy 3, then you have retained rather than forgotten about 80 percent of what you have studied. That's a good percentage for entering a test situation. However, you don't want to rely just on those frequent reviews of your notes to prepare for exams.

Here are ten do's and don'ts for exam preparation:

1. *Ask your instructor what the exam will cover and what type of test it will be.* Usually, except for "pop" quizzes, an instructor will tell you about a test in advance. Make certain you know on what material the test will be based. It doesn't hurt to ask if the test will be multiple choice or an essay exam. Knowing what type of test will be given can help you prepare for it. Some instructors let you look at past exam questions if you come to their offices.

2. *Start preparing for an exam at least a week before it is scheduled.* If you know the date of an upcoming test, don't wait until the night before to study for it. Plan ahead. You will still have to keep up with reading assignments from other courses. Don't sacrifice one class for another. Students who don't plan ahead often find themselves cutting classes in other courses to study for an exam. Or they fall behind in other class assignments because they concentrate on studying for a test. But these unwise moves can create anxiety and pressure both before and after a test.

3. *Don't try to reread assigned material.* Chances are, by the time you take an exam you have had to read several hundred pages of a textbook for one class alone. Use your notes to recall what you have read. If some of your notations seem fuzzy or don't make sense, reread only the pages covered by those notes to refresh your memory. Then fix your notes so that you will not need to reread those pages again before the final exam.

4. *Try to guess what questions the instructor will ask.* Think back over the course lectures. Did the instructor spend much time discussing a particular period or event? What was emphasized? What words or terms were defined or written on the board? On what sections in the textbook did the instructor make comments? Such questions help you recall what was stressed the most. Also, don't forget to use the questions in the assigned chapters of your textbook, especially those at the ends of chapters. Make certain you can answer them. Even if they are not stated the same way on the test, chances are you will recognize similar questions.

5. *Use the index and glossary as study aids.* If you are being tested on material that is contained in the first 150 pages of a textbook, for instance, look through the index for any entries that cover pages 1 to 150. If you don't remember the names, dates, terms, or places listed, then turn to those pages and review them. Make certain you check your notes to see if they contain references to the items that seem important. Do the same thing with the glossary. Look it over for terms that you remember reading or hearing about in the lectures. Make certain that you understand the definitions.

6. *Spread your notes on a table or the floor and look for the whole picture.* (If you have written notes on both sides of the paper, then you can't do this very well.) If you are being tested on three chapters, for instance, make certain you understand the main idea of each chapter and how each is related to the others. Do the three chapters make up a larger whole? Are any of the details in one chapter related to main ideas in the other chapters? It's at this point that you realize those textbook markings and reading notes were really your first step in preparing for a test. That's why good notes are so important to studying and learning.

7. *Make up summary sheets for your notes.* Take all the notes you have from lectures and reading for a particular chapter and write up a one-page summary. Doing so will help you remember what you studied and process the main points once again into a larger whole.

8. *Form a study group.* Get together with other students who are concerned about succeeding in the course. Each person in the group might be responsible for presenting a certain part of the material studied. In the group, each person "teaches" what he or she knows, with the other members adding to, or correcting if need be, the information presented.

9. *Take care of yourself physically, especially a week before the test.* Naturally, you should always take care of yourself, not just before a test. But part of being prepared for a test is to be in good physical shape. Eat regularly. Get the sleep you need. Before any major test, take some time off from work or activities that may take up too much study time. Delay socializing or indulging in too much entertainment.

10. *Don't cram for a test.* If you follow the advice in the nine previous items, you won't have to cram.

What's wrong with cramming?

At one time or another most students find themselves in situations where they feel they have to cram for a test. Planning poorly, avoiding the inevitable, feeling that the test isn't all that important, disliking a course, being caught unprepared, or just being subject to life's little interferences often cause students to cram. Cramming is never advisable. If you have to learn a large amount of material at one time, you will soon forget it. It takes time, study repetition, and review to really commit something to memory.

Cramming is also much more tiring than steady, regulated study. Your mind can only handle so much information without blowing a fuse. Going into a test already mentally fatigued won't give you a very good chance of doing well.

And then there's this business of why you are even attending college. Cramming for a test might help you pass in the short term, but is that all you want? Cramming reflects a negative attitude, an opinion that what you're learning is not really important. When you find yourself having to cram for tests, it's time to examine your attitude and schedule.

Can test anxiety be avoided?

I don't think I've met anyone who doesn't suffer from some sort of anxiety either before or during a test. Some students actually panic during exams; their fear of failure causes nervous reactions such as headaches or stomachaches. Some students get so tense they go blank when they read the test questions. Others forget what they knew well before the test, make uncalled for mistakes, or blame the instructor for asking questions that seem unrelated to the course content. Exams for most students are menaces that must be overcome. After all, grades depend on examination results, so there is reason for some concern.

Although text anxiety probably can't be eliminated, it certainly can be lessened. If you follow the ten steps just listed, you will feel more confident as you enter an exam. You will know you have done all you could to be prepared. Psychologists Clifford T. Morgan and James Deese have this to say about test anxiety:

> Probably the best medicine for this disease [test anxiety] is to be prepared. If you go into an examination prepared as well as you can ever expect to be, you don't need to get upset. You'll do your best, and that's that!
>
> This point has an important psychological sidelight. Many a student does not realize that going to pieces during an examination is frequently an alibi he has given himself. He blows up not only because he isn't prepared and knows he isn't prepared, but also because he then doesn't need to feel guilty about not being prepared. Test anxiety is often a childish defense the student puts up against taking blame for his own lack of preparation.[1]

1. *Source:* Clifford T. Morgan and James Deese, *How to Study*, 2nd ed. McGraw, 1969, 74.

If you are prepared for a test, anxiety might still exist, but it will be reduced to the point that you can do your best.

If you have test anxiety so severe that it causes you to get ill or perform poorly, discuss this with a counselor or someone at your college who has experience helping students overcome such problems.

PROCESSING WHAT YOU JUST READ

✍ If you are using the *Student's Reading Journal* that accompanies this text, go to page 41 and follow the directions given.

If you are using your own notebook as a journal, answer the following questions as you were directed on page 8.

1. Do you have test anxiety? Describe it. What causes it? What can you do about it?
2. Use the information you have read so far to make your own checklist of things you should do to prepare for tests. Then remember to use it before your next test.

Any hints for reading test directions?

When taking tests, always be aware of the following four kinds of information that may be included in the directions.

1. *Check for the time allowed.* If there are several parts to a test, pay attention to how much time is permitted for each. Don't spend time on a part that is giving you difficulty until you have done the parts that you do know. There may be questions you can answer in another part of the test but never will get to because you spend too much time on problem questions.

2. *Read carefully for your choices.* Check to see if you have to answer all questions or just some. Usually on essay exams you have choices. Some tests have sets of questions in which you are allowed to pick those you wish to answer.

3. *Pay attention to the way you are supposed to mark your answers.* Directions may ask you to mark, circle, or write in your answers. Some true-false tests ask you to explain why an answer is false. If written answers are requested, make certain you understand whether to write one sentence, one paragraph, or a certain number of words. On math tests, you may have to show how you arrived at your answers. Notice if incorrect answers count for more points off than blank spaces do. Some students lose many points on a test simply because they were in a hurry to start answering questions and failed to find out how the answers were to be given.

4. *Note what tools you are allowed to use during the test.* Some instructors won't accept answers in pencil; others don't care what you write with. Ask if you're not sure. Some instructors want your answers in test booklets sold at the bookstore, often called blue books. Other tests may require that you purchase a special marking slip for electronic scoring. Also find out if you are allowed to use a dictionary, calculator, notes, or textbook. Of course, these are things you should know before coming to the exam. Taking an exam without the aids permitted could result in a lower score.

Are there any tricks to taking objective tests?

In addition to being prepared, it helps to know how to take tests. The two major types of tests are *objective tests*, which include true-false, multiple-choice, and matching questions, and *subjective tests*, such as essay and take-home exams. Different types of tests require different test-taking techniques. Not all failure to answer a question correctly is a result of lack of knowledge. Frequently a wrong answer has to do with the inability to read and interpret the question.

True-false tests

Many objective questions have clues that you can use to your advantage when you are not sure of the answer. True-false questions, for instance, have to be just that, either true or false. They often contain clue words that help you make a decision. Following are four true-false questions. Circle what you think are the clue words and then mark each statement *T* for true or *F* for false in the blank.

1.   Economic depressions have always followed wars.   _____

2.   Economic depressions have never followed wars.   _____

3.   Economic depressions have seldom followed wars.   _____

4.   Economic depressions have sometimes followed wars.   _____

Although there is no substitute for actually knowing the right answer, picking number 4 as true, and marking the others false, is a good guess because of the clue words. The words *always* and *never* are too restrictive, because the question as stated deals with all wars. Number 3 uses the word *seldom*, which might or might not make the statement true. But the best guess is that number 4 is true, because *sometimes* would include *seldom*.

Clue words such as *all, always, every, exactly,* and *invariably* mean no exceptions. When these words are used in a true-false statement, they mean in every case. For example:

All triangles have three sides. (If a figure has more or fewer sides, it's not a triangle.)

Every insect has six legs. (If the creature has more than six legs, it's not an insect.)

One foot is *exactly* 12 inches. (If not, I've been measuring incorrectly for a long time.)

If you read a test question using one of these clue words, keep in mind it is implying that the statement is true in every instance. If you know the statement isn't or can't always be true, then mark it false.

Some clue words indicate they are partially true or true in a limited sense: *few, frequently, generally, many, most, often, seldom, some,* and *usually.* Notice the use of clue words in these statements:

Mental disorders are *often* caused by physical illness. (Often, yes; always, no.)

It *seldom* snows in Los Angeles. (Weather records will bear this out as true.)

Frequent review of study notes *usually* makes test taking easier. (There are too many variables for frequent review always to make test taking easier, but usually it does!)

Another type of clue to look for and read carefully is the use of negative words and prefixes such as *never, none, not, cannot, dis-, un-, in-, il-,* and *non-.* The use of these words and word beginnings can make a statement seem confusing. When you see a statement using a double negative, such as

A nation can *never* consume more than it *cannot* produce.

simply cut out both negatives so that the sentence reads

A nation can consume more than it can produce.

Then deal with the truth or falseness of the statement. Or, in this case,

General George Patton was not without courage in the face of battle.

you need to decide if the question claims that Patton was brave or not. Eliminate the double negatives so that the sentence reads

General George Patton was with courage in the face of battle.

History reveals that he was, making the statement true.

Multiple-choice tests

In some ways, multiple-choice questions can be treated as true-false questions. A multiple-choice question might read

The first exploration of new water routes to the East was undertaken by
a. English adventurers.
b. Italian merchants.
c. Spanish traders.
d. Portuguese navigators.

Read each choice as a true-false statement, such as

The first exploration of new water routes to the East was undertaken by English adventurers.

Do this with each choice until you are clear which one is true. Then mark that choice.

If you are uncertain, try a process of elimination. In the preceding example, the key word is *first*. Reasoning from the choices, you probably would eliminate merchants and traders as the first to explore new water routes. Chances are they would be using established routes for their businesses. That leaves adventurers and navigators. A good guess would be navigators, because they are the ones who would explore and map new routes, whereas adventurers would have different primary intentions.

Watch out for questions that begin

Which one is not an example of . . .

Skipping over that little word *not* could cause you to choose an item that *is* an example rather than *isn't*.

When you see a test question that gives "all of the above" as a choice, many times it is the answer. *But don't rely on that.* Still, if you know that two of the other three items are correct but are unsure of the third, the answer has to be "all of the above," because that's the only choice that would include the other two correct items.

Source: Reprinted by permission: Tribune Media Services.

Multiple-choice questions often use numbers or dates, such as

When was Franklin D. Roosevelt elected president for a fourth term?
a. 1940
b. 1944
c. 1948
d. 1950

If you have no idea, go for the middle numbers. Research shows that usually, though not always, the highest and lowest numbers are not correct in such questions. That logic leaves only two choices, giving you a fifty-fifty chance to be correct.

A word of warning, though. Many test makers are aware of these little "tricks of the trade." Knowing the correct answer is the best, not guessing.

Matching tests

Matching tests usually ask you to match items in one column with items in another. It is important to read the directions very carefully to see if you can use items more than once. Also, look over both columns before you mark anything. Sometimes just seeing the items helps refresh your memory. Match the ones you know first. As you match each item, mark or check it off, provided you are not allowed to use any item twice. Then go through the unmatched choices. Don't waste time on questions whose answers you don't know until you have answered all the questions you are certain you do know.

PROCESSING WHAT YOU JUST READ

✍ If you are using the *Student's Reading Journal* that accompanies this text, go to page 41 in it and follow the directions given.

If you are using your own notebook as a journal, answer the following questions as you were directed on page 8.

1. Compare the way you prepare for tests with the way shown in this section.
2. What will you do in the future to perform better on tests?

Are there any helpful hints for taking essay exams?

For many students, essay exams are a real problem. Objective tests ask isolated questions about content, but the questions themselves often contain key words or supply the correct answer somewhere in the multiple choices or matching columns. Seeing the information often helps you recall the correct answer. But with essay exams, you have to *recall* the information with no helpful hints, *organize* the information, and then *write* it all up in complete sentences and paragraphs. Students who know an answer "cold" often miss many points on an essay question because they are too quick to start putting down what they know and fail to write clearly and grammatically.

The following mnemonic (memory) device can help you remember the steps involved in writing a good answer to an essay question. It's called SLOWER[2]. Each letter reminds you of a necessary step for writing an essay answer.

S = *Select* a question you can handle if given a choice.
L = *List* all the ideas related to that question that you can remember.
O = *Organize* your ideas into categories based on similarities or differences.
W = *Write* a first draft based on your organization of information.
E = *Examine* your draft for errors.
R = *Revise* or *rewrite* if time allows.

2. *Source:* Robert A. Carman and W. Royce Adams, *Study Skills: A Student's Guide for Survival*, 2nd ed. Wiley, 1984, 150.

The first step, *Select* a question you can handle, may not always be an option. Sometimes you are allowed to select from several essay questions. But when you are taking a test containing part objective and part essay, you often have very little choice and you must write on a specific question. That means that you have to be prepared with enough content to support an answer to whatever question may be assigned.

Good essay test questions are usually very specific, and the instructor wants you to show that you know all the important points the question calls for. For instance, if you are asked to write an essay answer to this question,

> What are "clue words" and how can knowing them help you do better on objective tests?

you have two tasks: (1) explain what clue words are, and (2) show how you can use them to do better on tests. Questions like these require that you get right to the point. See Table 4.1 for a list of key words used in essay test questions, such as *compare*, *discuss*, *evaluate*, or *explain*. Study the definitions so that you know what is expected of you in questions using those words. The importance of knowing exactly what those words call for in an answer cannot be stressed too strongly.

TABLE 4.1   The Most Common Essay Exam Clue Words and Their Meanings

Clue Word	*Action Required*
Analyze	Find the main *ideas* and show how they are *related* and *why* they are *important*.
Comment on	*Discuss*, *criticize*, or *explain* as completely as possible.
Compare	Show both the *similarities* and the *differences*.
Contrast	Compare by showing the *differences*.
Criticize	Give your *judgment* or reasoned *opinion* of something, showing its good and bad points. It is not necessary to attack it.
Define	Provide the *formal meaning* by distinguishing from related terms. This is often a matter of giving a memorized definition.
Describe	Write a *detailed account* or *verbal picture* in a *logical* sequence or *story* form.
Diagram	Make a *graph*, *chart*, or *drawing*. Be sure you *label* it and add a *brief explanation* if needed.
Discuss	Describe, giving the *details* and explaining the *pros* and *cons*.
Enumerate	*List*, naming the main ideas one by one and *numbering* them.
Evaluate	Give your *opinion* or some *expert's opinion* of the *truth* or *importance* of the concept. Tell the *advantages* and *disadvantages*.
Illustrate	Explain or make clear by *concrete examples*, *comparisons*, or *analogies*.
Interpret	Give the *meaning* using *examples* and *personal comments* to make it clear.

Justify	*Why you think it is so*. Give *reasons*.
List	Produce a *numbered list* of words, sentences, or comments. Same as *enumerate*.
Outline	Give a *general summary*. It should contain a *series of main ideas* supported by *secondary ideas*. Omit minor details. Show the *organization* of the ideas.
Prove	Show by *argument* or *logic* that it is true. The word *prove* has a specialized meaning in mathematics and physics.
Relate	Show the *connections* between things, telling how one *causes* or *is like* another.
Review	Give a survey or summary in which you look at the *important parts* and *criticize* where needed.
State	Describe the *main points* in *precise terms*. Be *formal*. Use *brief, clear sentences*. Omit details or examples.
Summarize	Give a *brief* condensed account of the *main ideas*. Omit details or examples.
Trace	Follow the *progress* or *history* of the subject.

The second step is to *list* briefly all the ideas or supporting points related to the question that you can remember. Don't try to write your answer without first thinking it through. Naturally, you feel the need to hurry with a written response, but it's far better to take a few minutes to think about your answer before trying to write it. Use scratch paper or the inside of your test booklet. I prefer students to list all their points inside the test booklet cover, because if time runs out before they finish writing, I can refer to their lists when I am grading exams and give some test points for what would have been included in their answers if they had had more time.

Here's a list of ideas that could be used to answer the sample essay question about clue words and their usefulness in taking objective tests:

Clue Words

all	only
always	most
never	un- (prefix meaning no, not)
few	il- (prefix meaning no, not)
many	double negatives

Once you have listed all the needed information you can remember to answer the question, *organize* the list into an order you can use to write, something like this:

Clue Words

No Exceptions	*Limited*	*Negatives*
all	few	il-
always	generally	non-
every	many	un-
exactly	most	not
never	often	none
none	seldom	double negatives
only	some	

Notice that the clue words have been organized into three categories. This now makes it easier to discuss their usefulness. As you organize your information, you may even recall more things to say, as is the case in the example.

At this point you are ready for the next step, *write*. If time permits or if you are doing a take-home exam, plan to write a first draft that you can change once you get all your ideas into an essay form. Seldom can any writer sit down and write a perfect draft off the top of her head. Good writing requires rewriting, revision of organization, editing, proofreading, and more revision. Your final draft never reads the way your first draft does.

In an in-class essay exam, you generally don't have time for more than one draft. Once you have a good outline to follow, as shown in the previous step, you can get started writing. Most important, *get right to the point by turning the question into your opening statement*. For example, notice how the question

> What are "clue words" and how can knowing them help you do better on objective tests?

is used to begin the answer:

> Taking objective exams can be made easier by paying attention to clue words used in the questions. There are three general categories of clue words: those that mean something is always so, those that limit the meaning, and those that create double negatives.
>   The first group of clue words, such as "all," "always," "every," "exactly," "never," "none," and "only," imply there are no exceptions. If a test question reads . . .

Now the answer should show how noticing these words can help you read questions better.

This may not be greatly original, but see how the essay question was turned into the opening statement of the answer. With time limits, you can't waste minutes trying to think of some clever opening. The instructor wants to know if you know the answer, so make certain what you say sticks to the question. By contrast, if you are given time outside of class to write an essay, the instructor will expect a more polished and thoughtful finished product, possibly even typed.

In any case, when you write, be neat. Neatness can have a positive psychological effect on the instructor. Skip every other line as you write, and use only one side of the page. Doing so makes your paper easier to read and also leaves room for you to insert material or make changes if necessary. Write clearly and without pretense, using words the way you do naturally.

Once you have finished writing, *examine* your answer for errors. Use the following checklist:

1. Have I covered the topic thoroughly enough to show that I know the answer to the question?
2. Have I organized my writing so the instructor can easily follow what I've said?
3. Do my ideas move smoothly from one point to the next?
4. Have I written in complete sentences and paragraphed properly?
5. Is my punctuation correct?
6. Have I checked my spelling with a dictionary?

If you have double-spaced, you can scratch through a misspelled or misused word and write in the correction on the line above.

With in-class essay exams, you may not have time for the last step: *revise* or *rewrite*. If you have time for revisions, fine. But many students misguidedly spend time trying to recopy exams rather than making sure they have said what is important. Revision does not mean making a neat copy of what you have written.

It requires rearranging paragraphs, rewriting sentences, and proofreading carefully. Take-home essays always should be revised.

Remember the SLOWER method the next time you have to write an essay exam.

Source: Reprinted by permission of UFS, INC.

FINAL THOUGHTS

Once you have prepared to study-read, comprehended, and then processed what you have read, you generally have to prove you understand what you have learned by taking quizzes and exams, or by writing essays or reports. In this chapter you have learned how to prepare for and take objective and essay exams. This completes the last of the four general study-reading strategies. Now that you know all four strategies, use them together to your advantage for making the grade you want.

PROCESSING WHAT YOU JUST READ

✍ If you are using the *Student's Reading Journal* that accompanies this text, go to page 42 in it and follow the directions given.

If you are using your own notebook as a journal, answer the following questions as you were directed on page 8.

1. Pretend that you are taking an essay exam on the following question and write an answer for it actually using the method:

    Explain the SLOWER method for taking essay exams.

2. Write a definition of each of the four study-reading strategies.

For more practice on **Strategy 4: Proving You Understand**, go to Part III, page 300. Make certain you understand thoroughly the four study-reading strategies in Part I before going on to Part II.

❧

SPECIFIC STUDY-READING STRATEGIES

FOR THE SOCIAL SCIENCES, SCIENCES, AND HUMANITIES

❧

Introduction to Reading the Social Sciences

(Chapters 5–7)

WHAT DO YOU THINK?

People say, what's the use of reading history? I say, well, what's the use of Beethoven's sonatas? You don't have to have a tangible use. You have to have something that gives you pleasure, makes you think, makes life more valuable. Reading history does that even though it only shows what is past. I think it was Coleridge who said, "History is only a lantern on the stern." It tells you where you've been. Well, that's worth knowing.

Barbara Tuchman, historian

What exactly are the social sciences?

The term *social sciences* refers to those subjects that attempt systematically to discover and explain the behavior patterns of people and groups of people. The social sciences contain several disciplines or subdivisions, such as anthropology, psychology, sociology, economics, political science, and international relations. Each discipline focuses on some aspect of human behavior that is separate and distinct from those the others concentrate on.

Why are these subjects labeled as *sciences*?

Some purists argue that the social sciences are not really sciences at all. You will read in some of the selections in this unit why social scientists claim they are scientific in their studies. The basic argument for the use of the term *social sciences* stems from the fact that social science research is conducted in three basic ways: (1) through *experimental design*, as in the so-called pure sciences; (2) through *observational research*, a systematic watching of the research subject with no attempt to alter who or what is being watched; and (3) through *participant observation*, in which the researcher becomes directly involved with what he or she is watching. Because researchers in the social sciences review the literature relevant to their studies, formulate hypotheses regarding answers to their research problems, use a research design, collect data, analyze it, then form conclusions, social scientists feel they are scientists.

What makes reading the social sciences different from reading other subjects?

Each subject area uses language in a special way to explain its terms, its methods of research, and its findings. Research in the way social science textbooks are written suggests that the following specific skills[1] are necessary for successful reading comprehension of social science materials:

1. Vocabulary development in the specialized terms used
2. Comprehension skills that include the ability to
    a. differentiate main ideas from details
    b. recognize examples and illustrations used to support main ideas
    c. identify comparisons and contrasts
    d. recognize cause-and-effect statements
    e. distinguish between fact, interpretation, and opinion
3. Study skills that include the ability to
    a. devise a purpose for reading the assignment
    b. use the table of contents, index, and glossary
    c. organize information
    d. take notes
    e. develop flexibility in reading, such as scanning and skimming when appropriate

Part I has already introduced you to these study-reading strategies in general terms. The following three chapters will help you develop your study skills and reading comprehension skills in the social sciences.

---

1. *Source*: Mary M. Dupuis, ed. *Reading in the Content Areas: Research for Teachers.* International Reading Association, 1984, 69.

CHAPTER 5

The Language of the Social Sciences

PREPARING TO READ

This chapter deals with the language of the social sciences. It discusses vocabulary and writing patterns used in social science textbooks, especially how social science writers use denotation and connotation. It shows how you can recognize a social scientist's attitude by noticing his or her choice of words and reminds you that you need to avoid placing your meanings and feelings into social science terms. Finally, it provides you with some words and word parts commonly found in social science writings. **Your objective in reading this chapter is to become aware of the distinction between the literal meanings of social science terms and the feelings attached to them, and to learn some of the words and word parts commonly used in the social sciences.**

Is social science language really so different from the languages of other subject areas?

As you know, some words change meaning entirely with their context. This holds true with social science terms as well. For instance, think about the word *drive*. Chances are you thought of the word in connection with driving a car. But golfers think of the word in terms of their "stroke"; a political campaign manager thinks of *drive* in terms of an event to raise money. Social scientists think of the word in terms of basic human urges, such as a hunger drive or sex drive.

Like *drive*, many social science terms are also general vocabulary words and can create comprehension problems if they are not understood in context. If you come across a social science term that you have never seen before, naturally you should learn its meaning. But if in reading a social science text you run across a word that you use in ordinary speech, it may not be obvious that you need to look up the definition to understand the passage.

Take the word *role*, for example. A *role*, as you know, is a make-believe part an actor plays. But if you don't know that the social science writer is using the word not to mean an actor's part but to refer to a pattern of behavior associated with a certain social position, you may have trouble understanding the point.

Another word with several meanings in social science writing is *interest*. Read the following passage and circle the number of the definition following the passage that you think *interest* has here.

We still profess ourselves to be committed to the idea of a public interest, a conception of the general or common welfare, which it is the function of our political systems to seek out and implement. Yet, the most striking characteristic of our actual politics is that the struggle for power is dominated by special-interest groups, each bent on advancing its own special claims; actual policies tend to be compromises of these partial and self-interested claims.[1]

✍ What does *interest* mean in this passage?

1. curiosity
2. benefit
3. money paid for borrowing money
4. share

The correct answer in this case, of course, is number 2. But did you notice that each answer is one possible meaning of the word *interest*? Depending on the context, any of the four answers could have been correct.

Knowing the meaning of a word in one context may not assure that you know the meaning in another context. The best way to avoid reading inappropriate meanings into social science terms is to learn them carefully when you read them in a new context. Authors of introductory texts usually explain the difference between the special social science meaning of a word and its common meaning the first time it's mentioned. For example, the term *culture* as it is used in sociology might be explained as follows:

> For the sociologist, *culture* is not just a term of value judgment. Culture includes the total of the standards, knowledge, skills, attitudes, and traditions inherited by a member of society.

The author is alerting us to the way he means to use the word *culture*, not the way the word is used in science, or the meaning it has when discussing art or classical music.

How exactly do social scientists use denotation and connotation?

Every word has a literal meaning, that is, the meaning provided in a dictionary. But many words have certain ideas and emotions, not related to the literal meaning, associated with them. For example, most people associate the idea *green* with the word *grass*. When we read "The children were playing on the grass," most of us envision that the grass is green. But it could be brown or yellow. The concept of *green* is the connotation we have for the word *grass*. A **connotation**, remember, is the idea or feeling that we associate with a word. The exact or literal meaning of a word is its **denotation**.

In contrast to general vocabulary words, which have emotional connotations, social science terms are used to convey only information. For example, *monopoly* and *bureaucracy* are words with unfavorable connotations for many people. But when economists remark that the telephone company is a monopoly, they are not criticizing or praising. They are simply describing the position of the telephone company in the economic structure of our country. The same is true when political scientists describe the federal government as a bureaucracy. They are not attacking or defending the federal government, merely stating the nature of its administration.

Some social science terms have very strong emotional associations in general usage. Such words are almost worthless for conveying information unless the writer carefully defines them for the reader. *Democracy* is such a word. The political scientist or historian may use the word to mean "government by the people, directly or through elected representatives." But for many people, democracy stirs up noble feelings, echoes of "The Star-Spangled Banner," and feelings of patriotic pride.

1. *Source:* John C. Livingston and Robert G. Thompson, *The Consent of the Governed*. Macmillan, 1983, 10.

These associations can often interfere with understanding. For instance, suppose the author of a government text writes, "The United States is not a democracy." Earlier in the text, the writer may have defined democracy as only "direct government," instead of "government through representatives." But if you are not aware of the author's earlier specific use of the term, it would be easy to get the impression that something unfavorable is being said about the United States.

✍ See how easily you can detect different connotations. Following are four pairs of words and phrases. Both of the words or phrases in each pair refer to the same thing, but one has favorable connotations while the other has unfavorable ones. Write the words and phrases with favorable connotations in the left column and those with unfavorable connotations in the right.

a. **underdeveloped nation**   e. **backward country**
b. **egghead**   f. **intellectual**
c. **leftist agitator**   g. **social reformer**
d. **international organization** h. **world conspiracy**

Favorable   *Unfavorable*

1. _____   1. _____

2. _____   2. _____

3. _____   3. _____

4. _____   4. _____

You probably had little trouble classifying these terms, because each was placed beside a word or term with the opposite connotation. The favorable ones are *a, f, g,* and *d.* But sizing up a word is not always so easy.

Let's look again at *democracy,* a word that has a definite denotation but also has strongly favorable connotations. *Democracy* is often used for its connotative value alone. For instance, William Z. Foster, former head of the Communist party in the United States, made the following statement: "And in the Soviet Union . . . there exists a higher type of democracy than in any other country in the world." But you might read a sentence like this in a political science text: "The advocates of fascism and communism are the worst enemies of democracy."

If you assume that *democracy* is being used in its denotative sense in both sentences, you will be puzzled, because the statements obviously contradict each other. The first sentence states that the Soviet Union (in which the Communist party of that time was the only political party) is a democracy. The second sentence states that Communism is the enemy of democracy. But if you assume that both sentences are only using *democracy* in its connotative sense, to mean "a good form of government," the difference between the two boils down to a difference of opinion.

Why do social science writers use connotation?

Realizing that words can communicate attitudes and emotions, be alert to the use of words with different connotations in your social science reading. If you aren't, you may think you are reading for information when in reality you are absorbing the author's attitude or opinion. Most introductory textbooks, while expressing an author's attitude and opinion, do not try to trick you by using connotative language. However, social science instructors frequently assign outside readings in the field. With such readings, be alert to connotative language.

Here is a passage from a book frequently suggested as outside reading for history students interested in World War II. In it the author justifies the German National Socialist foreign policy aims before and during World War II. As you read it, underline words or phrases that contain connotative meanings.

> We National Socialists must cling unflinchingly to our foreign-policy aims, that is to guarantee the German nation the soil and territory to which it is entitled on this earth. And this is the only action which, before God and our German posterity, would seem to justify an investment of blood: before God, since we are placed in this world on condition of an external struggle for daily bread, as beings to whom nothing shall be given and who owe their position as lords of the earth only to the genius and courage with which they know how to struggle for and defend it: . . . The soil and territory on which a race of German peasants will some day be able to beget sons sanction the investment of the sons of today, and will some day acquit the responsible statesmen of blood and guilt and national sacrifice, even though they be persecuted by their contemporaries.[2]

✍ In the following space, write what you think the author means.

_____

_____

_____

_____

The writer, Adolf Hitler, chose his words carefully. Notice that he makes the Nazi foreign policy sound like a holy duty. To someone unaware, his message sounds noble because of connotative language such as *unflinchingly, entitled, God and our German posterity, genius* and *courage, sanction, sacrifice,* and *persecuted.* If he hadn't chosen words so carefully for their positive connotations, what he wrote would have sounded something like this:

> We Nazis must get on with our plan of territorial aggression; namely, to seize for Germany any land we want. Getting land is a good reason for going to war. We are justified because with the land we gain through deaths in battle, we can expand our population to replace those who die in the war. A future population growth justifies sending our men to be killed now, and it will later acquit the Nazi leaders of causing the deaths of our men, even though they are criticized now.

No doubt Hitler would have had a difficult time gaining followers if he had expressed himself in such straight-forward terms. But because his plans were expressed in connotative language, he gained a powerful hold over the German populace and even persuaded some people in other countries that the Nazis' cause was just.

To recognize bias in a writer with whom you do not agree or about whom you know something unfavorable is, of course, easy. History has revealed Hitler and his regime as fanatics and even criminally insane. Thus, we are likely to read critically anything written by him or his leaders. However, it is not so easy to be objective when we read something we agree with. For instance, if you substituted the word *Americans* for *National Socialists* and *the United States* for *Germany,* in the passage

2. *Source:* Adolf Hitler, *Mein Kampf,* trans. Ralph Manheim. Boston: Houghton, 1943, 947.

from *Mein Kampf,* and had it been spoken by the president of the United States, there would no doubt be some unaware American citizens who would agree with it. But I'd hope not too many!

Read the following passage from *Time* magazine. The writer is dealing with the problem of achieving peace in Vietnam in 1966. Underline the words and phrases that express an attitude.

> If a just and honorable peace guaranteeing the freedom of South Viet Nam can be obtained, all the world will benefit—and with it, the cause of freedom everywhere. If it should fail, the burden of blame will irrevocably rest where it has always belonged—upon the heads of the Communist aggressors, for all the world to see. Then, having tried everything in every possible place, and having enlisted every nation and office that might help in the cause of peace, the U.S. can resume reluctantly—but with clear conscience—the unwelcome and unwanted prosecution of the war.[3]

✍ Now answer the following two questions in the spaces provided.

1. List some of the emotionally loaded words and phrases you underlined in the passage.

2. What did you learn about Vietnam from the passage?

Now read this passage from the *New Republic.* It, too, deals with peace in Vietnam and was written the same week as the previous selection. Underline any connotative words and phrases.

> We will not get a cease-fire that amounts to more than a few days "truce" unless Mr. Johnson [the President then] and his advisors have some firmer and more realistic notion of the kind of South Vietnam we would tolerate, in preference to destroying and killing indefinitely and inconclusively. Is it a South Vietnam in which the Viet Cong who control so much of the country and its population are forced to submit unconditionally? As the Viet Cong have now been fighting on and off for 20 years, they are unlikely to submit even to American prower unless they are wiped out, which at the present rate of "body count" will take some time. Short of that, a South Vietnam in which the powerful National Liberation Front is outlawed from politics can be precariously main-

3. *Source:* "Diplomacy—In Quest of Peace," *Time,* January 14, 1966, 13.

tained only by a perpetual American military presence of at least six fighting divisions. That presence would undoubtedly keep alive the fiction of a sovereign Saigon government, but it would also mark the U.S. as a colonial master who dare not leave, and dare not take his hand off his gun while he stays.[4]

🖎 Now answer the following two questions in the space provided.

1. List some of the emotionally loaded words and phrases you underlined in the passage.

    _____

    _____

    _____

    _____

2. What did you learn about Vietnam from the passage?

    _____

    _____

    _____

    _____

Here are some of the words and phrases you might have underlined and listed. Compare these lists with yours.

From Time	*From the* New Republic
just and honorable peace	destroying and killing
freedom	forced to submit unconditionally
cause of freedom	wiped out
burden of blame	"body count"
Communist aggressors	outlawed
the cause of peace	precariously
reluctantly	perpetual . . . military presence
with clear conscience	fiction
unwelcome and unwanted	colonial master

Both passages deal with the U.S. military action in Vietnam, although neither tells you much about Vietnam. But the choice of words in the two pieces is so different that the attitudes expressed are exactly opposite. In the passage for *Time,* continued American military action in Vietnam is called "the unwelcome and unwanted prosecution of the war," done "reluctantly—but with clear conscience." The passage from the *New Republic* says the U.S. military in Vietnam is "destroying and killing indefinitely and inconclusively." Historically, these two passages reflect much of the difference that divided the American people during the Vietnam conflict. Today most historians agree that America's military intervention was a mistake, and evidence now reveals that our leaders lied to the public about our involvement and reasons for being in Vietnam.

4. *Source:* "Johnson's Choice," *New Republic.* January 8, 1966.

WHAT DO YOU THINK?

Joseph Heller, novelist: The emotions of people in a democratic society are no more rational than they are in any other type of society. They are manipulated. It is the function of a leader in a democracy, if he wishes to be a leader, to manipulate the emotions and the ideas of the population.

Bill Moyers: You remind me of the Gulf of Tonkin Resolution passed by Congress in 1964, which in effect gave Lyndon Johnson a blank check to go to war in Vietnam. Congress didn't intend it to be a blank check, but that's how LBJ interpreted it.

Joseph Heller: That's exactly what I'm talking about when I speak of the manipulation of emotions and the engineering of consent. Lyndon Johnson told Congress what had happened in the Gulf of Tonkin. And what he said had happened had not happened. I remember Senator Fulbright saying afterward, "I never believed that the President of the United States would lie to me."

You may have noticed that most of the examples of highly-charged connotative language used in this section were not taken from textbooks. Textbooks generally aim to inform rather than influence emotions, although writers can't keep their attitudes entirely out of their writing. Popular magazines and political writings, by contrast, often attempt to entertain the reader, or persuade, or both. Since words with strong connotations are more interesting and persuasive than strictly informative words, magazines and political writings usually contain a great deal of emotion-charged language. Be aware of such language, and don't be influenced unwittingly by it.

PROCESSING WHAT YOU JUST READ

✍ If you are using the *Student's Reading Journal* that accompanies this text, go to page 44 in it and follow the directions given.

If you are using your own notebook as a journal, answer the following questions:

1. List eight words that have both a denotative and a connotative meaning to you. Provide both meanings for each word.
2. Why is it important to recognize when you are reacting to a word on the connotative level rather than the denotative level? Give an example.

Is there really a social science "language"?

The language of social science contains many words made up of Greek and Latin word parts, some of which you probably already know. For instance, how many of the following words are familiar to you?

autograph	phonograph
biography	photograph
geography	telegraphy
mimeograph	graphic
paragraph	graphite

You may know every word on the list. But are you aware of what word part all these words have in common? Why do you suppose they all have the Greek root *graph* in them? Do you know why we call the lead in pencils *graphite*? Do you know why an autograph is called an *autograph*?

The root *graph* means to write, draw, or record. Each of the words in the preceding list has something to do with writing, drawing, or recording. *Auto* means "self," so *autograph* means "self-writing," or one's own writing, usually one's name. *Bio* means "life," so *biography* means "life-writing," or a written record of someone's life. *Geo* means "earth," so *geography* means "earth-record," or records about the earth.

Once you know the meanings of many Greek and Latin roots, you can figure out an unknown word's meaning by its root and the context. Use the following list of Greek word roots and affixes to develop your vocabulary skills in the social sciences.

Greek Word Roots and Affixes

Root or affix	Meaning	Word example
amphi	around, both sides	amphitheater
anti	against	antiunion
anthrop	man	anthropology
chrono	time	chronology
cyclo	wheel	cycle
demo	people	democracy
epi	upon	epidemic
gam	marriage	monogamy
geo	earth	geology
hemi	half	hemisphere
hetero	different, mixed	heterogeneous
homo	alike, same	homogeneous
iatry	medical treatment	podiatry
litho	stone	monolithic
log	word	prologue
macro	large	macrocosm
mania	craze for, madness	maniac
mega	great, large	megatrend
micro	small	microcosm
mono	one	monopoly
morph	shape	metamorphosis
neo	new, recent	neophyte
ortho	straight	orthodox
paleo	old	paleontology
pan	all	panacea
para	beside, equal	disparity
patho	suffering	pathology
phil	love	philosophy
phob	fear	phobia
polis, polit	city	metropolis
poly	many	polygamy
pseud	false	pseudoruler
psyche	mind	psychology
scope	examine	macroscopic
syn	together	synergy
theo	god	theology

PROCESSING WHAT YOU JUST READ

✍ Using the preceding list of Greek word roots and affixes, define the following words in the spaces provided.

1. amphibious   _____

2. philanthropic   _____

3. synchronize   _____

4. geography   _____

5. psychiatry   _____

6. megalomaniac   _____

7. monarch   _____

8. neoclassical   _____

9. anthropology   _____

10. demophobia   _____

Your wording may be different, but compare your answers with these: (1) capable of going on land and water; (2) kind, generous [loves humankind]; (3) coordinate, accompany; (4) study of the earth; (5) medical practice that deals with the mentally ill; (6) mentally ill person who thinks he or she has great power; (7) king or queen, head of state, ruler; (8) revival of a classical period in art, music, or literature; (9) study of the origin and development of human cultures; (10) fear of people.

Before going on, make certain you learn the words you had difficulty defining. Keep a list of the words and word parts you need to learn in your reading journal.

Now read the following list of Latin word roots and affixes which also make up many words used in the social sciences.

Latin Word Roots and Affixes

Root or affix	Meaning	Word example
act	do	transact
ambi	both ways	ambiguous
ante	before	antedate
ann, enn	year	annual, biennial
art	skill	artifact
bene	good, benefit	benevolent
circum	around	circumnavigate
cogn	know	cognition
credo	belief	credo
dict	speak	dictator
domin	master	dominate
equ	equal	equilibrium
homo	man	Homo sapiens
inter	between	interstate
junct	join	conjunction
lib	free, book	liberty, library
locus	place	locality

mag	great	magnitude
mater	mother	maternal
mortis	death	mortality
multi	many	multitude
opt	best	optimist
pater	father	paternity
plur	more	pluralist
pop	people	populist
reg	king	regal, reign
rupt	break	bankrupt
scribe, script	write	inscription
subter	under, secret	subterfuge
sum, sup	superior,	summit
term	end	exterminate
terr	land	terrain
trans	across	transcontinental
turb	confusion	turbulence
voc	voice	advocate

PROCESSING WHAT YOU JUST READ

✍ Using the preceding list of Latin word roots and affixes, define the following words in the spaces provided.

1. circumference _____

2. artisan _____

3. benefactor _____

4. dictate _____

5. equality _____

6. junction _____

7. magnitude _____

8. optimum _____

9. population _____

10. interrupt _____

Your wording may be different, but compare your answers with these: (1) the boundary around a circle; (2) artist, craftsperson; (3) helper, promoter, ally, friend; (4) command, order, speak; (5) evenness, parity, sameness; (6) a joining, linking, merger; (7) importance, significance, power; (8) superior, top, best; (9) masses, people, society; (10) halt, interject, break in.

Before going on, make certain you learn the words you had difficulty defining. Keep a list of the words and word parts that you need to learn in your reading journal. Take some time to learn them. Chances are your instructor will quiz you on them.

FINAL THOUGHTS Many social science terms are general vocabulary words with special definitions. It is important to learn the social science definitions for these terms and to avoid projecting emotional associations onto them. Social science sources use connotative language to express ideas and emotions more than introductory textbooks do, but, as an intelligent reader, you must be alert to both the writer's biases and your own.

Take the time to learn many of the Greek and Latin word roots and affixes that make up much of the language of social science. Knowing these word parts can often help you figure out a word's meaning without a dictionary.

PROCESSING WHAT YOU JUST READ

✍ If you are using the *Student's Reading Journal* that accompanies this text, go to page 45 in it and follow the directions given.

If you are using your own notebook as a journal, answer the following questions:

1. Pick at least ten words or word parts from the Greek list of roots and affixes (pages 85–86) and ten from the Latin list (pages 86–87). Write them in your journal so you can refer to them frequently. Make a conscious effort to learn them.
2. Summarize the main point of each of the headings in this chapter.

Review your journal notes, then go to Part III, page 308, and practice what you have learned.

CHAPTER 6 Writing Patterns in the Social Sciences

PREPARING TO READ

The theory behind this chapter is that your comprehension of social science textbooks will improve if you learn to recognize the writing patterns most used by social scientists. Some more general patterns were discussed briefly in Part I, but social scientists have their own way of writing, vocabulary, and approaches to expressing their knowledge. This chapter introduces you to five writing patterns found frequently in history, political science, economics, sociology, psychology, and anthropology texts. To help you better understand these patterns, selections from social science textbooks are used as illustrations. Each section concentrates on a particular pattern and provides examples and practice exercises to learn from. Don't try to read this chapter in one study session. Divide it into several parts, mastering one part at a time. **Your objective in reading this chapter is to learn the five basic writing patterns presented so that you can study-read your social science textbooks efficiently.**

Why spend time learning writing patterns?

All writing reflects an attitude. Since most social scientists are complicated thinkers and writers, it is important to learn how they think and write. If you can recognize the thought patterns they use most often, your comprehension will begin to improve, making your studying easier.

A typical college textbook contains around 800 pages, or more than 400,000 words. Just one book can treat a vast subject, such as the whole history of a country or a civilization or an entire field of knowledge, such as sociology or psychology. You cannot possibly learn everything in a book and still have a sane social or work life. You have to be selective, learning to identify the main ideas rather than to get bogged down in all the details. You have to learn to get to the core of a reading assignment, to connect it with the main ideas of each chapter in the book.

You can do this by being aware of the writing pattern used. If you understand the pattern, you can more easily recognize the main ideas. And once you identify the main ideas, you'll be surprised at how the smaller ideas and details will be easier to remember, because you will see them in relationship with main ideas, which become parts of a whole story.

Can you give an example?

Among the most common writing patterns found in social science texts is the use of an **example** or detailed incident to explain a main idea. Often easy to recognize, this writing pattern usually contains phrases such as *for example, for instance, in order to illustrate,* or *a recent incident illustrates.* Such wording alerts you that an example will support or explain the main idea. However, writers do not always use such phrases, making the pattern less easy to identify. But knowing that the examples are not as important as the main idea they are explaining can help you concentrate on the point of the passage. Your objective in this section is to identify how examples are used to support a main idea.

Read the following excerpt from an economics textbook. Underline the main idea.

> Everyone should realize from the start that economists are not all-knowing deities who can always give accurate predictions. For instance, those of use in the professions are constantly plagued at social gatherings by people who want infallible advice on what stocks to buy in order to get rich quickly and without any risk whatever. Although studies have shown economists do better than the average investor, very few have enough confidence in their skills at predicting market trends to substitute investing for making a living as an economist.[1]

In this example, the main idea is in the first sentence: Everyone should realize that economists cannot always correctly foresee what the economy will do. Everything that follows "*For instance*" in the second sentence serves as support for that main idea. The author gives the example of people at social gatherings asking economists for nonrisk stock tips and refers to examples of studies which show that while economists make more successful investments than average investors do, they don't do well enough to make their living from the stock market. Thus, the two examples help us understand and remember the main point: We can't expect economists' predictions always to be correct.

Here is a passage from a sociology textbook that uses an example to explain the effects of social changes. Again, underline the main idea.

> Social change involves complex patterns of response, since a change in one part of society forces changes in other parts. For example, a sharp decline in the birth rate during the 1960s soon caused a crisis in American schools. Suddenly there were too many teachers and classrooms for the number of students. Thus, many teachers had to be let go, and many schools had to close. Ex-teachers had to find new occupations, and some use had to be found for unused school buildings.[2]

This passage is structured like the previous passage. The main idea is stated in the first sentence, and an example follows, in this case, after the phrase *For example*. Here is an outline of the passage:

Topic:	Social change
Main Idea:	Social change is complex, a change in one part of society changes another part.
Example:	The sharp decline in birthrate in the 1960s caused changes in schools.
	a. Many teachers were let go and had to find new jobs.
	b. Many school buildings were closed and new uses for them had to be found.

Not all examples are announced, however. See if you can separate the main idea from the example in the following passage from an American history textbook dealing with early colonial settlers. Underline the main idea.

1. *Source:* Sanford D. Gordon and George G. Dawson, *Introductory Economics*, 6th ed. D. C. Heath, 1987, 5.
2. *Source:* Rodney Stark, *Sociology*, 2nd ed. Wadsworth, 1987, 437.

Life in the American wilderness was nasty, brutish, and short for the earliest Chesapeake settlers. Malaria, dysentery, and typhoid took a cruel toll, cutting ten years off the life expectancy of newcomers from England. Half the people born in early Virginia and Maryland did not survive to celebrate their twentieth birthdays. Few of the remaining half lived to see their fiftieth—or even their fortieth, if they were women.[3]

You probably underlined the first sentence as the main idea, which is correct. The rest of the paragraph gives examples of the "nasty, brutish, and short" life of the earliest Chesapeake settlers. Here is an outline of the passage:

Topic:	Life in the American wilderness for Chesapeake settlers
Main idea:	Life for Chesapeake settlers was nasty, brutish, and short.
Examples:	a. Malaria, dysentery, and typhoid killed many, and took ten years off life expectancy.
	b. Half the people in early Virginia and Maryland did not live to be twenty.
	c. Few lived to see their fiftieth birthday.
	d. Few woman lived to see their fortieth year.

Here's another passage from the same history text. Read it and underline the main idea.

Religious leaders wielded enormous influence in the 17th century Massachusetts "Bible Commonwealth." They powerfully influenced admission to church membership, by conducting public interrogations of persons claiming to have experienced conversion. Prominent among the early clergy was fiery John Cotton. Educated at England's Cambridge University, a Puritan citadel, he emigrated to Massachusetts to avoid persecution for his criticism of the Church of England. In the Bay Colony he devoted his considerable learning to defending the government's duty to enforce religious rules.[4]

The vocabulary used makes this passage seem more complex than the previous three examples. However, it really isn't when the passage is outlined.

Topic:	Religious leaders in 17th century Massachusetts
Main Idea:	Religious leaders had a great deal of influence in Massachusetts government.
Examples:	a. They had a strong influence on who could be admitted to the church.
	b. John Cotton, one of the more prominent church leaders, defended the government's duty to enforce religious rules.

Of course, if you have trouble understanding the meanings of words such as *wielded, interrogations, conversion,* and *citadel,* you need to look them up before you can truly understand the passage.

The following passage from a U.S. history textbook discusses one aspect of the agricultural revolution in this country between 1860 and 1890. The author uses several kinds of information to illustrate the main point. Read the passage and see if you can recognize the main point and how the details and illustrations support it.

The westward movement of farming spelled hardship, of course, for the farmers of the East and the seaboard South. Unable to compete

---

3. *Source:* Thomas Bailey and David M. Kennedy, *The American Pageant,* 8th ed. D. C. Heath, 1987, 39.
4. *Source:* Bailey, 25.

with the rich virgin soil of the West, burdened with higher taxes and investment charges, farming in these regions entered upon a decline from which it has never entirely recovered. Much of tidewater Virginia was given over to broom sedge and became that Barren Ground which Ellen Glasgow has described in her novel; large areas in Pennsylvania and New York reverted to wilderness or to a playground for vacationers. Hundreds of thousands of acres of New England were abandoned to brush and forest: in the half century after the Civil War, farm land under cultivation in this section declined by almost fifty per cent. A traveler through New England in 1889 wrote:

> Midway between Williamstown [Massachusetts] and Brattleboro [Vermont] I saw on the summit of a hill against the evening sky what seemed a large cathedral. Driving thither, I found a huge old-time two story church, a large academy, a village with a broad street, perhaps 150 feet in width. I drove on and found that the church was abandoned, the academy dismantled, the village deserted. The farmer who owned the farm on the north of the village lived on one side of the broad street, and he who owned the farm on the south lived on the other, and they were the only two inhabitants. All of the others had gone — to the manufacturing villages, to the great cities, to the West. Here had been industry, education, religion, comfort and contentment, but there remained only a dreary solitude of forsaken homes.[5]

A passage such as this one shouldn't be too difficult to read. It makes an easy-to-understand point and supports it with a wealth of detailed examples. To check your comprehension, number the following points from the selection in the order of their importance.

a. Ellen Glasgow wrote a novel called *Barren Ground*. _____

b. Farming in the East couldn't compete with the better soils and lower costs in the West. _____

c. A whole village in New England became a ghost town. _____

d. Much of the farmland in the East reverted to uncultivated land and has never been reclaimed. _____

Did you list *b*, *d*, *c*, and *a* in that order? The last two items are similar, but since item a is an example of item c, it is best listed as the least important. If you got those items in the right order, you recognized that the passage makes its point with the opening sentences, then elaborates on it. You weren't confused by the relative amount of space given to any one idea; the quotation describing the village takes up nearly half the passage, yet it is only an illustration.

You've probably noticed by now that the main idea or point being made often comes in the first or second sentence of a paragraph. However, some paragraphs may not have a main idea, but rather be a part of a longer passage or topic. A main idea can come anywhere in a passage. How do you find it when such a pattern occurs? Read the following selection and see if you can find the main idea.

5. *Source:* Allen Nevins and Henry Steele Commager, *A Pocket History of the United States*, 8th ed. Washington Square Press, 1986, 314–315.

The Planting of the Colonies

The history of English settlement in America began on a beautiful April morning in 1607, when three storm-beaten ships of Captain Christopher Newport anchored near the mouth of Chesapeake Bay, sending ashore men who found "fair meadows, and goodly tall trees, with such fresh waters as almost ravished" them to see. With these ships were George Percy, the active, handsome son of the Earl of Northumberland, and Captain John Smith. Percy records how they found noble forests, the ground carpeted with flowers; fine strawberries, "four times bigger and better than ours in England"; oysters "very large and delicate in taste"; much small game; "stores of turkey nests and many eggs"; and an Indian town, where the savages brought them corn bread and tobacco smoked in clay pipes with copper bowls. For a time these first experiences in Virginia seemed enchanting. Percy's *Observations* describes the delight of the newcomers in the richly colored birds, the fruits and berries, the fine sturgeon, and the pleasant scenery. But his brave narrative, full of a wild poetry, ends in something like a shriek. For he tells how the Indians attacked the settlers, "creeping on all fours from the hills, like bears, with their bows in their mouths"; how the men were seized by "cruel diseases, such as swellings, fluxes, burning fevers"; and how many died of sheer famine, "their bodies trailed out of their cabins like dogs to be buried."

The planting of a new nation in America was no holiday undertaking. It meant grim, dirty, toilsome, dangerous work. Here was a great shaggy continent, its Eastern third covered with pathless forests; its mountains, rivers, lakes, and rolling plains all upon a grandiose scale; its Northern stretches fiercely cold in winter, its Southern areas burning hot in summer; filled with wild beasts, and peopled by a warlike, cruel, and treacherous people still in the Stone Age of culture. In many respects it was a forbidding land. It could be reached only by a voyage so perilous that some ships buried as many as they landed. But despite all its drawbacks, it was admirably fitted to become the home of an energetic, thriving people.[6]

✍ Circle the number of the statement that comes closest to expressing the main idea of the preceding passage.

1. The history of English settlement in America began in April 1607.
2. George Percy's *Observations* tells us much about early English settlement.
3. Beginning a new nation in America was not easy for the early English colonists.
4. The English colonists were delighted with what they found in America.

Although all of the ideas in these statements are mentioned in the selection, item 3 comes closest to being the main point. The first sentence in the first paragraph lets us know when the first English colony arrived in America. A description of what the settlers found is provided with examples from George Percy's *Observations*. But, as we are told later in the paragraph, the settlers' delight at what they first saw "ends in something like a shriek" when examples of difficulties they faced are quoted from Percy. The first sentence in the second paragraph connects what is said in both paragraphs regarding the fact that this settlement was "no holiday undertaking." Your first real clue, however, is the heading itself, "The Planting of the Colonies," which alerts you to what the passage is about. As you read chapter assignments, realize that headings can give you clues about the topic being discussed. You should

---

6. *Source:* Nevins and Commager, 1–2.

then read for main ideas related to the topic, realizing that some paragraphs are merely laying groundwork.

Here is a longer selection from a sociology textbook[7] that uses examples. As you read it, practice marking the passage and look for the main idea and the support provided.

CHANGE AND CULTURAL LAG

There can be considerable delay before a change in one part of a society produces a realignment of other parts. During such a period of delay, parts of a society can be badly out of harmony — such as when education departments continue to pump out waves of new graduates after there are no employment opportunities for them. William F. Ogburn (1932) described such periods as **cultural lags**. According to Ogburn, cultural lags are times of danger for societies because severe internal conflicts can result.

Cultural lag and the Iranian revolution

The recent history of Iran illustrates the explosive potential of times of cultural lag. During the 1960s and 1970s, the Shah of Iran made an immense effort to rapidly modernize his country. Thousands of young people were sent to the West for advanced technical educations. Many new industries were founded, and many foreign experts were brought in to train Iranians to operate them. Indeed, the Shah encouraged the importation of Western culture generally — movies, music, books, clothing, and the like. For these reasons, most Western observers regarded Iran as the most modern and Western of Middle Eastern societies and a model of development for other nations in the region. Indeed, the Shah received unqualified praise for realizing that he had only a few years to modernize his country's economy before Iranian oil reserves were exhausted. Instead of spending the huge oil income of Iran on importing luxury goods (as many other less developed nations have done), the Shah was thought to be using it to build a modern society, able to provide a high standard of living for Iranians after the oil wells were pumped dry (Halliday, 1979).

But the Shah fell victim to cultural lag. Beneath the gleaming surface of rapid modernization, which was all Westerners could see of this society, the majority of Iranians remained deeply committed to their traditional culture and to an unusually strict form of Islam. From this perspective, Western clothing and manners, especially for women, were intolerably evil. Since Islamic doctrine prohibits the making of images (which is why Islamic art excels in floral and geometric designs, but does not depict humans), movies and TV were regarded as blasphemous. In short, the mass of Iranian society was not readjusting to the rapid modernization fostered by the Shah and was instead increasingly scandalized and angry.

This anger led to constant opposition. Sometimes the opposition was mainly symbolic, such as shunning women in Western dress. At other times, acts of terrorism occurred — several times angry Muslim fundamentalists chained the doors of movie theaters during a movie and then burned down the buildings, killing those inside. Of course, the opposition produced countless conspiracies to overthrow the Shah. In response, the Shah resorted to increasingly repressive measures, using his growing secret police forces to uncover and punish his enemies. These measures aroused opposition among many of the most Westernized Iranians, who, educated in the United States, Canada, and Europe, aspired to greater democracy.

The Shah was caught between two irreconcilable forces, one reflecting cultural change and the other cultural lag. He could not democratize without the society exploding in civil war. But as protest in demand of increased democracy attracted support from Western governments, he was forced to try. Despite these efforts, civil unrest rapidly increased.

7. *Source:* Stark, 437–439.

In hopes of regaining the support of the most Westernized citizens, the Shah appointed the opposition leader Shahpur Bakhtiar to the premiership on December 29, 1978. Still the public protests continued, and riots broke out between traditionalist and modernist factions. On January 16, 1979, the Shah and his family left the country on an extended "vacation," hoping to give the new government a chance to gain support.

But then on February 1, 1979, the Ayatollah Khomeini, the most militant Muslim opponent of the Shah, returned from years of exile in France. The Ayatollah directed a civil war against the Shah's supporters and, in less than two weeks, seized the government.

Now the Westernized opponents of the Shah faced a day of reckoning, for the Ayatollah was a much more deadly enemy. Music broadcasts were prohibited as "no different from opium." Women were commanded to don veils or at least the *chador* (a large head scarf). Swimming pools and movie theaters were shut down (Ismael and Ismael, 1980). Firing squads began the bloody task of purging not only former supporters of the Shah but also all "blasphemers and servants of the devil" who opposed the Ayatollah.

In the midst of this terrible purge, the United States embassy was stormed by a mob, and American citizens were taken hostage. It took more than a year to secure their release and safe return. Meanwhile, war broke out between Iran and Iraq and has continued ever since. The oil has not run dry, but a breakdown of Iranian industry has reduced exports to a trickle.

Looking back, analysts now agree that the Shah failed because he tried to do too much too rapidly, creating intolerable internal strains. Iranian culture had no time to adjust to changes.

✍ In the space provided, summarize what you think is the main idea of the selection you just read.

_____

_____

_____

_____

You should have had no trouble recognizing the most important point. The headings, the underlined main idea, and the key word *illustrates* used in the first sentence of the second paragraph make comprehension easy. The topic of the passage is "Change and Cultural Lag." The first sentence states the main idea: "There can be considerable delay before a change in one part of a society produces a realignment of other parts." As a way to illustrate what is meant by *cultural lags*, the author recounts what occurred in Iran in the 1960s and 1970s.

As you can see from the examples you have just read, social scientists frequently used detailed examples and illustrations to support a main idea. Since examples themselves are seldom the main idea, learn to connect all examples and illustrations with a main idea. You will discover that the main idea is thus supported and highlighted rather than lost in a mass of details.

PROCESSING WHAT YOU JUST READ

✍ If you are using the *Student's Reading Journal* that accompanies this text, go to page 47 in it and follow the directions given.

If you are using your own notebook as a journal, answer the following questions:

1. List some of the ways writers alert a reader that an example is going to be used to support a main idea.

2. Give your own example of cultural lag based on the definition in the sample sociology passage, "Change and Cultural Lag."

Can you define that for me?

A second writing pattern frequently found in social science texts is **definition**. The special terms used in the social sciences often need to be explained or defined to clarify their meaning. Some definition patterns may be as brief as a one-word synonym or a phrase. These are **simple definitions**. More often than not, complete definitions require one to several paragraphs. These are called **extended definitions**. In some cases an entire chapter is devoted to defining a subject, theory, or principle. These are known as **special definitions**. Clue words and phrases that alert you that a definition is coming are *is, called, known as, is defined as, a term meaning.* Your objective in this section is to understand the three basic ways social scientists define their terms so that you will better understand your social science textbooks.

Simple Definitions

As I discussed in Chapter 5, social scientists often use words and terms that have special meanings in context. For instance, an economist writing about a "run on a bank" uses the word *run* much differently from the way a sportswriter would use it when describing a baseball game. To explain the term in the context of economics, an author might provide the definition along with an example or two to help make the meaning clear. Can you see how the following passage from a history text uses simple definition?

> The framers of the Constitution, Madison included, had not thought well of [political] parties. "Faction" was a word generally used for party in the eighteenth century, and a faction meant, by Madison's own definition, a group organized to procure selfish advantages at the expense of the community. Denunciation of factions or parties was a standard ingredient in every discussion of politics in the eighteenth century, as safe and as platitudinous as denunciation of corruption and praise of honesty.[8]

✍ Circle the number of the statement that best summarizes the preceding passage.

1. Madison, one of the authors of the Constitution, did not think well of political parties.
2. *Faction* was the word used in the eighteenth century for what we now call political parties.
3. Factions, or political parties, were equated with corruption and selfishness by the framers of the Constitution.

All the statements are true, of course, but the one that best summarizes the paragraph is statement 3. Statement 1 is too narrow and focuses on Madison more than on what is being defined: faction. Statement 2 provides the definition given in the paragraph but leaves out the reason the word is being defined. Statement 3 provides both the definition of *faction* and the point the paragraph is making about the word's meaning in eighteenth-century America. As you read the definitions in your textbooks, make certain that in addition to learning the word or term being defined you understand why it is being defined.

8. *Source:* John M. Blum, et al. *The National Experience,* 7th ed. Harcourt Brace Jovanovich. 1989, 145.

Sometimes, the definition of a word or term is provided so subtly that you may miss it. See if you can tell what is being defined in this selection about the tobacco industry in the early American colonies:

> More tobacco meant more labor, but where was it to come from? Families formed too slowly to provide it by natural population increase. Indians died too quickly on contact with whites to be a reliable labor force. African slaves cost too much money. But England still had a "surplus" of displaced yeoman farmers, desperate for employment. Many of them, as "indentured servants," voluntarily mortgaged the sweat of their bodies for several years to Chesapeake masters. In exchange they received transatlantic passage and eventual "freedom dues," including a few barrels of corn, a suit of clothes—and perhaps a small parcel of land.[9]

✍ In the space provided, write what is being defined.

_____

_____

_____

Actually, two terms are being defined: *indentured servants* and *freedom dues*. You probably noticed that these phrases had quotation marks around them, a way of catching your attention. (Often authors use quotation marks, underlining, bold-faced type, or italics to call your attention to important points.) The paragraph begins with a question, then answers it by showing where the labor force will *not* come from. The transition word *but* alerts us that a change is coming: "But England still had a 'surplus' of displaced yeoman [considered a lower class in English society] farmers, desperate for employment." They were so desperate for jobs that they were willing to "mortgage" themselves for years as indentured servants, hoping for eventual freedom dues.

From such a context, definitions are formed. We can infer that indentured servants "sold" themselves for a certain period of time to pay for their passage to America. Once they had worked off their contracts, they hoped for payment of some type of "freedom dues."

Extended definitions

Now let's look at the use of extended definition. All this means is that the term being defined requires more than one or two sentences. Read the following example of an extended definition.

What Is a Family

A **nuclear family** is a kinship group of two or more persons who live in the same household and are related by marriage, blood, or adoption. A childless couple, a couple with two children, and a mother and her child are all different types of families. A couple with children is probably the most popular conception of the family, although other family types are common. The number of single-parent families in America has increased substantially in recent years.

9. *Source:* Bailey, 40.

Most individuals belong to at least two different family systems during their lives. The **family of orientation** is the family in which one was born and raised. The **family of procreation** is the system created by a couple who marry.

The **extended family** is a combination of two or more nuclear families across generations. For example, a grandmother living with her married son, his wife, and their children would be described as an extended family.[10]

✍ In the space provided, write how you would define a family.

_____

_____

_____

_____

Despite all the information given in the passage, the question "What is a family?" is answered in the first sentence. The rest of the information has to do with the three types of family systems: the family of orientation, the family of procreation, and the extended family. (Did you notice how the definition of the extended family used an example to help clarify the meaning?) The point of the passage is to provide an extended definition of family, to go beyond that simple definition of the first sentence.

Here is another extended definition. What do you think is the main idea of the passage?

What Is Sociology?

What we call **sociology** is one of several fields known as the **social sciences**. They share the same subject matter: human behavior. They are called the *social sciences* because the human is not a solitary beast. Our daily lives intertwine with the lives of others—what we do, even much of what we hope, is influenced by those around us. To study ourselves, we must study our social relations. . . .

Despite their common subject matter, there are a number of different social sciences. Psychologists, economists, anthropologists, criminologists, political scientists, and even many historians, as well as sociologists, are social scientists. Divisions among these fields are often hazy. Indeed, sometimes it is impossible to tell to which field a social scientist's work belongs . . .

Yet, sociologists do have a distinct subject matter—a turf of their own. *Sociologists study the patterns and processes of human social relations.* Some of us concentrate on small groups and the patterns and processes of face-to-face interaction between humans. This part of sociology is known as **micro sociology**—*micro* means small, as in microscope. Micro sociologists look at life close up. Others of us concentrate on large groups, even whole societies. This large-scope sociology is known as **macro sociology** (*macro* means "large"). Macro sociologists attempt to explain the fundamental patterns and processes of large-scale social relations.[11]

10. *Source:* Stephen J. Bahr. *Family Interaction.* Macmillan, 1989, 3–4.
11. *Source:* Stark, 7.

✎ It's obvious from the heading, the boldfaced type, and the italicized sentence that this passage is defining *sociology*. But which of the following items best states the main idea of the passage? Circle the number of the statement that best summarizes the main idea.

1. Sociology is the study of the patterns and processes of human social relations.
2. Sociology is one of the fields known as the social sciences, which share the same subject matter: human behavior.
3. Sociology, one of the social sciences, attempts to examine the patterns and processes of human social relations in small groups as well as in whole societies.
4. Despite the similarities found in the various fields of social sciences, sociology has its own distinct subject matter: the patterns and processes of human social relations.

All these statements are true. Statement 1, however, is too narrow. The selection's extended definition provides more information than that. Statement 2 is true, but it doesn't distinguish sociology from the rest of the social sciences, which also deal with human behavior. Statement 3 is the best selection, because it mentions that sociology is one of the social sciences, provides the definition of sociology italicized in the passage, and covers both the micro and macro aspects of sociology. Statement 4 comes in second, but it fails to mention the micro and macro aspects of the field.

Special definitions

Special definitions can be as short as a paragraph or as long as a book. In the following selection, the author uses the words *Populism* and *Progressivism*, but he wants to make clear how he means these words. As you read, notice how the author defines these terms differently from the way they are normally used.

> I should perhaps explain the unusually broad sense in which I use the terms "Populism" and "Progressivism." By "Populism" I do not mean only the People's (or Populist) Party of the 1890's; for I consider the Populist Party to be merely a heightened expression, at a particular moment in time, of a kind of popular impulse that is endemic in American political culture. Long before the rebellion of the 1890's one can observe a larger trend of thought, stemming from the time of Andrew Jackson, and crystallizing after the Civil War in the Greenback, Granger, and anti-monopoly movements, that expressed the discontents of many farmers and businessmen with the economic changes of the late nineteenth century. The Populist spirit captured the Democratic Party in 1896, and continued to play an important part in the politics of the Progressive era. I believe that Populist thinking has survived in our own time, partly as an undercurrent of provincial resentments, popular and "democratic" rebelliousness and suspiciousness, and nativism.
>
> Similarly, by "Progressivism" I mean something more than the Progressive (or Bull Moose) Party formed by the Republican insurgents who supported Theodore Roosevelt for the presidency in 1912. I mean rather the broader impulse toward criticism and change that was everywhere so conspicuous after 1900, when the already forceful stream of agrarian discontent was enlarged and redirected by the growing enthusiasm of middle-class people for social and economic reform.[12]

12. *Source:* Richard Hofstader, *The Age of Reform.* Knopf, 1985, 4–5.

✍ Check your comprehension by circling the letter of correct response in each of the following numbered items.

1. By *Populism* the author means
    a. the People's party of 1890.
    b. provincial resentments, "democratic" rebelliousness.
    c. belief in popular democracy.
    d. agrarian reform.
2. By *Progressivism* the author means
    a. broad impulse toward criticism and change.
    b. Bull Moose party.
    c. the philosophy of Theodore Roosevelt.
    d. agrarian discontent.

You understand the author's distinction between the usual definitions and his personal definitions if you circled *b* in question 1 and *a* in question 2. In the first paragraph, he says what he does not mean by *Populism*, eventually telling us, in the last sentence, what he does mean. He uses the same technique in the second paragraph when he provides a broader than usual definition of *Progressivism*.

It is important that you understand how the author uses these words or you could misread an entire section or chapter dealing with Populism and Progressivism, especially if you already knew the words in their more common definitions.

PROCESSING WHAT YOU JUST READ

✍ If you are using the *Student's Reading Journal* that accompanies this text, go to page 47 in it and follow the directions given.

If you are using your own notebook as a journal, answer the following questions:

1. Define the three types of definition commonly used by social science writers.
2. Provide some clue words that alert the reader to the definition writing pattern.

What's the difference between *comparison* and *contrast*?

Social scientists frequently **compare** two things by showing likenesses or **contrast** two things by showing differences. Doing so tells us not only what two things have in common but also what they do not. Some clue words and phrases that alert you to a comparison are *alike, also, likewise, similarly, in addition;* some clue words and phrases for contrast are *on the other hand, in contrast, however, nevertheless, whereas.* Your objective in this section is to recognize the comparison-and-contrast writing pattern so that you can better understand your social science textbooks.

Let's clarify what is meant by the words *compare* and *contrast.* As you know, *compare* means "to show similarities"; *contrast* means "to show differences." However, sometimes the word *compare* is broadly used in reference to both similarities and differences. In this section *compare* is used in its narrower sense. However, if you see the word on an essay test, ask your instructor if both similarities and differences are being requested.

Most of the time recognizing a comparison-and-contrast writing pattern is not difficult. When an author wishes to compare and contrast two people, two theories, two political parties, or two forms of government, naturally similarities and differences need to be shown. As a reader, your task is to make certain you see both.

Read the following example of the comparison-and-contrast writing pattern used to describe the North and the South around 1860.

An increasing body of Northerners believed in protective tariffs, while the rural South, wanting its manufactured goods cheaply, detested them. The North was interested in a quicker distribution of the public lands to small holders. A mighty demand for free homesteads to all settlers was arising: "Vote yourself a farm!" became a popular cry. The South wished to see the national domain held and sold only for good prices. The North wanted an efficient national banking system; the South, which accumulated little capital, was hostile to centralized banking. Socially the North, despite growing extremes of wealth and poverty in the large cities, was more democratic than the South, where the slaveholding oligarchy held most of the wealth and power.[13]

✍ Write the main idea of the preceding passage in the space provided.

_____

_____

_____

_____

The passage is contrasting the North and the South on four issues: protective tariffs, distribution of public lands, a national banking system, and social democracy. The basic pattern is easy to follow, alternating between what the North feels and what the South feels. There is no topic sentence here. As readers, we have to form the main idea on our own. However, it is not difficult to do so. The first sentence contrasts the North's and the South's views on protective tariffs; the following three sentences contrast their views on public lands; next, contrasting views on banking are given; finally, the differences in the regions' social structures are stated. When we are finished reading the passage, we realize there were wide differences between the North and the South at this time in history.

Not all comparison-and-contrast patterns are so simple, showing one side and then the other. Notice how comparison and contrast is done in the following selection:

What was it that gave the Old South its special identity? Not physical isolation, for it lacked natural barriers separating it from the rest of the country; nor geographic and climatic uniformity, for it had great diversity of soils, topography, mean temperatures, growing seasons, and average rainfalls. Not a difference in the origins of the white population, for the South, like the North, was originally settled mostly by middle- and lower-class people from northern and western Europe; nor contrasts in cultures or ideologies, for here, too, the similarities outweighed the differences. Not even the economies of the North and South were altogether dissimilar, for, although there were important differences, the majority of the white people of both sections were independent yeoman farmers who worked their own lands. However, fewer Southern farmers than Northern farmers benefited from improved transportation and became part of the national market economy. Wealth was less evenly distributed in the South than in the West; less money was invested in education; and the rate of illiteracy was higher. Fewer towns and less local industry developed. In short, the Old South remained more rural and economically less diversified than the North, and a larger

13. *Source:* Nevins and Commager, 209.

proportion of its small farmers lived a life of pioneer self-sufficiency and isolation.[14]

✍ Here is a list of points made in the passage you just read. In the blanks, write *S* after the items the North and South had in common and *D* after those that were different.

1. Money invested in education   _____

2. Origins of the white population   _____

3. Cultural backgrounds   _____

4. Independent yeoman farmers   _____

5. Rate of illiteracy   _____

6. Number of towns   _____

7. Industrial development   _____

8. Improved transportation   _____

9. Economic diversity   _____

10. Pioneer self-sufficiency and isolation   _____

The passage begins by asking a question: What gave the Old South its special identify? The first half of the selection outlines what was *not* different in the South and the North. But then comes the clue word *However*, and differences, things that gave the Old South its special identity, begin to appear. The final sentence begins "In short" and summarizes the main idea. If you saw this, your answers should read (1) D, (2) S, (3) S, (4) S, (5) D, (6) D, (7) D, (8) D, (9) D, and (10) D. If you had trouble with this selection, look it over again, using the answers as a guide.

Sometimes the comparison-and-contrast pattern can continue longer. So much information can be given that you become frustrated in deciding what is important to remember and what isn't. However, if you keep in mind that two things are being discussed at once, it will help to look for their similarities and differences.

Read this passage, which compares the president of the Southern Confederacy and the president of the United States.

Two New Presidents   Jefferson Davis of Mississippi, elected provisional president by the delegates to the Confederate Convention at Montgomery, Alabama, stepped out on the portico of the Alabama capital and was sworn in as President of the Confederate States of America on February 18, 1861. A week later Abraham Lincoln of Illinois arrived in Washington to become the sixteenth President of the United States. The two men, born a year and less than a hundred miles apart in Kentucky, were both products of the frontier experience. Their differences spoke the difference of North from South. Davis's father, taking his family to Mississippi, raised cotton and, when prospering, sent his son to Transylvania University. When financial reverses came, Jefferson transferred to West Point, which was free. Even before

14. *Source:* Blum, 193.

becoming a hero in the Mexican War, he had been elected to Congress and in the 1850s was first a senator, then Secretary of War, and then, again, a senator.

Tall and handsome, Davis was serious almost to the point of humorlessness, and he would not permit himself any emotional interchange with the men with whom he worked. As did the Lincolns, he and his much younger wife suffered the private anguish of the loss of a child during the public ordeal of the war. The Confederate President was proud of his family, but not sure enough of its aristocratic strength to be able to rely on it easily for self-confidence. Instead he demanded deference from colleagues and took criticism poorly. In his insistence on directing military actions, he provoked quarrels among his generals. He did not grow into greatness as President, instead he grew more and more reserved and remote from people who might have helped him. But in February 1861, the firm, upright Mississippian, well known to his colleagues, had inspired confidence. Introducing him on the Montgomery portico, William Lowndes Yancey said: "The man and the hour have met."

In contrast, Lincoln—having done virtually no campaigning, taken no public positions since the election, and forced to make a secret trip into Washington from Philadelphia to avoid an assassination threat in Baltimore—arrived in his capital an object of newspaper scorn and a man unknown to many people in government. Lincoln's father, poorer than Davis', had not provided for his son, who had to break from his family in order to escape poverty and succeed as a lawyer. Lincoln brought to the White House a confidence few, at first, guessed him to have. A deeply emotional man, he was perfectly in touch with his countrymen, from whom he demanded—and received—great sacrifices. Lincoln did, indeed, grow into greatness as President.

Jefferson Davis's Cabinet was never strong and was subject to constant change. Judah P. Benjamin, the first Jew in America to achieve cabinet rank, was Attorney General, Secretary of War, and finally, Secretary of State. He was perhaps the most able cabinet member, but it is telling that he was but one of six Secretaries of War. Alexander H. Stephens, the Vice President, was soon one of Davis's chief critics. Another weakness was that the states-rights doctrine led Southern governors to be more grudging in their support of the war effort than governors of the Northern states were to be.

Lincoln, in contrast, chose strong men and had far fewer changes in his Cabinet. Those who thought Secretary of State William H. Seward, Secretary of the Treasury Salmon P. Chase, or Secretary of War Simon Cameron—and later Edwin M. Stanton—would dominate the inexperienced President were wrong. Lincoln was soon in command, and he learned at the helm in one of the most difficult crises in American history.[15]

✍ In the spaces provided, write down some of the differences and similarities between Jefferson Davis and Abraham Lincoln.

Similarities	*Differences*
_____	_____
_____	_____

15. *Source:* Blum, 318.

_____   _____

_____   _____

_____   _____

If we look at one paragraph at a time, we see that the first paragraph of the selection mentions that both men were elected president and began serving their terms within one week. Both were born in Kentucky of frontier families. But then the author states, "Their differences spoke the difference of North from South." The rest of the paragraph is devoted to Davis's background.

The second paragraph deals entirely with Davis, except for the mention that both his family and the Lincolns suffered the loss of a child during the war. Then the third paragraph begins, "In contrast, Lincoln" and provides us with information about Lincoln's personality and performance that is different from what we are told about Davis.

The fourth paragraph goes back to Davis, his cabinet and weaknesses. The fifth and last paragraph begins, "Lincoln, in contrast" and reveals the differences in the way Lincoln dealt with his cabinet. Aware of that structure, we can now sort out the similarities and differences between the two men.

Compare the lists you just prepared with these:

Similarities	*Differences*
elected president	educational background
from Kentucky	emotional interchange with others
product of frontier experience	public reaction (Davis well-liked; Lincoln
lost a child during the war	scorned in the press)
	working relations with cabinet members

Your wording may be a bit different, but these items sum up the basic similarities and differences between Jefferson Davis and Abraham Lincoln, the leaders of the two sections of the country divided by civil war. Writing up your notes as shown for an assigned reading passage similar to this one, will force you to pull the key information from the text and organize it for future review.

When you read a passage that is comparing and contrasting two people, places, time periods, or events, your task is to recognize the similarities and differences being presented. Each of the two things beings compared or contrasted can be better understood in relation to the other.

PROCESSING WHAT YOU JUST READ

✍ If you are using the *Student's Reading Journal* that accompanies this text, go to page 48 in it and follow the directions given.

If you are using your own notebook as a journal, answer the following questions:

1. Explain the difference between comparing and contrasting.
2. Provide some clue words that alert the reader to the comparison-and-contrast writing pattern.
3. Based on your answers to the preceding questions, explain how the comparison-and-contrast writing pattern provides an organized way to take reading notes.

Don't social scientists try to explain what happened and why?

Social scientists search for logical reasons for the actions of people in the past, and then today they attempt to interpret human events and to re-create a story that makes sense. The economist tries to develop laws of economics by sorting out financial happenings. After analyzing contemporary life in society, the sociologist suggests theories of human social behavior. But all social science theories and laws begin with actual, disorderly human events. The problem for the social scientist is to give these events order.

You have already been introduced to three ways writers do this. You've seen how they make a general statement or claim and then back it up with examples. You've seen them introduce a useful term and define it. You've seen how they compare and contrast events and principles to clarify a position. These writing patterns are all ways to create order. Now you will learn another kind of order: **cause and effect**.

Generally, events or actions have causes, and usually they have effects as well. When social scientists try to find the causes of events, they must also deal with their effects. Clue words and phrases that alert you to the cause-and-effect pattern are *because, therefore, due to, is caused by, as a result of, resulted in, the effect was.* Your objective in this section is to learn the cause-and-effect pattern so that you can better understand your social science textbooks.

Cause-and-effect passages are seldom neatly ordered as the passages you've studied so far. They require close attention to each sentence because often no single sentence is the key one. You have to understand the relationships among the sentences. Social scientists are interested in historic events, so rather than merely state a conclusion they've drawn from some event, they like to provide the reasoning that led them to that conclusion. They are interested in why something happened, what caused it to happen, and then what the effect, result, or consequences of what happened were.

Because the social science writer looks closely at events, cause-and-effect passages are filled with references to times and places. These references are useful in recognizing the relationship that's being established. Practice your book marking skills and find the main idea in this passage, which deals with conscription, or the draft system, during the Civil War.

In March 1863, volunteering having fallen off, Congress passed a conscription act. The law applied to all men between 20 and 45, but it allowed draftees to hire substitutes and even to buy exemption for $300, a provision patently unfair to the poor, causing draft riots to erupt in parts of the nation. By far the most serious of these disturbances occurred in New York City in July 1863. Many workers resented conscription in principle and were embittered by the $300 exemption fee (which represented a year's wages). The idea of being forced to risk their lives to free slaves who would then, they believed, compete with them for jobs infuriated them. On July 13 a mob attacked the office where the names of conscripts were being drawn. Most of the rioters were Irish laborers who were desperately poor and no doubt resentful of what seemed to them the special attention blacks were suddenly receiving. For four days the city was an inferno. Public buildings, shops, and private residences were put to the torch. What began as a protest against the draft became a campaign to exterminate blacks. Over a hundred were run down "as hounds would chose a fox" and beaten.[16]

16. *Source:* John A. Garraty, *The American Nation,* 4th ed. Harper and Row, 1989, 379.

✍ In the space provided, write down the cause and the effect being described.

_____

_____

_____

_____

Most of this passage details the rioting that occurred in New York City in July 1863. However, the historian's purpose is to show the effect of the conscription act passed in March of that year. So the main point is not the rioting itself but the fact that there was deep resentment among many people regarding the draft law, the *cause* of the riot. The *effects* were destruction of property and bodily harm to blacks.

Read the following passage about the prohibition of alcohol in the 1920s, looking again for cause-and-effect relationships.

> In any case, prohibition widened already serious rifts in the social fabric of the country; its repressive spirit pitted city against farm, native against immigrant, race against race. In the South, where the dominant whites had argued that prohibition would improve the morals of the blacks, it was the blacks who became the chief bootleggers.
>
> Beside undermining public morality by encouraging hypocrisy, prohibition almost destroyed the Democratic party as a national organization; Democratic immigrants in the cities hated it, but southern Democrats sang its praises (often while continuing to drink).[17]

✍ In the space provided, write down the cause and the effects being shown.

_____

_____

_____

_____

In this selection, the writer shows the effects of prohibition. According to this historian's interpretation of history, prohibition [the cause] created "serious rifts" in this country, sparking disagreements that pitted "city against farm, native against immigrant, race against race" [the effects]. We aren't told, but we can assume the disagreements were over the pros and cons of prohibition. Another effect was that blacks became the chief bootleggers, ironically, the opposite of the effect dominant white Southerners expected. Other effects of prohibition were hypocrisy and the near destruction of the Democratic party as a national organization.

Here's another example of the cause-and-effect pattern. This one deals with certain Indian uprisings in the early American nineteenth century, during Andrew Jackson's presidency. Look for causes and effects as you read and mark the passage.

> Jackson proposed a bodily removal of the remaining eastern tribes— chiefly Cherokee, Creek, Choctaw, and Chickasaw—beyond the Mississippi [River]. Individual Indians might remain if they adopted white

17. *Source:* Garraty, 628

WHAT DO YOU THINK?

The public as a whole is not concerned with solving the problems of the poor, of the homeless, though they should be, because these ultimately can be dangerous to everyone's ordinary life. But something more seems to me to have happened, and that is the loss of a moral sense, of knowing the difference between right and wrong, and of being governed by it.

Barbara Tuchman, historian

---

society's ways. Emigration should be voluntary, since it would be "cruel and unjust to compel the aborigines to abandon the graves of their fathers."

Jackson's policy was high-sounding, but it led to the more or less forcible uprooting of more than 100,000 Indians in the 1830s. Many died on the "Trail of Tears" to the newly established Indian Territory (present Oklahoma) where they were "permanently" free of white encroachments. The Bureau of Indian Affairs was established in 1836 to administer relations with America's original inhabitants. But as the land-hungry "palefaces" pushed west faster than anticipated, the goverment's guarantees went up in smoke. The "permanent" frontier lasted about fifteen years.

Suspicious of white intentions from the start, braves from Illinois and Wisconsin, ably led by Black Hawk, resisted eviction. They were bloodily crushed in 1832 by regular troops, including Lieutenant Jefferson Davis of Mississippi, and by volunteers, including Captain Abraham Lincoln of Illinois.

The Seminole Indians of Florida, joined by runaway black slaves, retreated to the swampy Everglades. For seven years (1835–1842) they waged a bitter guerrilla war that took the lives of some fifteen hundred soldiers and proved to be the costliest Indian conflict in American experience. The spirit of the Seminoles was at last broken in 1837 when the American field commander treacherously seized their half-breed leader, Osceola, under a flag of truce.[18]

✍ In the space provided, state what you see as the major cause and effect in this passage.

_____

_____

_____

_____

This passage is not complicated, but to follow it requires considering every sentence; no main idea is stated. The first sentence states Jackson's proposal: remove the Indians beyond the Mississippi. The second and third sentences provide more information about the proposal. The second paragraph deals with the effect of the policy: a more or less forcible uprooting of over 100,000 Indians and the death of

18. *Source:* Bailey, 257

many other Indians. The *cause* is Jackson's proposal; the *effect* is what happened to the Indians.

Also in the second paragraph, we learn that the creation of the Bureau of Indian Affairs was another effect of Jackson's proposal. And an additional cause-and-effect pair is shown in this paragraph: Because the "palefaces" moved west faster than anticipated, promises to the Indians were broken. One thing followed from another. And this happened because, in historic fact, one thing caused another—or so the historian suggests.

The last two paragraphs of the passage also deal with cause and effect. If you were asked what caused the revolts of the Illinois and Wisconsin Indians, you could say their uprooting from their homes and being forced to suffer removal to lands west of the Mississippi. The historian doesn't say so in those exact words, but the writing pattern certainly suggests that the uprooting caused the rebellion.

Look again at the last sentence: "The spirit of the Seminoles was at last broken in 1837, when the American field commander treacherously seized their half-breed leader, Osceola, under a flag of truce." The word *when* implies "because." Two events occurred: their spirit was broken, and the American commander deceived them. The effect of these two causes was the end of the rebellion.

The *major cause* in this passage is Jackson's Indian removal proposal; the *effect* is the uprooting, destruction, and rebellion of the Indians affected by the proposal.

One of the ways social scientists organize human events is by linking what causes an event with the effects it brings. When social scientists propose that a certain event caused another, they must back up their statements with evidence. As a result, specific *examples* are an important part of this type of discussion, which cannot be summarized easily. Also, the *sequence* of events is very important, since an effect always follows its cause. Therefore, cause-and-effect passages require a reader's close attention and careful thought.

PROCESSING WHAT YOU JUST READ

✍ If you are using the *Student's Reading Journal* that accompanies this text, go to page 48 in it and follow the directions given.

If you are using your own notebook as a journal, answer the following questions:

1. Give two examples of cause-and-effect relationship. They don't have to be related to the social sciences.
2. Why are social scientists interested in causes and effects?

Don't social scientists have to deal in facts?

In the previous sections you have learned to analyze social science passages to discover how their meaning is revealed by the structure of the writing. In this section, you will analyze some social science passages with a different aim. Instead of structure, you will judge content. Your objective in this section is to find out how much "fact" each selection contains and how much is open to question, so that you can distinguish between fact and opinion or interpretation in all your social science textbooks.

What is fact?

Dictionaries tell us that a **fact** is "a piece of information presented as having objective reality." Then the question becomes "What is meant by objective reality?" An *objective statement* is one that is not colored or distorted by personal feelings or ideas. For instance, which of the following is an objective statement?

History is an exciting subject.

History is a required course for some college degrees.

Even though you might agree with both statements, one is a fact and one is opinion. The first statement is not objective; the word *exciting* makes it an opinion, because not everyone would agree with this view of history. However, the second statement can be verified as fact. Simply go to a college catalog and check it out. Facts, like the second statement, can be verified by checking the records. Opinions, like the first statement, cannot be verified. The only information they provide is the speaker's feelings.

Some statements tend to sound true because they may contain dates, events, or figures. However, which of the following statements is fact?

The Sixteenth Amendment to the Constitution was adopted in 1900.

The Sixteenth Amendment to the Constitution was adopted in 1913.

Can both be fact? Since, as you probably know, constitutional amendments are adopted only once, one of the statements has to be false. A check with a reliable source soon reveals that the second statement is true. As long as your knowledge is sound, two statements like this can easily be dealt with.

But suppose you read these two statements in a textbook:

James A. Garfield became president of the United States in 1881.

Chester A. Arthur became president of the United States in 1881.

You may not be sure enough of your history to know who became president in 1881. You might think that there was a printing error or that the author made a mistake. But if you checked with another source, or if you were already familiar with this period of history, you would know that both statements are fact. Garfield was assassinated in 1881, the same year he took office, and Arthur, his vice president, succeeded him.

The first criterion for accepting what you read is the reliability of the source. The second criterion is your own reading and background. The third is verification of suspect facts in other sources. The more you read, the more critical you can become, and the more you can rely on your knowledge. However, the more you read in the social sciences, the more you will discover that some facts, especially historic facts, are very difficult to check.

An example of this difficulty is found in the reported figures of war dead. Some texts, for instance, state that the United States lost more men in the Korean War than any other nation on its side. In some texts the number of the U.S. soldiers killed in action runs as high as 54,000. One recent text offers 23,000 as the number of U.S. dead, claiming that over a million Koreans and Chinese died in the conflict. Another text states that at least 50,000 South Koreans were killed, while still another work estimates conservatively that "at least 3000" South Koreans were killed. On the other side, the estimates for Communist casualties—both North Korean and Chinese—range from 1.5 million in one book to 5.0 million in another. Which authorities should you believe?

By checking the indexes of several books on the Korean War in the library, you might finally settle on your own estimate of the figures. Only by reading, checking, and thinking can you approach the truth. In some cases, the truth might no longer be available, or it might have to wait until more evidence is in. Just because a statement is printed—whether in a textbook, journal, or newspaper—it is not necessarily fact.

I'm not suggesting that historians make up figures or intentionally report unreliable information. The problem of reliability is a serious one. On the whole, historians use the tests of consistency and validation. But sometimes there isn't enough evidence, and what is reported as truth is found to be erroneous when new information surfaces which changes the "facts."

Looking for facts, read the following passage, which deals with the entry of the United States into World War II.

> The bitter wreckage of ships and planes at Pearl Harbor ended the illusion that the United States could be a world power and remain safe from world conflict. In the shocking strike from the placid Hawaiian skies, the Japanese crippled the Pacific fleet, destroyed nearly 200 planes, and killed nearly 2,500 men. The navy lost three times as many men in this single attack as it had lost in the Spanish-American and First World wars combined. Four days after Pearl Harbor, on December 11, 1941, Germany and Italy declared war on the United States and Congress declared war on them. America was now committed to global war.[19]

✍ Based on this passage, circle the numbers of any of the following statements that can be accepted as fact.

1. The Japanese attacked Pearl Harbor on December 7, 1941.
2. The United States Navy's Pacific Fleet was badly damaged.
3. Two hundred planes were destroyed and 2,500 men were killed.
4. The navy lost more men in this attack than it lost in the Spanish-American and First World wars combined.
5. Germany and Italy declared war on the United States on December 11, 1941.
6. Before this attack, the United States thought it could be a world power without being involved in world conflict.

This passage is almost entirely objectively stated. On the basis of the passage, all the items in the question are fact except number 3. The passage says *"nearly"* 200 planes were destroyed, and *"nearly"* 2,500 men were killed. Without that word *nearly* in front of the numbers, the statement is wrong. (Just a little trick there to see how alert you are before going on.)

WHAT DO YOU THINK?

Isn't it disgusting to realize that there are organizations and specialists who exist in grooming candidates for election to office? They tell candidates what to wear, how to stand, where to sit, what to say. But isn't it equally disgusting that we know about it, and that we're not revolted?

Joseph Heller, novelist

What is opinion?

In some ways, an opinion is easier to spot than a false fact. Here are two statements about a historic figure:

> Georges Clemenceau, often called "the Tiger," was twice premier of France, 1906–1909, and 1917–1919.

> Clemenceau drove bargains with the vulgar single-mindedness of a fishwife.

Obviously, the second statement, as worded, is someone's opinion, and a negative one. The language is "colored" by the author's opinion of Clemenceau. Other

---

19. *Source:* Blum, 667.

writers would disagree with such a subjective statement. The test of an **opinion**, then, is its *subjectivity*. Opinions are subjective, that is, personal, biased, or emotional reactions.

How subjective is the following passage?

> God has not been preparing the English-speaking and Teutonic peoples for a thousand years for nothing but vain and idle self-contemplation and self-admiration. No! He has made us the master organizers of the world to establish system where chaos reigns. He has given us the spirit of progress to overwhelm the forces of reaction throughout the earth. He has made us adept in government that we may administer government among savage and senile peoples. Were it not for such a force as this the world would relapse into barbarism and night. And of all our race He has marked the American people as His chosen nation to finally lead in the regeneration of the world. This is the divine mission of America, and it holds for us all the profit, all the glory, all the happiness possible to man. We are trustees of the world's progress, guardians of its righteous peace. The judgment of the Master is upon us: "Ye have been faithful over a few things; I well make you ruler over many things."[20]

If you had heard or read this speech in 1900, you might have been strongly moved by the force of the moral argument. Who wouldn't be on the side of "the spirit of progress"? And if we believe we have a "divine mission" (whatever that is), we must carry it out. But if you read carefully, you noticed that the speaker was trying very hard to persuade us at the expense of fact and logic. Many connotative words and expressions are used.

Notice the speaker's use of emotionally charged words: "master organizers," "chaos," "savage and senile," "barbarism and night," "divine mission,""judgment of the Master." Such words and phrases are intended to persuade and stir us into action. But scarcely a word used is capable of being verified. The speaker resorts to the old trick of taking a biblical quotation out of context, as though it had been written just for his purpose. There are no facts here; only feelings are presented, feelings which can stir many nonthinking people to action because they are credited to "God's will."

Politicians, of course, know very well the power of emotional language. Following is a portion of a speech given by President George Bush in 1990, shortly after Iraq invaded and took over a smaller neighbor, Kuwait. Worried that Iraq might also invade other oil-rich neighbors, Bush sent a large contingency of Americans troops, ships, and supplies to the Middle East as a protective measure. Whether this action was justified, only future events and historians can tell. Notice, however, the emotional language and method Bush used to rally Americans into accepting his preparations for a possible war.

> At this moment, our brave servicemen and women stand watch in the distant desert and on distant seas, side-by-side with the forces of more than 20 other nations.
>
> They are some of the finest men and women of the United States of America. And they're doing one terrific job.
>
> These valiant Americans were ready to leave at a moment's notice, to leave their spouses, their children, to serve on the front-line halfway around the world. They remind us who keeps America strong. They do.

20. *Source:* From a speech in the U.S. Senate by Albert J. Beveridge, January 9, 1900. *Congressional Record.* 33, Pt. 1, 711.

In the trying circumstance of the [Persian] gulf, the morale of our servicemen and women is excellent. In the face of danger, they are brave, well-trained and dedicated.

A soldier, PFC. Wade Merritt of Knoxville, Tenn., now stationed in Saudi Arabia, wrote his parents of his worries, his love of family and his hopes for peace. But Wade also wrote: "I am proud of my country and its firm stand against inhumane aggression. I am proud of my Army and its men. . . . I am proud to serve my country."

Let me just say, Wade, America is proud of you. And grateful to every soldier, sailor, Marine and airman serving the cause of peace in the Persian Gulf.

. . . So if ever there was a time to put country before self and patriotism before party, that time is now. Let me thank all Americans . . . for your support for our forces and their mission. So tonight, I want to talk to you about what is at stake—what we must do together to defend civilized values around the world, and maintain our economic strength at home.

God bless America.[21]

✍ In the space provided, list all the verifiable facts in this speech.

_____

_____

_____

_____

About the only verifiable facts in the speech itself are that American troops are in the Persian Gulf and that PFC. Wade Merritt wrote a letter to his parents expressing his feelings. Most of the speech appeals to our emotions. Using the letter of a serviceman who states he is proud of his country and loves his family is in itself an emotional device. To criticize such a letter, or to say our service personnel don't "keep America strong," are not "brave," and do not oppose "inhumane aggression" would seem "un-American" to many. The point here is not to argue for or against Bush's policy but to call attention to the deliberate use of emotion and opinion, not fact, to get support. Such language manipulates and distracts people from looking more deeply into the real issues.

Writers of most college textbooks try to avoid such connotative language, partly because it's poor scholarship and partly because it would confuse the reader. Besides, the writers know that other social scientists, critics, and teachers would be likely to call such statements to task. Usually, when writers do express their feelings, they make it clear that that's what they are doing and acknowledge that others disagree. Here's an example of one historian calling into question a viewpoint about the intent behind the Constitution held by other historians since 1913:

Charles Beard's Book, *An Economic Interpretation of the Constitution of the United States* (1913), has long defined the area around which debate on the constitutional period has revolved. Beard described the Constitution as the "reactionary" phase of the Revolutionary era—a shrewd maneuver by conservative property owners to curtail the democratic excesses let loose in 1776. Most modern scholars, if they accept Beard's argument at all, accept it only with severe qualifications. The

21. *Source: Los Angeles Times.*

most recent discussions of the Constitution have been cast in terms of reflections on the ancient riddle of republicanism: Does republican self-government rest on the virtue of the people or on the formal political institutions that control human behavior? Seen in this light, the framers of the Constitution appear more "radical" than their opponents.[22]

✎ In the space provided, write down what you think is significant about this passage.

_____

_____

_____

_____

_____

This writer explains a viewpoint held by historian Charles Beard and accepted by others for some time. Then the writer states that modern scholars either disagree with this viewpoint or accept it "with severe qualifications." The significant point seems to be that modern scholars are no longer in agreement with Beard's idea that the Constitution was "a shrewd maneuver by conservative property owners to curtail . . . democratic excesses." Modern scholars are coming up with opposing opinions based on their own historical interpretation.

What is interpretation?

Like an opinion, an **interpretation** cannot be verified. It's open to debate. But unlike opinion, interpretation is essentially nonemotional and nonpersonal. It often represents a widely held view, although this doesn't mean it's correct. Interpretations of history are constantly changing, as you just saw.

Are there qualities that distinguish opinion from interpretation? Often you have to rely on the "sound" of the writing. Opinion has a tendency to be emotional, full of the writer's feelings. Interpretation is more reasoned, more controlled. Opinion seeks to persuade the reader; interpretation tries to increase the reader's understanding. At what point interpretation slips into opinion it is impossible to say.

How do fact, opinion, and interpretation fit together? It might help to think of them as three separate levels of information:

1. **Fact:** basic information that can be objectively verified
2. **Opinion:** a writer's personal feelings about the facts
3. **Interpretation:** a writer's attempt to increase your understanding of the facts

All three are essential and, for that matter, inevitable. These three kinds of information serve different purposes. To use an absurd simile for a moment, reading can be like eating a bowl of chicken noodle soup. Sometimes you feel like eating only the meat, sometimes you want only the noodles, and on other occasions you want only the broth. But most of the time you consume them all at once. Just be alert for the presence in any reading selection of all three kinds of information, and be

22. *Source:* Bailey, 147.

prepared to sort them out. Otherwise you may accept an opinion or interpretation as the absolute truth.

As a student of the social sciences, you will need to develop the skill to judge what is fact, opinion, and interpretation. Read the following passage, looking for statements of fact, opinion, and interpretation.

The Rise of Kings and Commerce

If Columbus had sailed when the Norsemen did, his voyages would probably have had as little effect as theirs on the course of history. By 1492, however, Europeans were ready for new worlds. During the intervening centuries two important historical developments had prepared them. One was the rise of a large merchant class hungry for foreign trade. Spices, dyestuffs, textiles from India and the Orient traveled overland by slow, expensive caravan through Asia or partly by sail through the Red Sea or the Persian Gulf, passing from one dealer to another along the way until they finally reached the marketplaces of Europe. The prices people were willing to pay for these exotic imports were enough to send fifteenth-century sailors in search of sea routes to the source of the treasures. A direct sea route would permit importation in greater volume at less expense and would net the importer a huge profit.

Portugal took the lead in maritime exploration with an new type of vessel, the caravel—faster, more maneuverable, more seaworthy than any formerly known. Portuguese explorers, encouraged by their kings and by Prince Henry the Navigator (1394–1460), discovered the Azores and pushed their caravels farther and farther south along the coast of Africa. At first they were probably seeking only new trading opportunities in Africa itself, but by the 1480s they were searching for a way around the continent to the great riches of the Orient.[23]

✍ In the blank following each statement, place *F* for a fact, *O* for an opinion, and *I* for an interpretation.

1. If Columbus had sailed when the Norsemen did, his voyages would probably have had as little effect as theirs on the course of history. _____

2. By 1492, Europeans were ready for new worlds. _____

3. A direct sea route would permit importation in greater volume at less expense and would net the importer a huge profit. _____

4. Portugal took the lead in maritime exploration with a new type of vessel, the caravel. _____

5. At first they were probably seeking only new trading opportunities in Africa itself. _____

As I interpret the passage, numbers 1 and 5 are interpretations; note that the word *probably* is used in both statements. The second statement sounds factual with that date in it, but the content seems to be based on the author's interpretation of the "two important historical developments" that follow it; so I go for interpretation. I see both number 3 and number 4 as factual because they can be verified. In

23. *Source:* Blum, 4.

addition, from my own background reading of other historians, I know there is a consensus about these statements. You may read these statements differently, of course, but make certain your answers aren't based on opinion only.

FINAL THOUGHTS   This chapter has introduced you to five writing patterns found frequently in history, political science, economics, sociology, psychology, and anthropology textbooks. You should now understand how social scientists use examples, definitions, comparison-and-contrast, cause and effect, and fact, opinion, and interpretation in their writing.

You've learned that facts are verifiable statements, opinions are subjective, unverifiable statements, and interpretations are objective but unverifiable. Facts provide you with information, opinions tell you how the writer feels about the information, and interpretations increase your understanding of what the information means. Each kind of statement has its valid use and is necessary in the social sciences, but it is important not to mistake one for another.

WHAT DO YOU THINK?

Michael Josephson, ethicist: Success can be defined in so many ways. But right now people ask, how high is your position, how many people work for you, how high is your salary? When you get into that kind of yuppie version of success, you're going to sacrifice things along the way. There's not enough commitment to the ground rules of civic virtue.

Bill Moyers: Yet the people most conspicuous in the news for violating ethical imperatives have not been yuppies. They've been successful Wall Street brokers; career military officers; top middle-aged advisors to President Reagan. These have not been yuppies.

Michael Josephson: But they're the creatures of the yuppies. The yuppie is the constituency that makes it okay. They're the people who applaud success, who allow an Ivan Boesky to say, "Greed is good," and not be hooted down from the stage. They're the people who write books on how to win by intimidation and who can get on every TV show to teach people how to do that. Of course, the yuppie mentality is not really people, it's an approach. It's the philosophy of measuring our lives by what we get, what we acquire, who we know. It's a very shallow kind of life. People find that out in time. But during the period when that philosophy flourishes, we sacrifice a lot.

PROCESSING WHAT YOU JUST READ

✍ If you are using the *Student's Reading Journal* that accompanies this text, go to page 49 in it and follow the directions given.

If you are using your own notebook as a journal, answer the following questions:

1. Write two statements of fact and two statements of opinion about yourself. Then write a statement interpreting what you think those four statements say about you.
2. Write a brief explanation of each of the social science writing patterns as a way to summarize the contents of this chapter.

Review your journal notes, then go to Part III, page 318, and practice what you have learned. Use what you have learned to help you read your social science textbooks.

CHAPTER 7

Research Sources in the Social Sciences

PREPARING TO READ   It is not unusual for social science instructors to assign research projects or outside reading during the term. Outside reading is assigned to provide new, and often more detailed, information than you can get in lectures or your textbook. Since a textbook is often out of date as soon as it is published, instructors will assign extra readings or even research reports that require you to use current source material. Outside sources can range from the more familiar magazines, such as *Time, Newsweek*, and *U.S. News & World Report* to the *Congressional Record* and *Social Science Quarterly*. **Your objective in reading this chapter is to become more familiar with outside sources you can use for social science assignments.**

Source: Reprinted by permission of UFS, INC.

What's so important about outside reading assignments?

Writing a report on outside readings or doing a research paper several pages long, including footnotes and bibliography, can be seen as a real pain. But such projects can and should be interesting and are a way of exposing yourself to information and materials you never knew existed.

Most of what you learn about the social sciences, if you think about it, comes from only two sources: the instructor and the textbook. The textbook, even if it has a current copyright, is dated the day it comes off the press, because it can take a year or more after it has been written for a book to get into print. Most freshman and sophomore textbooks are written for survey courses, meaning they only touch on certain selected areas and are not able to cover many topics in detail. Your instructor is probably an expert in a specialized aspect of the social sciences and will no doubt have strong opinions on her specialty. But she won't know everything.

Your outside reading assignments and research projects provide a chance to broaden your knowledge in some area of personal interest. The more reading you do outside the textbook, the more knowledge you gain. After all, you probably won't be taking this course again, so when will you ever have the incentive and opportunity to learn more? You need outside reading assignments to help you separate fact from opinion, detect biases and prejudices, relate what you already know to what you are learning, and get a broader perspective on problems and situations you never knew existed.

The real reason outside readings and research projects can become a problem is procrastination, putting off the assignment until you feel pressured to complete it. When that happens, you just go through the motions of learning, doing "something" to get a grade. The time to begin such assignments is within a day or two of when they are given. Yes, it's easier said than done, but if you want to avoid making the assignment "busywork" rather than a chance to educate yourself (that *is* what you're here for, isn't it?), then begin on it immediately.

Where's the best place to get started?

The sources you need depend on what type of outside reading you have been assigned. If the reading is from the more popular magazines and journals you can buy at any newsstand, then you may need look no further. If, however, you are required to research a topic, then you will need to go to the library. If you are not familiar with the library on your campus, ask one of the librarians to show you helpful sources. Most librarians love their work and like showing students what materials are available and how to find them.

Two useful places to begin looking for sources are the card catalog or computer data bank and the *Readers' Guide to Periodical Literature*. Don't overlook the many encyclopedias that specialize in various aspects of the social sciences. In addition, numerous reference works contain bibliographies of printed works on various social science topics.

Here is a list of some sources helpful for research in the social sciences:

Bibliographies and Indexes

American Historical Association: Guide to Historical Literature
Foreign Affairs: 50-Year Index
Guide to American Historical Review
Sources of Information in the Social Sciences
World List of Historical Periodicals

Government Publications

Public Affairs Information Service Bulletin. Published monthly, this bulletin is good for finding references to social science publications on public affairs. You can then check your library to see if it has the publications mentioned.

Congressional Digest. This monthly publication presents controversial subjects that are being debated in Congress. A résumé of bills under consideration is presented with the pro and con arguments by members of the Senate and the House.

Congressional Directory. Printed annually, this directory gives biographical sketches of members of Congress, maps of congressional districts, membership of congressional committees, and election statistics.

Congressional Record. Published every day Congress is in session, the record is a collection of the speeches and comments made during the daily meetings. Congressmembers also contribute letters they receive and write, as well as articles and editorials they feel are interesting.

Statistical Abstract of the United States. A yearly publication of the Commerce Department, this work provides all types of statistical facts on population, unemployment, and the like.

The United States Government Manual. Published annually by the Government Printing Office, this publication outlines the organization and duties of the various branches of the government, the work they do, as well as the names of the people in charge.

History Journals

American Historical Review
Current History
English Historical Review
Hispanic American Historical Review
History Today
Journal of American History
Journal of Asian Studies
Journal of Economic History
Journal of Modern History
Journal of Southern History
Middle East Journal
Negro History Bulletin

Political Science Journals

American Political Science Review
Journal of Politics
Political Affairs
Political Science Quarterly

Economic Journals

American Economic Review
Business Week
Quarterly Journal of Economics

Sociology Journals

American Journal of Sociology
American Sociological Review
Social Problems
Social Research
Social Science Quarterly
Sociological Inquiry

Psychology Journals

Annual Review of Psychology
Journal of Educational Psychology
Journal of Personality and Social Psychology
Psychology Today
Psychological Review

Most of these sources are available in college libraries. You will be doing yourself a favor by finding a few of these reference works and seeing what they offer you beyond the textbook. If you are majoring in the social sciences, you will definitely want to familiarize yourself with current issues of the journals in your area of interest. Doing so is the best way to keep up to date with current events not covered in popular magazines or newspaper reports.

Once you find a useful source, make certain that you write down the full title, the volume number, and the pages you read. This information is usually required for written reports, but, more important, if you need to return to that source in the future to get more information or to check your notes, you will know exactly where to go.

If and when you need to do a research project, refer to the Appendix, "Procedure for Doing a Research Paper," page 450. It provides a step-by-step approach with examples of note taking.

Why is it so important to take good research notes?

One of the major reasons for taking research notes that include proper quotations and page references is to avoid unintentional plagiarism. Here is a passage from James D. Lester's book *Writing Research Papers: A Complete Guide* that best states why:

Avoiding Plagiarism

Plagiarism (the improper use of source materials) is a serious breach of ethics. Most instances of plagiarism are the result of ignorance of rules rather than a deliberate effort on the part of the researcher to deceive instructors and other readers of the research paper.

Purpose of Documentation of Source Materials

The inventor Thomas Edison depended upon documented research by others. He once said that he began his inventions where other men left off; he built upon their beginnings. How fortunate he was that his predecessors recorded their experiments. Scholarship is the sharing of information. The primary reason for any research paper is to announce and publicize new findings. A botanist explains her discovery of a new strain of ferns in Kentucky's Land Between the Lakes. A medical scientist reports the results of his cancer research. A sociologist announces the results of a two-year pilot study of Appalachian Indians. Similarly, you must explain your findings in a psychology experiment, disclose research into shoplifting, or discuss the results of an investigation into schizophrenia of preschool children. A basic ingredient of business and professional life is research, whether by a lawyer, boot maker, or hospital nurse. A management position demands research expertise as well as the ability to examine critically and to write effectively about an issue: a client's liability, a marketing decision, or the design of a work area.

Like Thomas Edison's, your research in any area begins where others leave off. You will report your findings, but whether or not somebody continues the research will depend upon two factors: the quality and significance of the research and the accuracy of the written document. In truth, an undergraduate paper probably will not circulate beyond the immediate classroom; yet the central purpose of all research remains the same—to disclose new findings to the research community. In the process you learn the conventions of scholarship, discover the multiple resources of the library, find methods for recording data, and learn more about a topic than associates and colleagues.

An Explanation of Plagiarism

Fundamentally, plagiarism is the offering of the words or ideas of another person as one's own. While the most blatant violation is the use of another student's work, the more common error is carelessness with reference sources because of mislabeled note cards or a failure to place quotation marks on a note card. Sometimes paraphrase never quite becomes paraphrase—too much of the original is left intact. The obvious form of plagiarism is to copy any direct quotation from a source without providing quotation marks and without crediting the source. The more subtle form, but equally improper, is to paraphrase material that is not properly documented. Remember that an author's ideas, interpretations, and words are his or her property; in fact, they are protected by law and must be acknowledged whenever borrowed. Consequently, the use of source materials requires conformity to a few rules of conduct:

1. Acknowledge borrowed material by introducing the quotation of paraphrase with the name of the authority. This practice serves to indicate where the borrowed materials begin.
2. Enclose all quoted materials within quotation marks.
3. Make certain that paraphrased material is rewritten into your own style and language. The simple rearrangement of sentence patterns is unacceptable. Do not alter the essential idea of the source.
4. Provide specific in-text documentation for each borrowed item. For example, MLA style requires name and page for all in-text references. Requirements differ for other fields . . .
5. Provide a bibliography entry in the "Works Cited" for every sources cited in the paper. Omit sources consulted but not used.

The examples provided below in MLA style should reveal the differences between genuine research writing and plagiarism. First is the original reference material; it is followed by four student versions, two of which are plagiarism and two of which are not.

Original Material

The extended family is now rare in contemporary society, and with its demise the new parent has lost the wisdom and daily support of older, more experienced family members. Furthermore, many parents are not as well equipped for parenthood as were their parents before them, since over the years most children have been given less responsibility in helping to care for younger siblings. [From Edward F. Zigler, "The Unmet Needs of America's Children," *Children Today* 5.3 (1976):42.]

Student Version A (Unacceptable)

Today's society and shifting patterns of social order may dictate, then, a climate for abuse. Many parents are just not equipped today for parenthood. For instance, the extended family is rare in contemporary society, and because of its disappearance new parents have lost the wisdom and daily support of the wise grandparents. In truth, a family such as that portrayed by the Waltons on television seldom exists today with grandparents, parents, and many children all living together under one roof. Therefore, today's young parents are not well equipped because as children they were given less responsibility in helping care for younger brothers and sisters.

This piece of writing is plagiarism in a most deplorable form. Material stolen without documentation is obvious, and even a casual reader will spot it immediately because of radical differences in the student's style and that of the source. The writer has simply borrowed abundantly from the original source, even to the point of retaining the essential wording. The writer has provided no documentation whatever, nor has the writer named the authority. In truth, the writer implies to the reader that these sentences are an original creation when, actually, only two sentences belong to the writer, and the rest belong to the source.

The next version is better, but it still demonstrates blatant disregard for scholarly conventions.

Student Version B (Unacceptable)

Too many parents are not equipped today for parenthood. The extended family with three or more generations under one roof is now rare. Thus parents have lost the wisdom of older, experienced persons. In truth, a family such as that portrayed by the Waltons on television seldom exists today with grandparents, parents, and many children living all together under one roof. Therefore, young parents of today do a poor job because as youngsters they did not help care for younger brothers and sister (Zigler 42).

Although this version provides a citation to the authority, it contains two serious errors. First, readers cannot know that the citation "(Zigler 42)" refers to most of the paragraph; readers can only assume that the citation refers to the final sentence. Second, the paraphrasing is careless with words that should be enclosed by quotation marks or rephrased into the student's language and style, such as: "not equipped . . . for parenthood," "extended family," and "lost the wisdom of older."

The next version is correct and proper.

Student Version C (Acceptable)

Public concerns for the whole fabric of society stand in conflict with the selfish, private needs of the abusive parent. On that point, Edward Zigler argues that many parents are just not equipped today for parenthood (42). He states that the "extended family is now rare in contemporary society, and with its demise the new parent has lost the wisdom and daily support of older, more experienced family members"(42). In truth, a family such as that portrayed by the Waltons on television seldom exists today with grandparents, parents, and many children all living together under one roof. If children do not learn by caring for their younger siblings, then, as Zigler warns, they cannot be prepared for handling their own children (42).

This version represents a satisfactory handling of the source material. The authority is acknowledged at the outset, the key phrases are directly quoted so as to give full credit where credit is due. The student has been completely honest to the source.

Let's suppose, however, that the writer does not wish to quote directly. The following example shows a paraphrased version:

Student Version D (Acceptable)

Today's society and shifting patterns of social order may dictate, then, a climate for abuse. Edward Zigler argues that many parents are just not equipped today for parenthood (42). He insists that the "extended family" with several generations under one roof no longer exists and parents, who have little experience and no wise adults around, are therefore ill equipped to handle their duties toward family members (Zigler 42). In truth, a family such as that portrayed by the Waltons on television seldom exists today with grandparents, parents, and many children all living together under one roof.

This shortened version also represents a satisfactory handling of the source material. In this case, no direct quotation is employed, and the authority is acknowledged and credited, yet the entire paragraph is written in the student's own language.[1]

The final form of your written reports will vary according to your instructor's whims and requirements. Just make certain you understand what is expected of you. If you don't, see your instructor during a scheduled office hour and get the information you need before you write up your paper.

Your campus bookstore or library will have books and manuals on information sources and how to write to research paper. Three widely used such books are

Jean K. Gates, *Guide to the Use of Libraries and Information Sources*. McGraw-Hill, 1989.
James D. Lester, *Writing Research Papers: A Complete Guide*, 5th ed. Scott, Foresman, 1987.
Michael Meyer, *The Little, Brown Guide to Writing Research Papers*. Little, Brown, 1987.

Your instructor may have one he or she prefers.

FINAL THOUGHTS When you are assigned outside reading or a research project, accept the assignment as an extension of your textbook. Don't wait until the last moment to begin; to do a credible job you will need all the time you are given. Familiarize yourself with publications that specifically deal with the social sciences rather than the more familiar *Time, Newsweek,* and *U.S. News & World Report.* Take accurate notes as you read, keeping track of the sources' full and correct titles, volume numbers, and page references.

PROCESSING WHAT YOU JUST READ

✍ If you are using the *Student's Reading Journal* that accompanies this text, go to page 50 in it and follow the directions given.

If you are using your own notebook as a journal, answer the following questions:

1. Write a brief description of plagiarism.
2. Go to the library and find at least four of the source materials listed in this section. In your journal, write a brief description of the contents and value of each work. Make certain you cite the author(s), full title, publisher, date of publication, and any page number references you wish to make.

Review your journal notes before going on to the next section assigned.

---

1. *Source:* James D. Lester, *Writing Research Papers: A Complete Guide,* 5th ed. Scott, 1987, 77–81.

INTRODUCTION TO READING THE SCIENCES AND TECHNOLOGY

(Chapters 8–10)

What's the difference between science and technology?

Science is often defined as a method of answering theoretical questions, whereas *technology* is a method of solving practical problems. As Paul G. Hewitt defines them:

> Science has to do with discovering the true facts and relationships between observable phenomena in nature, and with establishing theories that serve to organize these facts and relationships; technology has to do with tools, techniques, and procedures for implementing the findings of science. . . . What scientists discover may shock or anger people—as did Darwin's theory of evolution. But even an unpleasant truth is more likely to be useful; besides, we have the option of refusing to believe it! But hardly so with technology; we do not have the option of refusing to hear a sonic boom produced by a supersonic aircraft flying overhead; we do not have the option of refusing to breathe polluted air; and we do not have the option of living in a nonatomic age. Unlike science, progress in technology *must* be measured in terms of the human factor.[1]

In other words, science discovered the effects of splitting the atom; technology used the discovery to develop the atom bomb. Wise and humanistic application of science and technology, rather than their use as a destructive force, could go a long way toward bringing peace and prosperity to the world.

1   *Source:* Paul G. Hewitt, *Conceptual Physics.* Little, 1984, 4.

124

What subjects make up the sciences?

The word *science* comes from the Latin *scientia*, which means "knowledge." Science has two major branches: the physical sciences and the life sciences. As mentioned in the "Introduction to Reading the Social Sciences," some argue that the social sciences are a third branch of science; however, we've avoided that argument by giving the social sciences a section of their own. The *physical sciences* include areas such as astronomy, chemistry, geology, meteorology, and physics—all dealing with *nonliving* matter. The *life sciences* are concerned with areas such as anatomy, biology, botany, and zoology—all dealing with *living* matter. Physics is considered the most fundamental and inclusive of the sciences because it is concerned with the study of matter and energy, the root of every field of science.

What makes reading about technology and the sciences different?

Research reveals that the following specific skills are needed to read textbooks in the sciences successfully:[2]

1. A basic scientific literacy or knowledge of key words, terms, and symbols
2. Comprehension skills that include the ability to recognize the following writing patterns:
   a. **comparison and contrast**, in which concepts and things are shown to be alike or unlike
   b. **problem solving**, in which problems with or without solutions are provided
   c. **sequence**, in which explanations of steps in a procedure are explained
   d. **generalization**, in which a principle, hypothesis, or conclusion is supported with examples or details
   e. **classification**, in which things are placed under a common heading with subdivisions
3. Study skills that include the ability to
   a. develop a purpose for reading the assignment
   b. use the table of contents, index, and glossary
   c. organize information from reading and listening
   d. take effective notes
   e. develop flexibility in reading rate

Part I has already introduced you to the abilities listed in Item 3, general study-reading skills and strategies. The following three chapters deal with the language and the five basic writing patterns that appear with frequency in science textbooks. While you read about science language and writing patterns, remember to use what you have learned in previous chapters. The idea throughout this book is for you to build on each skill you learn. As you are introduced to new strategies and approaches, keep using and refining those you have already encountered.

2. *Source:* B. Morrison, *The Identification of Reading Skills Essential for Learning in Seven Content Areas at Postelementary Levels.* (ED 185 536), 1980.

CHAPTER *8*

The Language of the Sciences and Technology

PREPARING TO READ

This chapter discusses three aspects of scientific and technological literacy. First, you will learn to understand and use the specialized vocabulary of science, by finding the meaning of a word either in context or in a glossary, index, or dictionary. Second, you will learn to recognize words that stand for concepts rather than facts. Third, you will be introduced to the use of symbols in scientific writing. **Your objective in reading this chapter is to become familiar with these three aspects of scientific language.**

What is meant by *scientific literacy*?

Literacy is usually defined as the ability to read and write with a fair amount of proficiency. *Scientific literacy* is the ability to read and write scientific matter with some proficiency. You probably have acquired some scientific literacy already.

✍ Test yourself on the following words by writing brief definitions of the ones you know in the spaces provided. Don't take a lot of time for this.

1. aerodynamics

   _____

2. alloy

   _____

3. analog

   _____

4. antibodies

   _____

5. bar codes

   _____

6. biochemistry

_____

7. catalyst

_____

8. cathode

_____

9. cholesterol

_____

10. chromosomes

_____

11. data base

_____

12. DNA

_____

13. ecology

_____

14. electronic mail

_____

15. enzymes

_____

16. ergonomics

_____

17. fission

_____

18. fusion

_____

19. gestation

_____

20. glucose

_____

21. ionosphere

_____

22. micron

_____

23. node

_____

24. pathology

_____

25. plankton

_____

If you were able to define most of these words, you have a good beginning grasp of scientific literacy. Knowing these words is not so important in itself, but it does offer an advantage when reading biology or physics in particular. If you had trouble with many of them, you may find you need to spend more time studying scientific vocabulary as you read science textbook assignments.

Compare your answers with these:

   1. *Aerodynamics* is the branch of science that studies air and other gases acting on bodies moving through the air or on fixed bodies in a current of air.

   2. *Alloy* is a term used by metallurgists to denote a substance consisting of two or more metallic elements or of a metal and a nonmetallic element.

   3. *Analog* means having to do with a continuous range of possible values.

   4. *Antibodies* are chemicals in the blood that neutralize and counteract infectious diseases.

   5. *Bar codes* are a means of representing data as a series of white and black marks, such as you see an grocery products.

   6. *Biochemistry* is the science that deals with the chemical compounds and processes occurring in plants and animals.

   7. A *catalyst* is a chemical that speeds up or retards chemical reactions while remaining unchanged itself.

   8. A *cathode* is a negative electrode; in an electron tube the cathode emits electrons.

   9. *Cholesterol* is a fatlike chemical compound that collects in the blood vessels. (Some doctors consider it responsible for high blood pressure.)

   10. *Chromosomes* are strandlike bodies present in all cells which contain genes.

   11. *Data base* refers to one or more computerized files of interrelated or interdependent data items stored together efficiently.

   12. *DNA* is deoxyribonucleic acid, which is believed to carry the codes for all the hereditary traits of a species.

   13. *Ecology* is the investigation of the relationships of animals and plants in their environment.

14. *Electronic mail* is a data communications service that employs computers and telecommunications lines to send and store messages that would otherwise take the form of a phone call, memo, or letter.

15. *Enzymes* are organic catalysts responsible for the majority of the chemical changes in living matter, such as digestion.

16. *Ergonomics* is the study of people's physical, psychological, and anatomical relationships to their working environment.

17. *Fission* in biology is reproduction by the simple division of a cell into two cells. In physics, fission is the splitting of an atom into smaller particles, during which some of the matter is converted into energy.

18. *Fusion* is the act or operation of melting or blending together.

19. *Gestation* is the period of pregnancy.

20. *Glucose* is the chemical name for a natural sugar found in fruits and in the blood.

21. The *ionosphere* is a region of electrically charged (ionized) air beginning about 30 miles above the surface of the earth.

22. A *micron* is a unit of length, one-millionth of a meter.

23. A *node* is the joint of a stem (botany) or a swelling like a knot (anatomy and zoology).

24. *Pathology* is the science of diseases, their nature and causes.

25. *Plankton* refers to the tiny animals and plants that float or swim on the surface of a body of water.

This is certainly not a definitive list, but these words do appear with some frequency in introductory science and technology textbooks. And, because technology and science play such a large part in our everyday lives, the average person on the street should have some acquaintance with their language.

You may feel that there are too many words to learn and that scientific language is too technical. But remember, science attempts to be precise. Scientists use technical words because such words generally have only one meaning. For example, the words *aphasia* and *speechlessness* may appear to mean the same thing. But a doctor would never use the word *speechlessness* as a synonym for *aphasia*, because *speechlessness* implies a temporary inability to talk, usually because of fear or surprise, whereas *aphasia* is an abnormal loss of speech caused by brain damage. The scientist prefers a word that means only one thing.

There is another advantage to technical language. It is much easier to use the word *micron* than to say "one-millionth of a meter." It is easier to say, "He has hemophilia" than to say, "He has blood that is unable to clot." And it is easier for a chemist to use the symbol C_2H_6O than to say "two atoms of carbon, six atoms of hydrogen, and one atom of oxygen." As you can see, there is a need for scientific terminology. To learn to read scientific material, you will have to spend time developing your scientific literacy.

Don't scientists frequently define many terms in context?

In most scientific and technological textbooks, particularly those written for introductory courses, the authors attempt to define the terms they are using in the context of their writing. Here's an example from a textbook on computer technology:

Memory

The most important thing to keep in mind about a computer is that everything it deals with must be represented numerically—all it can do is manipulate numbers. The data, or raw information, that describe a problem and the step-by-step list of instructions that tells the computer how to solve that problem (the **program**) must be reduced to numerical form.

The **memory** is where all of these numbers — the data and the program — are stored, at the center of the computer system. In fact, this storage of data and program together is the defining characteristic of the modern computer, which was originally called the *stored-program computer*.[1]

✍ What three things are being defined in this passage?

_____

_____

_____

Within this short passage: the computer program, the memory, and the original term for computer memory are defined. As such terms are introduced, you need to learn them so that as they are used later, when new terms are presented, you understand their interrelationships.

Notice in this next passage from a botany textbook how the author tries to clarify his terms as he discusses molecular structure.

All matter (that which has mass and occupies space) is composed of submicroscopic particles, called **molecules**, which are in continuous motion. Such molecules are the smallest subdivision of a substance* which still possesses all of the specific properties or characteristics of that substance. Since these particles are not visible their motility has been determined by various indirect methods. However, a visible indication that water molecules are moving can be obtained by observing what has been termed **Brownian movement**. If small but visible particles (such as India ink) are suspended in a drop of water and observed through a microscope, these particles will be seen to "jiggle" about. Their nondirectional trembling movement is not a result of their own molecular composition but of the motion of water molecules striking first from one direction and then from another. The unequal collisions push the ink particles first to one side and then to another.[2]

*Substance: a material all samples of which have the same set of properties; it consists of but one kind of molecule.

From the beginning the author is defining terms for you. In the first sentence, he explains *matter* by inserting a definition in parentheses "(that which has mass and occupies space)." Then, in the same sentence, he states that all matter is composed of "submicroscopic particles, called **molecules**, which are in continuous motion." What he has done is define in context for you two words, *matter* and *molecules*.

In his second sentence, he elaborates on the word *molecules* and uses the word *substance*. Knowing that word is vague, he gives you the definition as he wants you to understand it in a footnote. The footnote is used instead of parentheses because it is less of an interruption.

Still another term is defined in this paragraph: *Brownian movement*. The author mentions this as a way of visibly observing water molecule movement. There is no

1. *Source:* Daniel L. Slotnick, et al., *Computers and Applications.* D. C. Heath, 1986, 13.
2. *Source:* Walter H. Muller, *Botany: A Functional Approach.* Macmillan, 1963, 13.

reason to be puzzled by the term, because he immediately follows through with its definition as well as its purpose.

As an alert reader, you should notice that the author here tries to make your reading easier. First, to emphasize their importance, he puts the two main terms he wants you to know—*molecules* and *Brownian movement*—in boldfaced type. Second, the author uses parentheses and a footnote to clarify terms that are less important, but necessary to an understanding of molecules and Brownian movement. Third, he defines words in context through two means. Take a look at the first sentence again. *Matter* is defined *after* the word is used. The definition of *molecules* is presented *before* the word is used.

All these methods are used widely in science textbooks to present technical words in context. Your reading will be easier if you are aware of these methods.

Here is another passage from the same textbook. How does it define words in context?

> Molecules in turn are composed of **atoms**, the building blocks, which are the smallest particles that will enter into a chemical reaction. Recent evidence indicates that atomic structure is more complicated than had been suspected, but for our purpose we may consider an atom to be made up of a sphere or swarm of electrons (negatively charged particles) surrounding a positively charged core.* The positive charge is due to **protons** (discrete units of positive charge), but the core also contains particles having no charge at all, the **neutrons**. This central portion contains practically the entire mass of the atom but occupies an extremely tiny portion of the volume; practically all the volume is occupied by electrons. In a neutral atom, the negative charge of the electrons is exactly balanced by the positive charge of the core; the number of electrons is equal to the number of protons. When an electron is removed from a neutral atom, the particle which remains behind is positively charged, or a **positive ion**:
>
> $$Na \rightarrow Na^+ + e^-$$
>
> The electron is shown as e-. When a neutral atom picks up an electron it forms a **negative ion**:
>
> $$Cl + e^- \rightarrow Cl^-$$
>
> The symbols Na and Cl refer to sodium and chlorine respectively. Such symbols are the chemists' method of abbreviating the name of an **element**, a substance which cannot be decomposed into simpler substances by ordinary action. Table 3-1 indicates some of the elements which are important in cellular structure and function.[3]
>
> *The term "nucleus" (rather than "core") is used by physicists and chemists, but this might lead to confusion in the mind of a beginning biology student, who is more familiar with a cellular nucleus than with an atomic nucleus.

✍ As a means of checking yourself, list at least four ways the author defines words in context in this paragraph.

1. _____

2. _____

3. _____

3. *Source:* Ibid., 13.

4. _____

The author uses the following aids: (1) designating the terms he is defining in boldfaced type; (2) employing parenthetical phrases to define terms; (3) adding a footnote to explain a term as he wants it used; (4) sometimes giving his definitions *before* the word he is defining appears and sometimes *afterward*; and (5) presenting symbols, as in Na $\rightarrow$ Na$^+$ +e$^-$. In addition, he refers the reader to Table 3-1 (not printed here), which elaborates on his definition of *cellular structure*.

Naturally, you must learn the terms being defined as you come to them or you will be lost later. If you pay attention to the way the authors of your science and technology textbooks define words in context, you can save yourself many trips to the dictionary or glossary.

How helpful is a glossary or an index in a science textbook?

Science textbooks generally have many reading aids. Before reaching for a dictionary to look up words you can't understand from context, check in the glossary of terms at the end of each chapter or at the end of your textbook. If the troublesome words are related to the subject you are reading, the author may have defined them for you in the glossary. An author generally knows when a reader will have trouble with a specialized word or term. She will usually explain it in context, in a footnote, or in a glossary.

Pretend for a moment that you are reading about asexual reproduction in your life sciences text, and you come to this passage:

> Some of the structurally simple vertebrates can reproduce asexually, most often by fission or budding. In animal **fission**, the entire body of the parent divides into two roughly equivalent parts, with each part then growing into a whole individual. When certain flatworms reproduce this way, the body may be divided in half in either the transverse or longitudinal direction. In **budding**, the new individual develops as an outgrowth of the parent body. When the bud develops a full set of the parental body structures, it breaks away. The buds of one cnidarian (*Hydra*) protrude from the parent body. The "buds" (gemmules) of sponges are produced internally, and each develops into a separate individual when the parent body disintegrates.[4]

Suppose when you get to the sentence "The buds of one cnidarian (*Hydra*) protrude from the parent body" that the names *cnidarian* and *Hydra* are familiar from a previous chapter, although you don't quite remember them. It is important that you remember, however, because they are related to the chapter that you are now reading.

The first place to look for definitions of these words is the **glossary**, an alphabetical list of names and terms that appears in almost all science textbooks. You look under *H*, but *Hydra* is not listed; and *cnidarian* doesn't appear under *C* either. Next, you turn to the **subject index** in the back of the book for help.

In the index, here's what you see under *Hydra*:

> *Hydra*, 321, 375–550; circulatory system in, 307; digestion in, 290, 291; gastrulation in, 230; locomotion in, 402, *402;* nerve net in, 376, 402; photosynthetic protists in cells of, *650;* radial symmetry in, 572; reproduction in, 246, *246*, 248, 265[5]

---

4. *Source:* Cecie Starr and Ralph Taggart, *Biology: The Unity and Diversity of Life,* 5th ed. Wadsworth, 1989, 489.

5. *Source:* Starr.

The quantity of page number listings may overwhelm you at first, but you don't need to read all the references. Notice the listing "reproduction in, 246, 246, 248, 265." Page 246 is listed twice; the italicized number means there is a picture or diagram on that page.

Your safest bet is to check the first page listed. Most of the time, though not always, the initial listing will refer to where the most is said about the subject. Once you turn to that page, don't try to read it all. Skim over it, letting your eyes search out the key words, in this case *Hydra* and *asexual reproduction*. Once you find these terms being used, read carefully. Ignore everything except passages dealing with what you are looking for. All you want is something that will help you remember hydras or cnidarian so you can connect them to your present reading assignment.

When you turn to the page reference, here is what you find. For practice, see how quickly you can find out how Hydra reproduce.

> The phylum Cnidaria, which consists of about 11,000 species, includes the hydras, jellyfishes, sea anemones, and corals. The oceans are home to most of these animals. Fewer than fifty species (including hydras) are adapted to freshwater lakes and ponds.

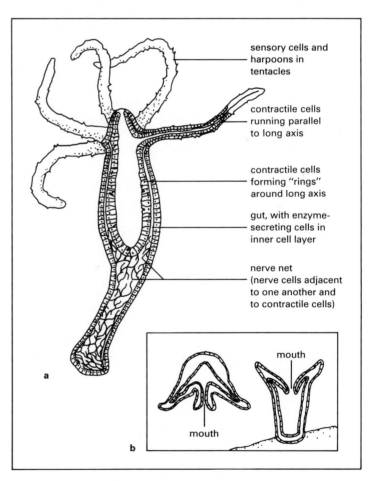

sensory cells and harpoons in tentacles

contractile cells running parallel to long axis

contractile cells forming "rings" around long axis

gut, with enzyme-secreting cells in inner cell layer

nerve net (nerve cells adjacent to one another and to contractile cells)

mouth

mouth

FIGURE 25.1 **(a) Nerve net, sensory cells, and contractile cells in Hydra, a type of cnidarian. (b) Regardless of whether a cnidarian is free-floating or sedentary, the nerve net is arranged radially about the mouth and gut.**

Cnidarians have two main body forms, called the **medusa** (plural, medusae) and the polyp. A medusa looks like a bell or an upside-down saucer. The mouth is centered under the bell, and the bell's edge has tentacles extending from it. Sometimes "oral arms" extend from the region of the mouth and assist in prey capture and feeding. **Polyps** are tubelike, and they have tentacles encircling the mouth. Typically they are sedentary, being attached by the end opposite the mouth end. Often the polyps are organized into colonies in which the tissues and gut of one member are continuous with those of its neighbors.

Many cnidarians have only a polyp stage or a medusa stage, either of which can reproduce sexually or asexually. Others have both polyp and medusa stages in the life cycle, the medusa being the sexual form. Regardless of whether it is the polyp or medusa that reproduces sexually, the resulting zygote nearly always develops into a swimming or creeping larva called a **planula**. With few exceptions, planulas have ciliated epidermal cells. Eventually a mouth opens up at its body surface and gradually the larva is transformed into a polyp or medusa, and so the cycle begins anew. Many biologists think that planula-like organisms may have given rise to bilateral animals.

The principle of asexual reproduction is always the same and is simple: a part of the parental organism, genetically identical with its other parts, develops into a separate organism. Neither fission nor budding promotes genetic variability; the offspring are clones, or genetically identical copies of the parents. Cloning is advantageous only so long as parents are well adapted to the surroundings, and only so long as the surroundings remain stable.[6]

You don't need to read the entire passage. By looking quickly at Figure 25.1, you can recall what hydras are, and, by skimming the page up to the third paragraph, you are reminded what hydras have to do with asexual reproduction. The best connection is in the first sentence of the fourth paragraph:

The principle of asexual reproduction is always the same and is simple: a part of the parental organism, genetically identical with its other parts, develops into a separate organism.

Once you have refreshed your memory, you are ready to return to your current assignment and continue reading with better comprehension than if you had skipped over these terms. However, too many trips back to previously read assignments via the index indicate poor initial reading of and note taking on those pages. You should find such trips less necessary the more you put the study-reading strategies in this book to work for you.

What about dictionaries and encyclopedias? Are they really useful?

It's up to you to learn important terms as you come to them in your reading. Imagine for a moment that the following statement is part of an assignment you are reading for the first time:

In both, haploid cells (or their nuclei) fuse and produce a new diploid individual.

This sentence may stop you because you can't understand *haploid* or *diploid* from their context. You check the textbook's glossary, but the words aren't defined there. If there is no helpful glossary or index listing, you must go beyond the textbook.

6. *Source:* Starr, 645-647.

This means going to a dictionary or an encyclopedia. Of course, you don't *have* to learn what *haploid* and *diploid* mean. After all, if you have a poor scientific vocabulary and you look up every word that you don't know, you can waste a lot of time. But reading without understanding isn't a very good use of your time either.

If you have been dodging the problem of poor vocabulary, this is the time to do something about it. Although it would be preposterous to stop and look up every word you don't know, you have to begin somewhere. At least look up the words that keep you from getting the main point of the passage. Many reading experts agree that if you read very much, a larger vocabulary comes almost automatically as you see words in context. But, because not all words can be understood from context, trips to the dictionary or encyclopedia are often necessary and helpful. Just accept them as part of the study process.

There are special dictionaries and encyclopedias that deal with only scientific language. No doubt your college library has several in the reference section. Here's what you would find if you looked up *haploid* in a scientific dictionary:

> **haploid**　A nucleus or individual containing only one representative of each chromosome of the chromosome complement. The haploid condition, denoted by the symbol *n,* is established by meiotic division of a diploid nucleus. In most plants (bryophytes, ferns, seed-plants, some algae) meiosis establishes a haploid generation, the gametophyte. Sooner or later the haploid gametophyte produces gametes by initosis. In lower plants the situation is extremely variable. Some, such as *Fucus,* follow the pattern more characteristic of animals, where meiosis results directly in the formation of gametes. In other cases, such as *Spirogyra,* the only form of the plant is haploid, and the diploid stage is restricted to a single-celled zygote. In flowering plants the haploid gametophyte generation is reduced to the pollen tube in the male and the embryo sac in the female. However, haploid plants can be obtained by culturing pollen grains under suitable conditions. Haploid plants may also be obtained when a zygote formed from an interspecific cross sheds all the chromosomes of one parent as it undergoes development. This phenomenon has been demonstrated when barley (*Hordeum vulgare*) is fertilized with pollen from the wild barley *H. bulbosum*. Haploid plants have great potential in plant breeding as it is possible, by doubling the chromosomes of a haploid plant, to obtain a completely homozygous plant. This may be impossible by other means, especially with self-sterile plants.[7]

Such a listing can be helpful, or it can be overwhelming, leading to more unknown words. How useful such an entry is to you depends on how much it relates to the textbook passage you want to clarify. If you are still confused, schedule a visit with your instructor. Your instructor, as well as a librarian, can give you the names of some useful specialized dictionaries and encyclopedias that relate to the science field you are studying.

What about scientific concepts and symbols?

Concepts

A **concept** in science is a generalized idea based on knowledge that explains a phenomenon. Scientists use analysis to develop certain concepts that help determine why and how. For example, in physics the conceptual unit is the atom, with its electrons, protons, and other particles; in biology, it is the cell.

---

7. *Source:* Elizabeth Tootill, *The Facts on File Dictionary of Botany.* Market House Books, 1984, 168.

Scientists approach their subject by taking facts and generalizing about them. Here is what one scientist has to say about science and concepts:

> Although facts are ultimate, their significance may alter. Facts are not phenomena; they are *descriptions* of phenomena. They are abstractions from the phenomena. They depend upon the *concepts*, the *ideas*, with which one approaches the phenomena. For example, the description of falling bodies is made in terms of certain concepts, such as time, distance, speed, and so on. With different concepts, different facts are obtained. Facts are ultimate, but only in the sense that in terms of a given set of concepts, certain things can be described as happening. What we choose to describe and the terms in which we describe it are *not* in the phenomena. The development of science is in large measure the development of concepts.[8]

If "the development of science is in large measure the development of concepts," it would be well for you to be able to identify scientific concepts.

Here is another passage from a science textbook. As you read it, try to identify the major words or terms used as concepts.

> The concept of energy helps us to unify all the possible changes that occur when work is done. When work is done, there is a change in energy. The amount of work being done is equal to the change in energy. Energy is one of the most fundamental concepts in science. It is a quantity that is possessed by objects: Work is *done*; objects *have* energy. When work is done on a system, the amount of energy possessed by the system changes. In general, we can define energy as the ability to work or simply as stored work.[9]

✍ In the spaces provided, place a check mark beside each of the following words from the passage that is a concept.

1. energy   _____

2. work   _____

3. science   _____

4. system   _____

5. stored   _____

All, of course, are concepts. You can't touch them, and they have no form or boundaries. But they are part of the vocabulary of science, and they are just as "real," in a scientific sense, as facts.

Symbols

A scientific **symbol** is an abbreviation that represents a word or a concept. Recognizing symbols is not new or difficult. These words you are reading are symbols that represent the sounds we make when we talk. You learned long ago what +, -, x, and ÷ mean. They too are symbols for words: add, subtract, multiply, and divide. Science simply uses more sophisticated or elaborate symbols. In science and tech-

---

8. *Source:* Theodore A. Ashford, *The Physical Sciences: From Stars to Atoms.* Holt, Rinehart and Winston, 1976, 34.

9. *Source:* James T. Shipman, et al. *An Introduction to Physical Science,* 5th ed. D. C. Heath, 1987, 54.

nology classes, you are expected to deal with symbols such as 10^{-6}, or m, or 1 cm = 0.3937 inches.

Here's a typical passage from a biology textbook that discusses acids and bases. Notice its use of symbols.

> Suppose you add hydrochloric acid (HCl) to water. The molecules of this acid dissociate (separate) into ionized parts (H+ and Cl-). The hydrogen ion is attracted to any neighboring water molecule, which thereby becomes a hydronium ion:

$$H^+ + = H_2O \rightarrow H_3O^+$$

hydronium ion

> In this reaction, water acts as a base. However, other basic substances besides water are present in cells, and they tend to be more powerful acceptors of hydrogen ions. Hence the hydronium ion quickly does an about face and acts as an acid, donating its extra hydrogen to its stronger neighbors.[10]

Note that the symbols for the elements are given immediately in parentheses. Of course, you are expected to remember or know where to find the meanings of these symbols once they have been introduced.

Most textbooks have appendixes with charts and diagrams of commonly used symbols. Frequently, such charts appear inside the front and back covers for easy reference. If your book doesn't have these, you might want to look for a copy of the *Handbook of Biological Data* or *Lange's Handbook of Chemistry*. Both contain tables, including the periodic system, the metric system, and astronomical values.

What scientific words and terms are used frequently?

Many scientific words have their basis in Greek and Latin word parts. Here is a partial list of Greek word roots and affixes that appear with frequency in science and technology textbooks. Study the list, learning the words you don't know.

Greek Word Roots and Affixes

Root or affix	Meaning	Word
anti	against, opposite	antibiotic
arthr	joint	arthritis
bio	life	biology
cardi	heart	cardiac
cephal	head	cephalopod
chlor	green	chlorophyll
chron	time	chronology
cyt	cell	cytology
dia	across, through	diameter
epi	upon, on	epidemic
gen	kinds, race, origin	genealogy
geo	earth	geology
graph	record, write	biography
hedron	solid figure with many faces	octahedron
helio	sun	heliotheraphy
hemo	blood	hemophilia

10. *Source:* Starr, 43.

hetero	mixed	heterogeneous
homo	same, alike	homogeneous
hydro	water	hydrolysis
itis	inflammation of	tonsillitis
log(y)	study of	biology
macro	large	macrocosm
meter	measure	chronometer
micro	small	microscope
mono	one	monopod
neuro	nerve	neurotic
octo	eight	octopus
ost; osteo	bone	osteopath
patho	disease of	pathology
phil	love	photophilic
phos; phot; photos	light	photosynthesis
poly	many	hydropoly
psyche	mind, soul	psychology
scope	examine	stethoscope
som; somat	body	chromosome
syn	together	synopis
tele	far, distance	television
thera	to nurse	therapy
zoo	animals	zoology

To make certain that you understand how this list of Greek word roots and affixes can be useful, test yourself on the following ten words. They all use word parts from the preceding list. Using the list, divide each word into its parts. For example: **perimeter**: *peri* = around, *meter* = measure. Then write what you think the definition is in the space provided. When you are finished, look up the word in the dictionary to see how close you came to its actual meaning.

1. psychotherapy   _____

2. hemophile   _____

3. biology   _____

4. geology   _____

5. polyphony   _____

6. anthropophilic   _____

7. arthritis   _____

8. neurology   _____

9. heliotherapy   _____

10. cytology   _____

The following partial list is made up of Latin word roots and affixes used frequently in the sciences and technology. Knowing these will help you read science material more easily.

Latin Word Roots and Affixes

Root or affix	Meaning	Word
ante	before	antecedent
aqua	water	aquatic
audio	hear	audiometer
aur	ear	aural
bene	well	beneficial
cap, cept, cip	take	capacity
carn	flesh	carnivorous
corpus	body	corpse
digit	finger	digital
dorm	sleep	dormant
duc, duct	to lead	conductor
inter	between	intervene
mitto, mit	send	transmit
mortis, mort	death	mortality
ocul	eye	oculist
pater	father	paternal
ped	foot	octoped
sanguin, sangui	blood	consanguinity
somn	sleep	insomnia
son	sound	ultrasonic
subter	under, secret	subterranean
trans	across	transport
utilis	useful	utility
video	see	videotape

The following list contains a mixture of useful Greek and Latin word parts used frequently in scientific and technological writing.

Greek and Latin Word Parts

Root or affix	Meaning	Word
a-, an-	without	asexual
caco	bad	cacophony
cosm	order, world	cosmos
etym	true meaning	etymology
eu	good	euphony
gnos	to know	agnostic
gon	angle	octagon
hepta	seven	heptagon
hexa	six	hexameter
latry	worship	heliolatry
path	feeling	apathetic
syn, sym	together	synergy

✍ To see how well you made sense of the preceding two lists, use them to divide each of the following ten words into its parts. For example: *transport: trans* = across; *port* = carry. Then write what you think the definition is in the space provided. Use the dictionary to check your answers.

1. postmortem _____

2. octoped _____

3. cacophony   _____

4. inaudible   _____

5. subsonic   _____

6. cosmos   _____

7. heliolatry   _____

8. transmit   _____

9. carnivorous   _____

10. dormant   _____

If you are interested in finding out more about the use of Greek and Latin word parts in the sciences, see Oscar E. Nybakken's *Greek and Latin in Scientific Terminology*. Your college library will probably have a copy.

FINAL THOUGHTS   Some knowledge of scientific vocabulary is essential to effective study-reading in the sciences and technology. As you read your assignments, make certain that you learn the new terms being used. Frequently, these words are defined for you as they are presented. At other times, you will need to use the textbook's glossary or index, or outside sources (such as a dictionary or encyclopedia) to define words necessary for good comprehension. Spending some time learning Greek and Latin word parts can be of help.

Don't worry about looking up every word you don't know as you read. Definitions often become clear as you read further. Look up only the words or terms that cause you to miss the main ideas of the text.

PROCESSING WHAT YOU JUST READ

✍ If you are using the *Student's Reading Journal* that accompanies this text, go to page 52 in it and follow the directions given.

If you are using your own notebook as a journal, answer the following questions:

1. Using the headings, summarize the main points of this chapter.
2. Discuss some of the ways scientific writers help readers understand scientific vocabulary.
3. Pick ten words from the list of Greek word parts and ten words from the list of Latin word parts. Write down the meaning of each word part and the definition of each word.

Review your journal notes, then go to Part III, page 349, and practice what you have learned.

WHAT DO YOU THINK?

Science is not an inhuman or superhuman activity. It's something that humans invented, and it speaks to one of our great needs—to understand the world around us. In the end, it makes you wonder whether people [who have negative images of scientists] have lost their curiosity, because that's all it is.

Maxine Singer, geneticist

CHAPTER 9

Writing Patterns in the Sciences and Technology

PREPARING TO READ

This chapter will introduce you to five writing patterns that appear with frequency in physical and life science textbooks: comparison and contrast, problem solving, sequence, generalization, and classification. Each pattern is explained with examples from college science textbooks. Learning how science writers define terms, explain principles and theories, and conduct experiments will help you get more from your science textbooks. **Your objective in reading this chapter is to learn the five basic science writing patterns so that you can study-read your science and technology textbooks efficiently.**

What's important about science writing patterns?

Unless we're among the "lucky" ones, most of us find reading the sciences none too easy. Here, for instance, is a typical passage from an introductory biology textbook:

> All atoms of an element have the same number of protons, but they can vary slightly in the number of neutrons. Most elements have these variant forms, which are called **isotopes**. For example, "a carbon atom" might be carbon 12 (containing six protons, six neutrons), carbon 13 (six protons, seven neutrons), or carbon 14 (six protons, eight neutrons). These can be written as ^{12}C, ^{13}C, and ^{14}C.
>
> Some isotopes are stable, in that they do not change into other atomic forms. **Radioactive isotopes** have unstable nuclei. Over a given period, they spontaneously give off subatomic particles and energy, and they break down (decay) into atoms of different types. For example, carbon 14 has too many neutrons for stability and it decays into nitrogen 14. It takes 5,730 years for half the carbon 14 atoms in a sample of material to do this. Such unvarying rates of decay are used to determine the age of rock samples and fossils.[1]

As a student, what are you supposed to get from such a passage? Much information is packed into the two paragraphs: particles of atoms (protons and neutrons), isotopes, carbon 12, carbon 13, carbon 14, their symbols, (^{12}C, ^{13}C, and ^{14}C), radioactive isotopes, nuclei, breakdown (defined as "decay"), carbon 14 decaying into nitrogen 14 after 5,730 years, decay rates used to determine the age of rocks and fossils. And this is only two paragraphs from an entire chapter, which means there are many other passages packed with similar information. What is the main idea

---

1. *Source:* Cecie Starr and Ralph Taggart, *Biology: The Unity and Diversity of Life,* 5th ed. Wadsworth, 1989, 27.

here? What is important to remember for a test? What notes should you take? How does this passage fit in with the rest of the chapter?

You can't possibly remember every single point made in your reading assignments. But by learning the writing patterns found in scientific materials, you will be better able to distinguish the main ideas from the details. Study-reading scientific material is not easy, especially if you have little background in the subject. Science and technology probably take more time, more effort, more rereading than any other subject. Approach science with that understanding, as well as information on the most common writing patterns, and you won't be so frustrated when reading your assignments.

Don't scientific textbooks use a lot of comparison and contrast?

Scientific textbooks do, indeed, use a lot of comparison and contrast, and you have already read something about this pattern in Chapter 6, on social science writing patterns. However, because the **comparison-and-contrast pattern** appears so frequently in science material to explain ideas or concepts introduced previously, it is worth looking at again. In this pattern, relationships between two similar or dissimilar things or characteristics are given. Sometimes this is done in a paragraph, sometimes over an entire chapter. Charts and illustrations are frequently employed with this writing pattern.

Here's an example of the comparison-and-contrast pattern at work in a science textbook:

> In structural terms, getting sperm and egg together is not too complicated among certain water-dwelling animals, including sea urchins and most bony fishes. Their gametes are simply released into the same region of water, and the motile sperm swim to an egg. Such *external fertilization* would be chancy if only one sperm and one egg were released each season. So energy outlays by each parent are required for the production of large numbers of sperm and eggs.
>
> In contrast, nearly all land-dwelling animals and even some aquatic forms depend on internal fertilization. (Sperm released on dry land obviously do not stand much change of swimming over to an egg.) The males have reproductive organs called **testes**, in which sperm are formed. Many male animals have a penis, a copulatory organ by which sperm are deposited into a specialized duct in the female. Many female animals have a **vagina**, a duct between the outside world and the ovary (an organ where the immature eggs grow). Thus the reproductive structures of reptiles, birds, and mammals protect sperm and eggs from harsh external conditions and enhance the probability of successful internal fertilization.[2]

In this passage two processes are being contrasted: getting sperm and egg together among water-dwelling animals and among land-dwelling animals, or, more specifically, *external* and *internal fertilization*. How do we know that? For one thing, both these terms are italicized, making it clear that they are key. For another, the second paragraph begins with "In contrast," making it clear that what is going to be stated is different from what was presented in the first paragraph. Once we recognize this, we can look for the differences between internal and external fertilization. Notes we take might look something like this:

2. *Source:* Starr, 491.

A. *water-dwelling animals* (no reproductive organs)
  – external fertilization, whereby eggs and sperm are released in same region of water
  – released in large numbers, no protection

versus

B. *land-dwelling animals* (have reproductive organs)
  – male deposits sperm (penis, testes) through female vagina
  – female carries fertile egg in ovary
  – process protects eggs from external conditions

Notice that the major headings show what is being compared and contrasted, and the different characteristics are listed under each item.

Here is a passage that compares more than it contrasts:

> The process of meiosis begins in very much the same way as mitosis. Here, too, the chromosomes shorten and thicken until the species number of chromosomes emerge from the tangled network. Here, too, each chromosome is doubled because every DNA molecule has duplicated itself. But in meiosis something happens that did not take place in mitosis. Each doubled chromosome is attracted to a very special partner.[3]

This passage makes it fairly obvious that the processes of meiosis and mitosis are being compared. It isn't until the last two sentences, when the authors say "But in meiosis," that a contrast is drawn. Here's how notes from such a passage might look:

Meiosis and mitosis

Similarities	*Difference in meiosis*
1. chromosomes shorten and thicken	each double chromosome attracted to special partner
2. species number emerge from network	
3. each chromosomes is doubled because every DNA molecule duplicated itself	

The notes demonstrate graphically that more comparisons than contrasts are being made.

Read the following passage about herds of wildlife in Africa. What is being compared and contrasted, and for what purpose?

> In order to catch the grazers, the predators on the plain have had to improve greatly their own running techniques. They have not taken to moving on the tips of a reduced number of toes perhaps because they have always needed their toes, armed with claws, as offensive weapons. Their solution is different. They have effectively lengthened their limbs by making their spine extremely flexible. At full stretch, traveling at high speed, their hind and front legs overlap one another beneath the body just like those of a galloping antelope. The cheetah has a thin elongated body and is said to be the fastest runner on earth, capable of reaching speeds, in bursts, of over 110 kph. But this method is very energy-consuming. Great muscular effort is needed to keep the spine

---

3. *Source:* A. Nason and P. Goldstein, *Biology: Introduction to Life.* Addison, 1979, 509.

springing back and forth and the cheetah cannot maintain such speeds for more than a minute or so. Either it succeeds in outrunning its prey within a few hundred yards and makes a kill or it has to retire exhausted while the antelope, with their more rigid backs and long lever-legs, continue to gallop off to a safer part of the plains.

Lions are nowhere near as fast as the cheetah. Their top speed is about 80 kph. A wildebeest can do about the same and keep it up for much longer. So lions have had to develop more complicated tactics. Sometimes they rely on stealth, creeping towards their victims, their bodies close to the ground, utilizing every bit of cover. Sometimes an individual works by itself. But on occasion, members of a pride will hunt as a team—and they are the only cats that do so. They set off in line abreast. As they approach a group of their prey—antelope, zebra or wildebeest—those lions at the ends of the line move a little quicker so that they encircle the herd. Finally, these break cover, driving the prey towards the lions in the centre of the line. Such tactics often result in several of the team making kills and a hunt has been watched in which seven wildebeest were brought down.[4]

✍ In the space provided, write an outline of some type that shows the similarities and differences between what is being compared and contrasted in this passage.

Your notes should show most of the following points:

---

4. *Source:* David Attenborough, *Life on Earth*, Little. 1979, 264.

Main point: Predators have had to improve their running techniques over those of grazers in order to catch them. **Support:** (1) Cheetahs (predators) have lengthy limbs and long, flexible spines; their hind legs and front legs overlap at high speeds; the great muscular effort required by high speeds restricts the time they can run, *as contrasted with* antelopes, which have rigid backs and long, leverlike legs. (2) Lions, *by contrast*, are not as fast as cheetahs and must rely on stealth more than speed. (3) Lions on occasion hunt in a pride, as a team, *unlike* cheetahs.

When you recognize the comparison-and-contrast pattern, look for signal words, such as *similarly, on the other hand, but, alike, differences, in contrast, by comparison,* and the like to help you clarify the comparisons and contrasts being drawn. Remember to look for the main idea or reason that the comparisons or contrasts are being made.

PROCESSING WHAT YOU JUST READ

✍ If you are using the *Student's Reading Journal* that accompanies this text, go to page 54 in it and follow the directions given.

If you are using your own notebook as a journal, answer the following questions:

1. Explain the difference between comparing and contrasting.
2. Write a comparison-and-contrast statement about the teaching styles of two of your instructors.

What about the problem-solving pattern?

The **problem-solving pattern** is not a difficult writing pattern to recognize or read. In a way, this pattern describes or recounts questions in science that have been answered through experimentation. Sometimes science textbooks provide a detailed account of a past problem in science, who solved it, and an explanation of the experiment used to solve it. Other times they merely provide a brief historical account of a famous person in science and state what his or her contribution to the field has been. When you notice this pattern in your studies, keep these three questions in mind:

1. What was the problem or question to be solved?
2. What kind of observation or experiment was done to solve the problem?
3. How was the question or problem answered or solved?

Read the following passage, looking for answers to these three questions:

In 1896, the French physicist Henri Becquerel was trying to find whether any elements emitted X-rays. To do this he wrapped a photographic plate in black paper to keep out the light, and then he put pieces of various elements against the wrapped plate. He thought that if these materials emitted X-rays, the rays would go through the paper and blacken the plate. He found that although most elements produced no effect, the mineral pitchblende did give out rays. It was soon discovered that similar rays are emitted by other elements, such as thorium, and actinium, and by two new elements discovered by Pierre and Marie Curie, polonium and radium. The emission of these rays was evidence of a much more drastic breaking apart of the atom than ionization. These rays were the result of a breaking apart and disintegration of the central core of the atom — radioactivity.[5]

5. *Source:* Paul G. Hewitt, *Conceptual Physics.* Scott, 1989, 591–592.

✍ See how well you read the problem-solving pattern by answering the following questions in the spaces provided.

1. What was the problem or question to be solved?

    _____

2. What kind of observation or experiment was done to solve the problem?

    _____

    _____

    _____

3. How was the question or problem answered or solved?

    _____

    _____

    _____

The problem: whether any elements emit X rays. **The experiment:** Becquerel wrapped black paper around a photographic plate, then placed pieces of various elements against the wrapped plate to see if any emitted X rays. **The results:** Most elements didn't, but pitchblende, as well as thorium, actinium, polonium, and radium, did. These results led to the discovery of radioactivity.

As you can see, keeping those three questions in mind once you recognize the problem-solving pattern makes comprehension easier.

Here now is a longer passage, using the problem-solving pattern in a different way. It is a brief historical account of the development of chemistry, but it uses a type of problem-solving pattern to show the major stages of development in that field.

One of the more interesting periods in the history of chemistry was that of the alchemists (500–1600 A. D.). People have long had a lust for gold, and in those days gold was considered the ultimate, most perfect metal formed in nature. The principal goals of the alchemists were to find a method of prolonging human life indefinitely and to change the base metals, such as iron, zinc, and copper, into gold. They searched for a universal solvent to transmute base metals into gold and for the "philosopher's stone" to rid the body of all diseases and to renew life. In the course of their labors they learned a great deal of chemistry. Unfortunately, much of their work was done secretly because of the mysticism that shrouded their activity, and very few records remain.

Although the alchemists were not guided by sound theoretical reasoning and were clearly not in the intellectual class of the Greek philosophers, they did something that the philosophers had not considered worthwhile. They subjected various materials to prescribed treatments under what might be loosely described as laboratory methods. These manipulations, carried out in alchemical laboratories, not only uncovered many facts of nature but paved the way for the systematic experimentation that is characteristic of modern science.

Alchemy began to decline in the 16th century when Paracelsus (1493–1541), a Swiss physician and outspoken revolutionary leader in chemistry, strongly advocated that the objectives of chemistry be directed toward the needs of medicine and the curing of human ailments. He openly condemned the mercenary efforts of alchemists to convert cheaper metals to gold.

But the real beginning of modern science can be traced to astronomy during the Renaissance. Nicolaus Copernicus (1473–1543), a Polish astronomer, began the downfall of the generally accepted belief in a geocentric universe. Although not all the Greek philosophers had believed that the sun and the stars revolved about the earth, the geocentric concept had come to be generally accepted. The heliocentric (sun-centered) universe concept of Copernicus was based on direct astronomical observation and represented a radical departure from the concepts handed down from Greek and Roman times. The ideas of Copernicus and the invention of the telescope stimulated additional work in astronomy. This work, especially that of Galileo Galilei (1564–1642) and Johannes Kepler (1571–1630), led directly to a rational explanation by Sir Isaac Newton (1642–1727) of the general laws of motion, which he formulated between about 1665 and 1685.

Modern chemistry was slower to develop than astronomy and physics; it began in the 17th and 18th centuries when Joseph Priestly (1733–1804), who discovered oxygen in 1774, and Robert Boyle (1627–1691) began to record and publish the results of their experiments and to discuss their theories openly. Boyle, who has been called the founder of modern chemistry, was one of the first to practice chemistry as a true science. He believed in the experimental method. In his most important book, *The Sceptical Chymist*, he clearly distinguished between an element and a compound or mixture. Boyle is best known today for the gas law that bears his name. A French chemist, Antoine Laviosier (1743–1794), placed the science on a firm foundation with experiments in which he used a chemical balance to make quantitative measurements of the weights of substances involved in chemical reactions.

The use of the chemical balance by Lavoisier and others later in the 18th century was almost as revolutionary in chemistry as the use of the telescope had been in astronomy. Thereafter, chemistry became a quantitative experimental science. Lavoisier also contributed greatly to the organization of chemical data, to chemical nomenclature, and to the establishment of the Law of Conservation of Mass in chemical changes. During the period from 1803 to 1810, John Dalton (1766–1844), an English school teacher, advanced his atomic theory. This theory placed the atomistic concept of matter on a valid rational basis. It remains today as a tremendously important general concept of modern science.

Since the time of Dalton, knowledge of chemistry has advanced in great strides, with the most rapid advancement occurring at the end of the 19th century and during the 20th century. Especially outstanding achievements have been made in determining the structure of the atom, understanding the biochemical fundamentals of life, developing chemical technology, and the mass production of chemicals and related products.[6]

✍ Answer the following questions in the spaces provided.

1.   What were the problems the alchemists wanted to solve?

6.   *Source:* Morris Hein, *Foundations of College Chemistry.* Brooks/Cole, 1986, 3.

_____

_____

2.   How did they go about solving the problems?

_____

_____

3.   Did they achieve their goals? Why?

_____

_____

4.   What did Boyle contribute to the advancement of chemistry as a science?

_____

_____

5.   What did Lavoisier contribute?

_____

_____

6.   What did Dalton contribute?

_____

_____

This type of passage is typical of many science textbooks. Rather than give scientific information, authors present information about some of the scientists who solved or discovered answers to earlier problems in their fields. In this passage, the author presents the names of several early scientists and credits them with their problem-solving solutions. Details on how they solved the problems are sparse.

Your answers to the previous questions are probably similar to these: (1) The alchemists were concerned with two problems: the search for a solvent to turn base metals into gold and the search for the "philosopher's stone" to rid the body of all disease. (2) Little is known about their methods; they worked in secrecy. (3) No, because, as far as we know, neither can be done. (4) Boyle was among the first to practice the experimental method; he distinguished between an element and a compound or mixture; and he's known for the Boyle gas law. (5) Lavoisier used chemical balance to make quantitative measurements of the weight of substances in chemical reactions; he also contributed to the organization of chemical data, to chemical nomenclature, and to the establishment of the Law of Conservation of Mass in chemical changes. (6) Dalton is credited with advancing the atomic theory we know today.

Generally speaking, an instructor is concerned not so much that you memorize all the dates or names in such passages but more that you see the progression of problem-solving occurrences over a long period.

Here is another passage that uses the problem-solving pattern. It's easy enough to recognize the pattern, because the passage begins with a question that requires a solution. This passage is taken from a chapter dealing with sexual reproduction. Apply the three questions as you read.

1. What was the problem or question to be solved?
2. What kind of observation or experiment was done to solve the problem?
3. How was the question or problem answered or solved?

> Nearly all land-dwelling animals and even some aquatic forms depend on internal fertilization. . . . Thus the reproductive structures of reptiles, birds, and mammals protect sperm and eggs from harsh external conditions and enhance the probability of successful internal fertilization.
>
> Another problem to consider: How is the embryo to be nourished? Almost all animal eggs contain yolk (proteins, lipids, and other nutritive substances), but some eggs contain more yolk than others. Following fertilization, sea urchin eggs develop into feeding-stage larvae within forty hours. Because these eggs are produced in large numbers, the biochemical investment in yolk for each one is limited. Hence there is a developmental premium on rapid development, with the self-feeding larval stage being reached in the shortest possible time. Bird eggs also are released from the mother's body, but these eggs are mostly a ball of yolk (the nonyolky cytoplasm and nucleus are positioned as a thin cap on the surface). The large yolk reserves nourish the embryo through a longer period of development, which proceeds inside a hard eggshell; unlike sea urchins, birds cannot feed on their own when they are hatched (Figure 34.2). Human eggs have very little yolk—but the developing embryo becomes attached to the mother's body and receives nourishment, and respiratory and excretory support, by physical exchanges with her tissues.
>
> The point of these few examples is that tremendous diversity exists in reproductive and developmental strategies. However, some patterns are widespread in the animal kingdom, and these patterns will serve as the framework for discussions to follow.[7]

Now answer the questions in the spaces provided.

1. What is the problem or question to be solved?

   _____

2. What kind of observation or experiment was done to solve the problem?

   _____

   _____

   _____

3. How was the question or problem answered or solved?

   _____

   _____

7. *Source:* Starr, 491–492.

The answer to the first question is stated for you in the first sentence of the second paragraph: "How is the embryo to be nourished?" In this case, the problem is not solved by experimentation but by nature. So the answer to Question 2 is that basically the embryo is nourished through yolk contained in the animal egg; however, bird eggs, sea urchin eggs, and human eggs all contain different amounts of yolk, causing developing embryos to receive their nourishment in different ways. The answer to Question 3 is not stated in the passage, but we can assume nature itself solved the problem of embryo nourishment through evolution.

As you can see from these examples, the problem-solving pattern is used to describe or recount questions in science that have been answered through experimentation or observation of the way nature works. Remember to apply the three basic questions when you recognize this pattern in your reading.

PROCESSING WHAT YOU JUST READ

✍ If you are using the *Student's Reading Journal* that accompanies this text, go to page 54 in it and follow the directions given.

If you are using your own notebook as a journal, answer the following questions:

1. Define the problem-solving writing pattern as it appears in science textbooks.
2. Write a paragraph of your own that uses the problem-solving writing pattern.

How does the sequence pattern differ from the problem-solving pattern?

The **sequence pattern** usually takes two forms: (1) the explanation of steps in a procedure or process, and (2) the presentation of steps in an experiment. Often, but not always, numbers are used to make each step of the sequence clear. The difficulty with reading such a pattern is that every step is as important as the others, meaning that you need to understand not only each step in the sequence but the interrelationships among the steps.

The following example is an explanation of the steps in what is often called the scientific method. The author is explaining how scientists know about organisms of the remote past when none exist today. Notice how each step in the sequence is explained.

> What, exactly, is a "principle"? The question is important for the answer provides insight into why the principle of evolution is used with such confidence. A principle is a way of explaining a major phenomenon of nature, one that has been synthesized from a large body of information. Thus the idea of evolution developed over centuries, as naturalists and travelers observed and collected specimens of living and extinct forms, then asked questions about the remarkable diversity those specimens represented. It became clear that almost all organisms alive today are very different from organisms of the remote past. Eventually there was overwhelming evidence that the difference was a consequence of evolution—of changes in lines of descent that have accrued since life began.

If we were to idealize the route from a question about such a major aspect of the world to a fundamental explanation, we might end up with a list like this:

1. Ask a question (or identify a problem).

2. Make one or more hypotheses, or educated guesses, about what the answer (or solution) might be. This means using the process of induction: sorting through cues, hunches, and observations, then combining bits of information and logic to produce a general statement (the hypothesis).

3. Predict what the consequences might be if a hypothesis is valid. This process of reasoning from a general statement to predicting consequences is called deduction (and sometimes the "if-then" process).

4. Devise ways to test those deductions by making observations, developing models, or performing experiments.

5. Repeat the tests as often as necessary to determine whether results will be consistent and as predicted.

6. Report objectively on the tests and on conclusions drawn from them.

7. Examine alternative hypotheses in the same manner.

This route represents what might be called a scientific approach to interpreting the natural world.[8]

The authors have made it easy to follow the sequence involved in what they call the "scientific approach" by numbering each step in the sequence. As readers, we have to understand each step, the proper order or sequence, and how each step relates to the others. We also have to understand that this approach or method is what scientists use to develop principles of science.

Here is another example of the sequence writing pattern at work. In this one, no numbered list is used. See if you can follow the steps in the sequence by a different author describing the scientific method.

The Scientific Method

Once you feel knowledgeable about your topic, begin planning your experiments. Biologists often work by following what is known as the scientific method. From reading and observing, biologists may raise a question or see a problem. To get an answer or find a solution, they start by forming a hypothesis. This is simply an educated guess, suggesting a possible answer to the question being investigated. Biologists next work out the detailed steps to follow in conducting their experiments. One thing they are always careful to include is a control whenever necessary.

A control is simply a standard of comparison. Biologists will set up two groups, identical in all respects but one. One group is subjected to the factor being investigated; the other group is not. For example, if you wished to test the effects of radiation on the growth of earthworms, you would expose some worms to X-rays. These make up the experimental group. You would keep other worms in identical physical surroundings, feed them the same way, and treat them exactly alike, but would not expose them to any radiation. These make up the control group. If the radiation had any effect, you should observe a noticeable difference between the experimental and control groups.

8. *Source:* Starr, 19.

Next, biologists collect data. Record everything you observe while conducting your project. Don't overlook anything. A chance discovery or casual observation may lead to some surprising findings. Record your data in a neat and organized manner in a book used only for your project. You may record your observations as notes, drawings, photographs, or in the form of numerical data. Make graphs and tables to organize your numerical data.

In the final step of the scientific method, biologists examine their data to see if they can reach some conclusion. This is where biologists try to explain their results, arriving at conclusions clearly stated and supported by the data. There should be no doubt that every conclusion is justified by the data collected. Therefore, experiments are always repeated to obtain sufficient data before reaching any conclusions.[9]

✍ See how well you understand the sequence just presented by answering the following questions in the spaces provided.

1. How many steps are mentioned? _____

2. Briefly state each step.

_____

_____

_____

_____

_____

_____

3. What words does the author use to help you follow the sequence?

_____

_____

Compare your answers with these: Five steps are mentioned: (1) Form a hypothesis about an answer or solution to a problem; (2) work out the detailed steps to conduct the experiment, including setting up control and experimental groups; (3) collect and record data; (4) examine data for any possible conclusions; and (5) repeat the experiment for verification of results. Words and phrases used to help follow the sequence are *start, by, next, in the final step,* and *therefore . . . are always repeated.*

No numbers are used in this sequence, but in Paragraph 1, the author helps us by saying "they start by" and "Biologists next work out." Paragraph 2 is just an elaboration of part of the second step mentioned in the previous paragraph. Paragraph 3 begins with "Next," and the final paragraph begins with "In the final steps." Such transitional words become very important in helping us follow the sequence pattern. You can see here how language usage works hand in hand with the sequence pattern.

9. *Source:* Salvatore Tocci, *Biology Projects for Young Scientists.* Franklin Watts, 1987, 10–11.

You might argue that only four steps are mentioned, especially because the author says, "In the final step" when referring to what I consider Step 4. In a sense, that's correct. But, if you read carefully, you noticed that the last sentence calls for repeating the experiment. And, because the author is explaining the scientific method, not just the steps in conducting an experiment the first time, repeating the experiment is actually the last step.

Frequently science textbooks incorporate charts or illustrations to help establish a sequence of events. Notice how the following passage presents a sequence in the stages of animal development and uses a chart to clarify that sequence.

Stages of Development

Animal development commonly proceeds through the stages listed in Figure 34.3, beginning with **gametogenesis**, or gamete formation. During this first stage, sperm or eggs form and mature within the parental reproductive system. **Fertilization**, the second stage, starts when a sperm penetrates an egg and it is completed when the sperm nucleus fuses with the egg nucleus. Next comes **cleavage**, a series of mitotic cell divisions that subdivide the fertilized egg into many smaller cells. Cleavage produces the early multicelled embryo (the blastula).

During **gastrulation**, the organizational framework for the whole animal is laid out as cells become arranged into two or more simple tissue layers. Interactions between cells in those layers permit the selective expression of specific genes — and this leads to organ formation, or **organogenesis**. Finally, organs increase in volume and acquire their specialized structural and chemical properties during **growth and tissue specialization**, which continue into the post-embroynic period of the life cycle.

gametogenesis	limited differentiation, under control of parental genes
↓	
fertilization	sperm activates the synthesis of proteins and DNA, initiating metabolic reactions
↓	
cleavage	gene activity largely under direction of cytoplasmic biochemicals
↓	
gastrulation	gene activity now proceeds according to control mechanisms operating in the nucleus of each differentiated cell — which activate different genes in the same set of DNA in different cells
↓	
organogenesis	
↓	
growth, tissue specialization	

FIGURE 34.3   Generalized overview of the stages of animal development described in this chapter.[10]

10. *Source:* Starr, 492.

Here the author provides three ways to help us follow the sequence: transitional words for each stage (first stage, second stage, next, and so on); boldfaced type for the name of or term for each stage; and a chart showing the sequence of the stages. Notice how Figure 34.3 does more than repeat the sequence mentioned in the text; it adds information for each step in development. Thus, you can see why it is important for you to refer to figures and charts when they are mentioned in the text.

As you read in your science textbooks, remember that the sequence pattern requires you not only to follow the actual order of steps or stages being presented but also to understand the importance of each step and how it relates to the others.

PROCESSING WHAT YOU JUST READ

✍ If you are using the *Student's Reading Journal* that accompanies this text, go to page 55 in it and follow the directions given.

If you are using your own notebook as a journal, answer the following questions:

1. Define the word *sequence* as it is used in the sequence writing pattern.
2. Using the sequence writing pattern, explain the "scientific method of experimentation."

Don't scientists generalize when they discuss principles and hypotheses?

The **generalization pattern** appears frequently in science textbooks. Most often, this pattern is used to present an explanation or an accepted principle or hypothesis. When you read this pattern, the supporting details are not as important to remember as the generalization being made. This is not to say that the supporting information is not significant. Rather, you should recognize the supporting details as an attempt to explain, clarify, or emphasize the generalization.

The following is an example of the generalization pattern at work.[11] As you read, look for the generalizations being made.

> The mass of air surrounding the earth is called the atmosphere. It is composed of about 78% nitrogen, 21% oxygen, and 1% argon, and other minor constituents by volume (see Table 12.1). The outer boundary of the atmosphere is not known precisely, but more than 99% of the atmosphere is below an altitude of 20 miles (32 km). Thus, the concentration of gas molecules in the atmosphere decreases with altitude, and at about 4 miles the amount of oxygen is insufficient to sustain human life. The gases in the atmosphere exert a pressure known as **atmospheric pressure**. The pressure exerted by a gas depends on the number of molecules of gas present, the temperature, and the volume in which the gas is confined. Gravitational forces hold the atmosphere relatively close to the earth and prevent air molecules from flying off into outer space. Thus, the atmospheric pressure at any point is due to the mass of the atmosphere pressing downward at that point.

11. *Source:* Hein, 254.

TABLE 12.1 Average Composition of Normal Dry Air			
Gas	*Percent by volume*	*Gas*	*Percent by volume*
N_2	78.08	He	0.0005
O_2	20.95	CH_4	0.0002
Ar	0.93	Kr	0.0001
CO_2	0.033	Xe, H_2, and N_2O	Trace
Ne	0.0018		

The boldfaced type for *atmospheric pressure* lets us know what this paragraph is primarily about. Two generalizations about atmospheric pressure are presented. One is "Thus, the concentration of gas molecules in the atmosphere decreases with altitude, and at about 4 miles the amount of oxygen is insufficient to sustain human life." The other is "Thus, the atmospheric pressure at any point is due to the mass of the atmosphere pressing downward at that point." The use of the word *thus* provides the clue in both cases. *Thus* is a summary word, so we know that the information presented before its use leads to a conclusion or generalization. The rest of the information, including the chart, is details that help support the generalizations, which lay the foundation for more information about the atmosphere to be presented later in the chapter.

Here's another example of the generalization pattern. What generalization is being made?

> It is an experimental fact that when only two neutrons are present in a nucleus, the nuclear force is not attractive. Of course, there is always a gravitational attraction, but it is negligible compared to the nuclear force. The nuclear force is generally attractive when there are several neutrons and protons present, but in the case of two it is weakly repulsive. Two protons will not attract each other, either. In this case, there is also an electric repulsion present. So two neutrons or two protons will not attract each other, but a neutron and a proton will attract.[12]

✍ In the space provided, state what you think is the generalization being made here.

_____

_____

_____

You probably had little trouble with this passage. The last sentence states the general principle regarding the attraction of two neutrons and two protons.

Try another passage. Look for the generalization being made here.

> A **motor** is a device that converts electric energy into mechanical energy. The basic principle involved is that a current-carrying wire will move in a magnetic field. This principle was illustrated in Fig. 8.28. Motors generally have many windings of wire around a piece of iron in order to enhance the basic effect shown in Fig. 8.28. The conversion of electric energy into mechanical energy is enhanced by more loops of wire and stronger magnets. Motors are heavy because of the iron that is used to concentrate and strengthen the magnetic field.[13]

12. *Source:* James T. Shipman, et al., *An Introduction to Physical Science*, 5th ed. Heath, 1987, 160.
13. *Source:* Shipman, 136.

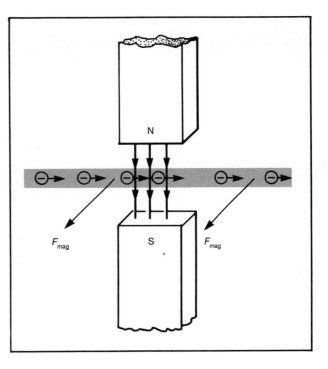

FIGURE 8.28 **A current-carrying wire in which the electrons are moving to the right as shown will be deflected out of the page by the vertical magnetic field. This is the basic principle of an electric motor.**

✐ Answer the following questions in the spaces provided.

1. What is the point of this passage?

_____

_____

2. What support is given?

_____

_____

The main point in this passage is to define a motor and show the principle behind how it works. Everything after the first sentence, including the illustration, supports the general principle of an electric motor.

In the generalization pattern, the support provided is important but not as important as the principle or definition being given. Once you recognize that the generalization writing pattern is being used, allow the explanations, illustrations, details, or definitions to help you understand the main point. Don't get stuck in all the details; grasp the principles or general statements.

PROCESSING WHAT YOU JUST READ

✍ If you are using the *Student's Reading Journal* that accompanies this text, go to page 55 in it and follow the directions given.

If you are using your notebook as a journal, answer these questions:

1. Summarize what you just learned about the generalization writing pattern in science textbooks.
2. Write a statement that makes a generalization about this textbook. (Be nice, now!)

The classification pattern: what is it?

The **classification pattern** is a writing pattern used by scientists to group and subgroup various things, objects, or areas. Readers of this writing pattern must be able to (1) recognize the topic being divided, (2) understand why it is being divided, (3) identify each of the subtopics, and (4) recognize the similarities and differences among subtopics. For example, writers may wish to discuss the structure of a plant. They may break their topic into various subheadings, such as roots, stems, leaves, and flowers. Even within these subheadings, they may break down their parts, providing more information about each subpart. Sometimes comparisons and contrasts are made to help classify subparts. Recognizing these structural parts in

FIGURE 9.1   Relationship of mammals to organic matter

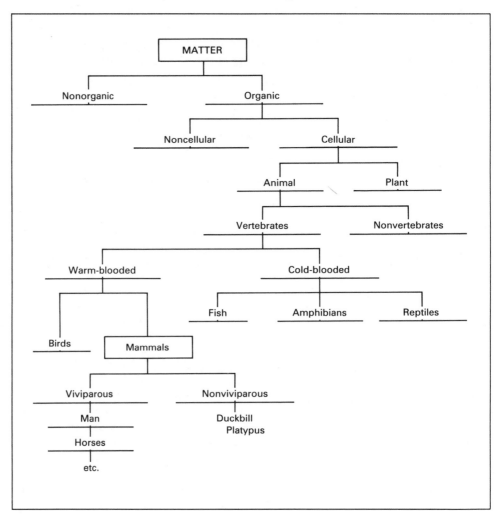

order of importance or position is vital to good comprehension and note taking when you are study-reading the classification pattern.

Frequently, charts, diagrams, and tables are used to classify and explain topics and subtopics. Shown in Figure 9.1, for instance, is an overview of the concept "mammals" and its relationship with "organic matter."

Such charts make the classification of things and their relationships with other things easier to understand. More often than not, however, you will have to recognize classification patterns as they are presented in writing. The classification writing pattern may appear in a single paragraph, two or more paragraphs, or even as an entire chapter.

Read the following single paragraph, which uses classification. What is being classified here?

> Physical science is the organized knowledge of our physical environment and the methods used to obtain it. Physical science is classified into five major divisions: astronomy, the science of the universe beyond our planet; chemistry, the science of matter and its changes; geology, the science of the Earth and its history; meteorology, the science of climate and weather; and physics, the science of energy and matter. Physical science studies the nonliving matter of the universe, while biological science studies the living matter.[14]

Here, the author wants to define *physical science*. But to do so requires classifying its various divisions. The author makes the classification pattern easy to spot by stating, "Physical science is classified into five major divisions," then discussing each division. An outline of this passage, if you were taking notes, might look something like this:

Topic:	Physical science
Subtopics:	1. astronomy
	2. chemistry
	3. geology
	4. meteorology
	5. physics

While such an outline reflects the correct division of subtopics, it lacks the real point of the passage, which is this: The five divisions of the physical sciences, each dealing with nonliving matter of the universe (as opposed to the biological sciences, which deal with living matter) work together to gain knowledge of the physical environment.

Truly to understand this passage, it is necessary to go beyond recognizing the subdivisions themselves and to understand why the topic is being divided and what the differences are among the subtopics. A better outline might look like this:

Topic:	Physical science (deals with *non*living matter)
Subtopics:	1. astronomy (deals with universe beyond our planet)
	2. chemistry (deals with matter and its changes)
	3. geology (deals with earth and its history)
	4. meteorology (deals with climate and weather)
	5. physics (deals with energy and matter)

In addition to showing the divisions, this outline reveals the similarity of the divisions (they all deal with nonliving matter) and the differences among the various physical sciences (what aspect of nonliving matter each deals with).

14. *Source:* Shipman, xiii.

Here is a longer passage using classification. Look for (1) the topic being divided, (2) why it is divided, (3) the subtopics, and (4) the similarities and differences among subtopics.

Oncogenes

Until a decade ago, the possibility of unraveling the secrets of cancer seemed remote, because cells of different cancers differ greatly in form, behavior, metabolic requirements, surface properties, and growth rates. However, it now appears that a small number of altered regulatory genes may contribute to at least some kinds of cancer.

Several viruses can cause cancerous transformations in vertebrate cells. They include the Rous sarcoma virus, or PSV (which causes cancer in chickens), papovaviruses (some species cause warts, others cause tumors), adenoviruses (which cause lung infections as well as tumors), and herpes viruses (different species cause fever blisters, chickenpox, genital infections, and cancer). In all cases, the viral genetic instructions become integrated into the DNA of a host cell and are subsequently expressed in all offspring of that cell.[15]

✍ Answer the following questions in the spaces provided.

1. What topic is being divided here?

   _____

2. What are the subtopics and what are their differences from other subtopics?

   _____

   _____

   _____

   _____

3. How are all the subtopics similar?

   _____

Compare your answers with these: (1) The topic being divided is cancer-causing viruses in vertebrate cells. (2) Four classifications of virus are presented, and the difference of each appears in the parentheses. You can reread the paragraph to check these. (3) The viruses' similarity, of course, is that they all produce cancer transformations in vertebrate cells.

Here is another example of the classification writing pattern. It is much longer than the previous examples but is rather typical of what you will find in science textbooks. Again, look for (1) the topic being divided, (2) why it is divided, (3) the subtopics, and (4) the similarities and differences among subtopics.

SUBVIRUSES

The smallest infectious agents known to researchers are termed **subviral infectious agents**, or **subviruses**. Scientists have identified at

---

15. *Source:* Starr, 231.

least six different strains: **satellite viruses, virinos, viroids, virusoids, virogenes**, and **prions**.

Members of one of the better understood strains, prions, range in size from considerably smaller than viruses, sometimes 100 times smaller, to almost as large as mitochondria and bacteria. Prions have been found to cause certain diseases and are implicated as the cause of others. Included in this list of diseases that prions seem to promote are scrapies and several similar degenerative brain diseases.

It has been theorized that prions may be radically different from any other known self-replicating entities. There is no evidence that prions contain any nucleic acids, DNA and/or RNA; instead, they appear to be little more than dots of protein. Even if they were found to contain nucleic acids, prions are so small that there is little chance they contain a nucleic acid any longer than 50 nucleotides. This is not large enough to encode a protein containing more than about 12 amino acids.

Despite indications to the contrary, it has even been suggested that prions may actually be conventional viruses, but this is quite unlikely. It appears equally unlikely that they will be found to represent a new category of protoorganismal material that reproduces in living cells, employing a technique that has yet to be elucidated. It has even been suggested that they may reproduce using a technique similar to that employed by viruses, without being viruses.

Some researchers have suggested that the mode of prion reproduction might involve fracture and continued growth, which would explain their small and uncertain molecular weights, their rod-like appearance, their varying lengths, and the unpredictability of which amino acid occurs terminally. The most recent work has shown that prions may be proteins produced somewhat abnormally by infected genes that somehow go awry.

Among the other subviruses are the viroids, minute rings of RNA that infect certain plants. Virusoids appear to be loops of RNA that occur inside regular viruses. Vironos, like viruses need an outer coat of protein, which they are unable to make on their own, but which they induce host cells to manufacture. Virogenes are otherwise normal genes that generate infectious particles under certain circumstances. Satellite viruses are tiny pieces of RNA that make full-size viruses work for them. These tiny nucleic acids multiply inside viruses that are inside cells.[16]

✍ Answer the following questions in the spaces provided.

1. What subject or topic is being classified:

   _____

2. Briefly describe each subtopic.

   _____

   _____

   _____

   _____

16. *Source:* Steven D. Garber, *Biology: A Self-Teaching Guide.* Wiley, 1989, 287.

_____

_____

3.   Which subtopic is given the most space? Why?

_____

_____

_____

4.   What do all the subtopics have in common?

_____

_____

The first question is answered in the first paragraph: subviral infectious agents, or subviruses. The second question requires more than writing down the six virus strains mentioned in boldfaced type in the opening paragraph, because it asks for a brief description of each. Except for prions, which get the most attention, the answer to Question 2 is found in the last paragraph, where the other five are described. Concerning Question 3, prions receive the most attention because they are radically different and are known to produce several diseases. As to the last question, they are all the smallest infectious agents known to researchers. Despite the length of such a passage, an application of the four guide questions will help your comprehension: (1) What topic is being divided? (2) Why is it divided? (3) What are the subtopics? (4) What are the similarities and differences among subtopics?

As I mentioned earlier, charts, diagrams, and tables are sometimes used to explain classifications. Read the following passage from a biology textbook and the table that accompanies it.

> Vitamins are classified into two groups: fat soluble vitamins and water soluble vitamins. Water soluble vitamins, when consumed in the diet in quantities greater than required, are readily passed through one's system and excreted, mostly through the urine. These include the various B vitamins, such as thiamine and riboflavin, and vitamin C. The fat soluble vitamins are A, D, E, and K. Most vitamins can be extracted from plants and animals, being concentrated especially in their most metabolically active tissues. Table 14.1 provides a listing of the water soluble and fat soluble vitamins.[17]

Notice that the author is classifying vitamins into two groups: fat soluble and water soluble. Table 14.1 provides more information on the similarities and differences than the paragraph does. In fact, the table is more important than the paragraph because of its detail and ability to show the two types of vitamins, their sources, their functions, their deficiency symptoms, and our daily need for them. So don't ignore references to charts, diagrams, and tables. They often make the point better than the text itself.

_____

17. *Source:* Garber, 242–243.

TABLE 14.1 Water Soluble and Fat Soluble Vitamins

Name	Sources	Function	Deficiency Symptoms	Daily Need
Fat soluable				
Vitamin A	Dairy products, egg yolk, green and yellow vegetables	Healthy skin, resistance to infection, formation of visual pigments	Scaly skin, susceptibility to infection, night blindness	5000 IU*
Vitamin D	Fish, liver, milk, sunlight action on the skin	Calcium metabolism	Rickets, muscular weakness	400 IU
Vitamin E	Green, leafy vegetables	Involved in electron transport chain	Anemia, male sterility	15 IU
Vitamin K	Leafy vegetables	Blood clotting	Excessive bleeding	Unknown
Water soluble				
Vitamin B$_1$ (Thiamine)	Organ meats, whole grains, green vegetables	Involved with Krebs cycle, normal growth and metabolism, appetite, nervous stability	Beri-beri, irritability, loss of appetite	1.5 mg
Vitamin B$_2$ (Riboflavin)	Dairy products, meat, green vegetables	Normal growth and metabolism, healthy skin, part of electron carrier FAD	Dermatitis	1.8 mg
Niacin	Whole grains, meat	Healthy skin, cell respiration, part of electron carrier NAD	Pellagra, nervous disorders	20.0 mg
Vitamin B$_{12}$	Liver	Red blood cell maturation	Pernicious anemia	0.003 mg
Vitamin C (ascorbic acid	Citrus fruits, tomatoes	Ground substance in cells	Scurvy, anemia, hemorrhage	45 mg

*IU = International Units

Source: Garber, 242–243.

Some science textbooks actually present classification charts as a way of introducing new material. Notice in the following passage how the author prepares you to read about animal phyla or divisions.

Representative Animal Phyla

It is possible to follow several trends in animal evolution without considering every single phylum (there are more than thirty). These are the groups we have chosen to illustrate the major body plans:

1.	Sponges	Asymmetrical, no gut
2.	Cnidarians, comb jellies	Radial, saclike gut
3.	Flatworms	Bilateral, saclike gut
4.	Nematodes, rotifers	Bilateral, pseudocoelomate, gut usually complete
5.	Mollusks, annelids arthropods, echinoderms, chordates	Bilateral (echinoderms also show radial chordates patterns), coelomate, gut usually complete

Taken together, the similarities and differences among these groups of animals help us perceive broad phylogenetic relationships.[18]

Here the author has already classified five selected divisions of animals from among thirty that he plans to discuss in more detail in the rest of the chapter. If you read more from this chapter, you would look for the similarities and differences discussed among the five groups. In effect, you would use comparison and contrast to help distinguish the classifications.

FINAL THOUGHTS

If you feel you need to review one or all of the five science writing patterns presented in this chapter—comparison-and-contrast, problem solving, sequence, generalization, and classification—do so before going on. As I've said before, this information will be of little use to you if you don't apply and practice what you've learned when you read your science textbooks.

PROCESSING WHAT YOU JUST READ

✍ If you are using the *Student's Reading Journal* that accompanies this text, go to pages 55–56 in it and follow the directions given.

If you are using your own notebook as a journal, answer the following questions:

1. Explain the classification writing pattern as used in science textbooks.
2. Make a chart or a table that classifies the five basic writing patterns often found in science textbooks.

Review your journal notes, then go to Part III, page 358, and practice what you have learned.

WHAT DO YOU THINK?

It's hard for a scientist to explain why it's interesting to learn about the universe. It just is. I don't understand how to explain that music is beautiful. It's a taste for wanting to understand why things are the way they are and where they came from. If you don't have the taste, talking about it can't give it to you. . . . There's a tremendous amount of interest in these questions. It gives us a sense of finding out what kind of drama we're actors in. I don't know how anyone could not want to know that.

Steven Weinberg, physicist

---

18. *Source:* Starr, 644.

10 *Research Sources in the Sciences*

Because science teachers frequently assign outside readings and written reports, you need to know some of the sources available to you in this subject area. This chapter introduces you to useful publications and references dealing with the sciences and technology. These publications can give you more detailed information on topics you are studying and keep you informed about current events in science, replacing dated information in your textbook. **Your objective in reading this chapter is to become more familiar with the outside sources you can use for science and technology assignments.**

Isn't it difficult to keep a science textbook up to date?

Most of the information in a first-year college science course is fairly standard stuff and deals with material that has been proved or generally accepted in the scientific community. However, scientists are always investigating and experimenting, making new discoveries and challenging old ideas. Because it usually takes a year or more to get a book in print after the author is finished writing it, your science textbook, even if it bears this year's copyright, is dated. That is not to say that the book is incorrect, only that it is not current.

Furthermore, one science textbook can't contain everything in its field. Science writers must select what they feel are the most fundamental areas. This means that Author A may want his science book to deal with contemporary fields of interest. He may cover historical and less contemporary scientific knowledge quickly in order to devote more space to the present trends of science. Author B may wish to give the most emphasis to the bodies of knowledge least likely to be challenged in the near future. Author C might want to emphasize people responsible for major scientific discoveries. The result is that we find textbooks, no matter how good, not including everything you or your instructor may want to cover. That's why outside reading is important and often assigned.

Your science instructor may provide a list of recommended outside sources. If so, don't wait too long into the term to locate some of those sources. I've frequently found that they are more interesting than the textbook!

Speaking of textbooks, we instructors usually have several textbooks for the same course on our office bookshelves. Publishers send us free "examination copies," hoping that we will select their books for use in our classes. We look them over, then chose the ones we feel are most appropriate for our students. If you are having trouble understanding passages from the textbook for a course you are taking, don't be afraid to ask the instructor if you can look over different textbooks on the same subject. Explanations in another book might be easier for you to follow.

In case you are unaware of science sources, here is a list that goes beyond the standard reference encyclopedias, such as *Compton's World Book*, or the *Encyclopaedia Britannica*. Look over this list and pick out two or three reference sources in your area of interest or coursework. Then go to your college library and become familiar with them.

Works Dealing with Science in General

American Yearbook: A Record of Events and Progress
Applied Science and Technology Index
Barnes and Noble Thesaurus of Science and Technology
A Century of Progress in the Natural Sciences: 1853–1953
Chambers's Dictionary of Scientists
A Dictionary of Scientific Terms (There is a dictionary for each of the following subjects: anatomy, biology, botany, cytology, embryology, genetics, physiology, and zoology)
Encyclopedia of Physical Science and Technology
Greek and Latin in Scientific Terminology
McGraw-Hill Encyclopedia of Science and Technology
Science Abstracts
Science Reference Sources
Scientific Terminology
Van Nostrand's Scientific Encyclopedia

Works Dealing with Biology

Biological Abstracts
The Columbia Encyclopedia of Nutrition
Encyclopedia of the Biological Sciences
The Facts on File Dictionary of Botany
Handbook of Biological Data
A Short History of Biology

Works Dealing with Chemistry

Chemical Abstracts
Encyclopedia of Chemical Technology
Guide to the Literature of Chemistry
Handbook of Chemistry and Physics

Works Dealing with Geology

Field Book of Common Rocks and Minerals
Geological Abstracts
Minerals Yearbook

Works Dealing with Physics

Glossary of Physics
Handbook of Chemistry and Physics
Reviews of Modern Physics

Journals and Periodicals in Science

American Journal of Anatomy
American Journal of Botany
American Journal of Physics
American Journal of Science
American Naturalist
American Scientist
American Zoologist

Animal Behavior Abstracts
Annals of Botany
Applied Microbiology and Biotechnology
Audubon Magazine
Biochemistry Journal
BioScience
Bulletin of Aquatic Biology
Bulletin of the Atomic Scientists
Ecology
General Science Index
Genetics
Journal of Animal Behavior
Journal of Bacteriology
Journal of Ecology
Journal of Geology
Journal of Marine Research
Journal of Natural History
Journal of Paleontology
Journal of Physiology
National Wildlife
Naturalist
Nature
Science
Science Digest
Science News
Scientific American
Scientific American Monthly
Scientific Monthly
Sea Frontiers
Sea Technology
Soil and WaterConservation News

These are only a few of the publications found in any good academic library. When you look through some of these works, you will find that they contain bibliographies mentioning even more publications. Make it a point to familiarize yourself with the resources available. Part of taking a course in science is to get to know sources that may be useful to you long after the course is over. Don't limit yourself to the course textbook.

Is that all there is?

Most of the sources listed in the previous section can be found in the reference section or periodical section of your college library. However, there are many other places to look.

If your library is computerized, all you need to do is look up the subject, such as biology, and you will be provided with dozens of options for finding sources. A number of academic libraries also have computerized data bases. For instance, if you wanted access to the most current research on the relationship between coffee and heart attacks, you could get a computer printout of the latest published information.

If and when you need to do a research project, refer to the Appendix, "Procedure for Doing a Research Paper," page 450. It provides a step-by-step approach with examples of note taking.

PROCESSING WHAT YOU JUST READ

✍ If you are using the *Student's Reading Journal* that accompanies this text, go to page 57 in it and follow the directions given.

If you are using your own notebook as a journal, answer the following questions:

1. Explain the value of reading outside sources in science.
2. How can looking at other textbooks for the same level science class be helpful?

What's the best way to read outside sources?

To close this section, here's an excerpt from a book entitled *Science Anxiety: Fear of Science and How to Overcome It* by Jeffry V. Mallow. I discovered it while looking over science materials available in the library in preparation for writing this book. You might be interested in reading it if you have any anxiety about learning science. In the following portion, Mallow discusses study-reading skills he feels are necessary for reading science and has some interesting things to say about outside reading as well as textbook reading.

Reading Science

There are various types of science writing, from popular science articles in newspapers and magazines to more detailed articles in *Science News*, *Science 81*, and *Scientific American* (articles that, however, require no prior knowledge of a subject) to textbook writing and, finally, to articles in scientific research journals. Each requires a different kind of reading style and different expectations about what can be learned from the content.

We shall not deal with research journal reading here. Of the other three, the easiest articles are those in the popular press. However, they have the least content and can sometimes be unintentionally misleading. In the first place, they are written in journalistic prose style. That is, the author's intention is to communicate the ideas to the reader in one fairly fast reading, just like nonscience articles. But, as we have emphasized in earlier chapters, you cannot learn science this way. What then is the popular article imparting to the reader? It is imparting the *results* of some scientific research. It cannot, in general, give the reader much insight into the process by which the research was conceived and carried out, nor about the logical train of thought underlying the research. We may read that an unmanned spacecraft is studying Jupiter; we will not learn how the particular problems to study were devised or why they are considered the essential ones or indeed how they fit into the general range of astronomical problems. The same can be said for science reporting on television: one sees results, but one does not get to follow the process of science.

There are two problems with this approach. The first is that it gives a somewhat misleading view of science. It appears as if the scientist can by magic choose the "right" problem to study and then quickly find a solution. Not so. Both the choice of problem and its solution are difficult tasks with no assurance of success—that's why it's called research! The second difficulty, especially for the person who wishes to understand the logical processes of science, is that the popular article may give the reader the impression that it contains more than it actually does. In particular, the article may look as if it is *explaining* something, when if fact it is only *describing* something. The reader, not understanding the logical process behind the scientific result, may then assume that he or she has missed something in the article, when in fact that something, the *explanation*, is not really present. Here is the beginning of a negative self-statement: "If I can't even understand this popular article, I must really be completely incapable of comprehending science!" The only effective way to combat this self-statement is to read the popular article the way it should be read: for results but not for explanation. Do not expect more than is there.

The next level of science writing is the more serious article in the science magazine. A good example is [an] article on black holes ... from *Scientific American*. Here, the author's purpose is indeed to give the reader some insight into the process of science as well as to present results. Although the author makes no demands that the reader have any prior background, except perhaps for a good general education, the author *does* demand a good deal of concentration on the part of the reader. Nobel Laureate Steven Weinberg, in his popular book about the origins of the universe, *The First Three Minutes*, makes this demand explicitly and articulately:

> However, this does not mean that I have tried to write an easy book. When a lawyer writes for the general public, he assumes that they do not know Law French or the Rule Against Perpetuities, but he does not think the worse of them for it, and he does not condescend to them. I want to return the compliment: I picture the reader as a smart old attorney who does not speak my language, but who expects nonetheless to hear some convincing arguments before he makes up his mind.

Thus as you read this kind of serious science writing for the nonscientist, you must read slowly, chew over each idea, and even go back and forth from earlier to later paragraphs to see if you follow the logical connections. You may not actually need pencil and paper in hand, since the articles may be fairly qualitative. But you will need to read slowly. When you have finished, however, you will have, if the writing is good, acquired more insight into how science is actually done than if you had read an article on the same topic in a newspaper. At all times, by the way, you should be assessing whether you think it is or is not good writing. Science writing, like any writing, is not of uniformly good quality, and it demystifies science to keep this in mind.

Finally, what about reading a science textbook? As we said in earlier chapters, this must be done slowly, with pencil and paper in hand, and must be done more than once. Ideally, a chapter should be read once before it is covered in a lecture, once during the time it is being covered, and once after it has been covered. Even before reading the chapter, you should read the chapter headings and subheadings just to get an overview of the material. At each step in which a new concept is presented, you must think it over, see if it makes sense to you, and work out an example if it is possible. Often in science texts the author will illustrate a concept by working an example. You should not only read the example for comprehension, but then work it for yourself without looking at the author's solution. When you can do this, and only then, can you feel sure that you have mastered the concept.

Keep in mind that it is not possible to skim the material for content. Skimming may provide a general overview, but it cannot provide the comprehension of the logical processes on which the material builds.

It is useful to look at more than one text's treatment of the same material. Find out what the instructor's second and third choices would have been for the course text and take a look at them. Often the auxiliary text will provide just a slightly different viewpoint, but one that makes more sense to you than the course text's treatment. Science, like art, is multifaceted. Each time you look at the same bit of work, you may see something different. So it is useful to read how various authors of science texts view the same concept. In fact, it is not dissimilar to reading two historians' views of the same series of events — except that the scientific data are reproducible.[1]

✍ Now answer the following questions in the spaces provided.

1. What is the difference between reading about science in a popular magazine and reading about science in a more serious science magazine or journal?

_____

_____

_____

2. How should you read serious science writing if you are a nonscientist?

_____

_____

_____

3. What recommendations are given for reading a science textbook?

_____

_____

_____

4. What is the difference between reading two historians' views of the same events in history and two scientists' views of the same scientific data?

_____

_____

_____

FINAL THOUGHTS

Remember that outside reading is an extension of your textbook. Take the time to familiarize yourself with the outside resources your library has: periodicals, journals, scientific encyclopedias, data bases, whatever. If you have a project to do for science class, use materials from more serious works rather than popular magazines and newspapers.

1. *Source:* Jeffry V. Mallow, *Science Anxiety: Fear of Science and How to Overcome It.* Thurmond, 1981, 153–156.

PROCESSING WHAT YOU JUST READ

✍ If you are using the *Student's Reading Journal* that accompanies this text, go to page 57 in it and follow the directions given.

If you are using your own notebook as a journal, answer the following questions:

1. If you are taking a science course and the instructor has assigned you a science project, make a list of all the possible sources in your college library that will be helpful. If you are not presently taking a science course, make a list of science resources available that sound interesting to you.
2. Look over the list of science journals beginning on page 166. Write down at least five titles that sound interesting. Go to the library and find a copy of the latest issue of each publication. Write a paragraph about the one you find most interesting.

Review your journal notes before going on to the next section assigned.

INTRODUCTION TO READING THE HUMANITIES

(Chapters 11–16)

Imagination is more important than information.

Robert Fulghum

What exactly are the humanities?

Like the social sciences and the sciences, the humanities are a body of knowledge. They deal with the study of humankind's intellectual and aesthetic creations. The word *humanities* comes from the Latin *humanus*, which means human, cultured, refined. Today, the area known as the humanities very broadly includes subjects such as literature, art, music, languages (including English), ethics, comparative religions, and philosophy.

In the social sciences, you study the institutions and processes of society. You study past problems and solutions that civilizations have found. You study people as individuals and as a group, with key personalities selected only because they are associated with certain events. When you read the sciences, you learn about the periodic table, the composition of elements, the difference between organic and inorganic matter, and what happens when you mix certain chemicals. What you learn is based on controlled observation and experimentation.

The study of humankind through the humanities tends to focus on humans as individuals. It does not reduce human life to its smallest particles or seek universal formulas that can be verified by experimentation. Rather, the humanities often reflect values and moral dilemmas. For this reason, the humanities can seem less structured, less uniform, and less easy to understand than biology or history. And because of their wide range of presentations, the reading tasks expected of students in humanities classes are probably more varied than in any other subject area.

What makes reading the humanities so different?

The reading material covered in humanities courses can be divided into two basic types: expository and imaginative. **Expository writing** presents information in a clear, precise form. Essays, magazine articles, textbooks such as this one—in fact, all the practice readings in the social science and science sections—can be classified as expository writings. Fortunately, all the writing patterns presented in those sections appear in introductory textbooks in art, music, philosophy, and comparative religions. So you're already familiar with expository writing.

Imaginative writing refers to fiction (the short story and the novel), poetry, and drama. Imaginative writing is often more difficult to read, especially for students who believe that novels and stories are "just pretend." But in good fiction, there is truth. A novelist can show you what an essayist can only tell about. A poet can make you feel an experience that you might otherwise only read about.

What skills are necessary for reading the humanities?

To study-read well in the humanities, you need comprehension skills that include the ability to

1. differentiate main ideas from details
2. recognize examples and illustrations used to support main ideas
3. identify comparisons and contrasts
4. recognize cause-and-effect statements
5. distinguish between fact, interpretation, and opinion
6. follow sequences of events
7. identify classification
8. differentiate the denotative and connotative uses of language
9. comprehend imaginative writings at the literal, interpretive, and affective levels

The differences between expository and imaginative writings are discussed in detail in the following chapter. If you have already finished the sections on the social sciences and sciences, then you have learned many of the strategies and skills just listed. The chapters in this section will familiarize you with the language used in the humanities, expository writing patterns frequently found in the humanities, and some strategies for reading fiction, poetry, and drama.

WHAT DO YOU THINK?

Perhaps, above all, we also want to know ourselves. And there are so many selves to know. There is, for example, the self studied by biology so that we can appropriate and become the masters of our bodies. There is the self studied by psychology, which tries to penetrate to the fundamental motives and intentions governing our behavior and to illuminate our opacities and irrationalities. There is the self studied by history, a most important self, because in a crucial sense we are our histories. . . . There is, finally, the self studied by literature, the imagined self, the uniquely individual self in contrast to the collective and general self of the social sciences. . . . Giving form to our lives is the way we integrate experience. What we do implicitly, literature does explicitly. This is why we have an affinity for it, and that is why we need it to understand ourselves.

Gerald Izenberg, educator at Washington University, St. Louis

CHAPTER 11

The Language of the Humanities

This chapter discusses the difference between expository and imaginative language. The meaning of words in fiction or in a poem may not be the meaning intended when the same words are used in expository writing. As a consequence, reading imaginative literature differs from reading other types of writing. Imaginative writing makes use of the suggestive power of words more than textbooks and essays do. Imaginative writing aims at words' emotional impact, at creating images in our mind's eye. Thus, words are often used more for their connotative meanings than for their denotative meanings. This does not mean, however, that connotations are not used in expository writing. More often than not, imaginative writing uses figures of speech, such as similes and metaphors. **Your objective in reading this chapter is to become familiar with language as it is used in the humanities.**

What makes the language of the humanities so different?

Actually, the only area in which the language used in humanities textbooks is different is imaginative writing: fiction, poetry, and drama. The use of language and the writing patterns in expository humanities books are much the same as you find in the social sciences and sciences. Because expository material in the humanities is so similar to material you have already encountered, let's concentrate mostly on the way language is used in imaginative literature.

You already know that words are like chameleons; they change color or meaning according to their surroundings. You already know that the best way to discover the meaning of an unfamiliar word is to look at the context in which the word is used. A word's **context**, remember, is how it is used in the sentence or paragraph in which it appears. The sentence or paragraph is the word's verbal environment. It sets the mood and helps define the word. Until a word is seen in context, it may have no particular meaning. In imaginative literature, a word may intentionally have many suggested meanings. It may connote meanings beyond its denotative definition.

Can you go over *denotation* and *connotation*?

A word's **denotation**, you may remember from Chapter 5, is what the word means in a narrow sense. Its **connotation** is what the word implies or suggests. Take the word *English*, for instance. The denotative meaning depends on how it is used in context. If you say *English*, you probably mean the language. If you say *the English*, you probably mean the people from England. These are denotative meanings, meanings you would find in a dictionary. If you have trouble remembering this, notice that *denotation* and *dictionary* begin with the same letter.

Now let's consider connotative meaning. What does the word *English* cause you to think about? Tea and biscuits? The Rolling Stones? "Masterpiece Theatre"? Stuffy, proper manners? A great summer you once spent in England? Depending on your experience, the word *English* can connotatively suggest feelings, thoughts, and experiences.

And what about English as a language? The experiences you have had in English classes have made the word mean something to you emotionally. If others have made fun of your speech, or if you have received poor grades in English classes, the word *English* may have a bad connotation. But, if you have had teachers who encouraged you in your writing, taught you to enjoy reading, or gave you good grades, no doubt *English* will have a positive connotation for you.

✍ Look at the following list of words. In the spaces provided, place a plus sign after those words that you feel have a positive connotation and a minus sign after those that have a negative connotation. Put a zero after words you feel have neither a positive nor a negative connotation.

1. God	_____	6. war	_____
2. youth	_____	7. communism	_____
3. love	_____	8. censorship	_____
4. welfare	_____	9. dentist	_____
5. money	_____	10. chocolate	_____

Chances are, you didn't put a zero after any of these words. After all, few people haven't tasted chocolate or been to the dentist. It is also unlikely that everyone using this book would make the same marks. To some people, *God* carries a positive, pleasant, comforting connotation; to others, the word connotes fear; to still others, God is a myth, an absurdity, a foolish notion, and the word conjures up a different negative connotation. Each word on this list has a "definition" that goes beyond what the dictionary says it means.

As a reader, you need to be alert not only to the dictionary meaning of a word and its use in context but also to the implications and feelings the word can arouse. Some authors load their writing with words full of connotative meanings. They play on our emotions. Politicians employ "imaginative language" when they use vague and clichéd phrases such as "the great American way of life handed down to us by our brave and valiant forefathers" or when they tell us about our "God-given rights." Advertisers use imaginative language when they tell us that a shampoo is "a velvet hair bath" or that a certain cigarette is "as refreshing as springtime green." The connotation of "springtime green," after all, is very different from the denotative statement that cigarettes are "cancer causing." An awareness of how you react to certain words is essential to full comprehension of what you read.

Imaginative writing in literature (novels, short stories, poems, and plays) makes use of the suggestive power of words more than most textbooks and essays do. The meaning given to words in a story or poem may not be the meaning given to them in a textbook. Therefore, your approach to the vocabulary of imaginative writing must be different from your approach to the language of expository writing.

Why do imaginative writers use so much connotative language?

In his novel *Hard Times*, Charles Dickens makes fun of the sort of person who can see only the "dictionary meaning" or denotation of words. At one point in the book,

Thomas Gradgrind, an old-fashioned schoolteacher, has called on a student named Bitzer to define a horse for another student:

> "Bitzer," said Thomas Gradgrind, "your definition of a horse."
>
> "Quadruped. Gramnivorous. Forty teeth, namely twenty-four grinders, four eye-teeth, and twelve incisive. Sheds coat in the spring; in marshy countries sheds hoofs too. Hoofs hard, but requiring to be shod with iron. Age known by marks in mouth."
>
> "Now, girl number twenty," said Mr. Gradgrind, "you know what a horse is."

Mr. Gradgrind accepts Bitzer's definition as a good one. But does "girl number twenty" *really* know now what a horse is? John Ciardi, a poet, said of Bitzer's idea of a horse: "No horseman ever rode a 'gramnivorous quadruped.' No gambler ever bet on one. No sculptor ever dreamed one out of a block of stone."[1]

Writers of imaginative literature are not Gradgrinds or Bitzers. They know that the connotation of a word can mean more to a reader than the word's denotation. The following poem shows a typical use of connotation. In it, words are more important for what they bring to mind and for what they make you feel than for what they "mean" in a narrow sense. The poem can thus have somewhat different meanings to different readers.

Composed upon Westminster Bridge
by William Wordsworth

Earth has not anything to show more fair:
Dull would he be of soul who could pass by
A sight so touching in its majesty.
This city now doth, like a garment, wear
The beauty of the morning; silent, bare,
Ships, towers, domes, theaters, and temples lie
Open unto the fields, and to the sky—
All bright and glittering in the smokeless air.
Never did sun more beautifully steep
In his splendor, valley, rock, or hill;
Ne'er saw I, never felt, a calm so deep!
The river glideth at his own sweet will.
Dear God! the very houses seem asleep,
And all that mighty heart is lying still!

Now suppose Mr. Gradgrind asked Bitzer what the words in Wordsworth's poem "really" mean. A line-by-line paraphrase, substituting a dictionary definition for each connotatively loaded word, might look like this:

Original	*Paraphrase*
Earth has not anything to show more fair:	Terrestrial globe reveals nothing more unblemished:
Dull would he be of soul who could pass by	Obtuse would he be of inner self who could ignore
A sight so touching in its majesty	A spectacular view so perceptually sensitive in its stateliness

---

1. *Source:* John Ciardi, *An Introduction to Literature.* Houghton, 1959, 665.

This city now doth, like a garment, wear	This incorporated municipality's boundaries are defined by a charter presently does, like wearing apparel, display
The beauty of the morning; silent, bare	That quality attributed to whatever pleases at the first part of the day: taciturn, naked

That's enough to give you the idea. The paraphrase is ridiculous, of course. Yet, peculiar as it sounds, it is a good job; it is *denotatively* the same as the original poem. But what's missing? The rhythm, the feeling, the images are all lost in the paraphrase. Wordsworth's use of language tells you much more about Westminster Bridge than Bitzer could.

What's more, you will probably remember what Wordsworth has told you. He has condensed ideas and feelings into a few words by choosing each word carefully.

Now read the following poem by Walt Whitman.

When I Heard the Learn'd Astronomer
by Walt Whitman

When I heard the learn'd astronomer,
When the proofs, the figures, were ranged in columns before me,
When I was shown the charts and diagrams, to add, divide, and
    measure them,
When I sitting heard the astronomer where he lectured with much
    applause in the lecture-room,
How soon unaccountable I became tired and sick,
Till rising and gliding out I wandered off by myself,
In the mystical moist night-air, and from time to time,
Looked up in perfect silence at the stars.

Like the previous poem, this one puts a lot of meaning into a few words. You could write a long essay expressing Whitman's vision when he left the stuffy lecture room and "Looked up in perfect silence at the stars" while the astronomer droned on inside. You might discuss at length the contrast between the scientist's attempt to describe the stars with charts and your own vision of real stars and clear night skies. You might even write pages about the limits of explaining the heavens with diagrams. You might explain your feelings in paragraphs of good prose. Or, like Whitman, you might condense your feelings into an eight-line poem. In fact, Whitman describes how all of us have felt in many lectures, not just those dealing with astronomy. The poem has meaning beyond the single lecture he discusses.

Connotation is just as important to the writer of imaginative literature as the proper placement of musical notes is to the musician or the correct blending of colors is to the painter. One of the qualities of a good writer is the ability to select the word that carries the exact feeling he or she wants the reader to have. Take any literary work and jumble up the words used in it. Then give those jumbled words to anyone, and see if he or she can use them as effectively as the original author. Maybe so, but the chances are pretty slim that anyone else would use the same words the same way.

Don't some words always mean the same thing?

To understand the words of imaginative writing, you have to remember that words change their meanings over time. When you read older works, you'll find some words that had meanings different from the ones they have today. If you study Samuel Taylor Coleridge's "The Rime of the Ancient Mariner," you find that a word such as *silly*, as used 200 years ago, cannot be read with the meaning it has for most people today. Coleridge used it to mean "plain" or "rustic," but today it is connected with words such as *stupid*. When over three centuries ago Samuel Pepys used the word *cheerful*, he didn't mean "happy" or "joyful"; he meant "calm."

You can often see the meanings of words change, in either their denotation or their connotation. Over the years, the word *dig* has come to mean "understand or enjoy," among other things. The word *key* usually refers to an instrument that opens a lock, a set of answers to a test, a lever on a hand-operated machine, or tonality in music. What kind of picture this word brings to mind depends on the context in which it is used. At the time this book was being written, *key* was taking on another meaning: "excellent, good, or cool." It was common to hear: "That's a key movie," or "She's real key, man." By the time you read this, such usage of *key* may have taken hold, or it might have been lost. The point is, we help create new meanings simply by using words in a way that is a little different from the way anyone else uses them. Everyone is a creator of definitions. The next time you're having trouble reading something from the 1700's, just remember that two hundred years from now another student will be trying to make sense of today's written words.

PROCESSING WHAT YOU JUST READ

✍ If you are using the *Student's Reading Journal* that accompanies this text, go to page 59 in it and follow the directions given.

If you are using your own notebook as a journal, answer the following questions:

1. Explain the difference between *denotation* and *connotation*.
2. Pick at least five words that have connotative meanings to you and explain what they are.

Why does a writer want to create mental images? Why not just write expository prose?

A good imaginative writer can bring to our minds impressions of sight, hearing, motion, touch, temperature, taste, and smell. Rather than just tell us something, the imaginative writer wants to *show* us, to help us *see* and *feel*, *remember* our own experiences. Notice the images created in the following stanza from John Keats's "The Eve of St. Agnes":

> St. Agnes' Eve—Ah, bitter chill it was!
> The owl, for all his features, was a-cold;
> The hare limp'd trembling through the frozen grass,
> And silent was the flock in wooly fold:
> Numb were the Beadsman's fingers, while he told
> His rosary, and while his frosted breath,
> Like pious incense from a censer old,
> Seem'd taking flight for heaven, without a death,
> Past the sweet Virgin's picture, while his prayer he saith.

Keats doesn't just tell us it is cold; his images—the owl, despite all his feathers, feeling the cold; the hare limping through cold grass; the still, silent flock of sheep; the cold, numb fingers and "frosted breath" of the Beadsman—all create the vivid sensation of cold for us to see and feel.

In "The Eagle," Alfred Lord Tennyson gives us a different kind of image, the swift motion of an eagle once he spots his prey far below him.

> He clasps the crag with crooked hands;
> Close to the sun in lonely lands,
> Ring'd with the azure world, he stands.
>
> The wrinkled sea beneath him crawls;
> He watches from his mountain walls,
> And like a thunderbolt he falls.

In the first stanza we see the eagle sitting high up, "close to the sun"; in the second, he falls "like a thunderbolt" from his mountain walls, presumably spotting a fish in the "wrinkled sea" far below him. Tennyson provides an image of swiftness as well as another definition of the term *eagle eyed*.

In the following poem, Langston Hughes creates feeling through familiar experiences:

Mother to Son
by Langston Hughes

> Well, son, I'll tell you:
> Life for me ain't been no crystal stair,
> It's had tacks in it,
> And splinters,
> And boards torn up,
> And places with no carpets on the floor—
> Bare.
> But all the time
> I'se been a-climbin' on
> And reachin' landin's
> And turnin' corners,
> And sometimes goin' in the dark
> Where there ain't been, no light.
> So, boy, don't you turn back.
> Don't you set down on the steps
> 'Cause you find it kinder hard.
> Don't you fall now—
> For I'se still goin', honey,
> I'se still climbin',
> And life for me ain't been no crystal stair.[2]

Hughes could have stated the basic idea of this poem in expository language: "Son, even though life is hard, don't give up. After all, life was hard for me, and I didn't give up." In effect, that's what the poem says. But the paraphrase simply doesn't duplicate the feeling in the poem. The mother's advice not to give up becomes very real, very moving in the poem.

The mother says, "Life for me ain't been no crystal stair." Life is compared to a stair, and stairs lead up as well as down. *Crystal* implies wealth and beauty. The image the line creates is one of wealth or beauty only dreamed about, as is appropriate to someone who has known only poverty and hard work. The image achieves its effect by a kind of reversal.

As the mother continues to compare life to stairs, we're told that some of the steps had tacks, some had splinters, some were torn up, some were without carpet. The images connote harshness, because we know tacks and splinters hurt when stepped on, torn-up stairs make the going difficult, and bare, uncarpeted floors are cold. It's that simple—and that real.

In spite of the bare, uncomfortable life, the mother has been "a-climbin' on." With the word *climbin'*, we know she chose to go up the stairs, not down. There have been "landin's" (stairway landings), where she stopped or rested before going on. There were "turnin' corners" where the unknown lay ahead in the dark, "where there ain't been, no light."

In spite of these hardships, though, she tells her son to go on, not to "set down on the steps/'Cause you find it kinder hard." Again the word *hard* reminds us of the difficult climb and the hard, bare stairs described earlier. Carefully selected words enable us to feel not only the hard life of this woman and the obvious despair of her son but also her powerful desire to overcome hardships and help her son survive. Perhaps for her there is something worth reaching at the top of those stairs. The poet helps us feel what the mother feels through the use of a few vivid words. He draws word pictures for us. Although the poem is about his mother and her hard life, chances are it made us think about our own mothers and things they have done for us.

Poetry isn't the only form of imaginative writing that uses images. Look at these early sentences from Ray Bradbury's novel *Dandelion Wine.*

> Douglas Spaulding, twelve, freshly wakened, let summer idle him on its early-morning stream. Lying in this third-story cupola bedroom, he felt the tall power it gave him, riding high in the June wind, the grandest tower in town. At night, when the trees washed together, he flashed his gaze like a beacon from this lighthouse in all directions over swarming seas of elm and oak and maple.[3]

Notice how certain words create an atmosphere and convey mental pictures for you to see and feel.

✍ In the spaces provided, jot down your own reaction to excerpts from this passage. List the words that create clear images in your mind. What are the images?

1. Douglas . . . let summer idle him on its early-morning stream.

   _____

   _____

   _____

   _____

2. . . . he felt the tall power it gave him, riding high in the June wind, the grandest tower in town.

   _____

3. *Source:* From *Dandelion Wine* by Ray Bradbury. Copyright 1957 by Ray Bradbury.

_____

_____

_____

3. . . . he flashed his gaze like a beacon from this lighthouse in all directions over swarming seas of elm and oak and maple.

_____

_____

_____

_____

Compare your comments with these:

1. The key words here are *summer, idle, early-morning stream*. The word *summer* connotes slowness or ease, thus, there is a connection between the words *summer* and *idle*. An *early-morning stream* fits in with the first day of summer. While this stream is literally a stream of sunshine, we think also of a stream of water, as in a lazy river. The stream has a long course to follow before summer is over. Douglas is lying idle in his bed, and he plans to let that early-morning stream of summer carry him along its course.

2. The key words here are *tall power, riding high, grandest tower*. The image created is one of height or elevation, and it fits the third-story bedroom Douglas is in.

3. The main image here is the boy's feeling of being the ray of light from a lighthouse. Douglas can see everywhere from his tall tower; his vision reaches out beyond the trees. From above, the trees look like "swarming seas" because the June wind is blowing their heavy foliage back and forth.

Mental pictures such as these, painted with words, are called **images**. By creating images, the author shows us rather than tells us what he or she has to say. The writer speaks directly to our senses.

As you read the following poem, notice its images.

The world is a beautiful place.
by Lawrence Ferlinghetti

> The world is a beautiful place
> > to be born into
> if you don't mind happiness
> > not always being
> > > so very much fun
> > if you don't mind a touch of hell
> > > now and then
> > just when everything is fine
> > > because even in heaven
> > > they don't sing
> > > all the time

> > The world is a beautiful place
> > > to be born into
> > > if you don't mind some people dying

all the time
or maybe only starving
some of the time
which isn't half so bad
if it isn't you

Oh the world is a beautiful place
to be born into
if you don't much mind
a few dead minds
in the higher places
or a bomb or two
now and then
in your upturned faces
or such other improprieties
as our Name Brand society
is prey to
with its men of distinction
and its men of extinction
and its priests
and other patrolmen
and its various segregations
and congressional investigations
and other constipations
that our fool flesh
is heir to

Yes the world is the best place of all
for a lot of such things as
making the fun scene
and making the love scene
and making the sad scene
and singing low songs and having inspirations
and walking around
looking at everything
and smelling flowers
and goosing statues
and even thinking
and kissing people and
making babies and wearing pants
and waving hats and
dancing
and going swimming in rivers
on picnics
in the middle of the summer
and just generally
'living in up'

Yes
but then right in the middle of it
comes the smiling
mortician[4]

4. *Source:* Lawrence Ferlinghetti, *A Coney Island of the Mind.* Copyright 1955, 1956 by Lawrence Ferlinghetti. Reprinted by permission of New Directions Publishing Corporation.

✍ In the space provided, write down some of the images you felt or enjoyed while reading this poem.

_____

_____

_____

_____

_____

It's not hard to see the images in this poem. "A bomb or two/ . . . in your upturned faces," "congressional investigations/ and other constipations," "kissing people and/ making babies"—the word pictures are clear and effective. Some of them are also humorous. The humorous pictures raise a question about the poem: Is it really just funny? There are a couple of other things going on in this collection of images created by the use of **figures of speech**.

THE FAR SIDE   By GARY LARSON

"Hang him, you idiots! Hang him! . . . 'String-him-up' is a figure of speech!"

Source: The Far Side Cartoon Features, San Francisco, California.

What are figures of speech?

When someone angrily tells you to "buzz off," the person usually doesn't expect you to go away making a buzzing noise. He or she expects you to respond to the connotative meaning, not the denotative, or literal, meaning of these words. *Buzz off* is a figure of speech expressing annoyance or anger. In other words, the **figure of speech** says one thing but means something else.

This is what Ferlinghetti does when he says, "The world is a beautiful place/to be born into." It is a beautiful place, he says, if you don't mind all the stupid and ugly things, such as bombs and dead minds, that human beings fill the world with. This obvious way of saying one thing and meaning another is called **irony**. You use irony when you say, "I just *love* to take exams!" You used it when you come to class unprepared and your instructor gives a pop quiz and you respond with "That's just *great*." Irony probably appears more in the humanities than in other disciplines.

Two other figures of speech frequently found in the humanities are metaphors and similes. A **metaphor** implies a comparison between two unlike things. When Shakespeare wrote "All the world's a stage," he was using metaphor to say something about the way people behave—or act. When Ulysses in Tennyson's poem says "I will drink/Life to the lees," he means metaphorically that he will experience life as deeply as possible, or down to the sediment (lees) at the bottom of the cup (life).

Like a metaphor, a **simile** is a stated comparison between two unlike things, but a simile uses words such as *like, as,* or *resembles* to make the comparison. A simile makes a comparison more obviously but less directly than a metaphor. For instance, instead of saying, "All the world's a stage" (metaphor), you might say, "All the world's *like* a stage (simile). When you remark that he "eats like a horse" or her hair is "smooth as silk," you're using similes. When you say, "The ice was smooth as glass," you're using simile; when you say, "The ice was glass," you're using metaphor.

✍ See if you can identify the figures of speech used in the following statements. In the spaces provided, place an *M* for metaphor or an *S* for simile, then explain what each statement means.

1. Sherry is a walking encyclopedia. _____

   _____

2. She's as sweet as Tupelo honey. _____

   _____

3. Tim works at a snail's pace. _____

   _____

4. Her brother is as deep as space. _____

   _____

5. The test was as rough as sandpaper. _____

   _____

6. In her diapers, Sherri waddled like a duck. _____

   _____

Compare your answers with these: (1) *M,* meaning she knows quite a lot; (2) *S,* meaning she has a nice disposition; (3) *M,* meaning Tim is a slow worker; (4) *S,* meaning he's engrossed in esoteric, profound, or mysterious thoughts; (5) *S,* meaning it was not an easy test; (6) *S,* meaning her walk resembled that of a duck.

There are other kinds of figurative language. "This class is like Christmas at Macy's" is a simile, but it is also grossly exaggerated. The often heard statement "I'm so hungry I could eat a horse" is also an exaggerated figure of speech. Such statements are called **hyperbole.**

To give you a better example of hyperbole at work in literature, here's a passage from James Thurber's "The Secret Life of Walter Mitty." Mitty, the main character, often slips off into a dreamworld where he imagines himself to be great at something. Here, he is visualizing himself as a surgeon performing a tricky operation:

> A huge, complicated machine, connected to the operating table, with many tubes and wires, began at this moment to go pocketa-pocketa-pocketa. "The new anesthetizer is giving way!" shouted an intern. "There is no one in the East who knows how to fix it!" "Quiet, man!" said Mitty, in a low, cool voice. He sprang to the machine, which was now going pocketa-pocketa-queep-pocketa-queep. He began fingering delicately a row of glistening dials. "Give me a fountain pen!" he snapped. Someone handed him a fountain pen. He pulled a faulty piston out of the machine and inserted the pen in its place. "That will hold for ten minutes," he said. "Get on with the operation."[5]

Thurber has the mild-mannered Walter Mitty in an extreme exaggeration of reality. A writer's use of hyperbole may be as simple as "They were packed into the bus like sardines" or as involved as Walter Mitty.

In the excerpt from Thurber's story, we find another word device that a writer can use. Thurber invented words to let us "hear" a sound: *pocketa-pocketa-pocketa.* And when the machine gets worse, it goes *pocketa-pocketa-queep.* This formation of words used to imitate sounds of an object or an action is called **onomatopoeia.** Imaginative writers use their imaginations. As imaginative readers, we need to use ours.

There are other ways a writer can use words. If he wants sound effects, a writer may use **alliteration,** as Shakespeare does in this line from *The Tempest.* Notice the repetition of certain letters.

> Full fathom five thy father lies.

This is not very different from a more familiar example of alliteration:

> Peter Piper picked a peck of pickled peppers.

A writer can use all these devices and more to make us feel, hear, smell, taste, and see through words. You'll learn more about these devices in your English and literature classes. Now you know what you as a reader must do when you read stories, poems, or plays. Let the words create mental pictures, listen to the sounds, and allow yourself to feel.

Not all language used in humanities textbooks is imaginative, is it?

What I've been discussing pertains to fiction, poetry, and drama. Because expository writing in humanities textbooks is similar to the language usage in other subject areas, the emphasis here had been on imaginative writing. Other sections in this

---

5. *Source: My World—And Welcome to It.* Harper, 1942.

book deal adequately with expository language, so there's no need to repeat it all here.

FINAL THOUGHTS   Writers of imaginative literature use words to connote feeling, create visual images, and suggest sounds. Devices such as irony, metaphor, simile, hyperbole, and alliteration are among the tools of the imaginative writer. Poets use these tools to say much in a few words or to create feelings in us that can't really be described in denotative terms. In themselves, the names of these figures of speech are not important. What is important is that you understand how figures of speech work and how they contribute to meaning in imaginative writing.

PROCESSING WHAT YOU JUST READ

✍ If you are using the *Student's Reading Journal* that accompanies this text, go to pages 59–60 in it and follow the directions given.

If you using your own notebook as a journal, answer the following questions:

1. Define these terms and give an example of each: (a) figure of speech, (b) simile, (c) metaphor, (d) hyperbole, (e) alliteration.
2. Make up or pick a figure of speech and explain its denotative and connotative meanings.

Review your journal notes, then go to Part III, page 381, for more practice in reading imaginative language.

CHAPTER 12

Expository Writing Patterns in the Humanities

PREPARING TO READ

This chapter deals with the expository writing patterns found most frequently in humanities textbooks. In the humanities, as in other subject areas, writers often develop their ideas by using the following writing patterns: example, comparison and contrast, cause and effect, definition, description, and combinations of these patterns. Except for the content, you will find that these patterns are similar to those discussed in the sections on reading the social sciences and the sciences. These are not all the possible expository writing patterns, of course, but they appear with enough frequency to be worth learning or reviewing. **Your objective in reading this chapter is to understand how the writing patterns mentioned can help you study-read your humanities textbooks more efficiently.**

Isn't example an easy writing pattern to spot?

Usually, **example** is a very easy writing pattern to spot. Expository writers often use examples or illustrations to make a point more clear. The types of examples can vary from statistics to diagrams or pictures. Notice the type of example used in the following paragraph from a humanities textbook:

> The humanities constitute one of the oldest and most important means of expression developed by man. Even if we go back to those eras called prehistoric because they are older than any periods of which we have written records, we find works to which we give an important place in the roster of the humanities. In 1879, a Spaniard, accompanied by his little daughter, was exploring a cave. Suddenly she began to cry, "Bulls! Bulls!" He turned his lantern so that the light fell on the ceiling of the cave, and there he saw the pictures of wild boar, hind, and bison which we now know as the Altima cave paintings (Figure 1). Since that time, similar paintings have been found in other caves, and the experts have given their judgment that these belong to the Upper Paleolithic Age, ten to twenty thousand years before Christ.[1]

✍ In the spaces provided, answer these questions about this paragraph.

1. What is the main idea of the paragraph?

   _____

   _____

---

1. *Source:* Louise Dudley and Austin Faricy, *The Humanities*, McGraw, 1967, 3.

FIGURE 1.   Galloping wild boar.

2.   What examples are used to support the main idea?

_____

_____

_____

The first sentence states the main idea. The humanities are "one of the oldest and most important means of expression developed by man." To support this statement, the authors provide two examples: (1) an account of the 1879 discovery of prehistoric cave paintings; (2) a picture of a prehistoric cave painting.

Here is still another example of the use of this writing pattern. (See, even I'm using the pattern!) This passage is taken from a humanities textbook that discusses "modernist literature," a name given to a literary movement in the early twentieth century. Look for the main idea and the example being used to support it.

A certain world weariness invades much of modernist writing. The devastations of World War I seemed to confirm already present philosophical assumptions about the futility and fragility of man's existence. . . . One of the best chroniclers of this state of emotional vacuum is T. S. Eliot. Eliot's most ambitious poem on this theme, "The Waste Land," portrays the spiritual desolation of a modern city, London, through references to ancient literature and oriental mythology. His earlier "Love Song of J. Alfred Prufrock" portrays a typically "modern" man, unable to make decisions, to act, or even to feel. Prufrock is an overcivilized human being in an overcivilized society, representative, before Freud's book, of "civilization and its discontents."[2]

2.   *Source:* Mary Ann Frese Witt et al. *The Humanities*, vol. 2. Heath, 1985, 305.

✍ In the spaces provided, answer the following questions about this paragraph.

1. What is the main idea of the paragraph?

    _____

    _____

    _____

    _____

2. What examples are used to support the main idea?

    _____

    _____

    _____

In this paragraph, the first two sentences present the main idea. Taken together, they make the point that the modernist writers, after experiencing the devastations of World War I, reflect a certain world weariness, a feeling that human existence is futile and fragile. T. S. Eliot is used as an example of the modernist writer. Two of Eliot's works, "The Waste Land" and "The Love Song of J. Alfred Prufrock," exemplify the point being made about modernist writers.

One last example follows. Taken from a book about poetry, it discusses figurative language. Read for the main idea, looking for any examples used to explain it.

> Though metaphor works first on an intuitive level, it also must work on a logical level. . . . Figurative language jumps off into imaginary territory but should not cut free from connections to reality. When the poet pushes an image too far, this can happen:
>
> > The wild tulip, at the end of its tube, blows out its great red bell
> > Like a thin clear bubble of blood for the children to pick and sell.
> >
> > Robert Browning
>
> Children selling a bubble of blood? No. We don't *believe* that. Lovely as the first glass-blowing image is, the poor logic in the second line spoils the image.
>
> When the metaphors are poorly conceived this kind of confusion results:
>
> > **The Vine**
> > The wine of love is music,
> >   And the feast of love is song:
> > When love sits down to banquet,
> >   Love sits long:
> > Sits long and rises drunken,
> >   But not with the feast and the wine;
> > He reeleth wityh his own heart,
> >   That great rich Vine.
> >
> > James Thomson, 1700–1748

These doubled-up metaphors get confusing. Vine, wine, feast, music, love—just what is the metaphor for what? None of the functions for figurative imagery are fulfilled; the tangle of imagery only obscures whatever significance the capital-letter "Vine" was supposed to have. The result is vague metaphors.[3]

The two poem examples are easy enough to identify in this passage, but what about the main idea? If you read carefully, you realize the author is using the examples to define *vague metaphors.*

✍ In the space provided, write down the author's definition of that term.

_____

_____

_____

_____

The two examples of vague metaphors show us that some metaphors don't work well when pushed too far or are so vague as not to be connected to reality. Vague metaphors, then, reflect poor use of figurative language, the author's main idea.

One last word about this writing pattern. Although the examples used here do not contain them, often phrases such as *for example, for instance, to illustrate,* or *to reflect my point* will clue you to this writing pattern. When such words are used, identifying this pattern becomes quite easy. If you need more explanation of this method, review pages 89–95.

PROCESSING WHAT YOU JUST READ

✍ If you are using the *Student's Reading Journal* that accompanies this text, go to page 61 in it and follow the directions given.

If you are using your own notebook as a journal, answer the following questions:

1. Explain the example writing pattern and why expository writers use it.
2. Using the example pattern, write a paragraph about any experience you have had with some aspect of the humanities.
3. Define *vague metaphor.* Give an example.

What about the use of comparison and contrast in humanities books?

Comparison and contrast is also used frequently in the humanities. Usually, to **compare** two things means to discuss how they are alike. To **contrast** means to show differences. Notice how comparison and contrast is done here:

It is almost impossible to formulate a set of rules for evaluating romantic art because it is a spirit of revolt, of individualism. There are many contrasts and paradoxes within the movement itself. If any guide can be suggested, it is contrast to the classic. The classic tendency in music and visual arts is toward a centralization, toward closed form; in the romantic, we find open form, the predilection for action and soaring

---

3. *Source: Frances Mayes, The Discovery of Poetry, Harcourt, 1987, 97–98.*

emotions. The classical is logical and intellectual, while the romantic is irrational, untypical, and often experimental. The classic deals in sharply defined lines and melodies: the romantic in vague, shadowy, conjectural forms and suggestive harmonies. One may also contrast the strong positive objectivity of the classic to the often loosely formed subjectivity of romanticism.[4]

✍ In the spaces provided, answer the following questions about this passage.

1. What is the main idea in this passage?

   _____

   _____

   _____

   _____

2. List the differences between *classical* and *romantic* in the appropriate columns.

   Classical   *Romantic*

   _____   _____

   _____   _____

   _____   _____

   _____   _____

   _____   _____

   _____   _____

Did you notice how the paragraph is constructed? It begins by stating that it is almost impossible to formulate a set of rules for evaluating romantic art, but, if any effort can be made, it is in *contrast* with classical art. Then the author follows a pattern by saying, for the classical, we find this; for the romantic, we find that. The pattern of giving the classical "rules" followed by the romantic "rules" is continued through the rest of the passage.

Read the following passage from a music textbook, looking for the main idea and how comparison and contrast is used to support the point being made.

It is interesting to note that, while Bach and Handel were contemporaries, they represented two entirely different personalities. Both were considered among the greatest organists of their day; they both produced lasting choral music. Bach admired Handel a great deal. He knew Handel's music and was anxious to know him personally. Handel, on the other hand, never had any desire to know Bach and probably knew very little of his music. The two men never met. Bach had no wish for

4. *Source:* Milo Wold and Edmuund Cykler. *Introduction to Music and Art in the Western World.* Brown, 1985, 200.

fame and fortune. Handel wanted fame and luxury, and it was only after fate had made him poor that he found his true artistic expression.[5]

✍ In the spaces provided, answer the following questions.

1. What were the three similarities between Bach and Handel?

   a. _____

   b. _____

   c. _____

2. What were two differences between Bach and Handel?

   a. _____

   b. _____

3. What is the main idea of the passage?

   _____

   _____

   _____

   _____

The main idea of the passage is that although Bach and Handel were contemporaries and produced similar music, they were very different personality types. They were alike in that both (1) lived during the same time, (2) were considered good organists, and (3) wrote lasting choral music. They were different in that (1) Bach admired Handel, but Handel never wanted to know Bach, and (2) Bach had no desire for fame and fortune, but Handel did.

Whenever you find passages that use the comparison-and-contrast pattern, list the likenesses and differences as you did for the preceding paragraph. Doing so not only helps you comprehend the passages better but provides a good note-taking technique.

What about the cause-and-effect writing pattern?

A **cause**, as you probably remember, is an event, an action, or a person that makes something else happen. The **effect** is the result of the action of cause. For example (what pattern am I using?), science has evidence that, if you spend time in the sun without sunscreen, you risk getting skin cancer.

   the cause: spending time in the sun
   the effect: risk of skin cancer

Look for the cause-and-effect pattern in the following passage, discussing the status of monarchies after the Middle Ages.

5. *Source:* Wold and Cykler, 166.

Farther to the east, in countries like Brandenburg-Prussia and Austria, the monarchies had emerged from the Middle Ages much weaker and more unstable than those in the west; as a result, eastern rulers were forced to go even further in order to obtain absolute political power. They granted the nobility (the middle class was really insignificant in numbers) the right to reduce the local rural populations to the status of serfs. In Brandenburg-Prussia, moreover, the *Junkers*, or nobility, were made the only class legally allowed to own land.[6]

✍ In the spaces provided, answer the following questions.

1. What is the main idea of the paragraph?

2. What is the cause?

3. What are the effects?

In this paragraph, the *cause* is the weakened and unstable monarchies that emerged from the Middle Ages. The *effects* are that eastern rulers were forced to grant the nobility the right to reduce the local rural populations to the status of serfs and in some places only the nobility were allowed to own land. The main idea is that some unstable and weak monarchies were forced to give concessions to the nobility.

Look for the cause-and-effect relationship in the following passage:

This philosophy of romanticism gave men the freedom to give voice to their passion, fear, love, and longing. Artists could now celebrate natural man and break the bounds of formalism imposed by classicism. This meant that new subjects for art were now available. All kinds of subjects and experiences, previously considered in bad taste, now found artistic expression. There was a renewed interest in nature. Landscape again became a favorite theme, as it had been in the seventeenth century. Folklore and folk song found a place as expressions of the simple, unaffected peasantry. The mysteries of love and death brought passion and drama back into the arts. The new ideals of freedom were drama-tized, both visually and tonally. The untypical experience fascinated the

6. *Source:* Witt, 13.

romantic artist because of its mystery and supernaturalism. Violence and shocking events were often used because such subjects gave more opportunity for the projection of strong emotions.[7]

✍ In the spaces provided, answer the following questions.

1. What is the main idea of the paragraph?

_____

_____

_____

2. What is the cause?

_____

_____

_____

3. What are the effects?

_____

_____

_____

The main idea of the paragraph is that the rise of romanticism gave people a freedom to voice their emotions. Of course, by stating the main idea, you have actually stated both cause and effect. The rise of romanticism (the *cause*) allowed artists to express their emotions in ways that before were considered bad taste (the *effect*). The passage offers many effects: the bonds of formalism imposed by classicism were broken, new artistic expression emerged, interest in painting landscapes was renewed, passion and drama were brought back to the arts, and so on.

Whenever you notice a cause-and-effect relationship, separate the cause from the effect. Doing so will help you understand the main idea. However, be wary when you read some uses of the cause-and-effect writing pattern. Sometimes the causes an author finds for events may not be the only or true causes. Without much background in a subject, you can accept a cause-and-effect viewpoint without realizing there may be other causes or effects. That's why reading sources outside the textbook is important.

PROCESSING WHAT YOU JUST READ

✍ If you are using the *Student's Reading Journal* that accompanies this text, go to page 61 in it and follow the directions given.

If you are using your own notebook as a journal, answer the following questions:

1. Compare or contrast the comparison-and-contrast writing pattern with the cause-and-effect pattern.
2. Give two examples of a cause and its effect.

7. *Source:* Wold and Cykler, 198–199.

How is definition used as a humanities writing pattern?

The use of **definition** as a writing pattern is easy to spot. You know how dictionaries and most textbooks define words. In the humanities, writers must define words or concepts for which words are only labels. Take the word *romanticism*, for example. Here's how one humanities book defines it in the glossary.

> A movement in all the arts as well as in philosophy, religion, and politics that spread throughout Europe and America in the early nineteenth century. The romantics revolted against Neoclassical emphasis on order and reason and substituted an inclination for nature and imagination. See Chapters 26 and 27.[8]

This is a nice definition to memorize for a test, but does it really *define romanticism*? Notice that the definition refers you to Chapters 26 and 27, which means there is a lot more to understand about romanticism than the simple explanation given here. To define romanticism truly, the author must explain what it means in the arts, in philosophy, in religion, and in politics.

Here is an attempt to define romanticism in Chapter 26, of the same humanities text. Notice how involved it gets.

> The varied, often contradictory [eighteenth century] cultural movement that swept over Europe and America and became known as romanticism had profound effects on the humanities—effects still very much felt in the contemporary world. The individualism, sense of isolation, and alienation of which we are now so aware have their roots in the Renaissance and Reformation period, but they were cultivated and brought to flower by the romantics.
>
> Romanticism as a movement may be said to have originated in Germany, but the word romantic first appeared in England in the mid-eighteenth century. It originated from an association with medieval "romances," the (predominantly French) stories of knights and ladies. As the word became coined in all European languages, it took on connotations of fanciful, picturesque, rugged, spontaneous, natural, and sentimental. During the early nineteenth century it was applied to groups of rebellious young artists promoting creativity, individualism, and free expression of emotion in opposition to classical canons and the regulations and standards based on "enlightened" reason that their parents' generation had espoused. For the romantics, life and art were one: as they threw out the old standards for art, so they lived their lives with bohemian freedom, following their passions or imagination rather than their reason or the "artificial" rules of society. Artistic and political ideals also intertwined: the French writer Victor Hugo called romanticism "liberalism in literature" and proclaimed that words, like postrevolutionary human beings, were now free from tyranny. By the middle of the century, however, many romantics had grown conservative, Catholic, or nationalistic, or they had retreated into an asocial dream world. This was partly because of the political scene in Europe: many who had first adored Napoleon as the bearer of the revolution became disillusioned with Napoleon the emperor. Yet some romantics were intensely conservative from the beginning, looking back toward the Middle Ages as an ideal period of order and spirituality. (The liberals, too, liked medieval themes but for other reasons.) It is impossible to attribute an exact beginning and end to this complex, varied, pan-European and American movement; but the French revolution gave impetus

8. *Source:* Witt, vol. 2, 528.

to its latent beginnings, and it died out in most places before 1850. In Slavic countries, however, the romantic movement in literature (and in nationalistic politics) continued longer, and romantic music flourished in Germany, France, and Italy throughout the nineteenth century. It is hardly possible to attempt a global history or definition of romanticism here. We will concentrate instead on the artistic expression of some major romantic themes: in this chapter, revolution, the hero, and nature; and in the following chapter, women and love.[9]

In spite of all this information, the passage ends with "It is hardly possible to attempt a global history or definition of romanticism here."

Definition, then, can be as brief as a sentence, as long as the preceding passage, or as complex as an entire chapter. As a reader, make certain that you can write a definition of every key term as well as know where the term fits historically, who was involved, and what its historical cause and effect were.

Don't art and music textbooks frequently use description?

You'll find a heavy use of description in the humanities, particularly in art and music textbooks. **Description** is often used to compare and contrast artistic styles, to illustrate artistic forms, or to help define terms. In other words, description is used in combination with some of the writing patterns already mentioned in order to make a point.

Notice how description is used here:

No matter how straightforward a work may seem, it is influenced tremendously by the artist's own perspective and by his or her culture. This may be a difficult idea to grasp at first. We can look at a beautiful painted landscape, for example, and think, "But that's just the way it *looks*. The artist isn't expressing anything." Is this really true?

To test the idea, we might compare two landscapes painted just four years apart—one by the American Thomas Cole, the other by the Englishman J. M. W. Turner. At first glance we are tempted to say that Turner is expressive and that Cole is not. Turner's landscape [*Rockets and Blue Lights*] is a fantasy of light and vapor and cloud and mist. We can scarcely identify any details. Cole's *Oxbow*, on the other hand, is a recognizable and very pretty scene on the Connecticut River. You could go there, find the right place, and it would look very much like the painting. The casual observer might say that Turner was inventing, whereas Cole was just recording nature.

The task of "just" recording nature, however, begins to seem rather formidable when we realize how many decisions Cole had to make in painting the scene. Why choose that particular spot? Why take the exact vantage point that he did? Why paint the scene by day instead of making a moonlit panorama? Why include a rainbow—wouldn't a violent storm have been more dramatic?[10]

✍ In the spaces provided, answer the following questions.

1.   What is being described in this passage?

_____

9.   *Source:* Witt, vol. 2, 218–219.
10.   *Source:* Rita Gilbert, *Living with Art.* Knopf, 1988, 48–49.

_____

_____

2. What is the point of the description?

_____

_____

_____

Although we get some description of both Turner's and Coles's paintings through comparison and contrast, the purpose or point of this passage is that an artist is influenced tremendously by the artist's own perspective and by his or her culture. The description is used to make a point.

Notice how description is used in the following passage to describe Islamic architecture:

The Architecture of Islam

. . . One of the best preserved examples of Muslim architecture is the Alhambra Palace in Granada in southern Spain, which was built in the mid-fourteenth century.

The Alhambra Palace

Perched on a promontory outside Granada in southern Spain, high above the city and cooled by the breeze that comes down from the snowcapped Sierra Nevada mountains, stands the Alhambra, the palace of the sultans who ruled this portion of Andalusia. It consists of an asymmetrical, rather rambling arrangement of halls, rooms, and corridors, grouped around two large and several smaller open courts, sometimes on one level and sometimes on two. The palace consists of three parts: first a public section where affairs of administration and justice were conducted, next the official residence of the sultan, and last his private residence and the harem, or apartments of his wives and concubines. As one walks through the palace, now almost empty of furniture and, of course, lacking the richness of carved woodwork, damask curtains, Persian carpets, glittering glass and metal utensils and vessels, one is still astounded at the richness of surface and subtlety of color harmonies. Brightly lit courtyards contrast abruptly with the dark, cool rooms into which light is sometimes filtered through grilled windows. Almost everywhere one looks one can see through a window or balcony a cool garden patio where the splashing of a fountain adds to the magic of the architecture. . . .

The Court of the Lions

The heart of the harem, or private apartments of the sultan, was the large court whose central fountain, supported on the backs of twelve lions . . . gives the court its name. It is rectangular, measures 115 by 66 feet, and is surrounded on the sides by an arcade whose arches rest alternately on single and double columns. The great number of these columns (eighteen in each portico alone) and their thinness reminds one of a line of young saplings whose sunlit trunks stand out against the cool shade of the forest beyond them. The spreading of the arches above them and the vegetal forms of the decoration heighten this impression.[11]

✍ In the spaces provided, answer the following questions.

1. What is being described in this passage?

   _____

   _____

   _____

2. How does the author use comparison and contrast as part of the description?

   _____

   _____

   _____

3. What is the point of the description?

   _____

   _____

   _____

To answer Questions 1 and 2, the Alhambra and particularly one of its parts, the Court of the Lions, are being described to provide an example of Islamic architecture. In this case, the description gives you a feeling for not only the Alhambra but Islamic design as well.

Within the descriptive example, the author uses comparison and contrast. In the first paragraph, he contrasts the emptiness of the palace today with a description of what it must have looked like in the fourteenth century, with its furniture, curtains, and carpets. He also contrasts the "brightly lit courtyards" with "the dark, cool rooms" and their filtered light. In the second paragraph, he uses what is virtually a figure of speech to compare the columns to young saplings "whose sunlit trunks stand out against the cool shade of the forest beyond them."

Description, then, is often used in a combination of writing patterns to compare or contrast, to explain terms, or to provide examples to support a main point.

FINAL THOUGHTS   In this chapter you have learned the expository writing patterns most frequently found in humanities textbooks. In the humanities, as in other fields, writers often develop their ideas by using the following patterns: examples, comparison and contrast, cause and effect, definition, description, and combinations of these patterns. Except for the content, you will find that these patterns are similar to those discussed in the sections on reading the social sciences and the sciences.

11. *Source:* Jon D. Longaker, *Art, Style, and History,* Scott, 1970, 115–116.

PROCESSING WHAT YOU JUST READ

✍ If you are using the *Student's Reading Journal* that accompanies this text, go to page 62 in it and follow the directions given.

If you are using your own notebook as a journal, answer the following questions:

1. Write a definition of expository writing and give some examples of writing patterns that appear in the humanities.
2. What did you learn in this chapter that will help you read humanities textbooks?

Review your journal notes, then go to Part III, page 397, for more practice in reading expository writing in the humanities.

CHAPTER 13

Strategies for Study-Reading Fiction

PREPARING TO READ

The purpose of this chapter is to show that close analysis of imaginative writing, such as a short story or a novel, requires more than a single reading. You will be given three types of comprehension questions to ask when you read imaginative writing: literal, interpretive, and affective. *Literal questions* ask about the basic facts of a story: the names and relationships of characters, the major events, where the story takes place, and so on. *Interpretive questions* ask you to analyze the story, to discuss how the story "works" and what it means. *Affective questions* ask you to explain how the story affects you personally—what it does to you, how it makes you feel, what you like and dislike about it. **Your objective in reading this chapter is to learn and apply the strategies for study-reading fiction.**

What's the point of studying fiction?

Some people think that reading **fiction**, "made up" stories, is a waste of time because fiction doesn't deal with "facts" about life. One of the things I found early in my college career was that I was often learning more truth about myself and others, more about the human condition in general, in my literature classes than in my introductory courses in sociology, psychology, and history. Those so-called factual subjects deal with how and why we behave as we do, what causes our actions, but so does good fiction. Fiction just does so in a different way.

It's not that literature has all the answers. Far from it. Some fiction merely entertains us for a while. We use it to escape temporarily from ourselves. But good fiction offers flashes of insight, hints, suggestions, reminders, awareness of the human condition. We enter an author's fictional world and come out with a broader understanding of and feeling for the "real" world.

Literature's ability to imitate life also gives us pleasure. Authors of fiction provide us with various visions of life, helping us stretch our imaginations. They tap into our emotions and our intellect. The more we learn about the various styles and creativity of imaginative writers, the more pleasure we get, not just from a momentary escape into stories, but from their artistic merit.

The first novel I read was James T. Farrell's *Studs Lonigan*, the story of a young man growing up in the Chicago area. Even after all these years, I haven't forgotten Studs. He is a part of me, just as much as if he had been someone I knew in high school. Many of the problems and feelings Studs experiences are ones that I experienced. His feelings toward his family, his religion, his sexual awareness, his relations with his peers, his fears—were more real to me than anything I had ever read. More than any introductory psychology book could, Studs showed me that I wasn't alone in my adolescent discontent and confusion. More than any sociology book could, Studs showed me the effects that peer group pressure, religious teachings, and ethnic backgrounds have on us all. More than any history book could, Studs taught me what life was like for inner-city families in a large city like Chicago.

WHAT DO YOU THINK?

If you look at the world in terms of storytelling, you have, first of all, the man who agitates, the man who drums up the people—I call him the drummer. Then you have the warrior, who goes forward and fights. But you also have the storyteller who recounts the event—and this is the one who survives, who outlives all the others. It is the storyteller, in fact, who makes us what we are, who creates history. The storyteller creates the memory that the survivors must have—otherwise their surviving would have no meaning.

Chinua Achebe, Nigerian novelist

Good fiction has very real things to say, with the added attraction of doing it pleasurably.

Since I read *Studs Lonigan*, hundreds of fictional characters in books and stories have become my guides, my companions, my enemies, my teachers, my entertainment. I am who I am in large part because of the fiction I have read. I hope in your study of fiction you will find the value I find in it.

OK, so what are some strategies for study-reading fiction?

To take the long way around to find out what some strategies for study-reading fiction are, read the following short story. Just read the way you normally would.

Sunday in the Park
by Bel Kaufman

It was still warm in the late-afternoon sun, and the city noises came muffled through the trees in the park. She put her book down on the bench, removed her sunglasses, and sighed contentedly. Morton was reading the *Times Magazine* section, one arm flung around her shoulder; their three-year-old son, Larry, was playing in the sandbox: a faint breeze fanned her hair softly against her cheek. It was five-thirty of a Sunday afternoon, and the small playground, tucked away in a corner of the park, was all but deserted. The swings and seesaws stood motionless and abandoned, the slides were empty, and only in the sandbox two little boys squatted diligently side by side. *How good this is*, she thought, and almost smiled at her sense of well-being. They must go out in the sun more often; Morton was so city-pale, cooped up all week inside the gray factorylike university. She squeezed his arm affectionately and glanced at Larry, delighting in the pointed little face frowning in concentration over the tunnel he was digging. The other boy suddenly stood up and with a quick, deliberate swing of his chubby arm threw a spadeful of sand at Larry. It just missed his head. Larry continued digging; the boy remained standing, shovel raised, stolid and impassive.

"No, no, little boy." She shook her finger at him, her eyes searching for the child's mother or nurse. "We mustn't throw sand. It may get in someone's eyes and hurt. We must play nicely in the nice sandbox." The boy looked at her in unblinking expectancy. He was about Larry's age but perhaps ten pounds heavier, a husky little boy with none of Larry's quickness and sensitivity in his face. Where was his mother? The only other people left in the playground were two women and a little girl on roller skates leaving now through the gate, and a man on a bench a few feet away. He was a big man, and he seemed to be taking up the whole bench as he held the Sunday comics close to his face. She supposed he was the child's father. He did not look up from his comics, but spat once deftly out of the corner of his mouth. She turned her eyes away.

At that moment, as swiftly as before, the fat little boy threw another spadeful of sand at Larry. This time some of it landed on his hair and forehead. Larry looked up at his mother, his mouth tentative; her expression would tell him whether to cry or not.

Her first instinct was to rush to her son, brush the sand out of his hair, and punish the other child, but she controlled it. She always said that she wanted Larry to learn to fight his own battles.

"Don't *do* that, little boy," she said sharply, leaning forward on the bench. "You mustn't throw sand!"

The man on the bench moved his mouth as if to spit again, but instead he spoke. He did not look at her, but at the boy only.

"You go right ahead, Joe," he said loudly. "Throw all you want. This here is a *public* sandbox."

She felt a sudden weakness in her knees as she glanced at Morton. He had become aware of what was happening. He put his *Times* down carefully on his lap and turned his fine, lean face toward the man, smiling the shy, apologetic smile he might have offered a student in pointing out an error in his thinking. When he spoke to the man, it was with his usual reasonableness.

"You're quite right," he said pleasantly, "but just because this is a public place. . . ."

The man lowered his funnies and looked at Morton. He looked at him from head to foot, slowly and deliberately. "Yeah?" His insolent voice was edged with menace. "My kid's got just as good right here as yours, and if he feels like throwing sand, he'll throw it, and if you don't like it, you can take your kid the hell out of here."

The children were listening, their eyes and mouths wide open, their spades forgotten in small fists. She noticed the muscle in Morton's jaw tighten. He was rarely angry; he seldom lost his temper. She was suffused with a tenderness for her husband and an impotent rage against the man for involving him in a situation so alien and so distasteful to him.

"Now, just a minute," Morton said courteously, "you must real-ize. . . ."

"Aw, shut up," said the man.

Her heart began to pound. Morton half rose; the *Times* slid to the ground. Slowly the other man stood up. He took a couple of steps toward Morton, then stopped. He flexed his great arms, waiting. She pressed her trembling knees together. Would there be violence, fight-ing? How dreadful, how incredible. . . . She must do something, stop them, call for help. She wanted to put her hand on her husband's sleeve, to pull him down, but for some reason she didn't.

Morton adjusted his glasses. He was very pale. "This is ridicu-lous," he said unevenly. "I must ask you. . . ."

"Oh, yeah?" said the man. He stood with his legs spread apart, rocking a little, looking at Morton with utter scorn. "You and who else?"

For a moment the two men looked at each other nakedly. Then Morton turned his back on the man and said quietly, "Come on, let's get out of here." He walked awkwardly, almost limping with self-consciousness, to the sandbox. He stooped and lifted Larry and his shovel out.

At once Larry came to life; his face lost its rapt expression and he began to kick and cry. "I don't *want* to go home, I want to play better, I don't want any supper, I don't *like* supper. . . ." It became a chant as they walked, pulling their child between them, his feet dragging on the ground. In order to get to the exit gate they had to pass the bench where the man sat sprawling again. She was careful not to look at him. With all the dignity she could summon, she pulled Larry's sandy, perspiring little hand, while Morton pulled the other. Slowly and with head high she walked with her husband and child out of the playground.

Her first feeling was one of relief that a fight had been avoided, that no one was hurt. Yet beneath it there was a layer of something else, something heavy and inescapable. She sensed that it was more than just an unpleasant incident, more than defeat of reason by force. She felt dimly it had something to do with her and Morton, something acutely personal, familiar, and important.

Suddenly Morton spoke. "It wouldn't have proved anything."

"What?" she asked.

"A fight. It wouldn't have proved anything beyond the fact that he's bigger than I am."

"Of course," she said.

"The only possible outcome," he continued reasonably, "would have been — what? My glasses broken, perhaps a tooth or two replaced, a couple of days' work missed — and for what? For justice? For truth?"

"Of course," she repeated. She quickened her step. She wanted only to get home and to busy herself with her familiar tasks; perhaps then the feeling, glued like heavy plaster on her heart, would be gone. *Of all the stupid, despicable bullies*, she thought, pulling harder on Larry's hand. The child was still crying. Always before she had felt a tender pity for his defenseless little body, the frail arms, the narrow shoulders with sharp, winglike shoulder blades, the thin legs, unsure but now her mouth tightened in resentment.

"Stop crying," she said sharply. "I'm ashamed of you!" She felt as if all three of them were tracking mud along the street. The child cried louder.

If there had been an issue involved, she thought, *if there had been something to fight for. . . . But what else could he possibly have done? Allow himself to be beaten? Attempt to educate the man? Call a policeman? "Officer, there's a man in the park who won't stop his child from throwing sand on mine. . . ."* The whole thing was as silly as that, and not worth thinking about.

"Can't you keep him quiet, for Pete's sake?" Morton asked irritably.

"What do you suppose I've been trying to do?" she said. Larry pulled back, dragging his feet.

"If you can't discipline this child, I will," Morton snapped, making a move toward the boy.

But her voice stopped him. She was shocked to hear it, thin and cold and penetrating with contempt. "Indeed?" she heard herself say. "You and who else?"[1]

---

1. *Source:* Robert Shephard and James Thomas, *Sudden Fiction: American Short-Short Stories.* Peregrine Smith, 1986, 20–23.

PROCESSING WHAT YOU JUST READ

✍ If you are using the *Student's Reading Journal* that accompanies this text, go to page 63 in it and follow the directions given.

If you are using your own notebook as a journal, answer the following questions:

1. Describe your thoughts, feelings, and reactions to the story. How did you like it?
2. What did the story make you think about? Why?
3. Have you ever felt the way any of the characters do in the story? Explain.

Now let's look at some strategies for study-reading stories like this one. No doubt every English instructor you have will approach literature from a different perspective. However, there are some guide questions you can use to make certain you read fiction carefully. The questions can be placed in three categories: literal, interpretive, and affective.

Literal comprehension questions

The term **literal comprehension** refers to the basic level of understanding, which ensures a recognition of the facts: names, places, dates, events that occur, for example. Before you can understand a story at the interpretive or affective level, you have to make certain you have all the necessary literal information. For a story or novel, literal comprehension questions deal with the main elements of fiction, which are character, setting, plot, and point of view.

Such terms are simply tools that readers use to talk about what they have read, just as the names for the parts of a molecule help a physicist or chemist talk about the molecule. These terms are the ones you'll meet most often in literature classes. Because they come up so frequently and because they do help you analyze literature, you should recognize these terms and be able to use them.

✍ In the spaces provided, answer the following questions in terms of the story you just read, "Sunday in the Park." Each question deals with a particular element of the story. As you answer the questions, feel free to look back at the story whenever necessary.

1. Who is the main person in the story? (*character*)

   _____

2. What other characters are important in the story?

   _____

3. Where and when is everything happening? (*setting*)

   _____

4. What is happening? (*plot*)

   _____

   _____

   _____

5. Through whose eyes do we learn what is happening? (*point of view*)

_____

Compare your answers with these: (1) The main **character** in this story has no name. "She" is the little boy Larry's mother and Morton's wife. (2) Other characters in the story include Larry, Morton, the other little boy in the sandbox (Joe), and Joe's unnamed father. (3) The story takes place in a city park, probably in New York City, because of the reference to the *Times Magazine*, a supplement in the Sunday *New York Times*. It is Sunday, around 5:30 in the afternoon. It's probably summer, because there is reference to warm, late-afternoon sun. This, then is the **setting**. (4) The **plot**, or events that occur in the story, is fairly simple: A family enjoying an afternoon in the park is forced to leave rather than engage in violence with another person in the park. (5) In this story, we see everything through the eyes of Morton's wife. The descriptions of the park, the other characters, and the events that occur are primarily shown as she sees them. This is known as **point of view**.

Although it is necessary to have all these literal facts straight to understand the story, they aren't all there is to the story. The author seems more interested in what goes on inside the main character's head than in physical actions.

Interpretive compre-
hension questions

Interpretive comprehension questions ask the *whys* and the *hows* of a story or an author's style. They force us to go beyond the literal level. To understand better what is meant by interpretive comprehension, answer the following questions in the spaces provided. Reread the story if you need to do so.

1. How does the author develop the main character? What things does Morton's wife say and do that let us get to know what she is like?

_____

_____

_____

2. What do we learn from the characters about human nature? What change in the main character's attitude reflects human nature?

_____

_____

_____

3. Stories often show some type of *conflict*, either within the main character or among the characters. What's the conflict in this story? Why do Morton and his wife act toward each other as they do at the end of the story?

_____

_____

_____

4.   What seems to be the point or *theme* of the story? What is the author saying about "the human condition"?

_____

_____

_____

See what you think about these answers:

1. The author develops the main character through her thoughts and her dialogue. As the story begins, she seems content, satisfied with her life. We're told she "almost smiled at her sense of well-being." She squeezes Morton's arm "affectionately," thinking he needs to get out in the sun more often. When Joe throws sand at her son, she says self-righteously, "No, no, little boy. . . . We mustn't throw sand. . . . We must play nicely." After the second time it happens, she's more stern: "You mustn't throw sand!" She expectantly looks around for a parent to reprimand the troublemaking little boy.

Her actions also reveal her character. When the boy's father spits, she "turns her eyes away." When she leaves the park, she does so "with all the dignity she could summon" and "with head high." Also, when Larry is hit by a spadeful of sand, he looks at his mother, and, we're told, "her expression would tell him whether to cry or not." Put together, all these things indicate to me that she believes in "proper" manners, in what she would call a civilized code of conduct, and that she perhaps feels a sense of power, protectiveness, self-satisfaction in her life. We get to know the main character through her actions, the scenes, and the dialogue.

2. Of course, the main character changes her attitude during the story. In the beginning, Morton's wife is enjoying herself in the park, watching her son play and her husband read the Sunday paper. "*How good this is,* she thought." She delights in watching her little boy play. She is content. We're told she always felt a "tender pity" for her son's "defenseless little body." But, by the end of the story, her mouth "tighten[s] in resentment" at her screaming son and her defeated husband. "I'm ashamed of you!" she yells at the child (and probably subconsciously at Morton). Morton and she are snapping at each other, and her final words echo the big bully's when she challenges Morton, in a thin, cold, contemptuous voice with "Indeed? . . . You and who else?" She is now the bully. As we watch her change, we are reminded or made aware of human nature.

3. The reason the main character acts as she does is perhaps a mystery even to her. She's having a **conflict** of feelings. On the conscious level, she is opposed to violence. She reasons, "*If there had been an issue involved . . . if there had been something to fight for. . . . But what else could he possibly have done?*" She knows that Morton would have been no match for Joe's father if they had fought. Morton's comments about broken glasses and "perhaps a tooth or two," make sense on a rational level. But on the subconscious level, she is angry, embarrassed, and disappointed that Morton didn't fight back. Her sense of propriety gives way to her baser instincts. She wants vengeance.

4. So what's the point or **theme** of the story? I think there are several. The story shows the domino effect of one person's actions on another. The bully father's attitude spreads to the main character's whole family. The author taps into our baser instincts to fight back, to not be taken advantage of. Revenge movies, such as the *Death Wish* and the *Rambo* series, are popular in part because they show the bad guys getting their due. Morton's wife wants Joe's father to "get his." The story also shows the power of the physically strong over the weak, civilized attitudes challenged by uncivilized attitudes, reason against unreasonableness. The story causes me to think of all these aspects of the human condition, because I've felt them myself at some level.

In reading literature at an interpretive level, there are no easy answers. That's because good fiction is like an onion. There are many layers to it, each part of another.

"If you want to send a message," a movie producer once said, "call Western Union." He had a point. It is better to "feel" the theme of a story than to reduce it to a single sentence. If the theme of a story can be stated effectively in one sentence, why write a story?

If you read "Sunday in the Park" carefully on an interpretive level, you see that the themes of the story are tied up closely with the characters, the plot, and even the point of view. This is one reason the story is effective.

Affective compre-hension questions

Maybe the most important question you can ask about any fiction you read is, "What does the story have to do with me?"

✍ Here are some affective questions to help you answer that question. In the spaces provided, answer them in terms of "Sunday in the Park."

1. What feelings do you have for the main character or characters?

_____

_____

_____

2. What passages do you feel are well written? Why do they seem effective?

_____

_____

_____

3. Why do you (or do you not) like the story?

_____

_____

_____

These questions ask for your personal reaction to the story. If you think carefully about the story and reply seriously, your answers can't be "wrong." They can, however, reveal a lot about you.

The first question asks what you feel about the main character. Does the mother-wife seem real? Is she like someone you know? Do you feel sympathy for her or her family? Do you see part of yourself in her actions or thoughts? Have you ever felt as she feels? The only correct answers to these questions are your own feelings. Maybe you are unable to feel anything about her. If so, wait awhile. Sometime you or someone you know may be in a similar situation. The story may become meaningful to you then. The characters and their feelings seem very real to me. I've had such feelings myself.

Your answer to the second question depends on your reaction to the author's *style*. In literature, style refers to the way an author uses words to tell a story, develop characters, or describe places. One writer might use short, apparently simple sentence structure and only a few descriptive adjectives and then rely on dialogue to develop characters and story. Another writer might use long, flowing sentences and an abundance of figurative language, and then use little or no dialogue. The more fiction you read, the more you'll notice stylistic differences. A question like this gives you a chance to use what you've learned about the language of imaginative writing. Here are a few examples of what you might see as effective images or well-written passages:

a. *sound* "The city noises came muffled through the trees in the park"; "His insolent voice was edged with menace"; "She was shocked to hear it, thin and cold and penetrating with contempt."

b. *sight* "Morton was so city-pale, cooped up all week inside the gray factorylike university"; "He put his *Times* down carefully on his lap and turned his fine, lean face toward the man, smiling the shy, apologetic smile he might have offered a student in pointing out an error in his thinking"; Larry's "frail arms, the narrow shoulders with sharp, winglike shoulder blades."

c. *emotional feeling* "She was suffused with a tenderness for her husband and an impotent rage against the man for involving him in a situation so alien and so distasteful to him."

d. *touch* "a faint breeze fanned her hair softly against her cheek."

You probably listed different passages. There are many others, of course. How words affect you is a personal matter. The more attention you pay to the use of imaginative language, the more sensitive you will become to a writer's style.

The last question is strictly personal. Just because a story is considered "great" doesn't mean you have to think it is. If you don't happen to like a story because it doesn't move you or entertain you, there is not automatically something wrong with you. No two readers ever react the same way to imaginative literature.

Still, the more carefully you analyze what you read, the more you will get out of literature. It is always possible that the fault is yours, not the author's. If you don't like an author's style or don't agree with what the story seems to say, at least after analyzing the work carefully you will know why.

One final point: It may be you lack both the experience in life and the experience in reading literature to appreciate what a writer has done. The more life experiences you have, the more the reading of good literature may come to mean to you. After all, literature, as an art form, is a way of mapping human experience. Some of the works you read in school may not have meaning for you not because the writer failed but because you lack the knowledge or the experience to make them meaningful. The rewards of reading aren't always immediately apparent. Give yourself and the work some time to gel.

PROCESSING WHAT YOU JUST READ

✍ If you are using the *Student's Reading Journal* that accompanies this text, go to page 63 in it and follow the directions given.

If you are using your own notebook as a journal, answer the following questions:

1. Define *literal, interpretive,* and *affective comprehension.* List some guide questions at each level that you can use for reading fiction.
2. Reread your last journal entry, about your reaction to the story "Sunday in the Park." Has applying the guide questions at the three levels of comprehension changed your feelings about or reactions to the story? Explain.

How is reading a novel different from reading a short story?

In both novels and short stories, writers create characters who act in certain settings. The characters and their actions are seen through one or several possible points of view. Both the novelist and the short story writer use language in a particular style to develop themes or express attitudes toward their characters and toward life. Both forms can be used to entertain, to inform, even to instruct the reader. Both forms are "unreal" versions of real situations. Thus, much of what you just learned can be useful in analyzing a novel.

However, there are some differences between novels and short stories. The most obvious is that novels are longer than short stories. A **short story** such as "Sunday in the Park" concentrates on a very brief period of time. It usually develops only one major character, whose relationship with other characters isn't explored very much. In the short story, there are usually few settings and limited descriptions of people and events.

A **novel**, by contrast, can cover a long period of time. John Galsworthy's *The Forsyte Saga*, for example, tells about several generations of the Forsyte family over many years in many settings. Or a novel may take close to a thousand pages to cover the events of one day, as James Joyce's *Ulysses* does. A novel can have several main characters, some of whom may never come to know each other in the book. All this means that there is more to analyze in a novel. It's not more difficult. All you have to do is adjust yourself to the length of the book and the length of your involvement in it.

Doesn't reading a novel take lots of time?

It's not unusual to run into instructors who expect their students to read a novel within a week, and English instructors aren't the only teachers who assign novels. Most of the time, however, instructors assign novel reading well in advance. Don't procrastinate; start reading immediately, making the assignment a daily part of your schedule.

Often history, philosophy, and art instructors ask you to read a novel or biography to gain an understanding of a particular period. For several reasons, you may feel discouraged when you face such assignments. One, you may feel pressed for time—time you feel you need for other classes. Two, you may not like to read novels anyway. Many college students manage to graduate from high school without ever reading a novel. With no experience in reading a novel, they think the task will be painfully time consuming. Three, you may feel that you could spend your time more profitably by reading about the novel than by reading the novel itself. Don't!

True, college bookstores and libraries are stocked with "study guides" or "notes" that give brief critical commentaries on almost every major novel. A typical study guide explains the plot, characters, style, and theme of a novel and provides some information about the author. Such a guide might be helpful, provided that you use it *as a guide* and *not as a substitute for reading*. The critical notes are usually brief, and they reflect the ideas of the study guide's author; they are often not correct or in agreement with your instructor. They are not *your* reactions, nor are they the "correct" reactions. Still, there is no denying that many college students do not read assigned novels and manage to get by on what they read about them. But there is no substitute for reading the novel itself. What's that old saying? "Cheaters never prosper."

How, then, do you approach the reading of a novel? Use the same three levels of comprehension presented for the short story. Keep in mind that you will have several characters to get to know and analyze. There may be subplots branching out

---

WHAT DO YOU THINK?

If you or I read a book, and we learn about someone else's life and torment, to the extent that the book is effective and good, we will be participating in that character's suffering. Presumably, when we close the book, it will give us an enlarged understanding of people we don't usually think of looking at. We are at the level, the depth, of the universal. In others we see ourself. So fiction really enlarges our humanity. Poetry, too, shares its perception of what life is, and raises to illumination our awareness of its profundity. That's why political diction and aesthetic diction are always antithetical. Because to get elected or to do what he wants to do, the politician has to appeal to prejudices, symbols, biases, fears — all the ways we have of not thinking. But the artist is always saying, "Wait, this is too simple, this is a lie, this is an untruth, this is a fraud." His diction is more like the texture of real life. Politics scants reality. It diminishes it and makes it small. That's the problem with political discourse.

E. L. Doctorow, novelist

---

from the main plot. There will be more events and character interactions than in a short story, to help you get to know the people and places better. All the basic elements of short fiction are found in novels.

Mark your novel as you read. When you see a well-written passage, underline it or make a check mark beside it. Look up words you don't know. As you read, write down your feelings and reactions in your reading journal or in the back of the book. Some of the novels I own are so marked up with personal comments I would never loan them out. Above all, try to get into the story and enjoy it.

FINAL THOUGHTS

To understand any fiction, apply these three sets of questions:

Literal Comprehension Questions

1. Who is the main *character*? What is she or he like?
2. What other characters are important?
3. Where and when is everything happening? (*setting*)
4. What is happening? (*plot*)
5. Through whose eyes do we learn what is happening? (*point of view*)

Interpretive Comprehension Questions

1. How does the author use actions, scenes, or dialogue to develop the main character? (*character development*)
2. What do we learn from the characters about human nature? (*awareness*)
3. What, if any, conflict occurs in the story? (*conflict*)
4. What is the point of the story? (*theme*)

Affective Comprehension Questions

1. What feelings did you have for the main character or characters?
2. What passages do you feel are well written? Why do they seem effective?
3. Why do you (or do you not) like the story?

These questions give you a place to start in analyzing fiction. As you answer them other questions will probably come up. Your own questions will help you even more.

PROCESSING WHAT YOU JUST READ

✍ If you are using the *Student's Reading Journal* that accompanies this text, go to page 64 in it and follow the directions given.

If you are using your own notebook as a journal, answer the following questions:

1. What novel have you read at some time in your life that has stayed with you? Why has it? What did you learn from it about yourself or others? (If you've never read a novel, discuss why you haven't.)
2. Why do you think that reading fiction should or should not be part of the college curriculum?

Review your journal notes, then go to Part III, page 415, for more practice in reading fiction.

14 *Strategies for*
Study-Reading Poetry

PREPARING TO READ
This chapter will present strategies for reading poetry as well as literal, interpretive, and affective comprehension questions for analyzing poetry. The purpose and form of poetry require an approach different from that for study-reading fiction and drama. **Your objective in reading this chapter is to learn and apply the strategies for study-reading and analyzing a poem.**

Why do people write and read poetry?

Many people shy away from reading poetry because they think they cannot understand it, believing that poetry contains "hidden" meanings beyond their grasp. True, some poems seem to require a certain reading background or language experience for a fuller understanding, but, like tennis, bowling, chess, or any activity requiring a skill, practice helps. This chapter provides you with some strategies for developing a proficiency in reading and understanding poems.

Actually, many poems can be understood and enjoyed on the first reading, even though a second, third, or fourth reading may yield more meaning than you saw at first. Read the following poem aloud:

To look at Any Thing
by John Moffitt

To look at any thing,
If you would know that thing,
You must look at it long:
To look at this green and say
"I have seen spring in these
Woods," will not do—you must
Be the thing you see:
You must be the dark snakes of
Stems and ferny plumes of leaves,
You must enter in
To the small silences between
The leaves,
You must take your time
And touch the very peace
They issue from.[1]

---

1. *Source:* John Moffitt, *The Living Seed.* Harcourt, 1961.

🖎 In the space provided, write a statement that reflects what you think this poem is saying.

_____

_____

_____

_____

Basically, this is a "how-to" poem. The poet, Moffitt, tells us that to really "know" anything, "You must look at it long." But more than that, you must "Be the thing you see . . . You must enter in . . . take your time/And touch . . . " He could be talking about how to look at a painting, how to listen to a piece of music, how to get to know someone better, how to study history, or even how to read a poem. There is nothing really mysterious here. Moffitt communicates what he wants to tell us by using language differently from the way he would in expository writing. We'll come back to this poem later to see what another reading might reveal.

Why do poets write like this, you might ask. An answer might be, Why do some people play football or attend football games? Why do some people express themselves by writing and playing music? But these aren't really answers. Here's one person's attempt to explain why:

> Perhaps the commonest use of language is to communicate *information*. We say that it is nine o'clock, that we liked a certain movie, that George Washington was the first president of the United States. . . . This we might call the *practical* use of language; it helps us with the ordinary business of living.
>
> But it is not primarily to communicate information that novels, short stories, plays, and poems are written. These exist to bring us a sense and a perception of life, to widen and sharpen our contacts with existence. Their concern is with *experience*. We all have inner needs to live more deeply and fully and with greater awareness, to know the experience of others, and to understand our experience better. Poets, from their own store of felt, observed, or imagined experiences, select, combine, and reorganize. They create significant new experiences for their readers—significant because focused and formed — in which readers can participate and from which they may gain a greater awareness and understanding of their world. Literature, in other words, can be used as a gear for stepping up the intensity and increasing the range of our experience and as a glass for clarifying it. This is the *literary* use of language, for literature is not only an aid to living but a means of living.[2]

As you gain more understanding of poetry and its function, you'll come to an answer of your own regarding the purpose of and need for poetry.

---

2. *Source:* Laurence Perrine, *Sound and Sense: An Introduction to Poetry,* 7th ed. Harcourt, 1987, 4.

Source: Reprinted by permission of UFS, INC.

How should you read a poem?

Here are five strategies for reading a poem that will help you switch from *practical* reading to the *literary* reading required for poetry:

1. *Always read a poem more than once.* Remember, you're not reading just for information; you're reading to "know that thing," the poem. Although some poems require only one reading, most demand several readings, each revealing more insights.

2. *Use a dictionary or thesaurus to look up key words.* As mentioned in Chapter 11, poets play on words, using connotative meanings and words that suggest, imply, hint, or symbolize something or some idea. Words you may know denotatively might bear connotative suggestions you aren't familiar with. A good dictionary or thesaurus can offer other possible meanings for a word used in a poem.

3. *Read the poem aloud, listening to its sounds and rhythm.* Poems are meant to be heard, so meanings often come through the sounds and the rhythm of the words and lines. That's why poems are not written in paragraph form. Don't read too flatly or fast, and don't read too slowly. After one or two readings, you'll begin to get a feel for the way the lines should be read. The length of lines and where they break are clues to the poem's rhythm. Pay attention to the punctuation at the end of a line. If there is none, that means read from the end of that line right in to the next line. If there's a period, colon, or semicolon, stop. If there's a comma, pause slightly. Remember that in poetry each line does not necessarily represent a unit of thought. Even though new lines often begin with a capital letter, a new sentence may not be starting. For instance, the poem "To Look at Any Thing" should be read like this:

> To look at any thing,   **(slight pause)**
> If you would know that thing,   **(slight pause)**
> You must look at it long: **(pause)**
> To look at this green and say   **(no pause, go on to next line)**
> "I have seen spring in these   **(no pause, go on)**
> Woods," will not do—you must   **(no pause, go on)**
> Be the thing you see: **(pause)**

The line of a poem is a rhythmic unit. Don't make the mistake of thinking that poems must have rhyming words and a *dah-ta-dah-ta-dah* beat to them.

4. *Try to follow the thoughts stated or implied by the words and sounds.* While listening to the sounds of the words and feeling the rhythm of the poem, pay attention to what the words are saying. Poems are compact and say much in a small space. That's why more than one reading is often necessary. Let's look again at "To Look at Any Thing." Read it through another time, pausing at each unit of thought.

To Look at Any Thing
by John Moffitt

To look at any thing,
If you would know that thing,
You must look at it long: **(What does this mean?)**
To look at this green and say
"I have seen spring in these
Woods," will not do—you must
Be the thing you see: **(What does this mean?)**
You must be the dark snakes of
Stems and ferny plumes of leaves,   **(What does this mean?)**
You must enter in
To the small silences between
The leaves,   **(What does this mean?)**
You must take your time
And touch the very peace
They issue from.   **(What does this mean?)**

What does Moffitt mean by "To look at this green and say / 'I have seen spring in these / Woods,' will not do"? Is he referring only to looking at a green woods in the spring and saying "I" have seen it before? Because the title is "To Look at Any Thing," we can infer that Moffitt is just using those lines as an example of Any Thing we look at and say we "know," not just a spring woods. We can also infer that "To look at" implies seeing more than physical objects, seeing ideas, relationships, knowledge, ourselves—again, anything we want to know better.

Moffitt goes on: "Be the thing you see: / You must be the dark snakes of / Stems and ferny plumes of leaves." Notice his use of *snakes, stems, ferny plumes, leaves*—all words related to the woods. Their use fits in nicely with the idea of a green, spring woods. But, again, we can infer that Moffitt means we must "Be the thing" we want to know by looking closely at all its parts, whether it is a physical thing or an abstract idea.

5. *Don't get carried away with looking for "symbols" and "hidden meanings."* Most poets don't "hide" their meanings. They are using words as an art form. A painter may not wish to paint a horse in a way that looks like a photograph of a horse, because that's been done. Instead, the artist may wish to paint an interpretation of a horse, to find a different way of expressing the beauty of a horse in motion. A jazz musician may not want to play a melody the way it was written; any musician could do that. Rather, the jazz musician might use a different arrangement of notes to interpret the melody with a fresh sound. A poet may say something that's been said before, but say it in a new way, a way that makes the old saying fresh and memorable. Moffitt doesn't conceal his meaning. He may make us work for it a bit, but when we're finished examining the poem, we can say, "Yes, it's true. If I want to really know that—thing, person, idea—I have to look at it closely, more closely than I've ever looked before."

These five reading strategies can be useful for approaching poetry. Your literature instructor will probably provide you with additional ways.

PROCESSING WHAT YOU JUST READ

✍ If you are using the *Student's Reading Journal* that accompanies this text, go to page 66 in it and follow the directions given.

If you are using your own notebook as a journal, answer the following questions:

1. Discuss how you feel about reading poetry. Do you read it often? Why?
2. What are the five strategies for reading a poem?

What exactly is overinterpretation?

Some readers mistakenly tend to find something symbolic in every word. Usually, that's overinterpreting. But there's a fine line between *over*interpreting and *un-derinterpreting*. To see what I mean, let's consider this familiar poem. Read it aloud.

> Humpty Dumpty sat on a wall.
> Humpty Dumpty had a great fall.
> All the king's horses
> And all the king's men
> Couldn't put Humpty together again.

✍ In the spaces provided, answer the following questions.

1. Who is Humpty Dumpty?

   _____

   _____

2. What was he doing?

   _____

   _____

3. Why would the king's horses try to put Humpty together again?

   _____

   _____

4. Who are the king's men?

   _____

   _____

5. What does the poem mean?

   _____

   _____

   _____

Answers to these questions are not as easy as they may seem. Let's look more closely at the questions. To the first question, most people answer that Humpty Dumpty is an egg. Most children's books do depict Humpty as an egg, wearing a little bow tie and polka dot pants. From an artistic point of view, this interpretation makes sense. An egg can't be put together again once broken. But what in the poem says that Humpty is an egg? Nothing. So who is Humpty Dumpty? What's he or she doing sitting on a wall? Why is the king interested in putting Humpty back together? What happened, anyway? To find the answers to these questions, we must look more closely at the poem; we must "look at it long." If we dismiss the poem as nothing more than a child's nursery rhyme about an egg that fell off the wall, we may be underinterpreting.

✍ One way to begin is to look at the key words in each line. Whoever Humpty is, he or she *sat* on a *wall*. In the spaces provided, write down other words that *sat* and *wall* suggest to you. Use a dictionary or thesaurus if you like. A couple of examples are provided to give you the idea.

sat	*wall*
passive	*barrier*
unmoving	*divider*

Now let's say that Humpty, whoever he or she is, is immobile or inactive or passive. He or she sits, undecided about something. Humpty's a fence sitter, meaning he or she can't decide what move to make. Such an interpretation makes sense about the first line.

Finally, however, Humpty makes a move. In the second line we're told he or she had a great fall; not just a fall, a *great* one. What does *great fall* suggest to you? You might be reminded of the biblical account of the fall of Adam and Eve ("In Adam's fall, we sinned all," said early American reading books). In mythology, there is the fall of Icarus, the fall of Faust. In history, there's the fall of the Roman empire. In all these cases, the "fall" was irreparable. The harm was done, and nothing could remedy it. Put together what we have so far, and Humpty, an undecided person, finally makes a decision, but it's a wrong move, and unfortunately Humpty falls or fails or creates problems.

✍ But what of the king's horses and men? Again, "think long" about what horses represent. In the space provided, write down what you think king's horses and king's men might represent here.

_____

_____

_____

Even today we use the word *horsepower*. A king would have many horses, the best, which represent wealth, power, status. The king's men might include advisers, people with wisdom and knowledge, his soldiers, representing human potential and power, or perhaps all the people in his kingdom. But despite all this at his disposal, the king is powerless to change what Humpty has done.

Who, then, is Humpty Dumpty? He or she might very well be any person. Humpty becomes a symbol, just as *wall*, *great fall*, *king's horses*, and *king's men* are symbols. Humpty symbolizes anyone in a predicament so great that no one can help, not even the most powerful people on earth. We know that whatever decision or action Humpty took, the consequences were such that things could never be the same again.

Some readers say that Humpty is any overambitious politician who got caught with his or her fingers in the cookie jar. Some say Humpty could be Hitler, who decided to take on too many armies at once; others say Humpty could be Richard Nixon, who was forced to resign from the presidency because of his decision to cover up the Watergate episode. Would the poem be better or worse if we tried to label Humpty as any one person? Couldn't Humpty represent any one of us who falls or breaks because of a wrong move or decision that makes it impossible to go back to the way things were? This little nursery rhyme may originally have been written to refer to some specific person in history, but, when we look at the poem itself, we see it says something meaningful to us even today.

Is all this overinterpretation? Well, you don't have to take this rendering of "Humpty Dumpty" too seriously. Maybe it is just a nonsense rhyme, but don't make up your mind until you've "looked at it long."

If we stick with the poem itself, interpreting only what can be found or suggested there, we are not overinterpreting. However, if any part of a poem doesn't fit our interpretation, and we ignore a line or a unit of thought just to make our interpretation stick, then we are overinterpreting. We analyze a poem by looking at it in parts, but we do so in order to see it as a whole.

PROCESSING WHAT YOU JUST READ

✍ If you are using the *Student's Reading Journal* that accompanies this text, go to page 66 in it and follow the directions given.

If you are using your own notebook as a journal, answer the following questions:

1. Who do you think Humpty Dumpty is? Explain.
2. What is meant by *overinterpreting* a poem? How can you keep from over-interpreting?

Are there some questions to help with reading poetry?

Here is another poem. Read it aloud once or twice, applying what you have learned so far.

Corner
by Ralph Pomeroy

The cop slumps alertly on his motorcycle,
Supported by one leg like a leather stork.
His glance accuses me of loitering.
I can see his eyes moving like a fish
In the green depths of his green goggles.

His ease is fake. I can tell.
My ease is fake. And he can tell.
The fingers armored by his gloves
Splay and clench, itching to change something.
As if he were my enemy or my death,
I just stand there watching.

I spit out my gum which has gone stale.
I knock out a new cigarette—
Which is my bravery.
It is all imperceptible:
The way I shift my weight,
The way he creaks in his saddle.

The traffic is specific though constant.
The sun surrounds me, divides the street between us.
His crash helmet is whiter in the shade.

It is like a bull ring as they say it is just before the fighting.
I cannot back down. I am there.

Everything holds me back.
I am in danger of disappearing into the sunny dust.
My Levis bake and my T shirt sweats.
My cigarette makes my eyes burn.
But I don't dare drop it.

Who made him my enemy?
Prince of coolness. King of fear.
Why do I lean here waiting?
Why does he lounge there waiting?

I am becoming sunlight.
My hair is on fire. My boots run like tar.
I am hung-up by the bright air.

Something breaks through all of a sudden,
And he blasts off, quick as a craver,
Smug in his power, watching me watch.[3]

✍ In the spaces provided, answer the following questions.

Literal comprehension questions

1. What is going on in the poem?

   _____

   _____

   _____

2. Who is the speaker?

   _____

   _____

3. List some key words in the poem and define them at both the denotative and the connotative level.

Words from the poem	Denotative meaning	Connotative meaning
_____	_____	_____
_____	_____	_____
_____	_____	_____
_____	_____	_____

3. *Source: In the Financial District.* Macmillan, 1968.

4. What are some of the figures of speech (similes and metaphors) used in the poem to create particular images or emotions?

_____

_____

_____

Interpretive comprehension questions

5. What do some of the images imply or suggest to you?

_____

_____

6. What do all the images in the poem suggest as a whole; that is, how are they related?

_____

_____

7. What is the point of the poem?

_____

_____

Affective comprehension questions

8. What mood does the poem create in you?

_____

_____

9. Which lines are particularly effective for you? Which are ineffective?

_____

_____

_____

10. What is your reaction to the poem?

_____

_____

_____

Of course, wording and selection of figures of speech will be different, but compare your responses with these.

1. The poem's about a standoff between "I" (not necessarily the author) and a motorcycle policeman. Both are acting nonchalant, but each is worried about what the other will do. They silently challenge each other, but there is no resolution between them at the end.

2. The poem is told in the first person, but no name is used. When a poem is told in the first person, you can't assume that it is the author any more than you can assume it is the author talking in a first-person story or novel.

3. Here are some key words you may have picked:

Words from the poem	Denotative meaning	Connotative meaning
cop	police officer	authority, enemy, the establishment
slumps alertly	the words contradict each other in their denotation	a casual stance hiding a readiness for combat
armored	protected	supported by instruments of war or violence

4. Here are some figures of speech you may have picked:

supported by one leg like a leather stork
his eyes moving like a fish / In the green depths of his green goggles
fingers armored by his gloves
I knock out a new cigarette
he creaks in his saddle
My Levis bake and my T shirt sweats

5. Your wording will differ, but the images reflect that both characters are appearing unworried on the surface but are nervous, fearful of each other in reality. They are silently challenging each other: "His ease is fake. I can tell. / My ease is fake. And he can tell." Most of the images reflect these two contradictory feelings.

6. The images contribute to a feeling of tension between the two characters, who are enemies without really understanding why. The speaker asks, "Who made him my enemy?" But he adds, "I cannot back down. I am there." As readers we wait for the moment of truth. What will happen?

7. The poet seems to be dealing with the potentially violent relationship between "I" and the policeman. It is dangerous because each man is playing a role. Each expects the other to act according to his role. The cop "accuses me of loitering," his "fingers armored by his gloves / Splay and clench." In the end, "he blasts off... Smug in his power, watching me watch." That's the policeman's role. The "I" just stands there, watching: "I spit out my gum which has gone stale. / I knock out a new cigarette," which "makes my eyes burn. / But I don't dare drop it." The narrator plays his role. There is no resolution, no encounter, but the poem asks: "Why do I lean here waiting? / Why does he lounge there waiting?" As readers, we ask the same things and come to our own answers.

8-10. Answers to these three questions are subjective. But asking them of this or any poem can help you "look long" at a poem.

FINAL THOUGHTS

This chapter has presented five strategies for reading a poem and some literal, interpretive, and affective comprehension questions to help you enter into any poem you read. Remember that these are merely guides. They won't "explain" every poem you read, but they will help you "look at it long." They will prompt questions of your own about your reading.

Use the following questions the next time you read a poem.

Literal comprehension questions

1. What is going on?
2. Who is the speaker in the poem?
3. List some key words in the poem and define them at both the denotative and the connotative levels.
4. What are some of the figures of speech (similes and metaphors) used in the poem to create particular images or emotions?

Interpretive comprehension questions

5. What do some of the images imply or suggest to you?
6. What do the images in the poem suggest as a whole; that is, how are they related?
7. What is the point of the poem?

Affective comprehension questions

8. What mood does the poem create in you?
9. Which lines are particularly effective for you? Which are ineffective?
10. What is your reaction to the poem?

The best way to learn to understand and appreciate poetry is to read as much of it as you can. Don't so much worry about what a poem means as enjoy the adventure of reading it. The meanings of some poems become clear long after you have read them. That's because good poetry is an expression of the unchanging and universal essence of human experience.

PROCESSING WHAT YOU JUST READ

✍ If you are using the *Student's Reading Journal* that accompanies this text, go to page 67 in it and follow the directions given.

If you are using your own notebook as a journal, do the following:

1. Copy the comprehension questions so that you will have them available the next time you read a poem.
2. Discuss what you have learned in this chapter that will help you study-read poetry.

Now go to Part III, page 428, for more practice in reading and understanding poetry.

CHAPTER 15

Strategies for Study-Reading Drama

The word *drama* (from the Greek *dran*, "to do") means "action" or "deed" and is used when referring to intense excitement, tension, suspense, or conflict. Because of this, *drama* is often used as a synonym for *play*. Plays, unlike short stories or novels, are written to be seen, not read, and will generally have at least one if not all of the elements known as drama. Many literature anthologies used in English classes contain plays that you must read. This chapter presents strategies for reading them. **Your objective in reading this chapter is to learn and apply the strategies for study-reading drama.**

Why do people read plays if they are meant to be seen?

We know that plays and poetry were around a long time before short stories and novels. About 330 B.C., the Greek philosopher Aristotle began analyzing drama and found that the plays of his time had six basic elements: plot, character, thought, diction, spectacle, and music. Of these, Aristotle considered plot most important. He felt that without **plot**, the series of events that constitute the action of a drama, there can be no play. Next in importance, he claimed, are the **characters**, for without them there can be no action or speech to bring out the plot. Third is **thought**, by which Aristotle meant the ideas of the author and their ability to touch the audience emotionally through speech. Closely tied in with thought is **diction**, the choice of words used.

These four elements are also found in short stories and novels. What helps make drama different are the last two elements: **spectacle** and **music**. Although not all plays contain music, all drama requires some form of spectacle. These elements require an audience to see and hear.

A play is also a form of storytelling, but, unlike fiction, it requires (1) actors to represent the characters, not only in voice but in movements, appearance, and emotion; (2) physical scenery and lighting to provide a setting; and (3) the presentation of some kind of conflict between characters or events.

Plays, then, are meant to be seen or heard, not read. Playwrights hope that actors will make their characters and dialogue so lifelike that the audience will *feel* the atmosphere created onstage. Why, then, read plays?

For one thing, reading a play lets us get to know it the way the author wrote it. Seldom is a play produced without some changes being made by the director and the actors. Staging may be adjusted to fit the size of a theater or a director's artistic interpretation. Dialogue may be changed; entire lines may be cut. Minor characters may even be eliminated from a stage production. Shakespeare's plays, for instance, seldom are produced exactly the way they were written. Watch different productions of *Othello*, and you will see the character Iago played by one actor as total evil, by another as a person motivated by jealousy, by still another as mad. Costumes may range from Elizabethan to contemporary. Certain lines and scenes will be cut to fit the director's interpretation. As a consequence, the only way really to know the original play as written by the author is to read it.

Another reason for reading plays is that plays in production are not always available. Unless you live in an area where many theaters are constantly producing a variety of plays, the only way to familiarize yourself with drama is through reading. Even though plays are meant to be seen, a play is a piece of literature before it becomes alive onstage. Reading a play before seeing it or even after can help us get more from it. We often miss lines or get confused while watching a play; reading it can help us pause and consider the importance of certain lines or actions.

Of course, still another reason for reading plays is that you will be required to do so at some point in your literature classes. Perhaps the following information will make the task easier and more enjoyable. Reading plays can be fun.

PROCESSING WHAT YOU JUST READ

✍ If you are using the *Student's Reading Journal* that accompanies this text, go to page 68 in it and follow the directions given.

If you are using your own notebook as a journal, answer the following questions:

1. According to Aristotle, what are the elements that make up a play?
2. What makes reading a play different from reading fiction?
3. What is so important about the first question that you are being asked to write about it?

How is reading a play different from reading fiction?

If you have had some experience reading plays, you know that you have to stage them in your imagination. You are not only the audience but all the characters, the director, the set designer, the costume designer, the lighting designer, and the stage manager. However, in his anthology *Literature: An Introduction to Fiction, Poetry, and Drama*, X. J. Kennedy has this to say about reading plays:

> Although some readers find it enjoyable to imagine the play taking place upon a stage, others prefer to imagine the people and events that the play brings vividly to mind. Sympathetically following the tangled life of Nora in *A Doll House* by Henrik Ibsen, we forget that we are reading printed stage directions and instead find ourselves in the presence of human conflict. Thus regarded, a play becomes a form of storytelling, and the playwright's instructions to the actors and the director become a conventional mode of narrative that we accept in much the same way we accept the methods of a novel or short story. In reading *A Doll House* caring more about Nora's fate than the imagined appearance of an actress portraying her, we speed through an ordinary passage such as this (from a scene in which Nora's husband hears the approach of an unwanted caller, Dr. Rank):
>
> > Helmer (with quiet irritation): Oh, what does he want now? (Aloud.) Hold on. (Goes and opens the door.) Oh, how nice that you didn't pass us by!
>
> We read the passage, if the story absorbs us, as though we were reading a novel whose author, employing conventional devices for recording speech in fiction, might have written:
>
> > "Oh, what does he want now?" said Helmer under his breath, in annoyance. Aloud, he called, "Hold on," then walked to the door

and opened it and greeted Rank with all the cheer he could muster—"Oh, how nice that you didn't pass us by!"

Such is the power of an excellent play to make us ignore the playwright's artistry that it becomes a window through which the reader's gaze, given focus, encompasses more than language and typography and beholds a scene of imagined life.[1]

Of course, not all plays provide stage directions that allow for this type of reading, and inexperienced readers may find the typed format of a play difficult to act out in the mind.

Here, then, are five guidelines for reading a play that may help you read as Kennedy suggests.

1. *Read all the stage directions carefully.* **Stage directions** usually appear in italics and in parentheses or brackets. Many playwrights provide a list of all the characters and some opening remarks regarding these characters and the setting, sound, and lighting for the stage. As you read through a play, apply to your imagination what the playwright is telling the actors to do.

2. *Notice how the dialogue reveals characters' own habits, characteristics, personalities, and thinking, as well as those of other characters in the play.* Like first-person narrators in fiction, characters in a play reveal themselves and others to us. **Dialogue** tells us which characters oppose each other and which ones support each other. It lets us know which characters are strong and which are weak, who is honest and who isn't, who is trustworthy and who is not. Dialogue will also soon let us know who the main characters are.

3. *Be alert for the conflict, problem, or tension that the dialogue and actions reveal.* There is always some **conflict** or tension in a play. Usually the conflict is between people, because of the limitations of a stage setting. Opposition between the ideas expressed in speeches is often the basic conflict of a play.

4. *Notice the plot as the play unfolds.* The **plot** of the play is the series of events that establish the action. The plot may not always be presented in chronological order; it may use flashbacks or jump forward in time. Playwrights, like fiction writers, use inventive ways to develop their plots. A play may also have a double plot or subplots involving minor characters.

5. *Take your time as you read, and expect some confusion in the beginning.* Remember that the dialogue in a play is meant to be heard, so don't try to read faster than you can provide the feelings necessary to go along with the dialogue. If you were viewing a play, you would become acquainted with the characters by their appearance, actions, and voice mannerisms, making it easier to follow. There would be staging and lighting to add to the setting and mood. When you read a play, you must provide these visual aids yourself, so allow time to do so.

Do the five drama study-reading guidelines work?

Try using these guidelines as you read the following one-act play, *Death Knocks*, by Woody Allen.[2]

Death Knocks
by Woody Allen

(The play takes place in the bedroom of the Nat Ackermans' two-story house somewhere in Kew Gardens. The carpeting is wall-to-wall. There

1. *Source:* Little, 1987, 838.
2. *Source:* Woody Allen, *Getting Even.* Random House, 1968.

is a big double bed and a large vanity. The room is elaborately furnished and curtained and on the walls there are several paintings and a not really attractive barometer. Soft theme music as the curtain rises. Nat Ackerman, a bald, paunchy, fifty-seven-year-old dress manufacturer, is lying on the bed finishing off tomorrow's Daily News. *He wears a bathrobe and slippers, and reads by a bed light clipped to the white headboard of the bed. The time is near midnight. Suddenly we hear a noise, and Nat sits up and looks at the window.)*

Nat: What the hell is that?

(Climbing awkwardly through the window is a sombre, caped figure. The intruder wears a black hood and skin tight black clothes. The hood covers his head but not his face, which is middle-aged and stark white. He is something like Nat in appearance. He huffs audibly and then trips over the windowsill and falls into the room.)

Death (for it is no one else): Jesus Christ. I nearly broke my neck.
Nat (watching with bewilderment): Who are you?
Death: Death.
Nat: Who?
Death: Death. Listen can I sit down? I nearly broke my neck. I'm shaking like a leaf.
Nat: Who *are* you?
Death: *Death.* You got a glass of water?
Nat: Death? What do you mean, Death?
Death: What is wrong with you? You see the black costume and the whitened face?
Nat: Yeah.
Death: Is it Halloween?
Nat: No.
Death: Then I'm Death. Now can I get a glass of water — or a Fresca?
Nat: If this is some joke —
Death: What kind of joke? You're fifty-seven? Nat Ackerman? One eighteen Pacific Street? Unless I blew it — where's that call sheet? *(He fumbles through pocket finally producing a card with an address on it. It seems to check.)*
Nat: What do you want with me?
Death: What do I want? What do you think I want?
Nat: You must be kidding. I'm in perfect health.
Death (unimpressed): Uh-huh. *(Looking around)* This is a nice place. You do it yourself?
Nat: We had a decorator, but we worked with her.
Death (looking at picture on the wall): I love those kids with the big eyes.
Nat: I don't want to go yet.
Death: *You* don't want to go? Please don't start in. As it is, I'm nauseous from the climb.
Nat: What climb?
Death: I climbed up the drainpipe. I was trying to make a dramatic entrance. I see the big windows and you're awake reading. I figure it's worth a shot. I'll climb up and enter with a little — you know. *(Snaps fingers)* Meanwhile, I get my heel caught on some vines, the drainpipe breaks, and I'm hanging by a thread. Then my cape begins to tear. Look, let's just go. It's been a rough night.
Nat: You broke my drainpipe?

Death:	Broke. It didn't break. It's a little bent. Didn't you hear anything? I slammed into the ground.
Nat:	I was reading.
Death:	You must have really been engrossed. (*Lifting newspaper Nat was reading*) "NAB COEDS IN POT ORGY." Can I borrow this?
Nat:	I'm not finished.
Death:	Er—I don't know how to put this to you, pal. . .
Nat:	Why didn't you just ring downstairs?
Death:	I'm telling you, I could have, but how does it look? This way I get a little drama going. Something. Did you read *Faust*?
Nat:	What?
Death:	And what if you had company? You're sitting there with important people. I'm Death—I should ring the bell and traipse right in the front? Where's your thinking?
Nat:	Listen, Mister, it's very late.
Death:	Yeah. Well, you want to go?
Nat:	Go where?
Death:	Death. It. The Thing. The Happy Hunting Grounds. (*Looking at his own knee*) Y'know, that's a pretty bad cut. My first job, I'm liable to get gangrene yet.
Nat:	Now, wait a minute. I need time. I'm not ready to go.
Death:	I'm sorry. I can't help you. I'd like to, but it's the moment.
Nat:	How can it be the moment? I just merged with Modiste Originals.
Death:	What's the difference, a couple of bucks more or less.
Nat:	Sure, what do you care? You guys probably have all your expenses paid.
Death:	You want to come along now?
Nat (studying him):	I'm sorry, but I cannot believe you're Death.
Death:	Why? What'd you expect—Rock Hudson?
Nat:	No, it's not that.
Death:	I'm sorry if I disappointed you.
Nat:	Don't get upset. I don't know, I always thought you'd be . . . uh, taller.
Death:	I'm five seven. It's average for my weight.
Nat:	You look a little like me.
Death:	Who should I look like? I'm your death.
Nat:	Give me some time. Another day.
Death:	I can't. What do you want me to say?
Nat:	One more day. Twenty-four hours.
Death:	What do you need it for? The radio said rain tomorrow.
Nat:	Can't we work out something?
Death:	Like what?
Nat:	You play chess?
Death:	No, I don't.
Nat:	I once saw a picture of you playing chess.
Death:	Couldn't be me, because I don't play chess. Gin rummy, maybe.
Nat:	You play gin rummy?
Death:	Do I play gin rummy? Is Paris a city?
Nat:	You're good, huh?
Death:	Very good.
Nat:	I'll tell you what I'll do—
Death:	Don't make any deals with me.
Nat:	I'll play you gin rummy. If you win, I'll go immediately. If I win, give me some more time. A little bit—one more day.

Death: Who's got time to play gin rummy?
Nat: Come on. If you're so good.
Death: Although I feel like a game.
Nat: Come on. Be a sport. We'll shoot for a half hour.
Death: I really shouldn't.
Nat: I got the cards right here. Don't make a production.
Death: All right, come on. We'll play a little. It'll relax me.
Nat (getting cards, pad and pencil): You won't regret this.
Death: Don't give me a sales talk. Get the cards and give me a Fresca
          and put out something. For God's sake, a stranger drops in,
          you don't have potato chips or pretzels.
Nat: There's M & M's downstairs in a dish.
Death: M & M's. What if the President came? He'd get M & M's too?
Nat: You're not the President.
Death: Deal.

(*Nat deals, turns up a five.*)

Nat: You want to play a tenth of a cent a point to make it interest-
          ing?
Death: It's not interesting enough for you?
Nat: I play better when money's at stake.
Death: Whatever you say, Newt.
Nat: Nat. Nat Ackerman. You don't know my name?
Death: Newt, Nat—I got such a headache.
Nat: You want that five?
Death: No.
Nat: So pick.
Death (surveying his hand as he picks): Jesus, I got nothing here.
Nat: What's it like?
Death: What's what like?

(*Throughout the following, they pick and discard.*)

Nat: Death.
Death: What should it be like? You lay there.
Nat: Is there anything after?
Death: Aha, you're saving twos.
Nat: I'm asking. Is there anything after?
Death (absently): You'll see.
Nat: Oh, then I will actually see something?
Death: Well, maybe I shouldn't have put it that way. Throw.
Nat: To get an answer from you is a big deal.
Death: I'm playing cards.
Nat: All right, play, play.
Death: Meanwhile, I'm giving you one card after another.
Nat: Don't look through the discards.
Death: I'm not looking. I'm straightening them up. What was the
          knock card?
Nat: Four. You ready to knock already?
Death: Who said I'm ready to knock? All I asked was what was the
          knock card.
Nat: And all I asked was is there anything for me to look forward
          to.
Death: Play.
Nat: Can't you tell me anything? Where do we go?

Death: We? To tell you the truth, *you* fall in a crumpled heap on the floor.

Nat: Oh, I can't wait for that! Is it going to hurt?

Death: Be over in a second.

Nat: Terrific. (*Sighs*) I needed this. A man merges with Modiste Originals.

Death: How's four points?

Nat: You're knocking?

Death: Four points is good?

Nat: No, I got two.

Death: You're kidding.

Nat: No, you lose.

Death: Holy Christ, and I thought you were saving sixes.

Nat: No. Your deal. Twenty points and two boxes. Shoot. (*Death deals.*) I must fall on the floor, eh? I can't be standing over the sofa when it happens?

Death: No. Play.

Nat: Why not?

Death: Because you fall on the floor! Leave me alone. I'm trying to concentrate.

Nat: Why must it be on the floor? That's all I'm saying! Why can't the whole thing happen and I'll stand next to the sofa?

Death: I'll try my best. Now can we play?

Nat: That's all I'm saying. You remind me of Moe Lefkowitz. He's also stubborn.

Death: I remind him of Moe Lefkowitz. I'm one of the most terrifying figures you could possibly imagine, and him I remind of Moe Lefkowitz. What is he, a furrier?

Nat: You should be such a furrier. He's good for eighty thousand a year. Passementeries'. He's got his own factory. Two points.

Death: What?

Nat: Two points. I'm knocking. What have you got?

Death: My hand is like a basketball score.

Nat: And it's spades.

Death: If you didn't talk so much.

(*They redeal and play on.*)

Nat: What'd you mean before when you said this was your first job?

Death: What does it sound like?

Nat: What are you telling me—that nobody ever went before?

Death: Sure they went. But I didn't take them.

Nat: So who did?

Death: Others.

Nat: There's others?

Death: Sure. Each one has his own personal way of going.

Nat: I never knew that.

Death: Why should you know? Who are you?

Nat: What do you mean who am I? Why—I'm nothing?

Death: Not nothing. You're a dress manufacturer. Where do you come to knowledge of the eternal mysteries?

Nat: What are you talking about? I make a beautiful dollar. I sent two kids through college. One is in advertising, the other's married. I got my own home. I drive a Chrysler. My wife has whatever she wants. Maids, mink coat, vacations. Right now she's at the Eden Roc. Fifty dollars a day because she wants to be near her sister. I'm supposed to join her next week, so what do you think I am—some guy off the street?

Death: All right. Don't be so touchy.

Nat: Who's touchy?

Death: How would you like it if I got insulted quickly?

Nat: Did I insult you?

Death: You didn't say you were disappointed in me?

Nat: What do you expect? You want me to throw you a block party?

Death: I'm not talking about that. I mean me personally. I'm too short, I'm this, I'm that.

Nat: I said you looked like me. It's like a reflection.

Death: All right, deal, deal.

(They continue to play as music steals in and the lights dim until all is in total darkness. The lights slowly come up again, and now it is later and their game is over. Nat tallies.)

Nat: Sixty-eight. . . one-fifty. . . Well, you lose.

Death *(dejectedly looking through the deck):* I knew I shouldn't have thrown that nine. Damn it.

Nat: So I'll see you tomorrow.

Death: What do you mean you'll see me tomorrow?

Nat: I won the extra day. Leave me alone.

Death: You were serious?

Nat: We made a deal.

Death: Yeah, but—

Nat: Don't "but" me. I won twenty-four hours. Come back tomorrow.

Death: I didn't know we were actually playing for time.

Nat: That's too bad about you. You should pay attention.

Death: Where am I going to go for twenty-four hours?

Nat: What's the difference? The main thing is I won an extra day.

Death: What do you want me to do—walk the streets?

Nat: Check into a hotel and go to a movie. Take a *schvitz*. Don't make a federal case.

Death: Add the score again.

Nat: Plus you owe me twenty-eight dollars.

Death: *What?*

Nat: That's right, Buster. Here it is—read it.

Death *(going through pockets):* I have a few singles—not twenty-eight dollars.

Nat: I'll take a check.

Death: From what account?

Nat: Look who I'm dealing with.

Death: Sue me. Where do I keep my checking account?

Nat: All right, gimme what you got and we'll call it square.

Death: Listen, I need that money.

Nat: Why should you need money?

Death: What are you talking about? You're going to the Beyond.

Nat: So?

Death: So—you know how far that is?

Nat: So?

Death: So where's gas? Where's tolls?

Nat: We're going by car!

Death: You'll find out. (*Agitatedly*) Look—I'll be back tomorrow, and you'll give me a chance to win the money back. Otherwise I'm in definite trouble.

Nat: Anything you want. Double or nothing we'll play. I'm liable to win an extra week or a month. The way you play, maybe years.

Death: Meantime I'm stranded.

Nat: See you tomorrow.

Death (being edged to the doorway): Where's a good hotel? What am I talking about hotel, I got no money. I'll go sit in Bickford's. (*He picks up the* News.)

Nat: Out. Out. That's my paper. (*He takes it back.*)

Death (exiting): I couldn't just take him and go. I had to get involved in rummy.

Nat (calling after him): And be careful going downstairs. On one of the steps the rug is loose.

(*And, on cue, we hear a terrific crash. Nat sighs, then crosses to the bedside table and makes a phone call.*)

Nat: Hello, Moe? Me. Listen, I don't know if somebody's playing a joke, or what, but Death was just here. We played a little gin. No, Death. In person. Or somebody who claims to be Death. But, Moe, he's such a *schlep*!

CURTAIN

✍ In the space provided, write your reaction to the play.

_____

_____

_____

_____

Are there literal, interpretive, and affective questions that apply to drama?

As with other imaginative literature, there are literal, interpretive, and affective questions you can ask yourself when you have completed reading a play that will help you understand it more completely. You may need to modify the wording a bit depending on each play, but these questions should help you analyze whatever play you read.

✍ Get to know these questions by answering them about Allen's *Death Knocks* in the spaces provided.

Literal comprehension questions

1.   Who is the main character? What is he or she like? What values does he or she hold? Are there one or more other main characters? What are they like? What values do they hold?

_____

_____

_____

_____

2. What other characters are important in the play?

_____

_____

3. Where and when is everything happening? (setting)

_____

_____

4. What action (*plot*) is taking place?

_____

_____

_____

See how well your responses compare with these:

1. The main character is Nat Ackerman, a fifty-seven-year-old dress manu-facturer who apparently has done well in business. His name and his Yiddish language (for instance *take a schvitz*, meaning go soak in a steam room, and *schlep*, a dullard or idiot) imply he's Jewish. He appears self-confident, unafraid of Death. He seems proud of his earned wealth and is shrewd enough to outwit Death (that's not really saying much the way Death is portrayed here!). Nat shares the stage with the character Death, but it could be argued that Nat is more the main character, because the play takes place in his room, he prolongs Death's goal, and Death is a bumbling dolt.

2. In this play, the only other character is Death, who in some ways resembles Nat. Death, too, is middle-aged and paunchy; he is out of breath after his climb up the drainpipe. His taste in furnishings and art is revealed to be as bad as Nat's when he comments on the apartment and says, "I love those kids with the big eyes," a reference to one of the wall paintings. He and Nat speak in the same surly way:

Nat:	I'll take a check.
Death:	From what account?
Nat:	Look who I'm dealing with.
Death:	Sue me. Where do I keep my checking account?
Nat:	All right, gimme what you got and we'll call it square.
Death:	Listen, I need that money.
Nat:	Why should you need money?
Death:	What are you talking about? You're going to the Beyond.
Nat:	So?
Death:	So—you know how far that is?

Nothing about Death inspires the fear or dread normally associated with death.

Strategies for Study-Reading Drama

3. From the stage directions for Nat's apartment and the reference to Kew Gardens, which is in Queens, a New York City suburb, we know where the play is taking place. The dialogue is contemporary, but the reference to Rock Hudson, an actor who played leading-man roles in the movies, dates the play at fifteen or twenty years ago. (A director staging this play today might change that reference to a more contemporary movie idol.)

4. Basically, Death comes to get Nat, but Nat outwits Death by beating him at gin rummy.

You probably had little trouble with these literal questions, but if you did, look back at the spots in the play that provide the answers.

✒ Now answer the following interpretive questions in the spaces provided.

Interpretive comprehension questions

1. How does the playwright use events, characters, or dialogue to develop the play's conflict?

_____

_____

_____

2. What is the theme or message of the play?

_____

_____

_____

3. How is the title related to the theme?

_____

_____

4. What effect does the ending have?

_____

_____

Your answers may be worded differently, and may even be better, but see how close they come in content to these:

1. The conflict, of course, is between Nat and Death. Death has come to take him, but Nat manages to gain another twenty-four hours by beating Death at a game of gin rummy. Most of the play and the conflict are staged around the card game. Death, normally considered a serious subject, is treated comically here. Wanting to make a dramatic entrance, Death instead falls when his heel gets caught in a vine tangled around the drainpipe he is climbing outside Nat's window. Rather than scare Nat, he merely startles and puzzles him. We discover that this is Death's first time on the job, and he bumbles it badly because he thinks he's a great gin rummy player. When he leaves, he's broke, no place to go, and falls down the stairs. But more important than the events is the sarcastic, crusty dialogue Allen gives his characters. Humor and character are developed through opening lines such as

Nat:	Who *are* you?
Death:	*Death.* You got a glass of water?
Nat:	Death? What do you mean, Death?
Death:	What is wrong with you? You see the black costume and the whitened face?
Nat:	Yeah.
Death:	Is it Halloween?
Nat:	No.
Death:	Then I'm Death. Now can I get a glass of water—or a Fresca?

Of course, by the end of the play Nat has the upper hand:

Nat:	So I'll see you tomorrow.
Death:	What do you mean you'll see me tomorrow?
Nat:	I won the extra day. Leave me alone.
Death:	You were serious?
Nat:	We made a deal.
Death:	Yeah, but—
Nat:	Don't "but" me. I won twenty-four hours. Come back tomorrow.
Death:	I didn't know we were actually playing for time.
Nat:	That's too bad about you. You should pay attention.
Death:	Where am I going to go for twenty-four hours?
Nat:	What's the difference? The main thing is I won an extra day.
Death:	What do you want me to do—walk the streets?
Nat:	Check into a hotel and go to a movie. Take a *schvitz*. Don't make a federal case.

The actors' speech provides insights into the characters themselves, develops the action or conflict, and entertains.

2. The subject of the play is obviously Nat's impending death, but Allen's theme is not quite so easy to ascertain. At one point, Death asks Nat if he has read *Faust*, a dramatic poem by the German author Johann Wolfgang von Goethe in the nineteenth century; it is about a scholar who sells his soul to the devil in exchange for youth, knowledge, and magical powers. At another point, Nat says he saw a picture of Death playing chess, probably a reference to an Ingmar Bergman film, *The Seventh Seal*, in which a knight plays a game of chess for his life with a figure who looks much like Death does in this play. These works treat death seriously. Maybe Allen's point is simply to write a humorous parody of our concern about death. Because we know we can't really outwit death when our time comes, perhaps the theme is "Wouldn't it be nice if we could." Is Allen laughing at Death or at us through Nat for thinking (wishing) we could outwit Death? Discuss this with others who've read the play and see what they think.

3. The title, "Death Knocks," is a play on words. If you know how to play gin rummy, you know that knocking means you are holding unmatched cards that total less than ten points and are calling for a showdown of cards, hoping that your opponent has more unmatched points than you do. During the card game in the play, Death "knocks" and loses the hand. In a broader sense, Death "knocks" or makes a call to claim Nat and loses. Also, humorously, Death doesn't knock on the door when he comes to get Nat but climbs a drainpipe to enter his bedroom window.

4. The ending is effective because Allen ironically has Death on the offensive; he's broke, has no place to go, berates himself for getting involved in a card game, and can't even get away with Nat's newspaper. His tripping on the stairs just as Nat warns him about the loose rug mirrors his bumbling entrance at the beginning of the play. The last words in the play, spoken by Nat to his friend Moe, are "he's such a *schlep!*"—and we have to agree.

Naturally, these are not the only good interpretive questions, but asking them usually brings up more questions of your own and helps you begin to look analytically at whatever play you read.

Affective comprehension questions

✍ Now answer the following affective questions in the spaces provided. These are personal questions, so they have no right or wrong answers, but they are important for getting the most from reading drama.

1. What feeling do you have for the main character? the other characters?

    _____

    _____

    _____

2. What passages do you find well written?

    _____

    _____

    _____

3. Why do you like or not like the play?

    _____

    _____

    _____

Although, as I said, these questions have no correct answers, here are some comments that may help you see how to answer such questions for a class in the future:

1. Because this play is a comedy, there is little chance that you will feel sadness, pity, anguish, or sorrow for either of the characters. But you might have a smile on your face for Nat's ability to outfox Death. Nat apparently faces Death the same way he faced business associates—successfully. You might admire him for his straightforwardness, his lack of deceit. Still, you may not identify with Nat because of his values; he seems to equate success with making money: "I drive a Chrysler. My wife has whatever she wants. Maids, mink coat, vacations." He even wants to play gin rummy with Death for money as well as for more time. If *Death Knocks* were a two- or three-act play rather than a one act, there would be more room for character development, making this question more significant.

You might like the character of Death because he is so inept. He *is* a "schlep," messing up on his first job as Death. If you are a Woody Allen fan, you know that he usually plays just such a role, a sorrowful but likable bungler. While we laugh at him, we recognize our own failures and flaws.

2. Many passages here might be identified as well written, if you enjoy the humor in the play. The success of this comic drama depends more on the language than on actions. For instance, notice in this passage how character is developed:

Death: I climbed up the drainpipe. I was trying to make a dramatic entrance. I see the big windows and you're awake reading. I figure it's worth a shot. I'll climb up and enter with a little—you know. (*Snaps fingers*) Meanwhile, I get my heel caught on some vines, the drainpipe breaks, and I'm hanging by a thread. Then my cape begins to tear. Look, let's just go. It's been a rough night.

Nat: You broke my drainpipe?

Death: Broke. It didn't break. It's a little bent. Didn't you hear anything? I slammed into the ground.

Nat: I was reading.

Death: You must have really been engrossed. (*Lifting newspaper Nat was reading*) "NAB COEDS IN POT ORGY." Can I borrow this?

Look how much we learn in these few lines. For one thing, Death explains the noise we hear offstage, in essence describing his offstage action. The lines also reveal traits of both characters. We learn of Death's desire to make a dramatic entrance, how inept and defensive he is about damaging Nat's drainpipe, how easily he's distracted from his purpose when he sees what Nat was reading, and that he appears to have been afraid of dying in a fall from the drainpipe. We also see that Nat is not afraid of Death; he's more interested in what happened to his drainpipe than in what happened to Death and manages to put Death on the defensive. The result is a humorous first encounter that moves the plot along, develops character, and provides entertainment. The play has many such passages.

3. You are not required to like Woody Allen's kind of humor; it's entirely possible that you didn't enjoy reading the play. Certainly, this is not what some critics refer to as "high drama." Your reasons for liking or not liking it are your own. It's a bet, though, that if you saw this play acted out, or if your class decided to read it aloud, you'd find it fun to watch and hear.

FINAL THOUGHTS

You have learned in this chapter that reading a play is different from reading a short story or poem. Five reading strategies can help you get more from reading plays:

1. Read all the stage directions carefully.
2. Notice how the dialogue reveals characters' own habits, characteristics, personalities, and thinking, as well as those of other characters in the play.
3. Be alert for the conflict, problem, or tension that the dialogue and actions reveal.
4. Notice the plot as the play unfolds.
5. Take your time as you read, and expect some confusion in the beginning.

Remember these strategies the next time you are assigned a play to read.

PROCESSING WHAT YOU JUST READ

If you are using the *Student's Reading Journal* that accompanies this text, go to pages 68–69 in it and follow the directions given.

If you are using your own notebook as a journal, answer the following questions:

1. Make a list of the literal, interpretive, and affective comprehension questions you can use to analyze any play you read.

2. How many plays have you seen produced onstage? Would you like to see *Death Knocks* done onstage? Explain.

Now go to Part III, page 435, for more practice in reading drama.

CHAPTER 16

Research Sources in the Humanities

PREPARING TO READ   Probably more than in any other discipline, instructors in humanities courses, especially in literature classes, assign research papers requiring documented footnotes and bibliography. Numerous resources exist for research in literature, art, music, and philosophy. Critical and interpretive works on fiction, poetry, drama, and other disciplines in the humanities abound. This chapter explains the differences between primary and secondary sources and provides a list of helpful sources in four areas of the humanities. **Your objective in reading this chapter is to become more familiar with outside sources you can use for research papers in the humanities.**

Isn't doing library research just a lot of busywork?

Library research can be busywork. Who wants to do a research paper that requires a certain number of pages, footnotes, references, and hours spent in the library? Such work can be a waste of time and energy, just another grade in the instructor's book.

But a research project can also be worthwhile, an experience that can broaden your perspective on the subject you investigate. Most of what you learn about a subject comes from only two major sources: your textbooks and the instructor. The textbook, although it's probably a good one, can't tell you everything. It offers only selected information. Your instructor may be an expert in his or her field, but, because instructors are human, they generally express their opinions and biases. For your own sake, you need to go beyond the textbook and the classroom.

Outside readings for a research project give you a chance to compare your classroom knowledge with knowledge from other sources. The more sources you have the time to read, the broader and deeper your knowledge of a subject can be. Outside reading assignments let you know what other people think about the issues you are studying. They help you relate what you have learned in the past with what you are learning now, and they open your eyes to problems and situations you never knew existed. Additional reading can also help you decide whether you have based your opinions on fact or prejudice. For all these reasons, a research project or outside reading can be well worth the time.

What's the best way to begin?

Don't put it off! One of the reasons students have trouble with research projects is that they wait too long to get started. So-called term papers are usually assigned during the first days or weeks of class and are due near the end of the term. Students who wait until near the end of the term to get started often find these assignments pressured chores and end up doing a poor job.

Set up an appointment with your instructor so you can get a fuller explanation of the assignment. Share your ideas for a project with the instructor, or, if you're short on ideas, let the instructor help you decide on an appropriate research topic. Find out if you are supposed to use primary and secondary sources. After you and the instructor are satisfied with the idea for your research, you're ready to go to work.

What's the difference between primary and secondary sources?

When an instructor assigns a research paper in any area of the humanities, begin by reading the primary source. **Primary sources** are those materials which have not been interpreted by others. If, for example, you had to do research on Emily Dickinson's poem, "Because I could not stop for Death," you would begin by reading the primary source, the poem itself. You might also discover that Dickinson possibly made comments about her poem in letters that she wrote. Any of her own comments about the poem in other works of hers are still considered primary sources.

When you begin reading what others have to say about her poem, you are reading secondary sources. **Secondary sources** appear in scholarly journal articles, magazines, book reviews, biographies, encyclopedias, and critical books about writers and their works. Such sources are materials which have been reported, analyzed, or interpreted by other persons.

When instructors assign research papers, they do so for two major reasons: (1) to teach you how to do research and write up your findings with documentation of the works used; and (2) to introduce you to the world of critical commentary that exists about various fields of study.

When you read outside sources, try to read from several types of references. If you limit yourself to newspaper or magazine articles, for example, you may encounter only superficial, quick reviews that were written to meet publication deadlines. For instance, in the year that J. D. Salinger's novel *Catcher in the Rye* appeared, there were almost two hundred book reviews written about it, most of them describing the novel as nothing more than "a good read," enjoyable "summer reading." Only a few of the reviews touched on the greatness that this work is now known for. So make certain that you balance your outside reading with longer, more critically thoughtful explications of the work or the author you are researching. For most good works of literature, there is a wide range of opinions and critical interpretations. You must know the primary source well enough to prevent critics from swaying you to their way of thinking unless you, too, see the interpretations they are making.

What are some useful reference works in the humanities?

Here, by categories, are some library reference works in the humanities with which you should familiarize yourself. These, of course, are not the only resources available, but they will provide you with a good start. Read each list to get an idea of the sorts of sources available.

IN LITERATURE

Bibliographies and Information Sources on Literature

Abstracts of English Studies, 1958–present
Book Review Digest

Contemporary Literary Criticism
Essay and General Literature Index
Fiction Catalog
Magill, F. N. *Bibliography of Literary Criticism*
New York Times Review of Books
The New York Review of Books

American Literature

American Literature
The American Novel: A Checklist of Twentieth-century Criticism (2 vols.)
American Writers: A Collection of Literary Biographies (4 vols.)
Bibliographical Guide to the Study of Literature of the U.S.A.
Bibliography of American Literature
Evans, Charles. *American Bibliography* (14 vols.)
Guide to American Literature and Its Backgrounds Since 1890
Kazin, Alfred. *An American Procession: The Major American Writers from 1830 to 1930*
Literary History of the United States
Matthiessen, F. O. *American Renaissance*
Modern American Literature
The Oxford Companion to American Literature
Recent American Literature

Black Literature

Black American Fiction: A Bibliography
Black American Fiction Since 1952: A Preliminary Checklist
Black American Writers: Bibliographical Essays (2 vols.)
Black American Writers Past and Present
Conjuring: Black Women, Fiction, and Literary Tradition
Davis, Arthur. *From the Dark Tower: Afro-American Writers* (1900–1960)
Poetry of the Negro: 1746–1970
Whitlow, Roger. *Black American Literature: A Critical History*

British Literature

Baker, Ernest A. *History of the English Novel* (11 vols.)
Bibliographical Resources for the Study of Nineteenth Century English Fiction
British Writers (8 vols.)
British Writers and Their Work (11 vols.)
Cambridge Bibliography of English Literature (5 vols.)
Cambridge History of English Literature (15 vols.)
English Novel Explication: Criticisms to 1972
The English Romantic Poets: A Review of Research and Criticism
Evans, Gareth L., and Barbara Evans. *The Shakespeare Companion Garland Shakespeare Bibliographies* (18 vols.)
Karl, Frederick R. *A Reader's Guide to the Eighteenth Century English Novel*
Karl, Frederick R. *A Reader's Guide to the Contemporary English Novel*
The McGraw-Hill Guide to English Literature (2 vols.)
Modern British Literature (4 vols.)
Oxford History of English Literature

Drama

American Drama Criticism: Interpretations, 1890–1977
Cheshire, David F. *Theatre: History, Criticism, and Reference*
Contemporary Dramatists
Cumulated Dramatic Index (2 vols.)
Drama Criticism (2 vols.)

Dramatic Criticism Index
Index to Full Length Plays (3 vols.)
McGraw-Hill Encyclopedia of World Drama (5 vols.)
Modern Drama: A Checklist of Critical Literature on Twentieth-century Plays
Oxford Companion to the Theatre
Play Index (6 vols.)

The Novel

American Fiction: A Contribution Toward a Bibliography (3 vols.)
The American Novel
The American Novel: A Checklist of Twentieth Century Criticism (2 vols.)
Bradbury, Malcolm, ed. *The Novel Today: Contemporary Writers on Modern Fiction*
Chase, Richard. *The American Novel and Its Tradition*
The Contemporary Novel: A Checklist of Critical Literature on the British and American Novel Since 1945
English Novel: 1578–1956: A Checklist of Twentieth Century Criticism
Geismar, Maxwell. *American Moderns, From Rebellion to Conformity*
Holman, C. Hugh. *American Novel Through Henry James*
Mercier, Vivian. *A Reader's Guide to the New Novel*
Rahv, Philip, ed. *Literature in America: An Anthology of Literary Criticsm*
Wiley, Paul L. *British Novel: Conrad to the Present*

Poetry

Altenbernd, Lynn, and Leslie L. Lewis. *A Handbook for the Study of Poetry*
American and British Poetry: A Guide to the Criticism, 1925–1978
Granger's Index to Poetry
Poetry Explication: A Checklist of Interpretation Since 1925 of British and American Poems, Past and Present
Subject Index to Poetry for Children and Young People

The Short Story

American Short-Fiction Criticism and Scholarship, 1957–1977: A Checklist
Short Story Index (and supplements)
Twentieth-century Short Story Explication

Indexes to Articles in Scholarly Journals

Abstracts of English Studies
Abstracts of Folklore Studies
Book Review Digest
Book Review Index
Current Book Reviews in the Humanities
Humanities Index
MLA International Bibliography of Books and Articles on the Modern Languages and Literatures (annually since 1921)

IN ART

Bibliographies to Art Books and Other Sources

Annotated Bibliography of Fine Arts
Applied and Decorative Arts: A Bibliographic Guide
Art Books
Arts in America: A Bibliography
Bibliographic Guide to Art and Architecture
Fine Arts: A Bibliographic Guide

General Works and Encyclopedias

American Art Dictionary, 1952–present
Art Education: A Guide to Information Sources
Art Through the Ages (2 vols.)
Britannica Encyclopedia of American Art
Contemporary Artists
Dictionary of American Painters, Sculptors, and Engravers
Encyclopedia of American Art
Encyclopedia of World Art
Guide to the Literature of Art History
A History of Architecture
Larousse Dictionary of Painters
The New International Illustrated Encyclopedia of Art (24 vols.)
Research Guide to the History of Western Art

Data Bases

Artbibliographies Modern
International Repertory of the Literature of Art

Indexes to Articles in Scholarly Journals

Art Index
Humanities Index

IN MUSIC

General Guides

Baker's Biographical Dictionary of Musicians
Cyclopedia of Music and Musicians
Dictionary of Music
Encyclopedia of Pop, Rock, and Soul
The New Grove Dictionary of Music and Musicians (20 vols.)
The New Harvard Dictionary of Music
Information on Music
International Cyclopedia of Music and Musicians
Music Reference and Research Materials
The New College Encyclopedia of Music
The New Oxford Companion to Music (2 vols.)
Oxford History of Music (8 vols.)

Bibliographies to Music Books

Bibliographic Guide to Music
*The Literature of American Music in Books and Folk Music Collections: A Fully
    Annotated Bibliography*
Music Reference and Research Materials: An Annotated Bibliography
Source Readings in Music History

Data Base

RILM Abstracts of Music Literature

Indexes to Articles in Scholarly Journals

Music Article Guide
Music Index

IN PHILOSOPHY

General Guides

A Dictionary of Philosophy
The Encyclopedia of Philosophy (8 vols.)
The History of Philosophy, (9 vols.)
How to Find Out in Philosophy and Psychology
The Philosopher's Guide to Sources
Research Guide to Philosophy
Research in Philosophy
Who's Who in Philosophy

Bibliographies to Philosophy Books

A Bibliography of Philosophical Bibliographies
The Classical World Bibliography of Philosophy
Philosopher's Index
Philosophy and Psychology: Classification Schedule, Author and Title Listing
    (2 vols.)

Data Base

PHILOSOPHER'S INDEX

Index to Articles in Scholarly Journals

Humanities Index
Philosopher's Index

This is enough, although it is far from all the available sources. But these lists should give you an idea of the numerous sources out there waiting for you to discover them. The first chance you get, go to your local or college library and look through some of the titles that sound interesting or helpful for your project.

What else is available?

Take some time to get to know your library. The *circulation desk* is usually located near the entrance and exit. When you can't find a book you need, go to the circulation desk; someone may be able to tell you if what you want is available or checked out. Sometimes instructors place certain books and periodicals at the *reserve desk* so that large numbers of students will have access to them for limited amounts of time.

Find out if your library uses a *card catalog* system or computer terminals, which are *on-line catalogs* connected to data bases. Many libraries are in a state of change because of new technology and the availability of computer data bases. Both cataloging systems contain information on all the books in the library, listed by author, title, and subject. Every book is identified by a call number. The call number indicates in what section of the library you will find the book.

The *reference room* contains encyclopedias, biographical sources, and general reference works. Frequently this room also houses nonprint materials, such as videos, audiotapes, films, and information on microfilm. If, for instance, you are not familiar with much drama, you might want to see whether your library has any recordings or videos of plays you could listen to or watch.

Many libraries also make available *interlibrary loans*, whereby one library may borrow from another. This service supplements the library's resources and, with enough advance notice, can get material for you that your library doesn't own.

PROCESSING WHAT YOU JUST READ

✍ If you are using the *Student's Reading Journal* that accompanies this text, go to page 71 in it and follow the directions given.

If you are using your own notebook as a journal, do the following:

1. Look over the preceding lists of reference works. Write down at least six titles that you want to see the next time you go to the library. Write a paragraph about the one you find most interesting.
2. What is the difference between *primary* and *secondary* sources?

What happens when you find a good source?

Once you know where to look for sources for your research project, you have to know how to use them. There may be so much material on your topic than you can't possibly read all the references you find. Here are some good beginning research strategies for writing about literature offered by X. J. Kennedy in his book *Literature: An Introduction to Fiction, Poetry, and Drama.* Even though what he says relates to literature, it can apply to all areas of the humanities.

> Offered a choice of literary works to write about, you probably will do best if, instead of choosing what you think will impress your instructor, you choose what appeals to you. And how to find out what appeals? Whether you plan to write a short paper that requires no research beyond the story or poem or play itself, or a long term paper that will take you to the library, the first stage of your project is reading—and note taking. To concentrate your attention, one time-honored method is to read with a pencil, marking (if the book is yours) passages that stand out in importance, jotting brief notes in a margin (*"Key symbol—this foreshadows the ending"; "Dramatic irony"; "IDIOT!!!"*; or other possibly useful remarks). In a long story or poem or play, some students asterisk passages that cry for comparison; for instance, all the places in which they find the same theme or symbol. Later, at a glance, they can review the highlights of a work and, when writing a paper about it, quickly refer to evidence. This method shoots holes in a book's resale value, but many find the sacrifice worth-while. Patient souls who dislike butchering a book prefer to take notes on looseleaf notebook paper, holding one sheet beside a page in the book and giving it the book's page number. Later, in writing a paper, they can place book page and companion note page together again. This method has the advantage of affording a lot of room for note taking; it is a good one for short poems closely packed with complexities.
>
> But by far the most popular method of taking notes (besides writing on the pages of books) is to write on index cards—the 3 × 5 kind, for brief notes and titles; 5 × 8 cards for longer notes. Write on one side only; notes on the back of the card usually get overlooked later. Cards are easy to shuffle and, in organizing your material, to deal with. To save work, instead of copying out on a card the title and author of a book you're taking a note from, just keep a numbered list of the books you're using. Then, when making a note, you need write only the book's identifying number on the card in order to identify your source. (Later, when writing footnotes, you can translate the number into title, author, and other information.)
>
> Now that coin-operated photocopy machines are to be found in many libraries, you no longer need to spend hours copying by hand whole poems and longer passages. If accuracy is essential (surely it is)

and if a poem or passage is long enough to be worth the investment of a few cents, you can lay photocopied material into place in your paper with transparent tape or rubber cement. The latest copyright law permits students and scholars to reproduce books and periodicals in this fashion; it does not, however, permit making a dozen or more copies for public sale.

Certain literary works, because they offer intriguing difficulties, have attracted professional critics by the score. On library shelves, great phalanxes of critical books now stand at the side of James Joyce's complex novels *Ulysses* and *Finnegans Wake*, and T. S. Eliot's allusive poem *The Waste Land*. The student who undertakes to study such works seriously is well advised to profit from the critics' labors. Chances are, too, that even in discussing a relatively uncomplicated work you will want to seek the aid of the finest critics. If you quote them, quote them exactly, in quotation marks, and give them credit. When employed in any but the most superlative student paper, a brilliant phrase (or even a not-so-brilliant sentence) from a renowned critic is likely to stand out like a golf ball in a garter snake's midriff, and most English instructors are likely to recognize it. If you rip off the critic's words, then go ahead and steal the whole essay, for good critics write in seamless unities. Then, when apprehended, you can exclaim—like the student whose term paper was found to be the work of a well-known scholar—"I've been robbed! That paper cost me twenty dollars!" But of course the worst rip-off is the one the student inflicted on himself, having got nothing for his money out of a college course but a little practice in touch typing.

Taking notes on your readings, you will want to jot down the title of every book you might refer to in your paper, and the page number of any passage you might wish to quote. Even if you summarize a critic's idea in your own words, rather than quote, you have to give credit to your source. Nothing is cheaper to give than proper credit. Certainly it's easier to take notes while you read than to have to run back to the library during the final typing.

Choose a topic appropriate to the assigned length of your paper. How do you know the probable length of your discussion until you write it? When in doubt, you are better off to define your topic narrowly. Your paper will be stronger if you go deeper into your subject than if you choose some gigantic subject and then find yourself able to touch on it only superficially. A thorough explication of a short story is hardly possible in a paper of 250 words. There are, in truth, four-line poems whose surface 250 words might only begin to scratch. A profound topic ("The Character of Shakespeare's Hamlet") might overflow a book; but a topic more narrowly defined ("Hamlet's Views of Acting"; "Hamlet's Puns") might result in a more nearly manageable term paper. You can narrow and focus a large topic while you work your way into it. A general interest in "Hemingway's Heroes" might lead you, in reading, taking notes, and thinking further, to the narrower topic, "Jake Barnes: Spokesman for Hemingway's Views of War."

Many student writers find it helpful, in defining a topic, to state an emerging idea for a paper in a provisional thesis sentence: a summing-up of the one main idea or argument that the paper will embody. (A thesis sentence is for your own use; you don't have to implant it in your paper unless your instructor asks for it.) A good statement of a thesis is not just a disembodied subject; it comes with both subject and verb. ("The Downfall of Oedipus Rex" is not yet a complete idea for a paper; "What Caused the Downfall of Oedipus

Rex?" is.) A thesis sentence may help you see for yourself what the author is *saying about* a subject. Not a full thesis, and not a sentence, "The Isolation of City-dwellers in Edward Albee's *A Zoo Story*" might be a decent title for a paper. But it isn't a useful thesis because it doesn't indicate what one might say about that isolation (nor what Albee is saying about it). It may be obvious that isolation isn't desirable, but a clearer and more workable thesis sentence might be, "In *A Zoo Story* Albee shows how city-dwellers' isolation from one another prompts one city-dweller to action"; the writer might well go on to demonstrate just what that action is.

Discovering and Planning

Writing is not likely to proceed in a straight line. Like thought, it often goes by fits and starts, by charges and retreats and mopping-up operations. All the while you take notes, you discover material to write about; all the while you tool over your topic in your mind, you plan. It is the nature of ideas, those headstrong things, to happen in any order they desire. While you continue to plan, while you write a draft, and while you revise, expect to keep discovering new thoughts perhaps the best thoughts of all. If you do, be sure to let them in.[1]

What Kennedy offers here is fairly standard stuff, especially in English classes. But, as I said earlier, the best approach to doing a research project is to make an appointment with your instructor to discuss it. Make certain you understand the assigned project, what written form it is to follow, and how many references are required. If you can pick a topic that really interests you, the project can be fun.

If and when you need to do a research project, refer to the Appendix, "Procedure for Doing a Research Paper," page 450. It provides a step-by-step approach with examples of note taking.

Source: Reprinted by permission: Tribune Media Services.

FINAL THOUGHTS   As you have learned in previous chapters, accept outside reading assignments and research projects as an extension of your textbook and class lectures. Don't wait until the last minute to start doing your outside reading or to begin your search for sources. You will need all the time the instructor gives. Use publications that deal specifically with your subject rather than only popular or familiar sources. Take accurate notes. Keep track of the correct titles, volume numbers, and page references used. Copy any quoted material accurately to avoid plagiarism (see page 120 for advice on proper use of quoted material).

1. *Source*: 4th ed. Little, 1987, 1335–37.

PROCESSING WHAT YOU JUST READ

✍ If you are using the *Student's Reading Journal* that accompanies this text, go to pages 71–72 in it and follow the directions given.

If you are using your own notebook as a journal, answer the following questions:

1. What information does Kennedy provide in the preceding statement that is useful for a research project in any area?

2. Go to the library, learn the following, and record the information in your journal.

    a. What system does the library use for cataloging its contents (card catalog, computer, other)?

    b. How do you go about finding the book or reference you may want to check out?

    c. List five reference books mentioned in this chapter that deal with a subject of interest to you (literature, art, music, philosophy) and are in your library.

    d. What did you find out about the library that you didn't know before?

PART III

PRACTICES

Practices in Strategy 1: Preparing to Read

The following practices will help you develop the skills involved in the first general study-reading strategy, preparing to read, as discussed in Chapter 1.

PRACTICE 1

Directions: Look carefully at the student study plan shown in Figure S1.1. Then answer the following questions in the space provided.

1. In how many courses is the student enrolled?   _____

2. Based on this schedule, how many hours should the student spend studying each week?   _____

3. How many hours of study time are devoted to

   a. English?   _____

   b. math?   _____

   c. sociology?   _____

4. Why should the student not have scheduled classes back to back?

   _____

   _____

   _____

5. Has the student planned a study period for each course on the night before each class? Is this wise? Why?

   _____

   _____

   _____

   _____

FIGURE S1.1   Study plan

	MON.	TUES.	WED.	THURS.	FRI.	SAT.	SUN.
7:00 – 8:00 A.M.	Breakfast, Travel to school	————————————————————→					
8:00 – 9:00	English 1A	Business comm.	English 1A	Business comm.	English 1A	WORK	FREE
9:00 – 10:00	Sociology 1	↓	Soc. 1	↓	Soc. 1		
10:00 – 11:00	Math 5	Study English	Math 5	Study biology	Math 5		
11:00 – 12:00	Lunch	————————————————→					
12:00 – 1:00 P.M.	History 1A	Biology 1	History 1A	Biology 1	History 1A		
1:00 – 2:00	Bio. lab	↓		↓			
2:00 – 3:00	Word processing	————————————————→					
3:00 – 4:00	Get to work	————————————————→					
4:00 – 5:00	WORK	————————————————→				↓	
5:00 – 6:00	WORK	————————————————→				FREE	
6:00 – 7:00	WORK	————————————————→				FREE	↓
7:00 – 8:00	Dinner	————————————————→				FREE	Dinner
8:00 – 9:00	Study math	Study English	Study math	Study English	Study history	FREE	Study English
9:00 – 10:00	Study bus. comm.	Study soc.	Study bus. comm.	Study soc.	Study history	FREE	Study soc.
10:00 – 11:00	TV/bed	————————————————→				FREE	BED
11:00 – 12:00	↓						

6. If you were this student's adviser, what changes in this schedule would you recommend and why?

_____

_____

_____

PRACTICE 2

Directions: Using the study plan sheet in Figure S1.2, outline your present schedule. Examine it to see if you need to make any changes. Then answer the following questions in the space provided.

1. Does this schedule really meet your needs? Why?

_____

_____

_____

_____

2. How much time do you waste?

_____

_____

_____

3. Do you have your study times properly spaced so that you can review for a class both before and after it?

_____

_____

_____

4. What changes should be made so that you get the maximum benefit from your classes and study times?

_____

FIGURE S1.2   **Study plan**

	MON.	TUES.	WED.	THURS.	FRI.	SAT.	SUN.
7:00 – 8:00 A.M.							
8:00 – 9:00							
9:00 – 10:00							
10:00 – 11:00							
11:00 – 12:00							
12:00 – 1:00 P.M.							
1:00 – 2:00							
2:00 – 3:00							
3:00 – 4:00							
4:00 – 5:00							
5:00 – 6:00							
6:00 – 7:00							
7:00 – 8:00							
8:00 – 9:00							
9:00 – 10:00							
10:00 – 11:00							
11:00 – 12:00							

_____

_____

_____

PRACTICE 3

Directions: The table of contents for a textbook appears on pages 255–259.[1] Look it over, then answer the following questions. Circle the letter of the correct answer or fill in the blank as appropriate.

1. For what course is this textbook probably used?
    a. U.S. History
    b. art history
    c. comparative religions
    d. humanities

2. Into how many parts is the book divided?
    a. three
    b. four
    c. five
    d. six

3. Each part deals with a "root." State each of the roots.

    _____

    _____

    _____

4. On which of the following will the textbook provide information?
    a. Greek and Roman architecture
    b. Classical and Renaissance drama
    c. Greek, Roman, and African art and sculpture
    d. literature from various periods
    e. all of the above

5. The textbook contains a glossary of terms and an index.
    a. True
    b. False

---

1. *Source:* Mary Ann Frese Witt, Charlotte Vestal Brown, Roberta Ann Dunbar, Frank Tirro, Ronald G. Witt, *The Humanities*, Vol. I, 2nd ed., Heath, 1985, xi–xiii.

Contents

COLOR ILLUSTRATIONS

Following page 134:

MAPS

XV

PRACTICE 4

Directions: Read the part of the preface to a textbook that appears on page 261.[2] Then answer the following questions. Circle the letter of the correct answer or fill in the blank as appropriate.

1. For what course is this textbook intended?

    _____

2. What is the title of the book?

    _____

3. The author of the book has not had experience outside the classroom.
    a. True
    b. False

4. Which of the following does the author claim is necessary for a breakthrough in learning to communicate in business?
    a. a perception that communication begins with knowing who one is
    b. a perception that communication begins with knowing whom one is addressing
    c. a perception that communication begins with knowing what one hopes to accomplish
    d. all of the above
    e. both a and c

5. What basic premise does the textbook make about writers?

    _____

    _____

6. For whom does the preface seem to be written?
    a. instructors
    b. students
    c. both

2. *Source:* Ruth G. Newman, *Communicating in Business Today.* Heath, 1987, vii.

PREFACE

During the past twenty years or more, I have been a student, a teacher, a writer, manager of several communication functions within business firms, and more recently an entrepreneurial consultant in business communication. For most of my professional life, therefore, while preoccupied with words and their effects, I have shuttled between two separate worlds. The first of these is the academic world of students, teachers, and scholarship; the second is the world that students, and even some teachers, call the "real world" — the marketplace where business transactions take place.

For most students and for many employees, however, the latter world is not very *real* at all. They harbor an abiding and contagious suspicion that business has a special mystique. They expect that the business environment will require them to put on hold their commonsensical perceptions about how to make people respond well to their ideas and words. If they are industrious and ambitious, they are prepared at the outset to master a whole new set of rules about writing, speaking, and even thinking. For the most part, they are wrong in this expectation.

The first breakthrough in learning to communicate well is achieved with the perception that communication begins with knowing who one is, whom one is addressing, and what one hopes to accomplish. Further success is almost guaranteed if one aims to be as logical, persuasive, and personable as one's personal endowments permit . . . and then some.

A basic premise of this text is that all writers must work hard to master the traditional tools of their trade. And even when they have the requisite knowledge in place, the writing process is always highly individualized, filled with starts and stops, and pressing endlessly towards a moving goal. In a real sense, writers must rediscover a successful writing process with each new effort to communicate.

Communicating in Business Today makes no bones about the fact that confidence and skill in communicating are acquired through study, strenuous effort, and constant practice. And it makes it clear that for student writers, adding to their arsenal can be a strenuous and time-consuming enterprise. But, through many realistic cases and examples, it also strongly implies that the business environment rewards those individuals who possess these skills in abundance.

PRACTICE 5

Directions: On pages 263–264 is more of the preface excerpted in Practice 4.[3] Use it to answer the following questions. Circle the letter of the correct answer or fill in the blank as appropriate.

1. List at least four key features of the textbook.

    _____

    _____

    _____

    _____

2. What will students learn that will help them think independently?
    a. audience and situation analysis
    b. processes for resolving the case problems
    c. explanations of memos, letters, and reports related to the case studies
    d. all of the above
    e. none of the above

3. List at least five topics related to business writing that receive extensive coverage in the textbook.

    _____

    _____

    _____

    _____

4. Does this part of the preface seem to be written for students or instructors? Explain.

    _____

    _____

3. *Source:* Newman, viii–ix.

Key Features

In designing this text we have aimed to provide students with pathways to learning that, while strenuous, are also interesting and compelling. We have tried to challenge and motivate students to discover their best selves and to exert their individual powers to resolve problems that they typically will encounter in the workplace. Moreover, because *Communicating in Business Today* avoids cookbook solutions and stresses the uniqueness of each writer and each business situation, it challenges instructors to help students develop their special abilities.

Among the text's distinctive features are the following:

Process / Product Case Method. A new approach to the case method stimulates rapid learning:

- Although many opportunities are provided for students to think independently, they are first carefully trained in audience and situation analysis. At frequent intervals, both an appropriate process for resolving the case problem and examples of the resulting memo, letter, or report are discussed in detail.
- Cases mirror real workplace tasks; moreover, they place readers in roles that are appropriate to the professional aims and aspirations of entry-level employees across a broad spectrum of industries and business functions.

Readability and Accessibility. This text is written in a style that aims to emulate what it teaches:

- We have tried to speak directly to our readers in a clear, candid, conversational style.
- Both style and content reflect a close analysis of our reading audience; an important objective has been to help our readers perceive that they are in touch with an instructor who understands and to a great extent shares their attitudes and perspectives.

Exceptionally Broad Coverage. Along with close attention to all aspects of business writing, the text provides extensive coverage of the following critical topics:

- *The job campaign,* from preliminary brainstorming, résumés and cover letters, through the acceptance letter.
- *The preparation and use of graphics* for business writing and speaking, with multiple examples.
- *Collaborative writing efforts,* in a full chapter devoted to "The Politics of Report Writing."
- A detailed list of *business research sources,* with discussion of available on-line data bases.

- *Planning, preparing, and delivering the spoken presentation.*
- *Business meetings*, from the perspective of both leader and participant.
- *International communications.*
- *Office automation technology* and its benefits.

Realistic, Practical Discussion Problems and Tasks. The text includes an extremely broad selection of chapter-end exercises.

- *Discussion Problems*
  These do not simply invite students to regurgitate the chapter's content. Many are case related; others help students to share their own communication strategies with their peers.
- *Tasks*
  Many are related to the preceding discussion problems—allowing students to implement the strategies they have defended in discussions. Others provide opportunities for practicing the techniques demonstrated in the chapter.

Innovative Approaches. Although there are many innovations in our text, the following are perhaps most notable:

- *The Dialogues*
  Four dialogues, or short plays, vividly reveal how writers tackle business communication. Based on actual recorded transcripts, they show a group of students analyzing each other's writings. Their discussions provide exceptional insights into the minds of writers and editors. Each dialogue is based on an interesting and challenging case. Each is followed by additional student letters or memos to discuss and revise.
- *Dynamic Treatment of Proposals and Reports*
  In confronting an important contemporary issue, an entry-level employee helps resolve a critical problem at his company. As he masters essential communication skills, the text covers in detail research techniques (including use of on-line data bases), letter proposals and formal proposals, formatting, and all topics relevant to preparing a major report.
- *Unique Application of Rhetorical Modes to Business Writing*
  The "Patterns of Relationship" chapter provides new insights into methods by which writers create logical structure. Using real-world examples, the text clearly shows that the relationships we deal with most frequently in business writing are natural and familiar: space, time, comparison, analysis, cause/effect, and problem/solution.
- *Traditional and New Techniques for Prewriting and Planning*
  Not only the traditional outline but also modern methods taught to executives by business consultants and trainers are explained. Students are helped to see planning as a natural and inevitable part of the writing process.

PRACTICE 6

Directions: Select one of your textbooks for another course and explore or survey it by answering the following questions. Circle the letter or letters of the correct answer or fill in the blank as appropriate.

1. What is the full title of the book? (This is found on the *title page* at the beginning of the book.)

    _____

2. When was it published? (Look at the *copyright date* on the back of the title page.)

    _____

3. What is the purpose of this book, and for whom was it written? (Read the *preface* for this.)

    _____

    _____

    _____

4. How is this book divided and organized? (Look over the *table of contents*.)

    _____

    _____

    _____

5. Which of the following does the book have?
    a. index
    b. glossary of terms
    c. appendix
    d. other: _____

6. What did you learn about the book you didn't know before?

    _____

    _____

    _____

    _____

PRACTICE 7

Directions: Using the textbook you explored in Practice 6, survey your next assigned chapter and answer the following questions in the space provided.

1. What is the title of the textbook?

   _____

2. What are the number and the title of the chapter?

   _____

3. How many major headings divide the chapter?

   _____

4. What reading aids (objectives, subheadings, marginal comments, summaries, visual aids and so on) are provided?

   _____

   _____

   _____

   _____

5. Can you read the chapter in one study period? _____ If not, where would you stop for breaks?

   _____

   _____

6. List at least four questions you want to answer when you read the chapter.

   _____

   _____

   _____

   _____

   _____

PRACTICE 8

Directions: Select another of your textbooks and explore or survey it by answering the following questions. Circle the letter or letters of the correct answer or fill in the blank as appropriate.

1. What is the full title of the book? (This is found on the *title page* at the beginning of the book.)

   _____

2. When was it published? (Look at the *copyright date* on the back of the title page.)

   _____

3. What is the purpose of this book and for whom was it written? (Read the *preface* for this.)

   _____

   _____

   _____

4. How is this book divided and organized? (Look over the *table of contents*.)

   _____

   _____

5. Which of the following does the book have?
   a. index
   b. glossary of terms
   c. appendix
   d. other: _____

6. What did you learn about the book you didn't know before?

   _____

   _____

   _____

PRACTICE 9

Directions: Using the textbook you explored in Practice 8, survey your next assigned chapter and answer the following questions in the space provided.

1. What is the title of the textbook?

   _____

2. What are the number and the title of the chapter?

   _____

3. How many major headings divide the chapter? _____

4. What reading aids (objectives, subheadings, marginal comments, summaries, visual aids and so on) are provided?

   _____

_____

_____

_____

5. Can you read the chapter in one study period? _____ If not, where would you stop for breaks?

_____

_____

6. List at least four questions you want to answer when you read the chapter.

_____

_____

_____

_____

_____

PRACTICE 10

Directions: Using a pencil, fill in the study plan sheet in Figure S 1.3 with a schedule you would like to follow for the next *four weeks*. Keep in mind the advice in the text for proper scheduling. Before filling in the blanks, use the space below for notes or rough drafts of your study plan.

_____

_____

_____

_____

_____

_____

_____

_____

_____

_____

FIGURE S1.3   **Study plan**

	MON.	TUES.	WED.	THURS.	FRI.	SAT.	SUN.
7:00 – 8:00 A.M.							
8:00 – 9:00							
9:00 – 10:00							
10:00 – 11:00							
11:00 – 12:00							
12:00 – 1:00 P.M.							
1:00 – 2:00							
2:00 – 3:00							
3:00 – 4:00							
4:00 – 5:00							
5:00 – 6:00							
6:00 – 7:00							
7:00 – 8:00							
8:00 – 9:00							
9:00 – 10:00							
10:00 – 11:00							
11:00 – 12:00							

Practices in Strategy 2: Comprehending What You Read

The following practices will help you develop the skills involved in distinguishing main ideas and supporting details, making inferences, recognizing bias, and marking textbooks, as discussed in Chapter 2.

PRACTICE 1

Directions: First, apply Strategy 1 by taking a minute to look over this passage. Then apply Strategy 2, looking for main ideas and support, making inferences where needed, identifying any bias (the author's or your own), and marking and underlining as you were shown. Answer the questions that follow the passage in the space provided.

(1) Company X is a large manufacturer of computer software products. If today you were to stroll through its lengthy corridors, you would see employees at every level—from technicians to senior executives—putting their thoughts down on paper. Systems analysts are writing instructions to programmers, who are laboring to distill their thoughts into neat, compact phrases. Marketing people are presenting surveys to product managers. People in technical communications are compiling information for a new product brochure. The company president and the chief financial officer are tearing apart a ten-page rundown of company finances. A network of communication, much of it written, extends from employee to employee, upwards, downwards, and sideways. This network also reaches beyond headquarters to Company X's West Coast subsidiary, to customers and potential customers, to suppliers, the media, and government agencies, and to many other people who this day are the audience for the ideas, messages, and explanations important to the company's operations.

(2) Company Y does not manufacture a product, but it does have something to sell. It is a successful service organization, and its business is employment. On this day, counselors and recruiters are spending a great deal of time on the phone contacting potential employers and setting up interviews to screen job candidates. They are also participating in interviews and conferences. Nevertheless, in offices up and down the halls, at any odd minute when people are alone, you will probably spot them writing—jotting memos to each other about new clients and rumors of job opportunities, corresponding with employers, and drafting reports to senior members of the firm about potential growth markets, new ideas for attracting clients, and the many other subjects that preoccupy them.

(3) Company Z is not a large firm. It is a family-owned enterprise that rents and sells uniforms to hospitals, laboratories, and other medical facilities. Its office and management staff includes about 30 people, and virtually half of them are "jacks-of-all-trades." Today Carol Taylor is out of the office, visiting a new bio-tech facility where she believes many new kinds of protective uniforms will be required. When Carol returns to the office, she will file a trip report to be read by her co-workers and retained in the company's active file. Her regular officemate, Peter Jones, is at his desk putting the finishing touches on a lengthy report about the company's current public relations and advertising tactics. This report is important to Peter because he knows that Bob and Joan Green, the firm's owners, will be reviewing his ideas about how to get the company's name mentioned in the newsletters of several of the city's larger hospitals.

(4) In these three settings we catch a glimpse of some of the activities that in our system of free enterprise we call business. But if we ourselves are not part of the daily business scene (and often even if we are) business may be only an abstraction. Economics textbooks tell us: "Business is the production of goods and services to be sold for a profit," and, of course, business is precisely that. But it is also the daily reality of the people who produce those goods and services, men and women who get up in the morning with specific ideas and tasks on their minds and head out their doors bent on "making a living" — exchanging time, energy, skill, and insights for wages or salaries. To perform effectively throughout their workday, they must share information, ideas, and opinions with one another. In short, they must communicate.

(5) If anything is obvious about today's business environment, it's that words have more importance and power than ever before. If we had started with A and described a different firm for each letter of the alphabet, we still would not have exhausted the almost limitless number of verbal interactions that businesses require of their employees during a single day of normal operations. Business people communicate to describe ideas, processes, products, and services.

(6) The size and intricacy of our business organizations have made communication more essential than ever before, and our technology has made it more abundant. Even a simple instrument like the telephone offers communications options that once would have seemed astonishing — messages relayed to new locations, conference calls across great distances, and many other possibilities. Today, when a manager has something to say, the means to say it quickly are almost always at hand.

(7) Even though spoken communication has increased, today's technological revolution has diminished neither the volume nor the frequency of written communication. The written word, whether typed onto paper or entered onto a terminal screen, continues to lie at the heart of business communication. As in the past, the operation of a business continues to demand that people express their ideas in words and transmit those words in a form that can be retained if necessary, usually with some degree of permanence. For most employees, this requirement makes writing a critical skill.

(8) Rather than decreasing the amount of writing and reading that employees face, modern technology has added to its abundance by increasing the ease and speed with which we can collect, store, and transmit data. The copying machine alone has revolutionized the way business communication is handled — not just the author of a document but anyone with access to a copier can easily retain or transmit the information that document contains. And the computer has, of course, made information management a whole new business discipline. Even small companies are likely to have memory typewriters and word-processing equipment, and large establishments commonly make use of terminal-to-terminal electronic mail and desktop computers that allow managers and employees to access enormous pools of information.

(9) No wonder that effective communication (and especially effective writing) is given such a high priority in today's business environment. Brevity and clarity are watchwords, and the favorite edict of programmers — "garbage in, garbage out" — can be taken as an admonition to all business people. Mangled ideas, snarled sentences, and muddy verbiage are wasted effort. Moreover, if sent to the wrong person or badly timed or tactless, even a clear and succinct message can be counted as waste.[1]

1. In what way are the first three paragraphs alike?

    _____

    _____

2. What point or idea do they support?

    _____

    _____

3. What is the main idea of paragraph 5?

    _____

    _____

4. What is the main idea of paragraph 6?

    _____

    _____

5. Is the topic of paragraph 7 spoken or written language?

    _____

6. Fill in this outline for paragraph 8:

    Topic: _____

    Main idea: _____

    _____

1. *Source:* Ruth G. Newman, *Communicating in Business Today.* Heath, 1987, 3–5.

Supporting details: _____

_____

_____

_____

_____

7. What is the main idea of the entire passage?

_____

_____

_____

8. What bias toward business communication does the author reveal?

_____

_____

_____

PRACTICE 2

Directions: First, apply Strategy 1 by taking a minute to look over this passage. Then apply Strategy 2, looking for main ideas and support, making inferences where needed, identifying any bias (the author's or your own), and marking and underlining as you were shown. Answer the questions that follow the passage in the space provided.

Business Writing: How Is It Different?

(1) As human beings, we think with words, and our thoughts move so swiftly that it is difficult to be conscious of the words that contain them. But writing alters this state. As we write, we make our thoughts visible and accessible; we can refine, revise, or expunge them. All writers, whether business writers or poets, are engaged in this process of capturing thoughts by carving them into words. Nevertheless, people put their thoughts into writing for very different reasons, and these differences are rooted in the writers' feelings about potential readers.

(2) For instance, people who write in their diaries are capturing memories and impressions, perhaps to savor them later but rarely to share them. Poets and novelists normally hope for an audience, but with or without one, they generally feel compelled to write. Two groups of writers, however, write exclusively to be read: journalists and business writers. For both of these, the effect their words have on an audience is critical. This similarity can provide some provocative insights into the pressures and challenges that confront business writers. Because they write for an audience, both reporters and business writers are greatly concerned about clarity; they know that their readers have limited time and many distractions. Furthermore, as writers, both reporters and business people are working under severe time constraints: they know the importance of deadlines. And finally, despite the pressures on them, both groups are highly accountable for their accuracy.

(3)   It is interesting to compare the *lead* of a news story to the tightly constructed opening of a well-written business memo. Both are digests of critical information that cater to the reader's need to know what will follow. And, in a sense, both are contracts between the writer and reader — promises that the indicated information will be the writer's primary focus. The lead can, for the same reasons, also be compared to the *executive summary*, which introduces a long report and provides a capsule of its contents for executives who must set priorities concerning what documents to read, how thoroughly, and in which order.

(4)   Despite such similarities, there is an important difference in the outlooks of reporters and business writers. For reporters, events and their own reactions to those events provide the primary motive for writing. But for business writers, concern for the reader's response is usually paramount. If you ask business people why they write, nine times out of ten the answers you receive will focus on the reactions of prospective readers. The reason for writing will be described in words such as these:

"Because I want to persuade *them* to . . ."
"Because I need to ask *them* to . . ."
"Because I want to sell *them* a . . ."
"Because we want *them* to understand our . . ."
"Because we would like *them* to explain their . . ."
"Because we would like *them* to attend our . . ."

(5)   More than any other kind of writers, business people try to know as much as possible about their readers. A simple profile generally will not suffice; they must have information about their readers' particular situations, interests, and needs. And since they write to people inside and outside their own organizations, to people they supervise, to peers, and to superiors, business writers do not always have easy access to this information. For instance, to plan an ad campaign or design a sales letter for a specific audience, a marketing specialist will spend time and resources learning about that audience's concerns. Similarly, almost any business writer will usually need to appraise his or her intended reader before writing.[2]

1. What is the main idea of the first paragraph?

    _____

    _____

2. How do the examples in paragraph 2 relate to paragraph 1?

    _____

    _____

2. *Source:* Newman, 5–6.

3. What comparisons are being made in paragraph 3?

_____

_____

_____

4. How does paragraph 4 relate to paragraph 3?

_____

_____

_____

5. Fill in this outline for the passage:

   Topic: _____

   Main idea: _____

   _____

   Supporting details:_____

   _____

   _____

   _____

6. On a separate sheet of paper, write a one-paragraph summary that contains the main idea of the passage and the key support.

PRACTICE 3

Directions: Apply the skills involved in Strategies 1 and 2 to this passage. Then answer the questions that follow the passage by circling the letter of the correct answer or filling in the blank as appropriate.

Fascination with the increasing degree to which questions about nature have been answered and the educational demands created by scientific discoveries and technological inventions have contributed to putting the humanities in crisis. In previous centuries the unquestioned focus of our educational system, the humanities must now justify their existence. Humanists (those who work in the humanities and related fields) must explain to themselves and to others the role they will or should play in a world preoccupied with controlling and manipulating nature for man's knowledge and welfare.

In recent years a different sort of criticism has arisen to challenge the humanities. It comes from certain religious individuals and groups who see humanists as atheists manipulating the educational system for the purpose of destroying religion. This criticism appears to equate, or to confuse, the traditional definitions of "humanists" and "humanism" with groups such as the American Humanist Association, or signers of the "Humanist Manifesto," groups that *do* profess secularism as a substitute for religion. Attacks against the influence of "humanism" in the schools focus on issues such as the teaching of evolution versus creationism, school prayer, and sex education. The antihumanists express their feelings in strong terms: one warns that the humanists are involved in "an ongoing battle, a battle for the mind that threatens the future of every pro-moral American." Another states simply: "Humanism is basically Satan's philosophy and program." Although such attacks and such concepts of humanism would seem to have little to do with the humanities, they do, by association, contribute to the ongoing discussion of the nature and the role of the humanities in our educational system and in our society.[3]

1. We can infer that the authors believe the humanities should receive as much attention in our educational system as science.
   a. True
   b. False
2. The authors are biased toward the role the humanities should play in our educational system and in our society.
   a. True
   b. False
3. We can infer that the authors are in agreement with such organizations as the American Humanist Association and the signers of the "Humanist Manifesto."
   a. True
   b. False
4. Humanists, according to the authors, are atheists.
   a. True
   b. False
5. Explain why you agree or disagree with the authors.

   _____

   _____

   _____

   _____

   _____

6. On a separate sheet of paper, write a one-paragraph summary that contains the main idea of the passage and the key support.

3. *Source:* Mary Ann Frese Witt et al., *The Humanities*, vol. 1, 2nd ed. Heath, 1985, 2.

PRACTICE 4

Directions: Read this passage from an American history textbook. Then answer the questions that follow it by filling in the blank as appropriate.

Despite the mind-sapping chatter of the "boob tube," Americans in the postwar era were better educated than ever before. The GI Bill of Rights paid the college fees of millions of veterans in the 1940s and 1950s, thus stimulating a vast expansion of higher education. By the 1980s the nation's colleges were graduating nearly a million degree-holders a year, and one person in every four in the twenty-five-to-thirty-four-year-old age group was a college graduate.

This expanding mass of educated persons lifted the economy to more advanced levels while creating consumers for "high culture." Americans annually made some 300 million visits to museums in the 1980s, boasted about a thousand opera companies, and 1,500 symphony orchestras. Despite television, Americans bought books in record numbers, especially after the "paperback explosion" of the 1960s, when more than a million volumes a day were being sold. Increasingly, and ironically, educated Americans were reading the lamentations of writers who were protesting against the same affluent postwar society that had made possible these very cultural gains.

Harvard sociologist David Riesman criticized postwar Americans as conformists in *The Lonely Crowd* (1950), as did William H. Whyte, Jr., in *The Organization Man* (1956). The novelist Sloan Wilson explored a similar theme in *The Man in the Gray Flannel Suit* (1955). Harvard economist John Kenneth Galbraith questioned the relationship between private enterprise and the public good in a series of books beginning with *The Affluent Society* (1958) and extending to *Economics and the Public Purpose* (1973).[4]

1. What is the main idea of the total passage?

   _____

   _____

   _____

   _____

2. What can you infer about the author's attitude toward television?

   _____

   _____

   _____

   _____

4. *Source:* David Kennedy et al., *The Brief American Pageant,* 2nd ed. Heath, 1989, 544.

3. What is ironic about what educated Americans were reading during the 1950s?

_____

_____

_____

_____

PRACTICE 5

Directions: Using the two study-reading strategies you have learned, read the following passage from a government report entitled *An Open Letter to the American People: A Nation at Risk.*[5] Then answer the questions that follow it, circling the letter or letters of the correct answer or filling in the blank as appropriate.

A Nation At Risk

Our Nation is at risk. Our once unchallenged pre-eminence in commerce, industry, science, and technological innovation is being overtaken by competitors throughout the world. This report is concerned with only one of the many causes and dimensions of the problem, but it is the one that undergirds American prosperity, security, and civility. We report to the American people that while we can take justifiable pride in what our schools and colleges have historically accomplished and contributed to the United States and the well-being of its people, the educational foundations of our society are presently being eroded by a rising tide of mediocrity that threatens our very future as a nation and a people. What was unimaginable a generation ago has begun to occur—others are matching and surpassing our educational attainments.

If an unfriendly foreign power had attempted to impose on America the mediocre educational performance that exists today, we might well have viewed it as an act of war. As it stands, we have allowed this to happen to ourselves. We have even squandered the gains in student achievement made in the wake of the Sputnik challenge. Moreover, we have dismantled essential support systems which helped make those gains possible. We have, in effect, been committing an act of unthinking, unilateral educational disarmament.

Our society and its educational institutions seem to have lost sight of the basic purposes of schooling, and of the high expectations and disciplined effort needed to attain them. This report, the result of 18 months of study, seeks to generate reform of our educational system in fundamental ways and to renew the Nation's commitment to schools and colleges of high quality throughout the length and breadth of our land.

That we have compromised this commitment is, upon reflection, hardly surprising, given the multitude of often conflicting demands we have placed on our Nation's schools and colleges. They are routinely called on to provide solutions to personal, social, and political problems that the home and other institutions either will not or cannot resolve. We must understand that these demands on our schools and colleges often exact an educational cost as well as a financial one. . . .

THE RISK

History is not kind to idlers. The time is long past when America's destiny was assured simply by an abundance of natural resources and inexhaustible human enthusiasm, and by our relative isolation from the malignant problems of older civilizations. The world is indeed one global village. We live

5. *Source:* 1982, 5–23.

among determined, well-educated, and strongly motivated competitors. We compete with them for international standing and markets, not only with products but also with the ideas of our laboratories and neighborhood workshops. America's position in the world may once have been reasonably secure with only a few exceptionally well-trained men and women. It is no longer.

The risk is not only that the Japanese make automobiles more efficiently than Americans and have government subsidies for development and export. It is not just that the South Koreans recently built the world's most efficient steel mill, or that American machine tools, once the pride of the world, are being displaced by German products. It is also that these developments signify a redistribution of trained capability throughout the globe. Knowledge, learning, information, and skilled intelligence are the new raw materials of international commerce and are today spreading throughout the world as vigorously as miracle drugs, synthetic fertilizers, and blue jeans did earlier. If only to keep and improve on the slim competitive edge we still retain in world markets, we must dedicate ourselves to the reform of our educational system for the benefit of all—old and young alike, affluent and poor, majority and minority. Learning is the indispensable investment required for success in the "information age" we are entering.

Our concern, however, goes well beyond matters such as industry and commerce. It also includes the intellectual, moral, and spiritual strengths of our people which knit together the very fabric of our society. The people of the United States need to know that individuals in our society who do not possess the levels of skill, literacy, and training essential to this new era will be effectively disenfranchised, not simply from the material rewards that accompany competent performance, but also from the chance to participate fully in our national life. A high level of shared education is essential to a free, democratic society and to the fostering of a common culture, especially in a country that prides itself on pluralism and individual freedom.

For our country to function, citizens must be able to reach some common understandings on complex issues, often on short notice and on the basis of conflicting or incomplete evidence. Education helps form these common understandings. . . .

INDICATORS OF THE RISK

The educational dimensions of the risk before us have been amply documented in testimony received by the Commission. For example:

- International comparisons of student achievement, completed a decade ago, reveal that on 19 academic tests American students were never first or second and, in comparison with other industrialized nations, were last seven times.

- Some 23 million American adults are functionally illiterate by the simplest tests of everyday reading, writing, and comprehension.

- About 13 percent of all 17-year-olds in the United States can be considered functionally illiterate. Functional illiteracy among minority youth may run as high as 40 percent.

- Average achievement of high school students on most standardized tests is now lower than 26 years ago when Sputnik was launched.

- Over half the population of gifted students do not match their tested ability with comparable achievement in school.

- The College Board's Scholastic Aptitude Tests (SAT) demonstrate a virtually unbroken decline from 1963 to 1980. Average verbal scores fell over 50 points and average mathematics scores dropped nearly 40 points.

- College Board achievement tests also reveal consistent declines in recent years in such subjects as physics and English.

- Both the number and proportion of students demonstrating superior achievement on the SATs (i.e., those with scores of 650 or higher) have also dramatically declined.

- Many 17-year-olds do not possess the "higher order" intellectual skills we should expect of them. Nearly 40 percent cannot draw inferences from written material; only one-fifth can write a persuasive essay; and only one-third can solve a mathematics problem requiring several steps.

- There was a steady decline in science achievement scores of U.S. 17-year-olds as measured by national assessments of science in 1969, 1973, and 1977.

- Between 1975 and 1980, remedial mathematics courses in public 4-year colleges increased by 72 percent and now constitute one-quarter of all mathematics courses taught in those institutions.

- Average tested achievement of students graduating from college is also lower.

- Business and military leaders complain that they are required to spend millions of dollars on costly remedial education and training programs in such basic skills as reading, writing, spelling, and computation. The Department of the Navy, for example, reported to the Commission that one-quarter of its recent recruits cannot read at the ninth grade level, the minimum need simply to understand written safety instructions. Without remedial work they cannot even begin, much less complete, the sophisticated training essential in much of the modern military.

These deficiencies come at a time when the demand for highly skilled workers in new fields is accelerating rapidly. For example:

- Computers and computer-controlled equipment are penetrating every aspect of our lives—homes, factories, and offices.

- One estimate indicates that by the turn of the century millions of jobs will involve laser technology and robotics.

- Technology is radically transforming a host of other occupations. They include health care, medical science, energy production, food processing, construction, and the building, repair, and maintenance of sophisticated scientific, educational, military and industrial equipment.

Analysts examining these indicators of student performance and the demands for new skills have made some chilling observations. Educational researcher Paul Hurd concluded at the end of a thorough national survey of student achievement that within the context of the modern scientific revolution, "We are raising a new generation of Americans that is scientifically and technologically illiterate." In a similar vein, John Slaughter, a former Director of the National Science Foundation, warned of "a growing chasm between a small scientific and technological elite and citizenry ill-informed, indeed uninformed, on issues with a science component."

But the problem does not stop there, nor do all observers see it the same way. Some worry that schools may emphasize such rudiments as reading and computation at the expense of other essential skills such as comprehension, analysis, solving problems, and drawing conclusions. Still others are concerned that an over-emphasis on technical and occupational skills will leave little time for studying the arts and humanities that so enrich daily life, help maintain civility, and develop a sense of community. Knowledge of the humanities, they maintain, must be harnessed to science and technology if the latter are to remain creative and humane, just as the humanities need to be informed by science and technology if they are to remain relevant to the human condition. Another analyst, Paul Copperman, has drawn a sobering conclusion. Until now, he has noted:

> Each generation of Americans has outstripped its parents in education, in literacy, and in economic attainment. For the first time in the history of our country, the educational skills of one generation will not surpass, will not equal, will not even approach, those of their parents.

It is important, of course, to recognize that the average citizen today is better educated and more knowledgeable than the average citizen of a generation ago—more literate, and exposed to more mathematics, literature, and science. The positive impact of this fact on the well-being of our country and the lives of our people cannot be overstated. Nevertheless, the average graduate of our schools and colleges today is not as well-educated as the average graduate of 25 or 35 years ago, when a much smaller proportion of our population completed high school and college. The negative impact of this fact likewise cannot be overstated.

HOPE AND FRUSTRATION

Statistics and their interpretation by experts show only the surface dimension of the difficulties we face. Beneath them lies a tension between hope and frustration that characterizes current attitudes about education at every level.

We have heard the voices of high school and college students, school board members, and teachers; of leaders of industry, minority groups, and higher education; of parents and State officials. We could hear the hope evident in their commitment to quality education and in their descriptions of outstanding programs and schools. We could also hear the intensity of their frustration, a growing impatience with shoddiness in many walks of American life, and the complaint that this shoddiness is too often reflected in our schools and colleges. Their frustration threatens to overwhelm their hope.

What lies behind this emerging national sense of frustration can be described as both a dimming of personal expectations and the fear of losing a shared vision for America.

On the personal level the student, the parent, and the caring teacher all perceive that a basic promise is not being kept. More and more young people emerge from high school ready neither for college nor for work. This predicament becomes more acute as the knowledge base continues its rapid expansion, the number of traditional jobs shrinks, and new jobs demand greater sophistication and preparation.

On a broader scale, we sense that this undertone of frustration has significant political implications, for it cuts across ages, generations, races, and political and economic groups. We have come to understand that the public will demand that educational and political leaders act forcefully and effectively on these issues. Indeed, such demands have already appeared and could well become a unifying national preoccupation. This unity, however, can be achieved only if we avoid the unproductive tendency of some to search for scapegoats among the victims, such as the beleaguered teachers.

On the positive side is the significant movement by political and educational leaders to search for solutions—so far centering largely on the nearly desperate need for increased support for the teaching of mathematics and science. This movement is but a start on what we believe is a larger and more educationally encompassing need to improve teaching and learning in fields such as English, history, geography, economics, and foreign languages. We believe this movement must be broadened and directed toward reform and excellence throughout education.

EXCELLENCE IN EDUCATION

We define "excellence" to mean several related things. At the level of the *individual learner*, it means performing on the boundary of individual ability in ways that test and push back personal limits, in school and in the workplace. Excellence characterizes a *school or college* that sets high expectations and goals for all learners, then tries in every way possible to help students reach them. Excellence characterizes a *society* that has adopted these policies, for it will then be prepared through the education and skill of its people to respond to the challenges of a rapidly changing world. Our Nation's people and its schools and colleges must be committed to achieving excellence in all these senses.

We do not believe that a public commitment to excellence and educational reform must be made at the expense of a strong public commitment to the equitable treatment of our diverse population. The twin goals of equity and high-quality schooling have profound and practical meaning for our economy and society, and we cannot permit one to yield to

the other either in principle or in practice. To do so would deny young people their chance to learn and live according to their aspirations and abilities. It also would lead to a generalized accommodation to mediocrity in our society on the one hand or the creation of an undemocratic elitism on the other.

Our goal must be to develop the talents of all to their fullest. Attaining that goal requires that we expect and assist all students to work to the limits of their capabilities. We should expect schools to have genuinely high standards rather than minimum ones, and parents to support and encourage their children to make the most of their talents and abilities.

The search for solutions to our educational problems must also include a commitment to life-long learning. The task of rebuilding our system of learning is enormous and must be properly understood and taken seriously: Although a million and a half new workers enter the economy each year from our schools and colleges, the adults working today will still make up about 75 percent of the workforce in the year 2000. These workers, and new entrants into the workforce, will need further education and retraining if they—and we as a Nation—are to thrive and prosper.

THE LEARNING SOCIETY

In a world of ever-accelerating competition and change in the conditions of the workplace, of ever-greater danger, and of ever-larger opportunities for those prepared to meet them, educational reform should focus on the goal of creating a Learning Society. At the heart of such a society is the commitment to a set of values and to a system of education that affords all members the opportunity to stretch their minds to full capacity, from early childhood through adulthood, learning more as the world itself changes. Such a society has a basic foundation the idea that education is important not only because of what it contributes to one's career goals but also because of the value it adds to the general quality of one's life. Also at the heart of the Learning Society are educational opportunities extending far beyond the traditional institutions of learning, our schools and colleges. They extend into homes and workplaces; into libraries, art galleries, museums, and science centers; indeed, into every place where the individual can develop and mature in work and life. In our view, formal schooling in youth is the essential foundation for learning throughout one's life. But without life-long learning, one's skills will become rapidly dated.

In contrast to the ideal of the Learning Society, however, we find that for too many people education means doing the minimum work necessary for the moment, then coasting through life on what may have been learned in its first quarter. But this shouldn't surprise us because we tend to express our educational standards and expectations largely in terms of "minimum requirements." And where there should be a coherent continuum of learning, we have none, but instead an often incoherent, outdated patchwork quilt. Many individual, sometimes heroic, examples of schools and colleges of great merit do exist. Our findings and testimony confirm the vitality of a number of notable schools and programs, but their very distinction stands out against a vast mass shaped by tensions and pressures that inhibit systematic academic and vocational achievement for the majority of students. In some metropolitan areas basic literacy has become the goal rather than the starting point. In some colleges maintaining enrollments is of greater day-to-day concern than maintaining rigorous academic standards. And the ideal of academic excellence as the primary goal of schooling seems to be fading across the board in American education.

Thus, we issue this call to all who care about America and its future: . . . America is at risk.

. . . [It has to] reverse the current declining trend—a trend that stems more from weakness of purpose, confusion of vision, underuse of talent, and lack of leadership, than from conditions beyond our control.

1. Why do the authors of this report claim that our nation is at risk?
   a. Foreign powers are undermining our educational system.
   b. We are using up our natural resources without regard for the future.
   c. The lead the United States once held over world competitors in commerce, industry, and science has given way to mediocrity.
   d. We can no longer take pride in our educational system.
2. If an unfriendly power had attempted to impose on America the mediocre educational performance that exists today, we might well have viewed it as an

_____.

3. According to the authors, America's position in the world is
   a. no longer secure with only a few exceptionally well-trained men and women.
   b. still secure but beginning to decline.
   c. secure, based on the changes taking place in the educational system.
   d. not being threatened by competition for international standing and its share of the marketplace.
4. Which of the following are some of the indicators of our nation being at risk?
   a. International comparisons of student achievement on nineteen academic tests indicate that American students, never first in comparison with other industrialized nations, were last seven times.
   b. Some 23 million American adults are functionally illiterate.
   c. About 13 percent of all seventeen-year-olds in the United States are functionally illiterate.
   d. The College Board's SAT results demonstrate a virtually unbroken decline since 1963.
   e. Between 1975 and 1980, remedial math courses in public four-year colleges increased by 72 percent.
5. Concerned educational experts claim that knowledge of the humanities must be connected to science and technology if both areas are to remain relevant to the human condition.
   a. True
   b. False
6. The average graduate of our schools and colleges today is not as well educated as the average graduate of _____ years ago.

7. More and more young people emerge from high school ready for
   a. work but not college.
   b. college but not the work force.
   c. neither college nor work.
   d. none of the above
8. Explain how the authors define *excellence* in each of the following areas:

   a. **individual learner:** _____

   _____

   _____

   _____

   _____

   b. **school or college:** _____

   _____

   _____

   _____

   _____

   _____

   c. **society:** _____

   _____

   _____

   _____

   _____

9. The authors claim that educational reform should focus on the goal of creating a "Learning Society." What do they mean by this?

    _____

    _____

    _____

    _____

    _____

Practices in Strategy 3: Processing What You Read

The following practices will help you develop the skills involved in learning and applying what you read in Chapter 3 about Strategy 3: Processing What You Read. Some of the exercises require that you apply Strategies 1 and 2 as well.

PRACTICE 1

A. *Directions:* First, apply the skills in Strategy 1 by previewing or exploring the passage from a psychology textbook on the following pages.[1] Second, apply the skills involved in Strategy 2, marking the passage as you look for main ideas and supporting details.

B. Now apply the skills in Strategy 3 by writing up reading notes on a separate sheet of paper, using the outline-summary method.

PRACTICE 2

Directions: On a separate sheet of paper, make a one-page map of the textbook passage in Practice 1.

---

1. *Source:* Mark K. Holland, *Introductory Psychology.* Heath, 1981, 100–105.

Retaining What is Learned

Many students suffer memory lapses during exams, failing to remember material that they thought they had "down cold." Do you have difficulty remembering what you have read or heard in lecture? Even though you have learned and understand some important principles, retaining them can often be a challenge.

Levels of Processing and Encoding

According to the **levels-of-processing theory** (see Chapter 4), we analyze and process information at different levels—some "shallow" and some "deep"—and this determines how well we can remember things. Shallow levels of processing are involved when we listen to or read material with only half of our attention on the task. Shallow processing also occurs during rote memorization—that is, mindlessly repeating a definition over and over with little thought about

what the words mean. This "shallow" type of study is called **maintenance rehearsal.**

Greater depth of processing is involved when we actively think about what the words mean and when we try to relate new information to already-acquired information. Studying by going over meanings, associations, applications, and relationships requires greater depth of processing. This "deep" type of study is called **elaborative rehearsal.**

Teaching a concept or theory to someone else requires considerable depth of processing; in order to effectively explain an idea to another person, you must understand it fairly well yourself and must be prepared to answer questions about it. One way to improve your memory for material you are learning is to try to teach it to your friend, your mother, or your roommate.

Another way to achieve depth of processing is to paraphrase the definition or theory you are trying to learn. The act of putting it into your own words requires that you process the information deeply, at the meaning level. Try writing down the principle or concept in your own words. This kind of active working with the material ensures adequate depth of processing and thereby strengthens the way the material is encoded in memory.[4]

Encoding Specificity and Retrieval

Suppose you were taking an examination on this chapter and were asked the following fill-in type question:

As a technique for remembering a definition, word-for-word repetition is usually less effective than paraphrasing, according to the _____ theory.

How were you able to remember that the answer called for was "levels of processing?" In answering a question like this, you must retrieve previously learned material from memory. Your ability to retrieve information depends upon retrieval cues. A **retrieval cue** is something that helps you find information in memory. In the fill-in question above, the words in the question are retrieval cues because they help point to the answer called for. A problem for students is that the retrieval cues provided by instructors in exam questions are often either too different or too brief to be of much help. Sometimes, however, there is considerable overlap between the material as originally learned and the retrieval cues available at the time of testing. For example, you might have learned that "Psychology is the science of behavior." Later, on a quiz, you may have the test item, "_____ is the science of behavior." In this case there would be a complete overlap between the information available at the time of learning and the information (retrieval cues) available at the time of testing. The words you studied and the words in the exam question are exactly alike and completely overlap.

According to the **encoding-specificity principle,** the effectiveness of retrieval cues depends upon the degree of overlap between the information presented at the time of learning a concept and the information available later when you are trying to remember it.[5] Memory is best when the information encoded at the time of learning is the same as the information presented at the time of testing.

What are the implications of the encoding-specificity principle for academic learning and retention? As a student in a class, you have little control over the way questions are asked on examinations, and therefore you cannot make sure that exam questions are phrased according to the way you studied the material. You do, however, have control over the way material is encoded during the learning process. You can increase the likelihood of an overlap between the information given during the learning time and that given at testing time by thinking of questions to ask yourself about the material you are learning and by thinking of applications for this material. The questions and the applications you think of are likely to resemble the questions and applications that will appear on exams. Therefore, the exam questions will be more effective retrieval cues, and you will be better able to remember the material learned.

Overlearning

You may have had the experience of having had a principle or theory "down cold" the night before an exam and then failing to remember it during the exam. You apparently had not learned the material as well as you thought you had. This problem results from practicing the material only until you just barely learn it. Material that is just barely learned is vulnerable to forgetting.

Because of forgetting, learning the material is not enough. You must overlearn it. **Overlearning** involves continuing to study material for a while after you feel you have mastered it. You must assume that you will forget some of the material between the time you last study something and the time you are tested on it. When you study something just until you feel you know it, you will often forget it later. By overlearning the material, you give yourself a margin for forgetting.

Interim Summary   The levels-of-processing theory and the encoding-specificity principle point to ways that you can improve your retention of what you read and study.   According to the levels-of-processing theory, the information that we encounter as we study is processed at different levels.   Information processed at shallow levels—for example, through maintenance rehearsal—is not retained very well.   Information processed at deeper levels—for example, through elaborative rehearsal—is retained better and for longer periods.   According to the encoding-specificity principle, the ease with which memories can be retrieved for exams depends upon the similarity between the conditions of study and the conditions of the test.   Memory is best when the information present at the time of learning a concept is available during the test in the form of a retrieval cue.   Finally, memory is better if material is overlearned, since you need a margin for forgetting.

Learning from Lectures

In most college courses, the classroom is the learning center, the focus of instruction.   Success in college courses requires certain skills in learning from lectures.   Classroom lectures are designed not only to stimulate thought and to provide important facts and principles, but also to present information necessary for progress through the course: what to read and when, when exams are given, what the exams will cover, and so on.   For some students, however, coping with lectures can be a serious problem: they have difficulty keeping up, staying awake, or maintaining effective class notes.

Selective Attention and Active Listening

Attending a lecture will guarantee that the words spoken will reach your ears but will not guarantee that these words will be processed, understood, and remembered.

The human mind is limited in its capacity to attend to several things at once.   In general, we can attend to only one thing at a time, a process called **selective attention**.   Thus, in a lecture, we have the capacity to attend to the person sitting next to us but not—at the same time—to what is being said in lec-ture.   We have the capacity to attend to a daydream about a favorite person but not—at the same time—to the context of the lecture.

We can selectively listen to the lecture or to a conversation occurring behind us, but it is extremely difficult, if not impossible, to listen to both.   Our ability to tune in to different conversations occurring around us is quite remarkable.   Try to remember the last time you were at a party or in a crowded room with everyone talking at once.   You were able to attend to any one of several conversations without turning around or otherwise moving.   This feature of selective attention is called the **cocktail-party phenomenon**.

The cocktail-party phenomenon works to your disadvantage in a lecture class.   It is easy to tune out the lecture and tune in something else.   The problem is that you then will not recall what was said in lecture.   A research demonstration of this principle can be found in the studies of selective attention that involve **dichotic listening**.   Dichotic listening is a procedure in which an individual is given earphones playing two different messages, one in one ear and a different one in the other ear.   Such studies show that it is possible to remember one message or the other but not both.[6]   Other studies showed that it was not possible to read and listen effectively at the same time; individuals who were asked to try to do both were

Studying with the television on is highly inefficient. Studies show that people cannot effectively read and listen at the same time, so listening to the television must interfere with your efforts to pay attention to your books. (Richard Chase)

later able to remember what they read, or what they heard, but not both.[7]

In a large lecture, it's easy for your mind to wander. On occasion you may even have to struggle to keep yourself from dozing off. Keeping alert, paying attention, and listening are frequently difficult. One step toward improving your listening is to recognize that listening is not a passive reaction that you have to a speaker who is somehow responsible for "making you" listen or "capturing" your attention. Instead, listening is a skill; it is an activity , something that you *do*—either well or poorly. And it is not a skill you are born with (or without) but is learned, acquired through practice.

The key to *active listening* is to formulate and answer questions as you listen to what the speaker has to say. For example, you could start at the beginning of a lecture by asking yourself, "What is the lecturer going to talk about today?" Then you could continue by asking yourself, "What are the major points?" Or you could ask yourself, "Why did the

lecturer say that? What evidence is there for believing that?" Asking the instructor questions during lecture, if appropriate, can also be helpful. Taking an active approach to listening is also a way of keeping alert and interested during lectures.

The Encoding and Storage Function of Notes

Taking good notes from lecture is an important part of active listening. Notes serve two main functions: (1) an encoding function, in which the lecture is transformed into material more easily remembered; and (2) an external storage function, in which the content of the lecture is retained for later review. Aside from the benefit of using lecture notes as an aid to memory when preparing for an exam, taking notes appears to strengthen memory for the lecture material. The physical act of writing down your version of the main points covered will help you later, even if you never look at your notes again.

One experimenter compared the effect of several note-taking conditions.[8] One group of students did not take notes, but later reviewed the lecture mentally. On a subsequent test, this group showed the least recall. Another group of students took notes and later reviewed them. This group showed the most recall. In a second study, students listened to a lecture while (*a*) taking no notes, (*b*) taking notes, or (*c*) having a lecturer-generated summary.[9] Those students who kept their own notes and later reviewed them had the highest recall scores.

One reason that note taking helps is that it necessitates greater depth of processing. Research on the levels-of-processing theory shows that material that is dealt with at the meaning level (the semantic level) is better remembered than material dealt with at levels that require less analysis (for example, simply listening to what is said without understanding its meaning).

According to the levels-of-processing theory of memory, taking lecture notes that require paraphrasing main points serves to encode the major ideas of the lecture in memory more deeply and more permanently. Going over the notes by thinking of the relationships between the new material that was presented and what you already know further strengthens your memory. Paraphrasing and placing the new material within different contexts of meaning is a form of elaborative rehearsal, which has been demonstrated to be highly effective for retention.

Some students make the mistake of trying to write down everything that is said in a lecture. In the first place, you really won't be able to do this very well because you can't write fast enough. In the second place, trying to do this would distract you from listening to the lecture. Finally, even if you could do this, you will not have time later to go over the entire lecture word for word. Your notes should be a summary of the major points, facts, and principles that are covered. The best notes are highly selective and are taken in some form of outline.[10] Later, when you review what was said, you should go over these notes and extract from them an even simpler summary of main points. This process of review and summation is also an effective memory aid. Compare the two sets of notes shown in Figures 5-2 and 5-3.

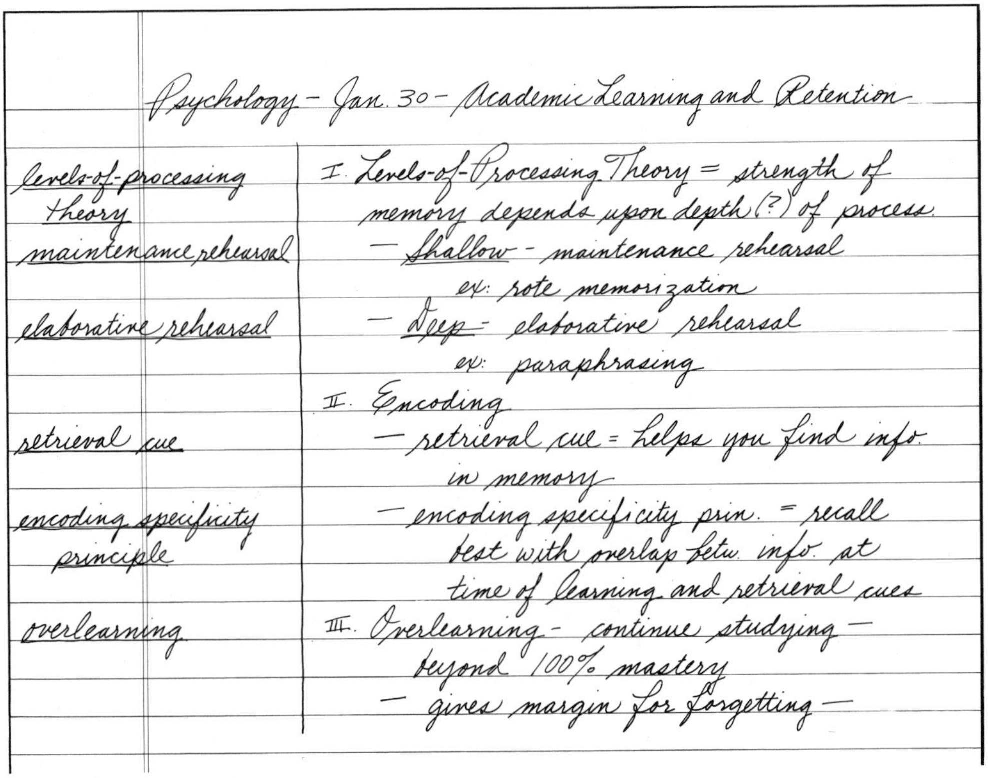
Psychology – Jan. 30 – Academic Learning and Retention
levels-of-processing theory
maintenance rehearsal
elaborative rehearsal
retrieval cue
encoding specificity principle
overlearning
I. Levels-of-Processing Theory = strength of memory depends upon depth (?) of process.
– Shallow – maintenance rehearsal
ex: rote memorization
– Deep – elaborative rehearsal
ex: paraphrasing
II. Encoding
– retrieval cue = helps you find info. in memory
– encoding specificity prin. = recall best with overlap betw. info. at time of learning and retrieval cues
III. Overlearning – continue studying – beyond 100% mastery
– gives margin for forgetting –

Figure 5-2 Effective lecture notes.

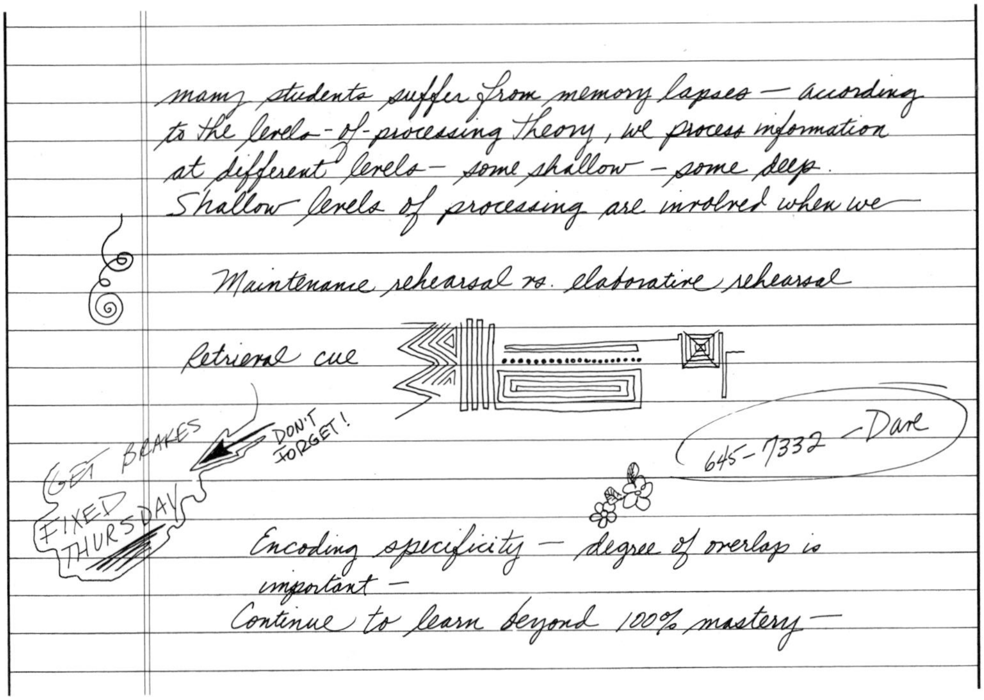
many students suffer from memory lapses – according to the levels-of-processing theory, we process information at different levels – some shallow – some deep. Shallow levels of processing are involved when we
Maintenance rehearsal vs. elaborative rehearsal
Retrieval cue
GET BRAKES FIXED THURSDAY
DON'T FORGET!
645-7332 – Dave
Encoding specificity – degree of overlap is important –
Continue to learn beyond 100% mastery –

Figure 5-3 Ineffective lecture notes.

PRACTICE 3

A. *Directions:* First, apply the skills in Strategy 1 by previewing or exploring this passage from a composition textbook.[2] Second, apply the skills involved in Strategy 2, marking the passage as you look for main ideas and supporting details.

B. *Directions:* Now apply the skills in Strategy 3 by writing up reading notes on a separate sheet of paper, using the outline-summary method or the mapping technique.

◆ COMPUTERS AND THE WRITING PROCESS

The computer is an essential tool in the workplace. Almost every type of business relies heavily on computers to generate, store, retrieve, and transmit information. Based on computer technology, the automated office today is likely to have word processors, microcomputers, teleconferencing equipment, fax machines, and even voice synthesizers that recognize and translate sounds into writing. Computers increase efficiency, save time, lower costs, and streamline the process of receiving and sending messages.

Knowing how to use a word processor is a requirement for most jobs. Em-

---

2. *Source:* Philip C. Kolin, *Successful Writing at Work*, 3rd ed. Heath, 1990, 35–40.

ployees either have word processors at their desks or have access to them. Gone are the days when you could do everything in longhand or on a typewriter and then turn over a rough copy to a secretary to edit and produce the finished product. Since you will most likely have access to a word processor, your employer will expect you to create, revise, and print a professional-looking document.

There are a variety of computers on the market, but common to all of them are an illuminated display screen (or monitor), a keyboard, a memory component using a computer chip, and a printer. These parts are known as the *hardware;* the various programs used to give instructions to the computer are known as the *software.* Various software programs will allow you to perform word processing, create graphics, and do accounting ledgers.

The word processor has been misleadingly called a typewriter with a memory. It is more than that; with a typewriter you are stuck with what you type on a given sheet of paper, and if you do not like it you have to start over. With a word processor you can make a large number of changes on a thin, flexible magnetic disk or on the computer's hard disk. The word processor saves what you want to keep while it makes room on the disk for any additions, deletions, or corrections. You are spared the drudgery of retyping a page each time you make a change or a mistake.

With the computer, the appropriate software, and a printer, you can make the following changes any time and anywhere in your document:

- insert or delete words, sentences, paragraphs
- move around lines or entire paragraphs
- search for and replace a word or phrase
- copy part of something in the document or in another document stored in the computer
- design and insert visuals
- use boldface or italic print; change the size of lettering; center headings and put information into columns
- set tabs and margins
- check and verify spelling and punctuation

Since you can watch all these changes on your screen, you will be able to visualize the writing process at work. You are thus able to interact with the text you are creating on the screen. And at any stage in the process you can *scroll* your document—roll the text up or down on the screen—to view different parts of the document.

The word processor assists you in every phase of the writing process by making it easier to complete. When you are prewriting, a word processor can help you to move items in your outline or brainstormed list quickly to organize them into categories. You might even use some of the software packages designed to generate and organize information so you can identify ideas easily. When you draft your document, the word processor can help you get some writing on the monitor screen quickly. In doing this the word processor keeps pace with the speed of your thought process. You will not have to worry about the time-consuming drudgery of having to return a typewriter carriage after every line or of retyping successive drafts. You do not have to stop to check spelling or punctuation since you can return to these matters later. And if you run into a snag on any draft, you do not have to stop to fix it and lose momentum. With a single stroke on the keyboard, the word processor will flag items that you want to return to or need more information about. During drafting and revising, some writers in fact move back and forth between a hard copy (the paper copy run off by the printer) and the text on the screen.

When you are revising, the word processor assists you in refining and refocusing your thoughts. Using a word processor can actually encourage you to make revisions since they can be accomplished easily and quickly. Again, you will be relieved of the burden of retyping what you want to save each time you make a change or spot an error. Since you can rearrange words, sentences, and paragraphs, or even the appearance of material, you can experiment with a number of versions of your work without having to type each separately. Some software packages even allow you to split your monitor screen into two or four parts (*windows*) to view different versions of a text or several pages of the text simultaneously. From that perspective you will be able to select the best version of a paper or format for your audience and also to see how a revision on one page might affect another page of your text. Finally, a word processor allows you to print a clean copy at any stage; it is always easier to catch errors on a clean copy than on a marked-up one.

The word processor was created with the needs of the business world in mind. It becomes an invaluable link in any collaborative writing venture; all you have to do is share your disk with a coworker, who can make changes on the disk and then return it to you. And if the boss asks you to change a word or two in the middle of a letter, add a new paragraph, or reverse the order of some paragraphs after seeing your "final" copy, you do not have to do the whole thing over. You can make these changes quickly and have a revised copy ready in no time. Figure 2.6 shows a letter an employee drafted on a word processor and on which her boss made a number of changes in wording, format, and content. Using the appropriate software, the employee was able to create the revised letter seen in Figure 2.7. If she had mailed the first draft, her reader very likely would not have been impressed with the company's professionalism and would have thought twice about placing an order. The revised final version of the letter is much more effective in its presentation of the material, in its individualized address, and in its formatting. Good writers benefit from constructive criticism of their drafts and know how to make effective changes during the revision process. In this example the employee benefited from the criticism of her boss. The final copy is the result of the suggested revisions.

Unquestionably, the word processor is a wonderful tool that will help you to increase and improve your writing. But it will not do your writing for you. You may use a software package to help organize your ideas, although you must first do research to discover what ideas are relevant for your audience. The word processor will enable you to produce more writing, but you are the one who must select the right words with appropriate tone and put them into readable sentences and logically organized paragraphs. As we saw, the word processor can greatly assist you in making revisions, but again you must decide what must be

38 CHAPTER 2 The Writing Process at Work

FIGURE 2.6 A draft of a letter prepared on a word processor and edited by an employer.

November 15, 1989

Terry Tatum
Manager
Consolodated Industries *i*
Houston, TX *add zip code*

Dear ~~Sir,~~ *Terry Tatum:*

Thank you for asking ~~I am taking the opportunity of answering your request~~ for a price list of Servitron products. Servitron has been in business in the Houston area for more than ~~twenty-two~~ *22* years and we offer unparalleled equipment and service to ~~any customer~~ *Consolidated Industries*. Utilizing a Servitron will *can* give you both efficiency and economy. *boldface*

Whatever model Servitron you choose carries with it a full one-year warranty *boldface* on all parts and labor. After the expiration date of your warranty you ~~should~~ *might* purchase our service contract for $75.00 a year.

~~Here are the models Servitron offers~~ *add boldface headings*

Zephyr	81072	$ 459.95
Colt	86085	$ 629.95
Meteor	88096	$ 769.95

Depending on your needs, one of these models should be right for you.

If I might be of further assistance to you, please call on me. *add phone number* I am also enclosing a brochure giving you more information, including specifications, on these Servitron products. *reverse the order of these two sentences*

~~Truly,~~ *Sincerely yours,*

SERVITRON *leave 4 spaces*
Randy Taylor
Sales Associate

FIGURE 2.7   The edited, final copy of Figure 2.6.

November 15, 1989

Terry Tatum
Manager
Consolidated Industries
Houston, TX 77005-0096

Dear Terry Tatum:

Thank you for asking for a price list of Servitron products. Servitron has been in business in the Houston area for more than 22 years and we can offer unparalleled equipment and service to Consolidated Industries. Utilizing a Servitron will give you both **efficiency** and **economy.**

Depending on your needs, one of these models should be right for you.

Model Name	Number	Price
Zephyr	81072	$459.95
Colt	86085	$629.95
Meteor	88096	$769.95

Whatever model Servitron you choose carries with it a **full one-year warranty** on all parts and labor. After the expiration date of your warranty you might purchase our service contract for $75.00 a year.

I am also enclosing a brochure giving you more information, including specifications, on these Servitron products. If I might be of further assistance to you, please call me at 580-1689.

Sincerely yours,

SERVITRON

Randy Taylor

Randy Taylor
Sales Associate

revised and how. And never be lulled into thinking that a clean, professionally printed document will hide or make up for incorrect content or poor writing.

◆ FOUR BASIC POINTS ON USING A WORD PROCESSOR

Throughout this book you will find a number of suggestions on how a word processor can help you to write better. But here are four basic points to help you escape some computer users' nightmares.

1. Give yourself adequate time to learn to operate your word processor and any software packages your employer uses. Read the manuals. A few hours of trial and error testing is time well spent.
2. Press the SAVE command every 10–15 minutes or you risk wiping out hours of hard work. Some word processors do so automatically.
3. Make a hard (paper) copy as a backup so that if an electrical storm knocks out the power or you make a keyboard error you will have a written record of your work. Also make a daily backup disk copy of your file.
4. Keep your disks away from magnetized surfaces (e.g., microwave ovens) and heat since these can destroy what you have recorded.

PRACTICE 4

Directions: On a separate sheet of paper, map the textbook passage in Practice 3.

PRACTICE 5

Directions: On a separate sheet of paper, map the passage from the business text on pages 23–24.

PRACTICE 6

Directions: On a separate sheet of paper, apply all three study-reading strategies to a chapter from one of your other textbooks. When you apply Strategy 3, select whatever method for taking reading notes you prefer.

Practices in Strategy 4: Proving You Understand

The following practices will help you develop the skills involved in mastering Strategy 4: Proving You Understand, as discussed in Chapter 4.

PRACTICE 1

Directions: Pretend that you are studying for a test in a business communications class. You will be tested on chapters that cover pages 19–240. Using the index from the book on page 300, answer these questions.[1]

1. Circle the letters of the subjects that you should review for the test.
   a. acceptance letters
   b. audience
   c. brevity in letters and memos
   d. cause and effect relationships
   e. clarity in writing
   f. coherence
   g. oral communication
   h. comparisons
   i. computers
   j. courtesy letters

2. What should you do if some of the items seem unfamiliar? Write your answer in the space provided.

_____

_____

_____

_____

_____

1. *Source:* Ruth G. Newman, *Communicating in Business Today.* Heath, 1987, 621.

INDEX

PRACTICE 2

Directions: Read this passage, applying the skills that make up the first three general study-reading strategies: (1) preview the passage; (2) read for main ideas and supporting details, marking as you read; (3) make reading notes in your journal.

Train Your Memory to Commit Itself

"I studied hard, but when I took that quiz, I couldn't remember a thing." "I knew the answer, but . . ." "How can the teacher expect us to remember all this stuff?" "I can't say it, but it's on the tip of my tongue." "I don't remember that ever being taken up in class." "I knew it cold yesterday, but today—."

Familiar remarks, aren't they? We've heard and expressed similar ones many times. And every time we've made such a statement, we've probably wished for a better memory; for the ability to recall what we assumed we once knew; for a mind, not a sieve. You are convinced, rightly, that a better memory would help you get better grades in any course you're taking.

Like the mind, memory is not an organ of the body. It is the mental capacity to recognize previous events and experiences, the faculty to retain and revive impressions and ideas of whatever kind. When we remember, we "recall," or "think of again," or "keep in mind," or "remain aware of." When we forget, we "cease to remember," or "fail to recollect," or are "unable to recall." Without memory, each of us would be a social and mental infant. Without the stored and shared memory of mankind, the world would be a savage wilderness.

No one possesses a perfect memory or even one that is regularly adequate. Everyone forgets. But some people apparently have better memories than others. We envy such persons and wish we could do something to improve our own. But can one improve his or her memory?

Psychologists and other students of mental processes generally agree that there is no such thing as a bad memory. Such a conclusion is shocking to everyone who uses his poor memory as an excuse for shortcomings and failures. It is an even greater blow to those who seem to pride themselves on their defective memories, somewhat as others are proud of their illegible handwriting. And yet there is such a thing as an "untrained memory." This is what everyone has who frequently lacks the ability to hold in mind what needs to be held. If your memory is not so much bad as it is untrained, how do you go about making it more efficient?

These suggestions may be useful:

1. *Make up your mind to remember.* As with several other approaches to studying, a determination, a mental set, an act of will is essential. If you "learn" something today, thinking that surely it will be gone from your mind by tomorrow or the next day, it probably will be. You must force yourself to want to remember. The motivation for, and interest in, remembering may be to avoid embarrassment, or feel more competent and assured in performing daily tasks, or getting higher grades. Whatever it is, it must be real and apparent to you. If you are fed up with your poor memory and determined to improve it, you are on your way. It is impossible to remember things one is not interested in remembering.

2. *You must "get" something before you can "forget" it.* When we say "I forgot" what we should be saying is "I never learned it in the first place." It is easy to get a snapshot impression of something, think we have it in mind, and fail to develop, print, and mount the picture. To remember something we must react positively and actively. We must really look, listen, stop, and think about anything we intend to get and keep in our minds. Observation and memory—close observation and good memory—go hand in hand.

Speed can be an enemy of memory, just as it can be (and often is) of reading or using a dictionary or any of several other approaches to study. You are wise, not stupid and not slow, when you take ample time to get something firmly fixed in mind. (Remember the fable of the tortoise and the hare.) If memory is an art as well as a skill, then that art depends upon the act of attention, of concentration. You can't expect to remember if you keep thinking "My mind is on something else." You can't remember unless you concentrate and take the necessary time to respond actively to what you're learning. You cannot forget something you've never really learned. Nor can you forget, except temporarily, anything you have genuinely mastered.

3. *Keep refreshing your memory.* Everything we learn tends to fade from our minds unless we keep bringing it back into consciousness. Some event from your childhood you can recollect in every detail—provided you have thought about it enough times since it happened. But how about thousands of other happenings that must have occurred of which you have no recollection? You probably know the multiplication table perfectly, but you wouldn't if you had learned it in elementary school and totally neglected it from then on.

Memory is not a camera which, snapped once, registers a permanent image. The three R's especially apply to reviewing, but they also have a direct bearing on our ability to remember: *read* (or see or do), *recite* (say to yourself or others), and *repeat* (continue the process). When reading a textbook, apply the three R's to each main point. Then repeat the act after you have completed a chapter. Memory depends far more upon attention and repetition than it does upon intelligence.

4. *Organize what you want to remember.* Experienced students of mental processes claim that the more you remember, the more you can remember. One's memory is like a muscle that can be trained, shaped, and exercised but cannot be overtrained. True, one's memory can become muscle-bound if it is required to retain numerous ideas, facts, and impressions that are unorganized and jumbled. Method (organization, outlining, structuring) may be called the "secret" of memory. William James once wrote:

> The one who thinks of his experiences most and weaves them into systematic relation with each other will be the one with the best memory.

In whatever you are studying, pick out main points—and only main points—and discard everything else. Then arrange these main points in a meaningful pattern or outline. Then, and only then, recite and repeat until you really "have" what you're trying to fix in mind. It is a misguided and hopeless practice to attempt to remember everything in an assignment or entire course of study. Select, organize, repeat—this is a time-tested, rarely failing process for remembering.

MEMORY TRICKS

Some persons have a remarkable ability to remember certain kinds of things such as telephone numbers, faces, names, dates, addresses, and the like. Others with phenomenal memories seem to rely, consciously or unconsciously, on various aids to memory. Memory experts who give public exhibitions use many and varied "tricks" to make their performances possible. It is likely, however, that most of us can improve our memories best by following the four suggestions already given.

One further comment should be made: What we remember most clearly is consciously or unconsciously associated with something known and remembered. That is, the surest means of remembering is through association. We are familiar with this fact: an odor "reminds" us of a place, event, or person with whom we instantly associate that odor. Some scene reminds us of something from our past. A person's face will cause us to recollect someone we knew years ago.

The memory device known as mnemonics is an aid in spelling. This aid is based on association: if you want to remember to spell *dessert* with a double *s*, associate the word with strawberry sundae and its two *s*'s. Such association, or linking, has applications other than in spelling.

For instance, if you want to remember the names of the Great Lakes, think of "homes" that dot their shores: *H*uron, *O*ntario, *M*ichigan, *E*rie, and *S*uperior. If you want to remember that you have twelve tasks to perform today, think of "month." If you need to remember that a certain river is 3365 miles long, associate its length with "year." A man whose initials are H.L. has no difficulty in recalling the five ingredients that he thinks make for happiness: he puts "ace" between his initials and readily recites the linked words "health, achievement, contrast, expectation, and love."

Such association, or linking, can be based on mental pictures that even appear ridiculous. On several occasions while studying U.S. history, the author attempted to learn the names of the presidents, in order. He never tried very hard and never succeeded. But several years ago, he learned them perfectly in ten minutes through a nonsense series of linkings:

Adam (*Adams*) was the first man but the second president after *Washington*. These two had a little dog named Jeff (*Jefferson*) who went mad (*Madison*). They got their "mon" (money, *Monroe*) and took him to the vet, Dr. *Adams*. The vet took their "Jack" (money, *Jackson*) and put it in a van (*Van Buren*). He then grabbed his son Harry (*Harrison*), tied (*Tyler*) him in a poke (*Polk*), and took him to a tailor (*Taylor*). The tailor's shop was filled (*Fillmore*) with stuff, but he calmly kept on piercing (*Pierce*) a buckskin (*Buchanan*) with his needle. He then got his *Lincoln* out of the garage, called his son, John (*Johnson*), and drove off without granting (*Grant*) a hello (*Hayes*) to his wife who was in the fields (*Garfield*). They picked up a boy named *Arthur* and drove toward *Cleveland*, where they stayed in the Hotel *Harrison* outside of *Cleveland*.

They then set off for Mt. *McKinley*, where they saw *Roosevelt* leading a group up the slopes with fat *Taft* lumbering behind. They couldn't see *Wilson* very well because it was hard (*Harding*) to make things out in the cool (*Coolidge*) fog. So they left and went on to the *Hoover* Dam, on which they saw sitting a man with a cigarette holder in his mouth (*Roosevelt*), a true man (*Truman*), a fellow named Ike (*Eisenhower*), a youngster named Ken (*Ken-*

nedy), and a boy named John (*Johnson*) who kept saying "nix" (*Nixon*). (Then they drove home in a *Ford*.)

Of course this sketch is silly, but time and again it has proved an infallible memory aid to the author at parties and among friends generally. It "makes no sense," but it is a method of linkage helpful in recalling a series of names. A scheme of your own composition will help you recall lists of ideas, formulas, dates, series of facts, or whatever needs recalling. Your method of linking can be sensible or nonsensical, as you please. But letting one item develop from the preceding one is an invaluable memory "trick." Try it.

A reliable memory will be an asset all your life. A good time to start developing and strengthening yours is right now when you need it in your quest for better grades. And as you work on training your memory, follow these steps:

1. Find a reasonable motive for wanting to remember.
2. Make up your mind to remember.
3. Take your time.
4. Really see what you look at.
5. Say it to yourself.
6. Write it in your own words.
7. Say or write it again.
8. Repeat the process.
9. Again.
10. And again.[2]

Set I: Objective Questions

A. *Directions:* Do not look back for answers. In the spaces provided, write *T* for true statements and write *F* False for false statements.

1. Some people possess a perfect memory.   _____

2. Like the mind, memory is not an organ of the body.   _____

3. There is no such thing as a bad memory.   _____

4. One of the keys to developing a better memory is to make up your mind to remember.   _____

5. Before you can forget something, you first have to know it.   _____

6. A relationship exists between the three R's of the SQ3R study-reading formula and what the author says about memory development.   _____

B. *Directions:* Circle the letter of the best answer or answers to the questions that follow.

7. Which of the following are suggestions for developing a better memory that appear in the textbook passage?
   a. Make up your mind to remember.
   b. You have to learn something before you can really forget it.
   c. Organize what you want to remember.

2. *Source:* Harry Shaw, *30 Ways to Improve Your Grades*. McGraw, 1976, 70–76.

  d. Keep refreshing your memory.

  e. none of the above

 8. Mnemonics refers to

  a. memory.

  b. memory devices.

  c. SQ3R.

  d. the ability to remember faces.

  e. all of the above

 9. Which of the following are examples of mnemonic devices?

  a. SQ3R

  b. association

  c. linking

  d. nonsensical stories

  e. all of the above

10. The author provides _____ steps for training your memory.

  a. 12

  b. 10

  c. 8

  d. 4

Set II: Essay Questions

Directions: On a separate sheet of paper, answer one of the following questions in a short essay. You may look back at the reading.

1. Summarize the main ideas on training memory offered in the passage.
2. Evaluate the information provided, discussing its relevance to you as a student and why you intend to use or not use it.
3. Discuss the four major suggestions for training your memory.
4. Comment on your reaction to the passage.

Source: Reprinted by permission of UFS, INC.

PRACTICE 3

Directions: Read this summary from an introductory textbook for a computer course, applying the skills that make up the first three general study-reading strategies: (1) preview the passage; (2) read for main ideas and supporting details, marking as you read; (3) make reading notes in your journal.

We solve problems every day. For a computer to solve a problem, not only must the solution be very detailed, it must be written in a form the computer can understand. An algorithm is a procedure for solving a problem. It is a step-by-step set of instructions that, if carried out, exactly solves the problem. While a computer follows instructions very rapidly, it does only and exactly what it is told. Algorithms are used to design these very specific instructions.

A program is an algorithm written in a programming language so that the algorithm can be carried out by a computer.

Learning to design algorithms and write programs is important for a number of reasons. First, the process of carefully designing an algorithm for a computer is a critical thinking technique that can be applied to any problem. Learning to design algorithms is not just a computer skill, it is a life skill. Second, no matter how many programs have been written, more are required to meet the needs of a changing world. Third, to make effective use of many of the most popular software packages, the user needs to develop a series of instructions to tailor the package to individual needs. Knowing how to design algorithms makes this process very straightforward.

Two different techniques are commonly used for designing algorithms. A flowchart is a pictorial method of depicting an algorithm in which the focus is on the program's logical flow. Pseudocode, on the other hand, is a written method using English phrases and formulas in outline form to indicate the step-by-step instructions necessary for solving a problem.

Large, complex tasks are unmanageable if attacked directly. Top-down analysis is a technique for breaking down problems into subtasks. These subtasks can be further divided, if necessary, until each subtask can be solved directly.

There are six steps needed to effectively design programs. They are: (1) Define the problem, (2) Define the output, (3) Define the input, (4) Define the initial algorithm, (5) Refine the algorithm, and (6) Define the program. The first five of these steps can be used to solve any problem in any field and are unrelated to computers.

Research in the artificial intelligence area of natural language processing is attempting to teach computers to speak and understand human languages such as English. Should such natural-language processing become commonplace, we would have no need for computer languages. However, we would still need to develop algorithms. Regardless of what language computers speak, they will still be machines requiring very detailed instructions.[3]

Set I: Objective Questions

A. *Directions:* Do not look back for answers. In the spaces provided, write *T* for true statements and *F* for false statements.

1. An algorithm is a very specific set of instructions.   _____

2. Carefully designing an algorithm requires critical thinking.   _____

3. There are three different techniques commonly used for designing algorithms.   _____

4. Learning to design algorithms is a computer skill.   _____

5. Top-down analysis of a problem is a technique for breaking down tasks into subtasks.   _____

---

3. *Source:* Helene G. Kershner, *Introduction to Computer Literacy.* Heath, 1990, 173.

B. *Directions:* Circle the letter of the best answer or answers to the questions that follow.

6. Which of the following is the best definition of an algorithm?
   a. An algorithm is a computer programming language.
   b. An algorithm is a pseudocode or written method using English phrases and formulas in outline form to indicate to the computer how to carry out an activity.
   c. An algorithm is a procedure for solving a problem.
   d. all of the above
7. Which of the following statements are true?
   a. A program is an algorithm written in a programming language so that the algorithm can be carried out by a computer.
   b. Algorithms are used to develop a series of instructions to make software packages usable.
   c. Once artificial intelligence can teach computers to speak and understand human languages, there will be no more need for algorithms.

Set II: Essay Questions

Directions: On a separate sheet of paper, answer one of the following questions in a short essay. You may look back at the reading.

1. Explain the difference between an algorithm and a computer program.
2. Give three reasons for the importance of learning to design algorithms.
3. Explain the techniques commonly used to design algorithms.

PRACTICE 4

Directions: On a separate sheet of paper, write an essay that explains the four general study-reading strategies.

WHAT DO YOU THINK?

But it seems to me that most of the human beings whose lives have stirred us and whom we admire are people who dedicated themselves not to the elementary pleasures, but to something noble, something fine, something that reaches beyond. Some encounter with necessity is the ground of taking one's life seriously. It's the ground of being sensitive to all of the really beautiful things in the world. It's the ground of being open to the call of something higher in which we have a chance to participate, whether it be perpetuation of our young, whether it be the arts or philosophy or music. And it's the ground, really, of transforming what is otherwise a mere necessity into an occasion of something really splendidly human.

Leon R. Kass, biologist and philosopher

Practices in Learning the Language of the Social Sciences

The practices in this section are related to the work you did in Chapter 5. They will help you understand the vocabulary of the social sciences, as well as increase your general vocabulary.

It is possible that building your vocabulary skills will benefit you more than any of the other reading skills discussed in this book. Although learning to explore accurately and to analyze writing patterns is very important for better comprehension, these skills are meaningless if you do not understand the vocabulary used in your reading.

Do not attempt to do too many of these practices at once. Before you leave one exercise, be certain you know the words in it that you didn't know before. Learn from your mistakes.

PRACTICE 1

Directions: Read this passage, and answer the questions that follow it in the space provided.

At the start of this chapter, we saw that scientific theories must be testable. Theories predict or prohibit certain things that can be checked by research. Put another way, theories direct us to examine certain things and they predict what we shall find. **Research** is the process of making systematic observations. Thus, researchers test a theory by comparing the results of their observations with those predicted and prohibited by the theory.

The testable statements derived from theories are *hypotheses*. **Hypotheses** are specific predictions about the empirical or observable world. While theories are general and abstract, hypotheses are specific and concrete. For example, a portion of micro sociological theory tells us that, *within human groups strong attachments to others will result in conformity to the norms while weak attachments will result in nonconformity*. That is a very general statement. It applies to all groups, all people, all attachments, and the norms of all groups. To test such a statement, we must formulate specific predictions. That is, we must deduce hypotheses that define where we should look and what we expect to find.[1]

---

1. *Source:* Rodney Stark, *Sociology*, 2nd ed., Wadsworth, 1987, 73.

1. How is *research* defined in this passage?

    _____

    _____

2. What are *hypotheses*?

    _____

    _____

3. What are *theories*?

    _____

    _____

4. What is the difference between *theories* and *hypotheses*?

    _____

    _____

PRACTICE 2

Directions: Read this paragraph and answer the questions that follow it in the space provided.

"Cow towns" like Abilene, Ellsworth, and Dodge City were as riotous and as venal as any mining camp. A local merchant characterized Abilene as a "seething, roaring, flaming hell"; its saloons, bearing names like Alamo, Applejack, Longhorn, and Old Fruit, were packed during the season with crowds of rambunctious, gun-toting pleasure seekers. Gambling houses and brothels abounded. When Ellsworth, Kansas, had a population of only a thousand, it had 75 resident professional gamblers. At dance halls like Rowdy Joe's, the customers were expected to buy drinks for themselves and their partners after each dance. Little wonder that McCoy wrote in his *Historic Sketches of the Cattle Trade* (1874): "Few more wild, reckless scenes of abandoned debauchery can be seen on the civilized earth than a dance hall in full blast in one of these frontier towns."[2]

1. Circle the words that indicate an attitude toward "cow towns."
2. What is meant by *cow town*?

    _____

3. Based on its context, what does the word *venal* mean?

    _____

2. *Source:* John A. Garraty, *The American Nation*, 4th ed., vol. 2, Harper, 1989, 439.

4. What other word or phrase could be used instead of *rambunctious*?

   _____

5. What is meant by "resident professional gamblers"?

   _____

6. Explain the phrase "reckless scenes of abandoned debauchery."

   _____

   _____

PRACTICE 3

Directions: Read this paragraph, and answer the questions that follow it in the space provided.

> The Indians, to their misfortune, stood in the path of the American settlers. Like the blades of mighty scissors, two lines of onward-moving pioneers were closing in simultaneously—one from the Pacific Coast, the other from the trans-Mississippi East. A clash was inevitable between an acquisitive civilization and a traditional culture, as the march of modernity crushed under its feet the hunting grounds and hence the food supply of the native inhabitants.[3]

1. Explain the phrase "like the blades of mighty scissors." Who or what is being compared to the scissor blades?

   _____

   _____

2. Who is being called "an acquisitive civilization" and who "a traditional culture"?

   _____

3. What does the author mean by "the march of modernity"?

   _____

   _____

4. In one sentence, explain the point of the passage.

   _____

   _____

3. *Source:* Thomas A. Bailey and David M. Kennedy, *The American Pageant*, 8th ed. Heath, 1987, 557.

PRACTICE 4

Directions: As you read this paragraph, circle the words in it that are *not* being used literally. Then answer the questions that follow it in the space provided.

> Washington, late in 1940, finally imposed the first of its embargoes on Japan-bound supplies. This blow was followed in mid-1941 by a "freezing" of Nipponese assets in the United States and a cessation of all shipments of gasoline and other sinews of war. As the oil gauge dropped, the squeeze on Japan grew steadily more nerve-racking. Protracted delay was on the side of the United States. Japanese leaders were faced with two painful alternatives. They could either knuckle under to the Americans or break out of the embargo ring by a desperate attack on the oil supplies and other riches in Southeast Asia. The ticking of the clock, while soothing to American ears, drove the Japanese to madness.[4]

1. Explain the following words or phrases as used in the passage:

   a. "Washington" _____

   b. "'freezing' of assets" _____

   c. "the oil gauge dropped" _____

   d. "the squeeze" _____

   e. "knuckle under" _____

   f. "ticking of the clock" _____

2. Based on the paragraph, what is an *embargo*?

   _____

   _____

PRACTICE 5

Directions: Read this paragraph, and answer the questions that follow it in the space provided.

> Less justifiable on grounds of efficiency was the technique of "horizontal integration," which simply meant consolidating with competitors to monopolize a given market. Rockefeller was a master of this stratagem. He perfected a device for controlling bothersome rivals—the "trust." Stockholders in various smaller oil companies assigned their stock to the board of directors of Rockefeller's Standard Oil Company. It then consolidated and concerted the operations of the previously competing enterprises. "Let us prey" was said to be Rockefeller's unwritten motto. Ruthlessly wielding vast power, Standard Oil soon cornered virtually the entire world petroleum market. Weaker competitors, left out of the trust agreement, went to the wall. Rockefeller's stunning success inspired

4. *Source:* Bailey, 789.

many imitators, and the word *trust* came to be generally used to describe any large-scale business combination.[5]

1. How does the author define a "trust"?

   _____

2. What are some other definitions of the word *trust*?

   _____

   _____

3. What does Rockefeller's motto, "Let us prey," mean?

   _____

   _____

4. What is meant by the statement "Weaker competitors . . . went to the wall"?

   _____

   _____

PRACTICE 6

Directions: As you read this paragraph, circle the words in it that have strong connotational or emotional appeal. Then answer the questions that follow it in the space provided.

> These are the times that try men's souls: The summer soldier and the sunshine patriot will, in this crisis, shrink from the service of his country; but he that stands it NOW, deserves the love and thanks of man and woman. Tyranny, like hell, is not easily conquered; yet we have this consolation with us, that the harder the conflict, the more glorious the triumph. What we obtain too cheap, we esteem too lightly: 'Tis dearness only that gives every thing its value. Heaven knows how to put a proper price upon its goods; and it would be strange indeed, if so celestial an article as FREEDOM should not be highly rated. Britain, with an army to enforce her tyranny, has declared that she has a right (not only to TAX) but "to BIND us in ALL CASES WHATSOEVER," and if being bound in that manner, is not slavery, then is there not such a thing as slavery upon earth. Even the expression is impious, for so unlimited a power can belong only to God.[6]

1. Place your circled words with favorable and unfavorable connotations in the appropriate columns.

5. *Source:* Bailey, 514.
6. *Source:* "The Crisis Papers," from *Selected Work of Tom Paine and Citizen Paine*, ed. Howard Fast. Modern Library, 1945, 43.

	Favorable	*Unfavorable*
	_____	_____
	_____	_____
	_____	_____
	_____	_____
	_____	_____
	_____	_____

2. What does Paine mean by "the summer soldier and the sunshine patriot"?

   _____

   _____

   _____

3. How does Paine make good use of the words *hell*, *heaven*, and *God*?

   _____

   _____

   _____

PRACTICE 7

Directions: There are probably times when you read or hear a word whose meaning you think you know. Yet when you try to define it, you can't. This practice provides an opportunity to see how many words from social science textbooks you can define in your own words. First, write out definitions to the words you think you know; then use a dictionary to look up all the words, comparing your answers with the dictionary definitions.

	Your definition	*Dictionary definition*
1. anarchy	_____	_____
2. suffrage	_____	_____
3. imperialism	_____	_____
4. arbitration	_____	_____
5. abolition	_____	_____
6. inalienable	_____	_____
7. communism	_____	_____

	Your definition	*Dictionary definition*
8. socialism	_____	_____
9. capitalism	_____	_____
10. reactionary	_____	_____
11. liberal	_____	_____
12. prejudice	_____	_____
13. diplomacy	_____	_____
14. dictatorship	_____	_____
15. depression	_____	_____
16. bureaucracy	_____	_____
17. nationalism	_____	_____
18. confiscate	_____	_____
19. monetary	_____	_____
20. conservative	_____	_____

PRACTICE 8

Directions: Select the proper word from the following alphabetical list to fill in the blank in each sentence. Use your dictionary if you need to.

appropriation	inflation
artisans	judiciary
authority	mediator
bureaucrat	pagans
caucus	proclamation
consumer	Reformation
dynasty	Renaissance
Industrial Revolution	testimony

1. The missionaries wanted the _____ to wear more clothing.

2. One group of Mexican _____ still uses the techniques of handicraft its ancestors used thousands of years ago.

3. The party leaders held a _____ to decide who their next candidate would be.

4. He was as poor a leader as the other members of the _____ that had reigned for years.

5. After the _____, factories were built and people moved to the cities.

6. One sign of _____ is a continual rise in prices.

7. Congress's _____ of large amounts of money for the space program was generally favored.

8. The _____ is the branch of our government that decides on the constitutionality of laws.

9. A _____ was called in to help settle the strike.

10. The _____ was an important movement during the sixteenth century that resulted in the formation of various Protestant churches.

11. From the respectful attitude of the congressmen, one could tell that this public figure commanded _____.

12. The selling success of any product ultimately depends on the

_____.

PRACTICE 9

Directions: In the questions that follow, circle the letter of the word or phrase that most closely defines the italicized word.

1. If a king *abdicates*, he
   a. assumes full command.
   b. trusts no one.
   c. resigns.
2. When a criminal is given *amnesty*, he is
   a. executed.
   b. pardoned.
   c. allowed special privileges.
3. An *amoral* person is one who has
   a. no sense of moral responsibility.
   b. much sense of moral responsibility.
   c. love for his homeland.
4. An *anarchic* ruler would
   a. cause chaos in government.
   b. satisfy the people's demands.
   c. have little power or control.
5. An *Anglo-American* is someone whose heritage is a combination of
   a. African and American.
   b. German and American.
   c. English and American.
6. *Anthropology* is the study of
   a. human beings.
   b. animals.
   c. ancient times.
7. Something dated *ante-Christian* would be
   a. against Christian principles.
   b. before the Christian Era.

   c.   after Christ.
8. An *alienated* person feels
   a.   rootless, wants to travel.
   b.   shiftless, restless.
   c.   estranged, powerless, worthless.
9. If you feel *apathetic* when you see a car hit a dog, you
   a.   laugh.
   b.   feel nothing emotionally.
   c.   cry.
10. When someone is called an *aristocrat*, it means he is
   a.   a member of a small privileged class.
   b.   an acrobatic performer.
   c.   a snob.
11. An *atheist* believes in
   a.   no god.
   b.   many gods.
   c.   God, but not Christ.
12. If a legislature is *bicameral*, it
   a.   consists of four branches.
   b.   consists of two branches.
   c.   consists of one branch.
13. To a lawyer, a *brief* is a
   a.   trial of short duration.
   b.   client.
   c.   concise statement of a case.
14. The *Bronze Age* follows the
   a.   Space Age.
   b.   Ice Age.
   c.   Stone Age.
15. *Canon law* refers to
   a.   church laws.
   b.   wartime laws.
   c.   ancient laws no longer in effect.
16. To *capitulate* is to
   a.   yield or surrender.
   b.   use your capital for further gains.
   c.   capture.
17. If a political party is *conservative*, it tends to be
   a.   concerned with changing things.
   b.   opposed to much change.
   c.   concerned with national forests.
18. If you are granted *franking* privileges by the post office, you can
   a.   send letters without charge.
   b.   send bulk mail at cheaper rates.
   c.   open a substation in your area.
19. An *edict* is
   a.   a building.
   b.   an obituary.
   c.   an official proclamation.
20. If you are a member of the *electoral college*, your function is to
   a.   elect the president and vice president of the United States.
   b.   run for office.
   c.   learn about voting rights and privileges.
21. If you are *indicted* for murder, you are
   a.   convicted.
   b.   charged.

    c. freed.
22. A *liberal politician* is one who
    a. belongs to the Republican party.
    b. is broad-minded, not restricted to policy.
    c. is extremely active.
23. If you are given a *mandate*, you get
    a. an acre of land.
    b. a fruit.
    c. an order.
24. If you are a *partisan* of a political party, you are a
    a. follower.
    b. foe.
    c. principal leader.
25. If you are tried for *sedition*, you are accused of
    a. owning slaves.
    b. treason.
    c. forming business monopolies.

PRACTICE 10

Directions: Select any words you are having trouble learning or remembering and make vocabulary flash cards for them. Get some three-by-five-inch cards. On one side, print the word you want to learn. On the other side, write the definition and a sentence using the word in context. Practice learning each word by looking at the front side of the card, pronouncing the word, and giving its definition. Then check the back side to see if you are correct. Keep adding cards to your stack, practicing them over and over. You may want to pair up with someone and practice this technique.

Practices in Reading the Social Sciences

The practices in this section will help you develop the comprehension skills necessary for successful study-reading in the social sciences as presented in Chapter 6. The practices begin with short passages from social science textbooks and end with an entire chapter.

PRACTICE 1

Directions: Read this paragraph from a book on childhood development. Look for the topic being discussed, the main idea, and the writing pattern. Then answer the questions that follow it by circling the letter of the correct answer or filling in the blank as appropriate.

> Researchers have further observed that children in the middle childhood period, and some older children and adults as well, often endorse moral standards which they do not necessarily follow (Alston, 1971) and that both children and adults do not always behave in ways that they think best (Hoffman, 1984). The fact is, how a person decides to behave in any given situation is influenced not only by moral reasoning but also by the behavior of others, by one's personality characteristics, and by the standards of society. For example, most school-age children know that cheating is wrong, and they can usually explain why it is, evidencing an intellectual awareness of the issues involved. Nevertheless, when their peers put pressure on them to cheat or when they do not think that they will be caught, some of them do cheat.[1]

1. What is the topic of the paragraph?

   _____

2. The main idea of this paragraph is stated in the
   a. first sentence.
   b. second sentence.
   c. third sentence.
   d. last sentence.
3. What writing pattern is used to support the main idea?
   a. comparison and contrast
   b. definition
   c. cause and effect
   d. example

---

1. *Source:* Edward F. Ziegler and Martia Finn-Stevenson, *Children.* Heath, 1987, 539.

4. What key words help you recognize the writing pattern?

_____

PRACTICE 2

Directions: As you read this passage from a sociology textbook, look for the topic, the main idea, and the writing pattern used. Then answer the questions that follow it by circling the letter of the correct answer or filling in the blank as appropriate.

Whereas American youth think that getting a job and getting married entitle them to independence, the case is quite different in many other societies. In old India, Ireland, China, and Japan, for example, the authority of the parent tended to continue until death. The end of adolescence did not mean a significant change in authority, and hence the adolescent phase, for that reason at least, did not stand apart as a separate period. In addition, there was little conflict over authority, not only because complete emancipation did not occur, but also because such emancipation as did occur developed by well-grooved, mutually accepted, publicly ritualized steps.

In modern society, by contrast, the child is supposed to become completely emancipated from the parental power, but the exact time, manner, and cause of such emancipation remain uncertain, a subject of dispute, recrimination, and remorse. The individual may become a full-fledged wage earner as early as childhood or as late as adulthood. Marriage often is postponed so long that there tends to arise a distinction between the adolescent and the unmarried adult. Neither employment nor matrimony, therefore, may be accepted as a standard criterion of emancipation. There is no such standard criterion. Each family must virtually settle the matter for itself as a result of private interaction. This in spite of the fact that the emancipation, once it does come, is relatively more complete than in most societies.[2]

1. What is the topic of the passage?

_____

2. What is the primary writing pattern used?
    a. definition
    b. example
    c. cause and effect
    d. comparison and contrast

3. What is the function of the first paragraph?

_____

4. What is the function of the second paragraph?

_____

2. *Source:* Harry C. Bredemeier and Jackson Toby, *Social Problems in America.* Wiley, 1972, 145.

5. What key words signal the writing pattern used?

_____

PRACTICE 3

Directions: This passage is from a sociology textbook. As you read it, look for the topic, the main idea, and the writing pattern used. Practice your marking techniques as you read. Then answer the following questions, circling the letter of the correct answer or filling in the blank as appropriate.

Crazes or fads, such as flagpole sitting, are instances of what sociologists call collective behavior. For a behavior to be classified as collective, each of the following elements must be present:

1. The act must be unusual.
2. The action must be taken by a group of people, not by lone individuals.
3. The people involved must influence one another in some way.
4. This influence must occur with little or no planning, and there must be little or no organization of the group.

Shipwreck Kelly was an out-of-work sailor and movie stuntman. One day in 1924 he hit upon flagpole sitting as a scheme for making money. It worked like this. When he sat on a flagpole crowds gathered and the news media gave him publicity. Therefore, sponsors would pay him to publicize a product, a new building, a fair—anything that could profit from a publicity gimmick. Soon he was able to earn $100 a day, a huge sum at that time. In his best year, 1929, he spent a total of 145 days on top of flagpoles and earned about $29,000. He wasn't really so crazy. It was the lure of money, too, that drew Hold 'em Joe and others to copy Shipwreck's novel actions.

Let's see how flagpole sitting fits the definition of collective behavior. First, the actions of flagpole sitters are unusual. That's why they attract so much public attention. If thousands of Americans celebrated every Fourth of July by sitting on their flagpoles, flagpole sitting would not be unusual. Instead of collective behavior, it would merely be behavior governed by custom and tradition. Second, Shipwreck was not the only person who sat on flagpoles; a number of people did so. Third, the flagpole sitters influenced one another. Hold 'em Joe and the others took up flagpole sitting when they saw that Shipwreck was on to a good thing. Soon they competed with one another for records of height and duration. Finally, the flagpole sitters never did get together to plan future activities, and they never formed a flagpole sitters' organization. Thus, all four characteristics of collective behavior apply to flagpole sitting.[3]

1. What is the function of the first paragraph?
   a. to define crazes or fads
   b. to define behavior
   c. to define collective behavior
   d. to introduce flagpole sitting

---

3. *Source:* Rodney Stark, *Sociology*, 2nd ed. Wadsworth, 1987, 547.

2. What is the function of the second paragraph?

_____

3. The third paragraph defines collective behavior.
   a. True
   b. False, because _____
4. The main idea of the third paragraph is expressed in the first sentence.
   a. True
   b. False, because _____
5. What key transition words in the third paragraph are also used to support the definition given in the first paragraph?

_____

_____

PRACTICE 4

Directions: This passage is from a history textbook. Practice marking as you read for the main idea and supporting details. Then answer the questions that follow, circling the letter of the correct answer or filling in the blank as appropriate.

More than any other single factor, the railroad network spurred the amazing industrialization of the post–Civil War years. The puffing locomotives opened up fresh markets for manufactured goods and sped raw materials to the factory. The forging of the rails themselves provided the largest single backlog for the adolescent steel industry.

The screeching iron horse likewise stimulated mining and agriculture, especially in the West. It took farmers out to their land, carried the fruits of their toil to market, and brought them their manufactured necessities. Clusters of farm settlements paralleled the railroads, just as earlier they had followed the rivers.

Railways boomed the cities and played a leading role in the great cityward movement of the last decades of the century. The iron monsters could feed enormous concentrations of people and at the same time ensure them a livelihood by providing both raw materials and markets.

Railroad companies also stimulated the mighty stream of immigration. Seeking settlers to whom their land grants might be sold at a profit, they advertised seductively in Europe and sometimes offered to transport the newcomers free to their farms.

Finally, the railroad, more than any other single factor, was the maker of millionaires. A raw new aristocracy, consisting of "lords of the rail," replaced the old southern "lords of the lash." The multiwebbed lines became the playthings of Wall Street; and colossal wealth was amassed by stock speculators and railroad wreckers.[4]

1. The passage deals with a historic cause and effect. What is the cause being discussed?
   a. "lords of the rail" versus "lords of the lash"
   b. the railroad network of the post–Civil War years
   c. the adolescent steel industry
   d. none of the above; the cause is _____

4. *Source:* Thomas A. Bailey and David M. Kennedy, *The American Pageant,* 8th ed. Heath, 1987, 510.

2. What are the major effects mentioned?

   _____

   _____

   _____

   _____

   _____

3. What words or phrases are used to refer to the railroads and trains?

   _____

   _____

PRACTICE 5

Directions: This passage is from a history textbook. Practice marking as you read it for the main idea and supporting details. Then answer the following questions, circling the letter of the correct answer or filling in the blank as appropriate.

The wage earner felt the full force of the tide, being affected in countless ways—some beneficial, others unfortunate. As industry became more important in the United States, the number of industrial workers multiplied rapidly: from 885,000 in 1860 to more than 3.2 million in 1890. While workers lacked much sense of solidarity, they exerted a far larger influence on society at the turn of the century than they had in the years before the Civil War. More efficient methods of production enabled them to increase their output, making possible a rise in their standard of living. Yet an unskilled worker still could not maintain a family decently by his own efforts. And the weight of the evidence indicates that industrial workers did not receive a fair share of the fruits of economic growth. Nevertheless, it is incontestable that materially most workers were improving their condition.

On the other hand, industrialization created problems for those who toiled in the mines, mills, and shops. When machines took the place of human skills, jobs became monotonous. Mechanization undermined both the artisans' pride and their bargaining power vis-à-vis their employers. As expensive machinery became more important, the worker seemed of necessity less important. As businesses grew larger, personal contact between employer and hired hand tended to disappear. Relations between them became less human, more businesslike and ruthless. The trend toward bigness also seemed to make it more difficult for workers to rise from the ranks of labor to become themselves manufacturers, as Andrew Carnegie, for example, had done during the Civil War era. Moreover, industrialization tended to accentuate swings of the business cycle. On the upswing something approaching full employment existed, but in periods of depression unemployment became a problem, striking workers without regard for their individual abilities. It is significant that the word unemployment (though not, of course, the condition itself) was a late-19th-century invention.[5]

1. What is the topic of this passage?
   a. the worker at the turn of the century
   b. industrialization
   c. mechanization in industry
   d. improved working conditions
2. The passage mentions some positive and negative effects of industrialization on the wage earner. List the important comparisons here:

Positive effects	*Negative effects*
_____	_____
_____	_____
_____	_____
_____	_____
_____	_____
_____	_____
_____	_____

3. The passage is mostly
   a. fact, because _____
   b. opinion, because _____

PRACTICE 6

Directions: This passage was written by a historian who witnessed a Nazi rally in Nuremberg, Germany, in 1934, when Adolf Hitler was gaining popularity. As you read it, look for statements of fact and opinion. Remember that an opinion is not necessarily a false statement. Then answer the following questions, circling the letter of the correct answer or filling in the blank as appropriate.

I'm beginning to comprehend, I think, some of the reasons for Hitler's astounding success. Borrowing a chapter from the Roman church, he is restoring pageantry and colour and mysticism to the drab lives of twentieth-century Germans. This morning's opening meeting in the Luitpold Hall on the outskirts of Nuremberg was more than a gorgeous show; it also had something of the mysticism and religious fervour of an Easter or Christmas Mass in a great Gothic cathedral. The hall was a sea of brightly coloured flags. Even Hitler's arrival was made dramatic. The band stopped playing. There was a hush over the thirty thousand people packed in the hall. Then the band struck up the *Badenweiler March*, a very catchy tune, and used only, I'm told, when Hitler makes his big entries. Hitler appeared in the back of the auditorium, and followed by his aides, Göring, Goebbels, Hess, Himmler, and the others, he strode slowly down the long centre aisle while thirty thousand hands

5. *Source:* John A. Garraty, *The American Nation*, 4th ed. Harper, 1989, 467.

were raised in salute. It is a ritual, the old-timers say, which is always followed. Then an immense symphony orchestra played Beethoven's *Egmont* Overture. Great Klieg lights played on the stage, where Hitler sat surrounded by a hundred party officials and officers of the army and navy. Behind them the "blood flag," the one carried down the streets of Munich in the ill-fated putsch. Behind this, four or five hundred S.A. standards. When the music was over, Rudolf Hess, Hitler's closest confidant, rose and slowly read the names of the Nazi "martyrs"— brown-shirts who had been killed in the struggle for power—a roll-call of the dead, and the thirty thousand seemed very moved.

In such an atmosphere no wonder, then, that every word dropped by Hitler seemed like an inspired Word from on high. Man's—or at least the German's—critical faculty is swept away at such moments, and every lie pronounced is accepted as high truth itself. It was while the crowd—all Nazi officials—were in this mood that the Führer's proclamation was sprung on them. He did not read it himself. It was read by Gauleiter Wagner of Bavaria, who, curiously, has a voice and manner of speaking so like Hitler's that some of the correspondents who were listening back at the hotel on the radio thought it was Hitler.[6]

1. The author of this passage witnessed in person what he wrote about.
   a. True
   b. False
2. The author was not able to understand how the 30,000 people at the meeting were inspired by Hitler.
   a. True
   b. False
3. Is this selection mostly fact or opinion?
   a. Fact
   b. Opinion
4. Read the following statements from the passage, and, in the spaces provided, write *F* for statements of fact and *O* for expressions of opinion.
   a. "Borrowing a chapter from the Roman church, he [Hitler] is restoring pageantry and colour and mysticism to the drab lives of twentieth–century Germans." _____
   b. "This morning's opening meeting in the Luitpold Hall on the outskirts of Nuremberg was more than a gorgeous show." _____
   c. "Hitler appeared in the back of the auditorium, and followed by his aides, . . . he strode slowly down the long centre aisle while thirty thousand hands were raised in salute." _____
   d. "Then an immense symphony orchestra played Beethoven's *Egmont* Overture." _____
   e. "Man's—or at least the German's—critical faculty is swept away at such moments, and every lie pronounced is accepted as high truth itself."
   _____
5. List some words, phrases, or sentences from the passage that show the author's bias.

_____

_____

_____

6. *Source:* William Shirer, *Berlin Diary.* Knopf, 1940, 1941, 18–19.

PRACTICE 7

Directions: Before reading this preface from a psychology textbook, take a minute or so to read the opening paragraph, the first sentence of each paragraph, and the last paragraph. In the space provided, write what you think you will learn when you read the preface carefully.

_____

_____

_____

Now read the preface, applying all the strategies you have learned.

How to Think Straight About Psychology

There exists a body of knowledge that is unknown to most people. This information concerns human behavior and consciousness in their various forms. It can be used to explain, predict, and control human actions. Those who have access to this knowledge use it to gain an understanding of other human beings. They have a more complete and accurate conception of what determines the behavior and thoughts of other individuals than do those who do not have this knowledge.

Surprisingly enough, this unknown body of knowledge is the discipline of psychology.

What can I possibly mean when I say that the discipline of psychology is unknown? Surely, you may be thinking, this statement was not meant to be taken literally. Bookstores contain large sections that are labelled "psychology." Television and radio talk shows regularly feature psychological topics. There are psychology columns in newspapers. In spite of this, however, there is an important sense in which it is true that the discipline of psychology is unknown.

Despite much seeming media attention, the discipline of psychology remains for the most part veiled from the public. The transfer of "psychological" knowledge that is taking place via the media is largely an illusion. Few people are aware that the majority of the books they see in the "psychology" sections of many bookstores are written by individuals with absolutely no standing in the psychological community. Few are aware that many of the people to whom the media apply the label "psychologist" would not be considered so by the American Psychological Association. Few are aware that many of the most visible psychological "experts" have contributed no information to the fund of knowledge in the discipline of psychology.

The flurry of media attention paid to "psychological" topics has done more than simply present inaccurate information. It has also served to obscure the very real and growing knowledge base in the field of psychology. The general public is unsure as to just what is and is not psychology and is unable to independently evaluate psychological claims. Adding to the problem is the fact that there are many people who have a vested interest in a public that is either without evaluative skills or that believes there is no way to evaluate psychological claims. The latter view, termed the "anything goes" outlook, is one of the fallacies discussed in this book, and it is one that is particularly costly to the public. Many pseudosciences are multimillion-dollar industries that are dependent on the fact that the public is unaware that claims about human behavior can be empirically tested. The general public is also unaware that many of the claims that are made by these pseudo-sciences (e.g., astrology, psychic surgery, speed reading, biorhythms, subliminal weight loss, talk-show psychics) have been tested and have been found wanting. The existence of the pseudoscience industry, which is discussed in this book, exacerbates the media's tendency toward sensationalistic reporting of science. This tendency is worse in psychology than in other sciences, and understanding the reasons for this is an important part of learning how to think straight about psychology. This book, then, is directed not at potential researchers in psychology, but at a much larger group: the consumer of psychological information. The target audience is the beginning psychology student and the general reader who has inevitably encountered information on psychological issues in the general media and has wondered how to go about evaluating its validity.

This book is not a standard introductory psychology text. It does not outline a list of facts that psychological research has uncovered. Indeed, telling everyone to take an introductory psychology course at a university probably is not the ultimate solution to the inaccurate portrayal of psychology in the media. There are many laypersons with a legitimate interest in psychology who do not have the time, money, or access to a university to pursue formal study. More importantly, as a teacher of university-level psychology, I am forced to admit that we often fail abysmally at the task of giving our beginning students a true understanding of the science of psychology. This is because lower-level courses often do not teach the critical analytical skills that this book is about. As instructors, we often become obsessed with "content" — with "covering material." Every time we stray a little from the syllabus to discuss issues such as psychology in the media, we feel a little guilty and begin to worry that we may not "cover all the topics" before the end of the term.

Consider the average introductory psychology textbook. Many now contain between 600 and 800 multi-columned pages and reference literally hundreds of papers in the published literature. Of course, there is nothing inherently wrong with this. It is simply a reflection of the increasing knowledge base in psychology. There are, however, some unfortunate side effects. Instructors are often so busy trying to cram their students full of the dozens of theories, facts, and experiments that they fail to deal with some of the fundamental questions and misconceptions that students bring with them to the study of psychology. The instructor (and the introductory textbook author), rather than dealing directly with each of these, often hopes that by simply exposing the student to enough of the empirical content of psychology, the student will simply induce the answers to his questions. The hope is that the student will realize that the instructor has implicitly answered these questions in his discussion of empirical research in several content areas. All too often this hope is frustrated. In a final review session — or in office hours at the end of the term — the instructor is shocked and discouraged to hear questions that he would have expected on the first day of the course, but not after having presented fourteen weeks of psychological facts: "But psychology experiments aren't real life; what can they tell us? Psychology just can't be a real science like chemistry, can it? But I heard a therapist on TV say the opposite of what our textbook said. I think this theory is stupid — my brother behaves just the opposite of what it says. But that experiment doesn't have anything to do with psychology. Psychology is nothing more than common sense. Everyone knows what anxiety is, why bother defining it? Psychology is just a matter of opinion, isn't it?" For many students, such questions are simply not implicitly answered by a consideration of the content of psychology. Perhaps they should be, but they are not. In this book we will deal explicitly with the confusion that underlies questions such as these.

Unfortunately, research supports the idea that the average introductory psychology course does very little to correct the many misconceptions about the discipline that are held by entering students (McKeachie, 1960; Vaughan, 1977). One researcher has stated, "I must conclude that the [introductory] course has little influence on their erroneous beliefs" (Vaughan, 1977, p. 140), and, further, drew the conclusion that, "there is little evidence for a generally heightened skepticism, which might lead students to question statements about which they have received no additional information" (p. 140). Vaughan's latter conclusion is important because it touches on the fundamental purpose of this book. Psychology, probably more than any other science, requires the application of critical thinking skills, skills that are necessary to enable the student to separate the wheat from the chaff that accumulates around all sciences. These are the critical thinking skills that the student will need to become an independent evaluator of psychological information. Years after the content of an introductory psychology course is forgotten, the fundamental principles covered in this book will still be used to evaluate psychological claims if its key points have been learned. Long after Erikson's stages of development have been forgotten, the student will be using the "thinking tools" introduced here to evaluate new psychological information that is encountered in the media or in course work. Once acquired, these skills confer the ability to at least partially evaluate knowledge claims. First, they provide the ability to conduct an initial gross assessment of plausibility. Secondly, these skills provide some criteria for assessing the reliability of "expert" opinion. Because the necessity for reliance on expert opinion can never be eliminated in a complex society, evaluation of an expert's credibility becomes essential for knowledge acquisition. Although these critical thinking skills can be applied to any discipline or body of knowledge, they are particularly important in the area of psychology because the field is so poorly represented by the general media.

Many psychologists are pessimistic about any effort to stem the tide of misinformation about their discipline. While, unfortunately, this pessimism is often justified, this "consumer's guide" to psychology was motivated by the idea that psychologists must not let this problem become a self-fulfilling prophecy.[7]

Now answer these questions in the space provided.

1. What did you learn from reading this preface?

_____

_____

_____

7. *Source:* Keith A. Stanovich, *How to Think Straight About Psychology.* Scott, 1986, Preface.

_____

_____

2. Explain why you would or would not be interested in reading more of the book from which this preface was taken.

_____

_____

_____

_____

_____

3. How does the author make his book sound different from traditional introductory psychology textbooks?

_____

_____

_____

_____

_____

4. Why does the author call his book a "consumer's guide"?

_____

_____

_____

_____

_____

5. Define these words and phrases used in the preface. Consult a dictionary if you need to.
   a. *discipline of psychology*

_____

   b. *psychological community*

_____

c. *pseudosciences*

_____

d. *empirically tested*

_____

e. *target audience*

_____

f. *laypersons*

_____

g. *independent evaluator*

_____

h. *gross assessment of plausibility*

_____

i. *stem the tide*

_____

PRACTICE 8

Directions: The following passage is from an introductory psychology textbook.[8] Before reading it carefully, look over the entire passage, reading the opening paragraphs, the headings, the first sentences of a few paragraphs, and the last paragraph. In the space provided, write what you think you will learn when you read the passage carefully.

_____

_____

_____

_____

Now read the passage, marking key points.

8. *Source:* Mark K. Holland, *Introductory Psychology.* Heath, 1981, 478–481.

Prejudiced Attitudes

Some of the most harmful social attitudes are prejudices. We live in a world that supports prejudice. In the home, in school, in magazines and books, and on radio and television, the images we have of members of different groups are shaped. These images are often negative. Do you have prejudiced attitudes toward members of different groups? Check your prejudices on the list below:

☐ men   ☐ blacks
☐ women   ☐ Hispanics
☐ children   ☐ Asians
☐ short people   ☐ Catholics
☐ tall people   ☐ Jews
☐ handicapped people ☐ Protestants
☐ old people
☐ whites

What Is Prejudice?

"A woman's place is in the home."

"All Jews care about is money."

"Children should be seen and not heard."

"Some of my best friends are blacks, but I wouldn't want my sister to marry one."

You have heard remarks like these before. What is similar about them? First, each statement groups people of a particular type together; it regards them all as the same even though each individual is unique. This tendency to see all members of a group as the same is called **overgeneralization.** Second, each statement reflects a negative attitude toward the people who have been grouped together: women are seen as incapable of acting productively in the world; Jews are seen as having selfish motives; children are seen as stupid; and blacks are seen as undesirable mates. Regarding members of groups as having such negative characteristics is called **devaluation.** When you deny the value or worth of people, you devalue them.

Prejudice is a preconceived and unfavorable attitude toward an entire group; it consists of a combination of overgeneralization and devaluation. For example, a person who is prejudiced against women sees all women as similar in having certain traits.

You are an individual, but sometimes people see you as a category instead of a person. When people respond only to your group category of black, white, male, or female, you lose your individuality. You have become stereotyped. A **stereotype** is a set of fixed ideas about a person that is based on group membership. It is the consequence of categorizing first and observing second. It is the product of prejudice.

About fifty years ago one hundred white college students were asked to describe the personalities of persons from various national and ethnic groups.[1] These students showed definite stereotypes about the typical personalities of each of ten groups. "Americans" were most commonly rated as hard-working, intelligent, materialistic, ambitious, and progressive. "Italians" were rated as artistic, impulsive, passionate, quick-tempered, and musical. "Jews" were rated as shrewd, greedy, hard-working, and intelligent. "Negroes" were rated as superstitious, lazy, happy-go-lucky, ignorant, and musical. These students had fixed ideas about what black Americans were like, ideas that contrasted sharply with their view of themselves as "Americans."

Stereotypes of blacks have changed somewhat in the past fifty years since this study was completed. The evidence of several studies shows that the stereotype of blacks is less negative than it was, although it is still negative.[2,3] Fixed ideas about racial and ethnic groups are remarkably resistant to change; they tend to be learned early in life and to last over the years.

What are your stereotypes? Do you have fixed ideas about the personality of another person you have not met? Do you tend to categorize first and observe later?

People can be divided into many different groups, and each group has its subgroups. Prejudice is commonly reflected in our attitudes toward these subgroups. Recently attention has been drawn to prejudice against blacks, Hispanics, Jews, and women. Prejudice against Irish, Catholics, Asians, Iranians, and American Indians has also been a serious problem. The prejudice shown against children and men has been, for the most part, entirely ignored. Yet children have no equality before the law, are often treated as property, and are clearly "second-class citizens." Prejudice against men takes the form of a prejudgment that any particular man will show his "masculinity" by being insensitive, vulgar, unexpressive, materialistic, and violent.

Learning How to Hate

Some people are extremely prejudiced and others are not. What causes these differences? Studies show that some parents and schools distort the minds of children and teach them prejudice.

Children learn what attitudes and beliefs they are expected to hold. For the most part, children learn their prejudices from other people with whom they interact: parents, friends, and teachers. Studies show that there is a strong relationship between the extent

of a child's prejudice and the extent of the parents' prejudice.[4] If parents are prejudiced, their child tends to be prejudiced also. In one study a psychologist invented a group of persons called the "Piraneans." Slides of people supposedly of this group were shown to 180 elementary school children; then their attitudes toward these people were measured and compared with their parents' attitudes toward blacks, Jews, and other subgroups. It was found that the attitudes of the children toward the imaginary group resembled the attitudes of their parents toward real groups; when the parents were prejudiced, the children were, too. These children had learned to be prejudiced not toward a particular group but in general.[5]

The learning of prejudice by children most likely takes place through the processes of modeling and identification. Children tend to imitate the behavior and beliefs of their parents and other significant adults. Furthermore, as children grow up, they typically identify with the parent of the same sex and adopt the attitudes and mannerisms of that parent. In this way, children can learn to hate from their parents.

Parents are not the only teachers of hate. Children adopt the attitudes of society that they experience around them. Until very recently, magazines, movies, and television consistently portrayed all persons except white Americans as inferior. The characters displayed to children conformed more to stereotypes than to reality. All blacks were shown in menial jobs; all Hispanics were shown as lazy. Recently, the representation of minorities in the media has improved, but it is still true that the hero of most stories is white and male and most servants on television are black and female.

Schools have taught a biased history. It has been, and to some degree still is, a history from the white person's point of view; it neglects important contributions made by nonwhites. Some school counselors still advise blacks and Hispanics to pursue careers as laborers and to take courses in school to prepare for menial jobs.

Schoolteachers speak for their culture; their attitudes and values reflect the attitudes and values of the rest of society.   But the attitudes held by teachers and taught by teachers are sometimes prejudiced.   One New York City school teacher classified a number of her Puerto Rican students as mutes, unable to speak. When questioned about this, she reported that they had not spoken a word to her in six months.   When asked if they talked to one another, she replied, "Sure, they cackle to each other in Spanish all day!"[6]   The school system, for the most part, is staffed by white English-speaking persons and reflects the values and beliefs of white English-speaking persons.   In a speech before the U.S. Senate, Dr. David Sanchez reported:

Equal education has been a fraud.   How can there be equal education if some of the students are looked on as defective?   The injuries of the Latin American child have been inflicted by those who claim to teach and motivate him, who have in reality alienated him and destroyed his identity through subtle rejection of his language which nobody speaks, his culture which nobody understands and ultimately him whom nobody values.[7]

Prejudiced Personalities

How can a person be prejudiced against a group that does not exist?   It cannot come from the experience of interacting with the people involved, since they are imaginary; such a prejudice cannot be learned, since no opportunity for learning was possible.   Yet studies have shown that many people are prejudiced against groups that do not exist, and these are the same people who are prejudiced against real groups.[5]   People who are prejudiced against one minority group tend to be prejudiced against other minority groups as well.[8] Findings such as these have led to the idea that prejudice has more to do with the personality of the person who is prejudiced than with present social conditions.   Prejudiced people may simply be different psychologically from other people.   From this point of view, the personality of the person who is prejudiced should differ from the personalities of others.

The personality pattern characterizing highly prejudiced people has been called the **authoritarian personality.** An individual with this type of personality keeps feelings under great control, is extremely conventional and resistant to change, and shows a dependence on and admiration of authority figures.

A massive study of the personalities of prejudiced people was undertaken during and immediately following World War II, and a report of this study was later published in a book entitled *The Authoritarian Personality.*[8]   For this study, about two thousand people took tests designed to measure prejudice, political beliefs, and personality.   One of the most important parts of the test was a set of questions called the **F scale,** designed to measure basic personality traits that were assumed to support prejudice.   High agreement with the items of this scale was supposed to reflect fascistic, authoritarian, or antidemocratic tendencies. Some of the items from the F scale appear below; check the ones that you agree with.

- ☐ Obedience and respect for authority are the most important virtues children should learn.
- ☐ Sex crimes, such as rape and attacks on children, deserve more than mere imprisonment; such criminals ought to be publicly whipped, or worse.
- ☐ When a person has a problem or worry, it is best for him not to think about it, but to keep busy with more cheerful things.
- ☐ People can be divided into two distinct classes: the weak and the strong.
- ☐ Nowadays when so many different kinds of people move around and mix together so much, a person has to protect himself especially carefully against catching an infection or disease from them.
- ☐ A person who has bad manners, habits, and breeding can hardly expect to get along with decent people.
- ☐ Young people sometimes get rebellious ideas, but as they grow up, they ought to get over them and settle down.

Prejudiced people tend to agree more with these items than nonprejudiced people.[9]   The results of this test and more intensive studies of prejudiced persons supported the idea that highly prejudiced people tend to have a particular personality pattern.   They tend to have unquestioning admiration for authorities and to hold in contempt persons they believe to have a status position lower than themselves. Interpersonal relationships for these people tend to be based on power and status. Highly prejudiced people show rigidity in their personality and thinking; they have little tolerance for unclear situations and prefer definite pat solutions to problems.[8]

What causes the prejudiced personality? One approach to this problem is to assume that prejudice is a form of displaced aggression and that the person who is prejudiced is scapegoating. According to the scapegoating theory, the prejudiced person has been frustrated or threatened by someone against whom retaliation was not safe; the impulse to fight back was inhibited because such action would be dangerous; and the aggression was therefore displaced or redirected to a relatively safe target, a minority group. The highly prejudiced person, then, should be someone who has been severely threatened or frustrated by someone against whom retaliation was dangerous or impossible.

Studies have shown that highly prejudiced persons tend to have aggressive and punishing parents.[8] The punishment they experienced as children was often arbitrary and violent. Whippings and beatings were commonly used punishments. One prejudiced person described her parents' disciplinary methods as follows:

. . . mother had a way of punishing me—lock me in a closet—or threaten to give me to a neighborhood woman who she said was a witch. . . . I think that's why I was afraid of the dark. . . .

Father picked upon things and threatened to put me in an orphanage.[8]

It is easy to believe that such punishment might provide a source of frustration that would later cause a prejudiced personality. The reactions of anger, hostility, and aggression that are inhibited in the child emerge later in the authoritarian adult as prejudice.

Map the passage from the psychology textbook on a separate sheet of paper. Then answer these questions, circling the letter of the correct answer or filling in the blank as appropriate.

1. List at least three things you learned from reading this passage.

   _____

   _____

   _____

   _____

   _____

2. How do we learn prejudice?

   _____

   _____

   _____

   _____

   _____

3. The personality pattern characterizing highly prejudiced people has been called the *authoritarian personality*, meaning that such people are very dependent and admire authority figures.
   a. True
   b. False, because _____

   _____

4. What is the *F scale*, and what is its purpose?

   _____

   _____

   _____

   _____

   _____

5. Highly prejudiced persons tend to be those who have been severely threatened or frustrated by someone against whom they were able to retaliate and continue to hate.
   a. True
   b. False, because _____

   _____

6. Studies have shown that when parents are prejudiced, their children are prejudiced too.
   a. True
   b. False, because _____

   _____

7. Define these words or phrases as they are used in the passage.
   a. *overgeneralization*

   _____

   _____

   b. *devaluation*

   _____

   _____

   c. *stereotype*

   _____

   _____

   d. *materialistic*

   _____

   _____

   e. *impulsive*

   _____

   _____

   f. *Piraneans*

   _____

   _____

   g. *menial jobs*

   _____

   _____

   h. *mutes*

   _____

   _____

i.   *extremely conventional*

_____

_____

j.   *scapegoating*

_____

_____

PRACTICE 9

Directions: Here is an entire chapter from Jules R. Benjamin's *A Student's Guide to History.*[9] As you read the chapter, apply everything you have learned about study-reading the social sciences: surveying, marking, identifying writing patterns, and mapping.

Chapter I:

The Subject of History and How to Use It

What Historians Are Trying to Do

Since the time when human beings invented writing, they have left records of their understanding of the world and of the events in their lives and how they felt about them. By studying the records that previous generations have left, we can find out about the kind of lives they led and how they faced their problems. We can use what we learn about the experiences of people who lived before us to help solve problems we face today. Though the modern world is quite different from the societies in which our ancestors lived, the story of their accomplishments and failures is the only yardstick by which we can measure the quality of our own lives and the success of our social arrangements.

All of us look into the past from time to time. We read historical novels or books about historical events. We gaze at old photographs or listen to the stories our grandparents tell. Historians, however, make a serious and systematic study of the past and attempt to use the knowledge they gain to help explain human nature and contemporary affairs. Professional historians spend their lives pursuing the meaning of the past for the present. To amateurs, historical research is like a hobby, but their occasional journeys into the past may contribute to the store of human knowledge and can greatly influence their own lives. Your study and research as a student qualifies you as an amateur historian. Your study of the past is part of the same search for knowledge carried on generation after generation.

---

9. *Source:* Jules R. Benjamin, *A Student's Guide to History.* St. Martin's, 1975, 1–10.

What History Can Tell You

Everything that exists in the present has come out of the past, and no matter how new and unique it seems to be, it carries some of the past with it. The latest hit recording by the newest group is the result of the evolution of that group's musical style and of the trends in music and society that have influenced them. Perhaps their style developed from earlier rock styles associated with the Beatles, or perhaps they are taking off from even older folk themes used by Bob Dylan. Well, Dylan was influenced by Woody Guthrie, who wrote his songs in the 1930s and whose music grew out of his contact with the heritage of American folk music from the nineteenth century, which in turn had come in great measure from earlier music in England and Scotland, some of which has its origins in the Middle Ages. So you can see that the house of the present is filled with windows into the past.

The car you ride in, although it may have been designed only a few years ago, carries within it the basic components of the "horseless carriage" of the turn of the century. Your car works because people who knew how to make carriages, bicycles, and engines put their ideas together in a new way. The knowledge necessary to make the carriages and bicycles came, in turn, from earlier inventions. Some, like the wheel, go back into the antiquity of human history.

Everything has a history. At least part of the answer to any question about the contemporary world can come from studying the circumstances that led up to it. The problem is to find those past events, forces, arrangements, ideas, or facts that had the greatest influence on the present subject you have questions about. The more you understand about these past influences, the more you will know about the present subject to which they are related.

History and the Everyday World

Most of us are curious. Children are always asking their parents the "why" of things. When we grow up we continue to ask questions because we retain our fascination with the mysteriousness and complexity of the world. Because everything has a history, most questions can be answered, at least in part, by historical investigation.

What are some of the things about which you are curious? Have you ever wondered why women's skirts in old movies are so long, or why Frenchmen often embrace one another whereas Englishmen almost never do? Perhaps you have wondered how the Kennedy or Rockefeller families came to be rich, or why the Japanese attacked Pearl Harbor. Have you thought about why most of the peoples of southern Europe are Catholic whereas most northern Europeans are not? Many oriental peoples bow when they greet one another; we shake hands. The questions could go on forever; all the answers are written somewhere in the record of the past.

The record of the past is not only contained in musty volumes on library shelves; it is all around us in museums, historical preservations, and the antique furnishings and utensils contained in almost every household. Our minds are living museums because the ideas we hold (for example, democracy, freedom, equality, competitiveness) have come down to us by way of a long historical journey. Though we are usually unaware of it, the past is always with us. Because history is literally at our fingertips, we can travel back into it without difficulty.

A Brief Journey into the Past

If you have ever driven any distance, you have probably ridden over a system of very modern superhighways with high speed limits and no cross traffic or stoplights. This national highway network, built within the last fifteen years, connects all the major United States cities and is known as the interstate system. These roads were planned by the Eisenhower Administration in 1955, and, though they are the newest highways in the country, they have a history two decades long.

Looking for the marks of history in the world around us is something like the task of the geologist or archaeologist. However, instead of digging down into the earth to uncover the past, the historical researcher digs into the visible, everyday elements of society to find the historical roots from which they sprang. The fact that the interstate highway system built in the 1960s and 1970s had its origins in the 1950s is just, so to speak, the uppermost layer of history. If a study of the newest highways can take us back twenty years, what about the historical roots of the older highways or of the country roads? How far into the past can we travel on them?

Turn off the eight-lane interstate, past the gleaming Exxon station, past the orange roof of the Howard Johnson restaurant, past the bright signs before the multistoried Holiday Inn, and onto, say, U.S. Route 51 or 66. These are older highways, built mostly in the 1940s and 1950s. Being from an earlier period, like older strata of rock, perhaps they can tell us something of life in an earlier period of America.

When you leave the interstate system for this older road network you first notice that the speed limit is lower and that many of the buildings are older. As you ride along at the slower pace there are no signs saying "Downtown Freeway 32 miles" or "Indiana Turnpike—Exit 26N." They say "Lubbock 38 miles," or "Cedar Rapid 14 miles." As you approach Lubbock or Cedar Rapids, you will see motels less elaborate than the Holiday Inn. They may be small wooden cottages with fading paint and perhaps a sign that says "Star Motor Court" or "Stark's Tourist Cabins." Instead of Howards Johnson's or McDonald's, you may pass "Betty's Restaurant" or "Little River Diner." If you pay close attention to these buildings and do not become distracted by the more modern structures between them, you can take a trip into history even as you ride along. All of the older restaurants, stores, and gas station you see were built before the large shopping centers and parking lots that separate them, and they are clues to the history of the highway on which you are riding. Places like the Star Motor Court and the Little River Diner probably were built when the road was new. Unless they have been modernized, they are relics of a previous historical period—when men named Roosevelt and Truman were president and when the cars that rode by looked like balloons with their big rounded hoods, trunks, and fenders. The diner isn't air-conditioned, and the sign over the tourist cabins proudly proclaims that they are "heated." This is the world of the 1930s and 1940s.

Now turn off the highway at State Route 104 where the sign says "Russell Springs 3 miles" or where it says "Hughesville 6 miles." Again the speed limit drops, and the bright colors fade further away. You are on a road that may have been built in the 1920s or 1930s or earlier (in older sections of America the country roads all go back a hundred years or more). Time has removed many of the buildings that once stood along this road, but if you look closely, the past is there ready to speak to you. The gas station here has only one set of pumps, and the station office sells bread, eggs, and kerosene. The faded advertisements on the wall display some products that you have never heard of — NeHi Orange and Red Man Chewing Tobacco. If you see a restaurant or motel, it may be boarded up because the people who used to stop in on their way to Russel Springs or Hughesville now go another way or may no longer live in the country but in a nearby city. However, many of the homes along Route 104 are still there. They were built when only farmland straddled the road, and they may go back to a time when horses and not internal combustion engines pulled the traffic past the front door. Such relics of early technology as old washing machines and refrigerators may stand on the tilting wooden porches, and a close look behind the tall weeds beside the dirt driveway may reveal the remains of a 1936 La Salle. As you stop before one of the old farmhouses, the past is all around you, and, although the place does not appear in its youthful form, a little imagination can reconstruct what life was like here on the day in 1933 when Roosevelt closed all the banks or the day in 1918 when the Great War in Europe ended.

The line linking past to present never breaks, and the house itself has a history, as do the people who once lived in it. In this sense, every house is haunted with its own past, and a keen eye can see the signs. Enter the house and you can see the stairway that was rebuilt in 1894, and the fireplace in the main bedroom upstairs, which was put in about 1878, the year the house was built. Perhaps the old Bible on the table near the bed notes the year the family came to the United States, and the dates in the early nineteenth century when the parents of the immigrants who built the house were born.

The story could go on forever, although the evidence would become slimmer and slimmer. You could find out from county records who owned the land before the house was built, going back perhaps to the time when the people who lived on the land were red, not white. In distance you may have traveled only ten or twenty miles from the interstate highway and it may have taken you less than an hour, but by looking for the signs of the past in the present, you have traveled a hundred years or more into history.

If you think and study about the passage of time between the old farmhouse on the country road and the gleaming service station by the interstate, you may come to understand some of the social, political, and economic forces that moved events away from the old wooden porch and sent them speeding down the interstate highway. The more you know about this process, the more you will learn about the times when the farmhouse was new and the more you will understand how the interstate highway came about, what you are doing riding on it, and into what kind of a future you may be heading.

Historians don't usually wander into history in such a casual fashion. They have to be trained in their methods of investigation and analysis. As an introduction to your own historical research and study, the next section will describe some of the tools employed by historians in their examination of the records of the past.

How Historians Work

Like you, historians are challenged by the complexity of the world, and many want to use their studies of the past to help solve the problems of the present. The questions that can come to mind are numberless, and serious historical investigators must choose wisely among them. They do not want to spend a lot of effort pursuing the kind of question to which history has no answer (for example, "What is the purpose of the universe?" "Am I a lovable person?" "Who is the smartest person in the world?"). Nor do they want to struggle to achieve the solution to a problem that is not of real importance. (Historical investigation can probably tell you who wore the first pair of pants with a zipper in it, but that might not be worth knowing.) The main difficulty facing historians is not eliminating unanswerable or unimportant questions, but choosing among the important ones.

A historian's choice among important questions is determined by personal values, by the concerns of those who support the historian's work, by the nature of the time in which the historian lives, or by a combination of all of these. The ways in which these influences operate are very complex, and often historians themselves are unaware of them.

Historians investigate the questions they choose to study in many ways. Their particular approach depends on their academic training and their belief about which aspects of human nature and the human environment are most important to an understanding of their subject. Traditionally, historians have been divided into those who saw social, cultural, intellectual, political, diplomatic, economic, or psychological matters as central to answer the question being investigated. The social historian investigates the development of human groups and communities and their interaction with the larger society in which they emerge. The cultural and intellectual historian deals with the meaning of ideas and attitudes and their effect upon social changes. The political historian focuses on the operation and acts of governments, parties, and institutions, whereas diplomatic historians deal with relations between governments. The economic historian studies developments in technology, production, consumption, and the division of wealth. Most recently, a group known as psychohistorians have centered their investigations on the emotional development of individuals and families.[1]

When the historian has chosen his or her subject, many questions still remain. For example, does historical evidence dealing with the subject exist, and if so, where can it be found? If someone wanted to study Gypsy music from medieval Europe, and that music was never written down or mentioned in historical accounts of the period, then little or nothing can be found about this subject through historical research. Even if records exist on a particular subject, the historian may be unaware of them or unable to locate them. Perhaps the records are in an unfamiliar language or are in the possession of individuals or governments that deny access to them. Sometimes locating historical evidence can be a problem.

Having determined that records do exist and that they can be located and used, the historian faces another and more important problem: What is the credibility or reliability of the evidence? Is it genuine? How accurate are the records, and what biases were held by those who wrote them? If sources of information are in conflict, which is correct? Or is it possible that most of the sources are in error? Historians must pick and choose among the sources they uncover, and that is not always easy to do. The historian's own biases, as well, cloud

---

1. Historians also have been divided according to their particular philosophies of history. These are complex systems that try to explain the larger course and meaning of history. If you wish to look into this question, seek advice from your instructor.

the picture, making impartial judgment extremely difficult.

There are two basic forms of historical evidence: primary and secondary. Primary evidence records the actual words of someone who participated in or witnessed the events described. These can be newspaper accounts, diaries, notebooks, letters, minutes, interviews, and any works written (or otherwise recorded, as in photographs) by persons who claim first-hand knowledge of an event. Another primary source is official statements by established organizations or significant personages, royal decrees, church edicts, political party platforms, laws, and speeches.

Secondary evidence records the findings of someone who did not observe the event but who investigated primary evidence. Most history books fall into this category, although some are actually tertiary evidence because they rely not on primary evidence but are themselves drawn from secondary sources. When your own history research paper is finished, it will be secondary, or more likely, tertiary evidence to anyone who may use it in the future.

The problem of determining the reliability of evidence is a serious one. Secondary and even primary evidence can be fraudulent, inaccurate, or biased. Eyewitness accounts may be purposely distorted in order to avert blame or to bestow praise on a particular individual or group. Without intending to misinform, even on-the-scene judgments can be incorrect. Sometimes, the closer you are to an event, the more emotionally involved you are, and this distorts your understanding of it. We can all recall events in which we completely misunderstood the feelings, actions, and even words of another person. Historians have to weigh evidence carefully to see if those who participated in an event understood it well enough to have accurately described it, and whether later authors understood the meaning of the primary documents they used. Official statements present another problem—that of propaganda or concealment. A government, group, or institution may make statements that it wishes others to believe, but that are not true. What a group says may not be what it does. This is especially true in politics.

To check the reliability of evidence, historians use the tests of consistency and corroboration: Does the evidence contradict itself and does it agree with evidence from other sources? Historical research always involves checking one source against another.

The bias of a source also presents difficulties. People's attitudes toward the world influence the way they interpret events. For example, you and your parents may have different attitudes toward music, sex, religion, or politics. These differences can cause you to disagree with them about the value of a rock concert, a Sunday sermon, or the president. Historians have their own attitudes toward the subjects they are investigating, and these cause them to draw different conclusions about the character and importance of religious, political, intellectual, and other movements. Later historians must take these biases into account when weighing the reliability of evidence.

In analyzing the evidence, the historian must find some way of organizing it so that he or she can make clear its meaning. A mass of facts and opinions concerning a subject is not a historical study. The task of the trained historian is to arrange the material so that it supports a particular conclusion. This conclusion may have been in the historian's mind at the outset, or it might be the result of investigation. If the evidence does not appear to support the conclusion, however, then the historian must either change that conclusion or seek other evidence to support it.

Once a historian is satisfied that research has uncovered sufficient evidence to support a particular conclusion, then he or she works to display the evidence in a manner that will clearly show that the conclusion drawn is a proper one. If any evidence that leads to other conclusions is uncovered, the historian has a responsibility to include it. In doing so, he or she must show how the supporting evidence is stronger than the nonsupporting evidence. There are many ways of organizing evidence in support of a conclusion. The historian's arguments in favor of a particular conclusion must be strong and convincing, and the logic of these arguments must not be faulty.

Recently, in an effort to eliminate error, bias, and faulty logic as much as possible, some historians have turned to techniques from mathematics and science to handle historical evidence and test conclusions. These historians prefer to deal with quantitative or uniform data that are easily comparable and that can be interpreted by mathematical formulas. Such researchers often use computers to analyze their data. They question historical findings involving opinion and judgment and look to types of evidence (usually statistical) that can test the more intuitive conclusions of other historians. The kinds of problems they deal with are usually narrow, and they have to be well trained in techniques of statistical analysis. Their tests of evidence are sophisticated and are becoming more so. The extent to which the study of history can or should become "scientific" is an important current debate among historians.

On a separate sheet of paper, write short answers to the following questions.

1. What are historians trying to do?
2. What can history tell you?
3. What does history have to do with the everyday world?
4. How do historians work?
5. Describe the two basic forms of historical evidence.

PRACTICE 10

Directions: The passage that follows is from a political science textbook.[10] As you read it, apply everything you have learned about study reading the social sciences: surveying, marking, identifying writing patterns, and mapping.

POLITICAL ANALYSIS: WHY? HOW? WHAT?

WHY ANALYZE POLITICS?

Whether a person likes it or not, virtually no one is completely beyond the reach of some kind of political system. A citizen encounters politics in the government of a country, town, school, church, business firm, trade union, club, political party, civic association, and a host of other organizations. Politics is an unavoidable fact of human existence. Everyone is involved in some fashion at some time in some kind of political system.

If politics is inescapable, so are the consequences of politics. That statement might once have been shrugged off as rhetorical, but today it is a brutal and palpable fact. For whether humankind will be

---

10. *Source:* Robert A. Dahl, *Modern Political Analysis,* 4th ed. Prentice, 1984, 1–6.

blown to smithereens or will design political arrangements that enable our species to survive is now being determined — by politics and politicians.

The answer to the question, "Why analyze politics?" is obvious then. We cannot really escape politics — though we may try to ignore it. That is a powerful reason for trying to understand it. You may want to understand politics simply in order to satisfy your curiosity, or to feel that you comprehend what is going on around you, or in order to make the best possible choices among the alternatives open to you — that is, in order to act wisely. Although, for most people, making better choices probably provides the strongest incentive for political analysis, human beings also tend to feel a powerful need to make sense out of their world. To be sure, anyone can make some sense out of politics; but politics is an exceptionally complex matter, quite likely one of the most complex matters human beings encounter. The danger is that without skill in dealing with its complexities, one will drastically oversimplify politics. It is fair to say, I think, that most people do oversimplify. Of course, because some simplification is unavoidable, this book also simplifies political complexities; but it does not, I believe, do so excessively. As we shall see, trying to acquire the elementary skills necessary for understanding politics is not a simple task.

HOW

At this point you might ask: If I want to understand politics, why shouldn't I plunge directly into political life and acquire the knowledge I need from direct experience? Doesn't political experience provide better knowledge about politics than books, analysis, theory, and abstractions? Since there is much to be said for knowledge gained from experience, perhaps an analogy will help to show its limits.

From ancient times, the skill of the statesman has been likened to that of the physician: the statesman cares for the political well being of the community, the physician for the health of the people in it. However, modern medicine distinguishes between the practice of medicine — what medical people often call "clinical" medicine — and research into the manifestations, causes, and treatment of disease — the "science" of medicine. Medical practitioners and scientists agree that treating patients requires the special skills of the practitioner, and that in acquiring those skills there is no substitute for direct experience. In premedical and medical training, in the classroom and the laboratory, the mind of the budding practitioner is stuffed full of scientific knowledge. Essential as this knowledge is, however, it is nonetheless inadequate for treating patients. Even after four years of academic training and some clinical exposure, newly minted medical graduates are still too unskilled to be fully entrusted with the treatment of patients. Further medical training therefore demands internship, and in fields of specialization, an additional period of clinical experience, nowadays typically a residency of three or four years. In ways not at all well understood, some physicians acquire an unusual capacity to make wise decisions about the treatment of sick people and may become known to their peers as excellent, even brilliant, clinicians.

Essential as the skills of the practitioner are in treating patients, however, the progress of medicine depends mainly not on the experience of practitioners but on the work of scientists. Many medical scientists have little to do with patients; some might even be inept practitioners. Only in rare cases, it seems, are both kinds of skills developed in the same person. Yet knowledge gained from direct experience with patients, valuable as it is, does not ordinarily lead to new discoveries in medicine: The Nobel prizes go to the great medical scientists, not the great practitioners. Without the work of medical scientists, then, the practitioner could acquire only a feeble understanding — little better than that of doctors in the eighteenth century — of the causes and treatment of diseases. The wise judgment of even the greatest practitioner is only in part — perhaps in small part — a product of direct experience. It is also a product of knowledge gained from generations of scientific research.

Although the analogy ought not to be pushed too far, a similar distinction might be made about ways of acquiring political knowledge. Experience in politics unquestionably provides knowledge that cannot be acquired in any other way. I have found that students who participate in political campaigns or work a stint for a member of Congress or of a state legislature are usually convinced that they have gained knowledge that is different from what they can learn from books and classrooms. They are right in thinking so. Yet, as in medicine, what one can learn from direct experience is necessarily very limited. For example, how could you learn only from your own direct experience what features of a country — El Salvador, let us say — make democracy there likely or unlikely? Or what policies of the United States, if any, would increase or reduce El Salvador's prospects for democracy? Because direct experience is inadequate, political practitioners, like medical practitioners, depend greatly on specialists, including academic specialists. Far more than may be commonly understood, political leaders today are required to make practical judgments about essential abstract or theoretical questions.

Just as in medicine, however, we must not mistake skill in systematic political analysis with skill in political practice, even though these skills overlap. As in the arts, an analyst, or critic, is not necessarily a gifted performer.

Skill in analyzing politics is not the same as skill in practicing politics. James Madison's speeches at the Constitutional Convention and his chapters in *The Federalist* demonstrate that he was a brilliant political analyst, yet he was a mediocre President. By contrast, Franklin Roosevelt had enormous skill, insight, and astuteness as a political leader and President; yet one cannot find in Roosevelt's messages, state papers, and letters an analysis of how he himself operated as President that seems as valid as the analysis contained in several later studies by scholars. Even if Roosevelt had tried to explain how he operated, could he have succeeded? Skilled artists are frequently unable to explain why or how they do what they do so superbly.

Sometimes, to be sure, skill in political practice does go hand-in-hand with skill in political analysis. Woodrow Wilson was a historian and political scientist before he was a politician. *Congressional Government*, which he wrote in 1884 at the age of twenty-eight, is still worth reading a century later. As governor of New Jersey and as President, Wilson also displayed a high order of skill as a political practitioner — until opposition to his goals during his second term brought out aspects of his personality that severely impaired his skills as a politician.[1] Moreover, all skilled political practitioners must have some capacity for political analysis, even though they may be unable to explain what they know. The rapidly increasing complexity of modern national and international politics requires a corresponding increase in the analytical competence of political leaders. Old fashioned wardheelers whose political knowledge was narrow and parochial were once an effective force in American politics; yet they have all but disappeared because the complexities of an age of high-speed computer technology, nuclear energy, and artificial satellites made them obsolete.

What is true for political leaders is also true for ordinary citizens. In making judgments about political leaders and their policies, understanding and choosing among alternatives, and making sense out of the world's confusing complexities, everyone needs more than direct experience. The aim of political analysis, therefore, is to go beyond what anyone can hope to learn from direct experience.

FOUR ORIENTATIONS

To understand and to act intelligently, we often ask a basic question that will of course vary from one situation to another. The question frequently goes something like this: How can I act in order to arrive at a better state of affairs (for me, my family, my business, my party, my country, the weak and suffering, the strong and able, the people, all of humanity, and so on)? But another question must be asked to answer the first: What would a better state of affairs be? More generally, what distinguishes the better from the worse? However, still a third question must be asked: How do things come about in the real world? For instance, if I believe that peace is better than war, and if I wish to prevent wars, I must therefore do something about the causes of wars. But what are the causes of wars? All three questions presuppose answers to a fourth, a question so fundamental that one often takes the answer for granted and is quite unaware that there is such a question: What do I mean by the key terms I use or the statements I make? For example, how do I define democracy? How do I distinguish it from other forms of government?

Each question represents a different orientation toward the world. In asking the first question, one is oriented to discovering a policy. In asking the second, one seeks to discover norms, values or criteria, to judge alternative policies. In asking the third question, one seeks to discover empirical relationships among elements in the real world. In asking the fourth, one tries to clarify meaning. Hence we can speak of a policy orientation, a normative orientation, an empirical orientation, and a semantic orientation. Depending on which question is the focus of attention at any given moment in political analysis, one can speak of policy analysis, normative analysis, em-

---

1. In his analysis of Wilson's personality and political conduct, Alexander L. George shows that when Wilson met genuinely threatening opposition, as he did during his second term, he "was unable to function expediently and proved singularly gauche as a politician. . . . Wilson became rigidly stubborn and tried to force through his proposal without compromising it." See "Power as a Compensatory Value for Political Leaders," Journal of Social Issues 24 (July 1968): 42. See also Alexander L. George and Juliette L. George, Woodrow Wilson and Colonel House: A Personality Study (New York: Dover Press, 1964).

pirical analysis, and analysis of meaning (sometimes referred to as conceptual or semantic analysis).

In actual political analysis, however, the boundaries are usually not sharply defined. Moreover, although the four orientations suggest a certain logical relation—choosing a policy presupposes some standards of evaluation, which in turn presuppose some empirical beliefs, which make sense only if the key terms have meaning—political analysis rarely if ever proceeds exactly in this fashion. As we shall see in a moment, while the plan of this book does presuppose the relations that I have just described, it seems to me easier to approach the questions in the reverse order: We shall begin by clarifying the meaning of some of the key terms used in political analysis, move on to some fundamental empirical questions, then proceed to normative analysis, and finally examine the problem of choosing policies.

Before saying more about the plan of the book, however, it will be helpful if we confront a question directed particularly to empirical analysis.

A Query About Empirical Political Analysis: Art or Science?

Is empirical political analysis a science?[2] Or is it an art? I believe it is both. To the extent that many aspects of political analysis are most easily of human beings is inherently different from the study of nature in its nonhuman manifestations, acquired by practice and training under the supervision of a person already skilled in this area, it is an art. Whenever students of politics scrupulously test their generalizations and theories against the data of experience by means of meticulous observation, classification, and measurement, then empirical political analysis is scientific in its approach. To the extent that this approach actually yields tested propositions of considerable generality, political analysis can be regarded as scientific in its results.

The extent to which empirical political analysis should be approached as an art or a science is a hotly debated issue. And if it is considered a science, there are important differences between those who seek to emulate the natural sciences like physics and chemistry, and those who believe that the study of human beings is inherently different from the study of nature in its nonhuman manifestations.

Many who hold the second view argue that we cannot really understand a human action unless we can grasp its subjective

---

2. American scholars who helped inaugurate the first departments of political science in this country were strongly influenced by scholarship in nineteenthh-century Germany, where the term *wissenschaft* connoted not only science but also learning, knowledge, scholar ship, and more generally, the intellectual product of any systematic inquiry. Thus the word "science" in "political science" was probably intended to mean something like "systematic study" and not, as it is more likely to be interpreted today, "empirical inquiry of the manner of the natural sciences." For a brief history, see Dwight Waldo, "Political Science: Tradition, Discipline, Profession, Science, Enterprise," in *The Handbook of Political Science*, vol. 1, (Reading, Mass.: Addison-Wesley Publishing Co., Inc., 1975).

In some countries, such as France and Italy, the term political science has been used to cover a number of specialized fields such as law, economics, and sociology. In these countries, political analysis was until recently assumed to be an aspect of each of these fields, but not an autonomous intellectual discipline. Consequently, among the "political sciences' there was no separate field of political science.

meaning: what it means to the person who performs it, what that person intended by it, and so on. An atomic particle does not intend anything; what it does has no subjective meaning to the physicist. Physics does well as a science by describing activity in purely external, physical terms. But even so simple an action as voting cannot be understood as merely a physical activity. Imagine how voting might be perceived by an invisible observer from Mars who knows no human language and hasn't the faintest idea what those peculiar earthlings are doing when they enter an enclosed booth and pull a little lever or scratch some black marks on a piece of paper. For all the Martian knows, a person who votes and a person who makes a call from a telephone booth are performing similar acts.

The incompleteness of purely external, physical descriptions of human activity, combined with the difficulty of arriving at an adequate understanding of the subjective features that give human action so much of its meaning, have led some scholars to the pessimistic view that a "scientific" understanding of human action is impossible. Others optimistically view the problems posed as difficult but not insuperable. The pessimistic view suffers from the usual weakness of perfectionism. In this case, the perfectionist appears to be saying that there is nothing worthwhile between utter ignorance, at one extreme, and knowledge of regularities as exhibited in the laws of physics and chemistry, at the other. This is absurd. Some reduction in our uncertainty is better than total uncertainty. No one seriously argues that systematic inquiry can never improve our knowledge, thus reducing our uncertainty.

It is true, however, that uncertainty appears to be a prime characteristic of all political life. Systematic political analysis can reduce some of that uncertainty. Yet even the best political analysis leaves a large element of uncertainty in our understanding of political life. For the foreseeable future, perhaps the only certainty about political life will be its uncertainty. Hence, intelligent political analysis will have to be based on the assumption that political knowledge has distinct limits, even though these are not permanent.[11]

On a separate sheet of paper, write answers to the following questions.

1. The author says that politics is inescapable and so are its consequences. Explain what he means and why you agree or disagree.
2. The aim of political analysis is to go beyond what anyone can hope to learn from direct experience. Why is this important, according to the author?
3. Define each of the following terms as used by political scientists: *policy analysis; normative analysis; empirical analysis; analysis of meaning* (sometimes called *semantic analysis*).
4. Explain why the author feels that empirical political analysis is both a science and an art.
5. If you were to read the rest of the political science textbook from which this chapter was taken, what would you expect it to teach you?

---

11. *Source:* Robert A. Dahl, *Modern Political Analysis*, 4th ed. Prentice-Hall, 1984, 1–6.

WHAT DO YOU THINK?. . .

And with the emphasis on fund raising for all elections, which is ruining the electoral system, we will be accepting entertainers as our candidates, not those who have learned the processes and practices of government. You can't govern without having the training in it. Even Plato said that a long time ago. You need to be trained in government, to exercise it, to practice it. But the American public is now satisfying itself with entertainers.

Barbara Tuchman, historian

Practices in Learning the Language of the Sciences and Technology

The practices in this section are related to the work you did in Chapter 8. They will help you understand the vocabulary of the sciences and technology, as well as increase your general vocabulary.

Do not attempt to do too many of these practices at once. Before you leave one exercise, be certain you know the words in it that you didn't know before. Learn from your mistakes.

PRACTICE 1

Directions: Read this passage, noticing in particular the boldfaced words. Using any context clues you can, answer the questions that follow the passage in the space provided. Refer back to the passage as you need to.

Metabolism

Raw materials do not assemble on their own to form each new organism. The assembly processes—indeed, all processes associated with life—are the result of *energy transfers* between substances. For example, in a process called **photosynthesis** plants absorb sunlight energy and use it to form compounds such as adenosine triphosphate, or ATP; then the energy of ATP is used to build sugar, starch, and other molecules. Here, energy is transferred from the sun, to ATP, and then on to molecules that the cell uses as building blocks or tucks away as energy reserves. In another process, called **aerobic respiration**, cells tap their energy reserves by breaking apart molecules so that some energy becomes available to form ATP—which in turn delivers energy to sites where specific cellular activities take place.

This example tells us something about the nature of energy transfers. Energy stores can be used up. Organisms cannot create "new" energy from nothing; to stay alive, they must tap an existing energy source from their surroundings (the sun, nectar from a flower, a chicken dinner), then transform the acquired energy into forms that can be stored and used to do cellular work.

All forms of life extract and transform energy from their surroundings, and they use it for manipulating materials in ways that assure maintenance, growth, and reproduction. More briefly, they show what is called "metabolic activity."[1]

1. Define *photosynthesis*.

   _____

   _____

2. Define *aerobic respiration*.

   _____

   _____

3. What is meant by *energy transfer*?

   _____

   _____

4. Define *metabolic activity*.

   _____

   _____

PRACTICE 2

Directions: Read this paragraph, noticing in particular the boldfaced words. Using any context clues you can, answer the questions that follow the paragraph in the space provided. Refer back to the paragraph as you need to.

Of a somewhat different social impact are the drugs contained in birth control pills, another success with complex molecules. The drugs used in these pills are synthesized and have proved to be more effective than similar natural compounds. The first one of these drugs to be synthesized was **norethynodrel**. It was known for some time that the hormone progesterone would prevent ovulation in the human female about 85% of the time; this, however, is hardly an effective contraceptive. By synthesizing compounds similar in structure to progesterone a compound was found, norethynodrel, which turned out to be virtually 100% effective at one-third the dosage of progesterone when given with a small amount of another hormone, estrogen.[2]

1. As used here, what does *synthesized* mean?

   _____

   _____

1. *Source:* Cecie Starr and Ralph Taggart, *Biology.* Wadsworth, 1987, 5.
2. *Source:* James T. Shipman and Jerry D. Wilson, *An Introduction to Physical Science,* 5th ed. Heath, 1987, 287.

2. What is *norethynodrel*?

    _____

    _____

3. What is *progesterone*?

    _____

    _____

4. What is *estrogen*?

    _____

    _____

PRACTICE 3

Directions: Read this paragraph, noticing particularly the underlined words. In the questions that follow the paragraph, circle the letter of the correct definition for each underlined word as it is used in context. Refer back to the paragraph as you need to.

Some substances are <u>compounds</u>: they are capable of being <u>decomposed</u> into simpler substances. Water can be broken down into its <u>constituents</u>, hydrogen and oxygen, but the latter two materials are elements, which cannot be decomposed further. In order to indicate the composition of a compound, a formula is written (e.g., H_2O). The formula, utilizing symbols and <u>subscripts</u>, provides the following information: (1) the elements in the compound; (2) the <u>relative</u> number of each atom (subscripts indicate the number of atoms, the number 1 being omitted); (3) the combining weights of the elements, since the symbol refers to an atom and the atomic weights are known; and (4) the molecular weight of the compound, if it is known.[3]

1. *compounds*
    a. powdered substances
    b. substances made of two or more parts
    c. compromises
2. *decompose*
    a. to break up
    b. to rot
    c. to let air out
3. *constituents*
    a. persons who vote
    b. costive ingredients
    c. components
4. *subscripts*
    a. symbols
    b. notations written underneath or lower
    c. foreign words

3. *Source:* Shipman, 287.

5. *relative*
   a. comparative
   b. a relation
   c. subordinate

PRACTICE 4

Directions: Use the information in the dictionary listings on page 353 to answer the following questions in the space provided.[4]

1. What is *biotherapy*?

   _____

2. From what language is the word *biotherapy* derived?

   _____

3. What are the two major word parts of *biotherapy*, and what do they mean?

   _____

4. What is a *bioscope*?

   _____

5. What is *bioscopy*?

   _____

6. What is the difference between *bi* and *bio*?

   _____

7. What is another word for *bionomics*?

   _____

8. What does *nomos* mean in Greek?

   _____

9. What is *bionomy*?

   _____

10. Judging from this sample listing of words in a dictionary, how important would you say that knowing Greek and Latin roots is for enlarging your science vocabulary?

    _____

4. *Source: Webster's New World Dictionary of the American Language,* College Edition. World, 1968, 72.

bi·ol·y·sis (bī-ol′ə-sis), *n*. [*bio-* + *-lysis*], the destruction of life as by bacteria or other microorganisms.

bi·o·lyt·ic (bī′ə-lit′ik), *adj*. of or produced by biolysis.

bi·o·met·rics (bī′ə-met′riks), *n.pl.* [construed as sing.], [< *bio-* + *metric*], that branch of biology which deals with its data statistically and by quantitative analysis.

bi·om·e·try (bī-om′ə-tri), *n*. [*bio-* + *metry*], 1. calculation of the probable human life span. 2. biometrics.

Bi·on (bī′ən), *n*. Greek pastoral poet; c. 3d century B.C.

bi·o·nom·ics (bī′ə-nom′iks), *n.pl.* [construed as sing.], [*bionomy* + *-ics*], the branch of biology that deals with the adaptation of living things to their environment; ecology.

bi·on·o·my (bī-on′ə-mi), *n*. [*bio-* + Gr. *nomos*, law], 1. the science that deals with the natural laws controlling life processes. 2. bionomics.

bi·o·phys·i·cal (bī′ō-fiz′i-k'l), *adj*. of biophysics.

bi·o·phys·ics (bī′ō-fiz′iks), *n.pl.* [construed as sing.], the branch of physics that deals with living matter.

bi·o·plasm (bī′ō-plaz'm). *n*. living matter; protoplasm.

bi·op·sy (bī′op-si), *n*. [see BIO- & -OPSIS], in medicine, the excision of a piece of living tissue for diagnostic examination by microscope, etc.

bi·o·scope (bī′ə-skōp′), *n*. [*bio* + *-scope*], a motion-picture projector.

bi·os·co·py (bī-os′kə-pi), *n*. [*bio-* + *-scopy*], in *medicine*, examination to find out whether life is present.

-bi·o·sis (bī-ō′sis, bī-o′sis), [< Gr. *biōsis*, way of life < *bios*, life], a combining form meaning *a* (specified) *way of living*, as in *symbiosis*.

bi·o·so·cial (bī′ō-sō′shəl), *adj*. of the communal or family relationships of animals, as bees, apes, etc.

bi·o·stat·i·cal (bī′ō-stat′i-k'l), *adj*. of biostatics.

bi·o·stat·ics (bī′ō-stat′iks), *n.pl.* [construed as sing.], [*bio-* + *statics*], the branch of physiology that deals with the relation of structure to function in plants and animals: opposed to *biodynamics*.

bi·o·ther·a·py (bī′ō-ther′ə-pi), *n*. [*bio-* + *therapy*], the treatment of disease by means of substances secreted by or derived from living organisms, as serums, vaccines, bile, penicillin, etc.

bi·ot·ic (bī-ot′ik), *adj*. [Gr. *biōtikos* < *bios*, life], of life; of living things.

bi·ot·i·cal (bī-ot′i-k'l), *adj*. biotic.

bi·o·tin (bī′ə-tin), *n*. [*biotic* + *-in*], a bacterial growth factor, $C_{10}H_{16}O_3N_2S$, found in liver, egg yolk, and yeast; vitamin H: the lack of it may cause dermatitis.

bi·o·tite (bī′ə-tīt′), *n*. [after J. B. *Biot* (1774–1862), Fr. naturalist], a dark-brown or black mineral of the mica family, found in igneous and metamorphic rocks.

bi·o·type (bī′ō-tīp′), *n*. [*bio-* + *-type*], a group of plants or animals with similar hereditary characteristics.

bi·pa·ri·e·tal (bī′pə-rī′ə-t'l), *adj*. of or connected with the prominent rounded part of the two parietal bones.

bi·pa·rous (bip′ə-rəs), *adj*. [*bi-* + *-parous*], 1. bearing two offspring at a birth. 2. in *botany*, dividing into two branches.

PRACTICE 5

Directions: Here is a list of Greek roots and their meanings. Use it to define the words that follow the list in the space provided. Don't consult a dictionary until you have tried to define the words by examining their Greek roots. Use a dictionary for words you still don't understand.

acou	to hear
anthrop	man, mankind
anti	against
arthr	joint
auto	self
bio	life
cardi	heart
cephal	head
chlor	color
chron	time
cyt	cell
derm	skin
dia	across, apart

epi	upon
gen	kinds, race
geo	earth
helio	sun
hemo	blood
hydro	water
itis	inflammation of
macro	large
meter	measure
micro	small
neuro	nerve
octo	eight
ost, osteo	bone
patho	disease of
phobos	fear
poly	many
scope	examine
som, somat	body (sleep)
thera	to nurse
zo	animals

1. acoustician _____

2. anthropology _____

3. antibiotics _____

4. arthritis _____

5. autogenesis _____

6. biochemistry _____

7. cardiac _____

8. cephalopod _____

9. chlorophyll _____

10. chronometer _____

11. cytology _____

12. diameter _____

13. epidermis _____

14. genetics _____

15. geophysics _____

16. hemorrhage _____

17. hydrometer _____

18. macrocosm _____

19. octagon   _____

20. polygon   _____

PRACTICE 6

Directions: Here is a list of Latin roots and their meanings. Use it to define the words that follow the list. Don't consult a dictionary until you have tried to define the words by examining their Latin roots. Use a dictionary for words you still don't understand.

aqua	water
audio	hear
aur	ear
carn	flesh
corpus	corpse, body
digit	finger, toe
dorm	sleep
duc, duct	lead
ex	out
locus	place
mitto, mit	send
mortis, mort	death
ocul	eye
ped	foot
port	carry
post	after
pro	before
sanguin	blood
sol	sun
somn	sleep
son	sound
video	see

1. aquarium   _____

2. aqueduct   _____

3. audiogram   _____

4. audiology   _____

5. aural   _____

6. carnivore   _____

7. conducive   _____

8. corpulent   _____

9. digitate   _____

10. dormant   _____

11. exogen   _____

12. locally   _____

13. mortal   _____

14. mortuary   _____

15. oculist   _____

16. pedometer   _____

17. portable   _____

18. post-mortem   _____

19. prognosis   _____

20. prophecy   _____

21. sanguine   _____

22. solar   _____

23. somnambulist   _____

24. transmitter   _____

25. video tape   _____

PRACTICE 7

Directions: Select any words you are having trouble learning or remembering and make vocabulary flash cards for them. Get some three-by-five-inch cards. On one side, print the word you want to learn. On the other side, write the definition and a sentence using the word in context. Practice learning each word by looking at the front side of the card, pronouncing the word, and giving its definition. Then check the back side to see if you are correct. Keep adding cards to your stack, practicing them over and over. You may want to pair up with someone to practice this technique.

WHAT DO YOU THINK?

Of all the animals, we are the one least dictated to by genetics or by nature. We have the capacity to shape ourselves for good or for evil. So that while we are endowed with certain caring features, we can create a corrupt race of human beings and eventually destroy ourselves.

Willard Gaylin, bioethicist

Practices in Reading the Sciences and Technology

The practices in this section will help you develop the comprehension skills you learned in Chapter 9 which are necessary for successful study-reading in the sciences and technology. The practices are taken from a wide variety of science textbooks and vary in length.

PRACTICE 1

Directions: Read this passage from an introductory chemistry text. Look for the topic being discussed and the main idea. Then answer the questions that follow it in the space provided.

The use of the scientific method is usually credited with being the most important single factor in the amazing development of chemistry and technology. Although complete agreement is lacking on exactly what is meant by "using scientific method," the general approach is as follows:

1. Collect facts or data that are relevant to the problem or question at hand, which is usually done by planned experimentation.
2. Analyze the data to find trends (regularities) that are pertinent to the problem. Formulate a hypothesis that will account for the data that have been accumulated and that can be tested by further experimentation.
3. Plan and do additional experiments to test the hypothesis. Such experiments extend beyond the range that is covered in Step 1.
4. Modify the hypothesis as necessary so that it is compatible with all the pertinent experimental data.

Confusion sometimes arises regarding the exact meaning of the words *hypothesis*, *theory*, and *law*. A hypothesis is a tentative explanation of certain facts that provides a basis for further experimentation. A well-established hypothesis is often called a theory. Thus a theory is an explanation of the general principles of certain phenomena with considerable evidence or facts to support it. Hypotheses and theories explain natural phenomena, whereas scientific laws are simple statements of natural phenomena to which no exceptions are known under given conditions.[1]

1. *Source:* Morris Hein, *Foundations of College Chemistry.* Brooks/Cole, 1986, 6–7.

1. What is the topic of the passage?

    _____

2. What writing pattern is used in the first paragraph?

    _____

3. What is the function of the second paragraph?

    _____

    _____

4. What writing pattern is used in the second paragraph?

    _____

PRACTICE 2

Directions: As you read this paragraph, look for the main idea, the supporting details, and the writing pattern used. Then answer the questions that follow it by circling the letter of the correct answer or filling in the blank as appropriate.

4.6 Law of Definite Composition of Compounds

A large number of experiments extending over a long period of time have established the fact that a particular compound always contains the same elements in the same proportions by weight. For example, water will always contain 11.2% hydrogen and 88.8% oxygen by weight. The fact that water contains hydrogen and oxygen in this particular ratio does not mean that hydrogen and oxygen cannot combine in some other ratio. However, a compound with a different ratio would not be water. In fact, hydrogen peroxide is made up of two atoms of hydrogen and two atoms of oxygen per molecule and contains 5.9% hydrogen and 94.1% oxygen by weight; its properties are markedly different from those of water.[2]

1. What is the topic of the passage?

    _____

2. What is the law of definite composition of compounds?

    _____

    _____

3. What support of the main idea is provided?

    _____

2. *Source:* Hein, 8.

4. What writing pattern is used?

PRACTICE 3

Directions: Read this passage, and answer the questions that follow it in the space provided.

The Branches of Chemistry

Chemistry may be broadly classified into two main branches: organic chemistry and inorganic chemistry. Organic chemistry is concerned with compounds containing the element carbon. The term organic was originally derived from the chemistry of living organisms: plants and animals. Inorganic chemistry deals with all the other elements as well as with some carbon compounds. Substances classified as inorganic are derived mainly from mineral sources rather than from animal or vegetable sources.

Other subdivisions of chemistry, such as analytical chemistry, physical chemistry, biochemistry, electrochemistry, geochemistry, and radiochemistry, may be considered specialized fields of, or auxiliary fields to, the two main branches.[3]

1. What is the main point of the passage?

2. What writing pattern is being used?

3. On a separate sheet of paper, draw a chart that contains the main ideas of the passage.

PRACTICE 4

Directions: Read this passage, and answer the questions that follow it in the space provided.

DNA is unique in three respects. First, it is a very large molecule, having a certain outward uniformity of size, rigidity and shape. Despite this uniformity, however, it has infinite internal variety. Its varied nature gives it the complexity required for information carrying purposes. One can, indeed, think of the molecule as if it had a chemical alphabet somehow grouped into words which the cell can understand and to which it can respond.

3. *Source:* Hein, 4.

The second characteristic of DNA is its capacity to make copies of itself almost endlessly, and with remarkable exactness. The biologist or chemist would say that such a molecule can *replicate*, or make a carbon copy of itself, time and again with a very small margin of error.

The third characteristic is its ability to transmit information to other parts of the cell. Depending upon the information transmitted, the behavior of the cell reflects this direction. As we shall see, other molecules play the role of messenger, so that DNA exercises its control of the cell in an indirect manner.[4]

1. What is the topic of the passage?

_____

_____

2. What are the characteristics of DNA?

_____

_____

_____

3. What does *replicate* mean?

_____

PRACTICE 5

Directions: This passage may require more than one reading to master. That's typical of many science passages. Read it looking for the main idea, then answer the questions that follow it in the space provided.

The nomenclature used to distinguish isotopes in nuclear and atomic physics is best described by an example. Let us consider the oxygen isotope $^{16}_{8}O_8$. The letter **O** is the chemical symbol for oxygen. The left superscript designates the mass number (many textbooks use a right superscript instead). The left subscript designates the atomic number and the right subscript the neutron number. (The right superscript position is left vacant because often there is a charge on the atom and the charge is indicated at this position. For instance, an oxygen atom with only seven electrons would have a total positive charge of 1 because it would have one more proton than electrons.)

The atomic number plus the neutron number must equal the mass number by definition. Usually, the neutron number is omitted from an isotopic symbol, as it can be easily determined by subtracting the atomic number from the mass number. The atomic number and the chemical symbol specify the same thing since all atoms of the same element have the same number of protons. However, only a few tenacious souls have memorized the number of protons in every element, so it is usually specifically designated. Some other possible

4. *Source:* James T. Shipman and Jerry D. Wilson, *An Introduction to Physical Science,* 5th ed. Heath, 1987, 291.

isotopes of oxygen are $^{15}_{8}O_9$, $^{17}_{8}O_9$, and $^{18}_{8}O_{10}$. Figure 10.4 summarizes the nomenclature just described.[5]

> Mass number → 16
> Atomic number → $_8$ O $_8$ ← Neutron number
>
> **Figure 10.4** Atomic nomenclature. The symbol for the chemical element is shown in the center.

1. What is the topic of the passage?

   _____

   _____

2. What is meant by *nomenclature*?

   _____

   _____

3. What does the left superscript designate?

   _____

4. What does the left subscript designate?

   _____

5. What does the right subscript designate?

   _____

6. What does the right superscript designate?

   _____

7. Why is the neutron number usually omitted from the isotopic symbol?

   _____

   _____

8. How can Figure 10.4 help you understand the passage?

   _____

   _____

PRACTICE 6

Directions: Read this passage, and answer the questions that follow it in the space provided.

5. *Source:* Shipman, 160.

The characteristics of a substance are known as its properties. There are two basic types of properties, physical and chemical. **Physical properties** are those that do not involve a change in the chemical composition of the substance. Among these properties are density, hardness, color, melting point, boiling point, electrical conductivity, thermal conductivity, and specific heat. These properties may change with a change in pressure or temperature. Those changes, which do not alter the chemical composition of the substance, are called **physical changes**. The processes of freezing or boiling water are good examples of physical changes brought about by changing the temperature. Other examples of physical changes are dissolving table salt in water, heating a piece of metal, and evaporating water.

The properties involved in the transformation of one substance into another are known as **chemical properties**. When wood burns, oxygen in the air unites with the different substances in the wood to form new substances. When iron corrodes, it combines with oxygen and water to form a new substance commonly known as rust. These are examples of chemical properties of wood and iron, respectively. Changes that result in the formation of new substances are known as **chemical changes**. The fermenting of wine, burning of gasoline, souring of milk, discharging of a battery, and the exploding of gun powder are all examples of chemical changes. All chemical changes involve a production or absorption of energy.[6]

1. Define *properties* as used in the passage.

    _____

2. What is the difference between *physical properties* and *chemical properties*?

    _____

    _____

3. What is the difference between *physical changes* and *chemical changes*?

    _____

    _____

4. List some examples of both types of changes that do not appear in the passage.

    Physical changes   *Chemical changes*

    _____   _____

    _____   _____

    _____   _____

    _____   _____

6. *Source:* Shipman, 242.

Physical changes	*Chemical changes*
_____	_____
_____	_____

PRACTICE 7

Directions: Read this paragraph, and answer the questions that follow it in the space provided.

If the total mass involved in chemical reaction is precisely weighed before and after the reaction takes place, no change can be detected. This law is known as the **law of conservation of mass** and is stated as follows:

> **There is no detectable change in the total mass during a chemical process.**

This law was formulated in 1774 by Antoine Lavoisier. Lavoisier had developed balances which could measure 1/100 the weight of a drop of water. He put tin in a vessel, sealed it, and carefully weighed it. The vessel was then heated so that the tin reacted with the air in the vessel to form a new compound. Lavoisier next reweighed the sealed container and found the weight to be identical with the original weight. Because the container had been sealed, no air could go in or out. When Lavoisier opened the vessel, air rushed in. This showed that the tin had reacted with the air inside, or something in the air, to form the new compound. This experiment of Lavoisier's was one of the first great quantitative chemical experiments. Now, two centuries later, Lavoisier's law of conservation of mass is still almost exactly true.[7]

1. What was the problem or question Lavoisier wanted to solve or answer?

   _____

   _____

2. What experiment did he perform to solve the problem or answer the question?

   _____

   _____

3. What was the result of the experiment?

   _____

   _____

7. *Source:* Shipman, 242.

4. Of what importance was the experiment?

_____

_____

PRACTICE 8

Directions: Read this passage from a science laboratory manual, and answer the questions that follow it in the space provided.

> You can study what controls the movement of materials across the cell membrane with the use of dialysis tubing. This tubing is used in dialysis machines to filter out waste products from the blood of people with kidney disease.
>
> Dissolve some sugar, starch, salt, and gelatin or egg white (protein) in distilled water. Pour the solution into a piece of dialysis tubing. Insert a 10-ml pipette into one end of the tubing and place it in a beaker of distilled water. . . . After 30 minutes, record the height of the water in the pipette. Test the contents of the beaker and dialysis tubing for sugar, starch, salt, and protein. If the solution turns cloudy when a few drops of 5% silver nitrate are added, salt is present. Based on your results, determine which substances crossed the membrane. Explain why only certain substances crossed the membrane. Explain why only certain substances can diffuse through the membrane. Investigate the effects of increasing the temperature or pressure on the diffusion of these substances.[8]

1. What is the point of the experiment described in the passage?

_____

_____

2. What materials would you need to have on hand to begin the experiment?

_____

_____

_____

3. List in numerical order the sequence of steps in this experiment.

_____

_____

_____

_____

8. *Source:* Savatore Tocci, *Biology Projects for Young Scientists.* Watts, 1987, 56.

_____

_____

4.   What must you do when you have completed the experiment?

_____

_____

PRACTICE 9

Directions: This passage contains figures and tables to clarify the concepts being presented.[9] Use them to help you answer, in the space provided, the questions that follow the passage.

3.2 Physical States of Matter

solid

Matter exists in three physical states: solid, liquid, and gas. A **solid** has a definite shape and volume, with particles that cohere rigidly to one another. The shape of a solid can be independent of its container. For example, a crystal of sulfur has the same shape and volume whether it is placed in a beaker or simply laid on a glass plate.

Most commonly occurring solids, such as salt, sugar, quartz, and metals are *crystalline*. Crystalline materials exist in regular, repeating, three-dimensional, geometric patterns. Solids such as plastics, glass, and gels, because they do not have any particular regular internal geometric pattern, are called

amorphous

amorphous solids. (*Amorphous* means without shape or form.) Figure 3.2 illustrates three crystalline solids: salt, quartz, and gypsum.

liquid

A **liquid** has a definite volume but not a definite shape, with particles that cohere firmly but not rigidly. Although the particles are held together by strong attractive forces and are in close contact with one another, they are able to move freely. Particle mobility gives a liquid fluidity and causes it to take the shape of the container in which it is stored. Figure 3.3 shows equal amounts of liquid in differently shaped containers.

gas

A **gas** has indefinite volume and no fixed shape, with particles that are moving independently of one another. Particles in the gaseous state have gained enough energy to overcome the attractive forces that held them together as liquids or solids. A gas presses continuously in all directions on the walls of any container. Because of this quality a gas completely fills a container. The particles of a gas are relatively far apart compared with those of solids and liquids. The actual volume of the gas particles is usually very small in comparison with the volume of the space occupied by the gas. A gas therefore may be compressed into a very small volume or expanded almost indefinitely. Liquids cannot be compressed to any great extent, and solids are even less compressible than liquids.

9.   *Source:* Hein, 46–48.

(a)

(b)

(c)

Figure 3.2 These three naturally occurring substances are examples of regular geometric formations that are characteristic of crystalline solids: (a) halite (salt), (b) quartz, and (c) gypsum.

When a bottle of ammonia solution is opened in one corner of the laboratory, one can soon smell its familiar odor in all parts of the room. The ammonia gas escaping from the solution demonstrates that gaseous particles move freely and rapidly and tend to permeate the entire area into which they are released.

Although matter is discontinuous, attractive forces exist that hold the particles together and give matter its appearnace of continuity. These attractive forces are strongest in solids, giving them rigidity; they are weaker in liquids but still strong enough to hold liquids to definite volumes. In gases the attractive forces are so weak that the particles of a gas are practically independent of one another. Table 3.1 lists a number of common materials that exist as solids, liquids, and gases. Table 3.2 summarizes comparative properties of solids, liquids, and gases.

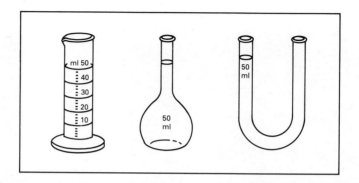

Figure 3.3 Liquids have the property of fluidity and assume the shape of their container, as illustrated in each of the three different calibrated containers.

Table 3.1 Common materials in the solid, liquid, and gaseous states of matter

Solids	*Liquids*	*Gases*
Aluminum	Alcohol	Acetylene
Copper	Blood	Air
Gold	Gasoline	Butane
Polyethylene	Honey	Carbon dioxide
Salt	Mercury	Chlorine
Sand	Oil	Helium
Steel	Vinegar	Methane
Sulfur	Water	Oxygen

Table 3.2 Physical properties of solids, liquids, and gases

State	*Shape*	*Volume*	*Particles*	*Compressibility*
Solid	Definite	Definite	Rigidly cohering; tightly packed	Very slight
Liquid	Indefinite	Definite	Mobile; cohering	Slight
Gas	Indefinite	Indefinite	Independent of each other and relatively far apart	High

1. What are the three physical states of matter?

   _____

2. Explain the distinguishing characteristics of each state.

   _____

   _____

   _____

   _____

3. Which of the three states of matter is the most compressible? Why?

   _____

   _____

   _____

4. Why is it possible to smell an opened bottle of ammonia in all parts of a room?

   _____

   _____

   _____

5. What is meant by the statement "Matter is discontinuous"?

   _____

   _____

   _____

6. What writing pattern is used in this passage?

   _____

PRACTICE 10

Directions: Read this passage from a textbook for a computer class, and answer the questions that follow it by circling the letter or letters of the correct answer or filling in the blank as appropriate.

Computer-Assisted Instruction

Computer-assisted instruction, or **CAI**, is the use of computers to assist in the process of learning. CAI is derived from the work in *behavior modification* done by B. F. Skinner. Educators were quick to see the possible classroom applications of his theories of reward and punishment. If students receive immediate positive response to their work, they will tend to learn material more rapidly and retain information longer. Although instant feedback can be virtually impossible for one teacher faced with 30 students, it's a piece of cake for a computer. Thus the development of computer-assisted instruction.

Initially, computer-assisted instruction consisted of quizzing, or "drill-and-practice," routines. The computer presented a question to the student, who responded. If the student's answer was correct, the computer displayed "yes" or some similar positive message and went on to the next question. If the student was wrong, the computer indicated that, gave the right answer, and presented another question similar to the first. Although such simple formats are still in use today, for example, in the kindergarten reading program we described above, more intriguing and sophisticated educational uses of computers are being developed every day. Computers are used for foreign language drills (in which the student and computer engage in a Spanish or French or German dialogue), tutoring (in which concepts are explained and wrong answers are corrected at length), and problem solving in physics and higher mathematics. Computers can provide students with realistic decision-making scenarios (as we'll see in a later section of this chapter on physician training) or engage them in complex *Socratic dialogues* (interchanges in which questions and answers, from both student and computer, run along a logical line to a clear conclusion). In history classes, students can refight the Battle of Gettysburg or rule a feudal manor, in which case the computer will inform them of the effects of their decrees on the economy, agriculture, or political climate of their fiefdom.

Math teachers have found that computers perform a doubly valuable role in their classrooms, since writing a program to solve a problem requires that a student be completely comfortable not only with programming techniques but also with the basic mathematical concepts represented by the problem. Some high school students have become such practiced programmers that they have produced customized software for their teachers in geography, economics, calculus, and history. One of these precocious programmers made over $40,000 his first year out of high school by writing a game for an Apple computer.

Some colleges and universities, such as Carnegie-Mellon, Boston College, and Dartmouth, require some or all of their entering students to purchase a personal computer along with their textbooks and notepads. More and more college libraries are installing computer systems to replace bulky and unmanageable files of index cards. Shelf location and whether or not the book is in circulation can be accessed by keying the book's title, call number, or author. Systems in some libraries feature subject searches as well. College-level CAI applications—such as the PLATO instructional system developed at the University of Illinois, which stores over 8000 hours of course material in every area from physics to Swahili—are increasing every day. College departments across the country are participating in programs in which professors are loaned personal computers that they can keep if they develop an application appropriate to their discipline. The benefits are threefold: increased production of home-generated software for colleges, innovative course material for students, and free personal computers for professors.[10]

1. The letters *CAI* stand for _____

2. CAI is derived from B. F. Skinner's work in behavior modification, a learning theory whereby students who receive immediate positive feedback will learn more rapidly and retain information longer.
   a. True
   b. False, because _____

3. CAI consists mostly of "drill-and-practice" routines.
   a. True
   b. False, because _____

4. Which of the following subjects are mentioned in the passage as using CAI beneficially with students?
   a. foreign languages
   b. physics
   c. math
   d. history
   e. English

5. Some colleges and universities now requires students to purchase a

   _____ along with their textbooks.

6. What success story is mentioned as an example of the programming skill level some high-school students have achieved?

   _____

   _____

7. Which of the following is *not* listed as a benefit when colleges participate in programs whereby college professors are loaned personal computers that they can keep if they develop an application of CAI materials for their discipline?
   a. increased production of home-generated software
   b. innovative course material for students
   c. free personal computers for professors
   d. money made from writing computer programs

PRACTICE 11

Directions: This passage is longer than the others. Read it, applying everything you have learned about study-reading, then answer the questions that follow it by circling the letter of the correc answer or filling in the blank as appropriate.

10. *Source:* Daniel L. Slotnick, Evan M. Butterfield, Ernest S. Colantino, Daniel J. Kopetzky, Joan R. Slotnick, *Computers and Applications*. Heath, 1986, 571.

CHAPTER 4

REPRODUCTION

ASEXUAL REPRODUCTION

Asexual reproduction is quite simple compared to sexual reproduction in that it requires only one organism: no partner is necessary. Therefore, in most asexual species, every mature individual can reproduce, enabling the population to increase far more rapidly than the otherwise comparable sexual species that require two individuals to reproduce.

Many organisms take full advantage of asexual reproduction. For instance, each time an *amoeba* divides, it produces two genetically identical replicas of itself. And many species of single-celled as well as multicellular organisms produce asexually reproductive cells known as **spores** that float in the air or water and eventually produce genetic replicas of the parent.

Another asexual mode of reproduction involves budding, as illustrated in Figure 4.1. In **budding**, part of the parent sprouts smaller offspring that separate and become distinct individuals. Many plants reproduce **vegetatively**, sprouting new plants from leaves, roots, or some other part of the parent. In **parthenogenesis**, an egg can develop into an adult without being fertilized by a sperm cell.

Another form of asexual reproduction is **fragmentation**, in which part of an organism separates from the whole, and a new individual regenerates from that part. Such fragmentation sometimes

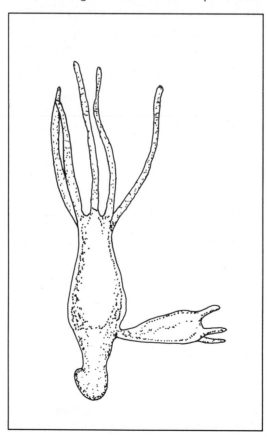

Figure 4.1 Budding is illustrated here, where a parent hydra is "sprouting" a smaller hydra.

occurs when an organism is in danger: pieces of the injured organism then regenerate into whole organisms. Starfish, for example, have this preproductive capacity. Worms and planaria can also fragment and then **regenerate** the missing portion of their body.

Cloning is another type of asexual reproduction that involves the production of copies that are genetically identical, although they may not look identical. This happens with many plant species—such as when one plant grows from a seed and then many other plants sprout up from the roots.

There are many benefits as well as drawbacks to both asexual and sexual reproduction. Through natural selection, some sexually reproducing organisms have been able to survive and continue to flourish because they benefit from the genetic variability that this mode of reproduction promotes. For instance, should the environment change so that one variation were unable to survive, the entire species would perish if the species consisted of a clone. When, however, the species consists of genetically variable individuals within each population, different populations can adapt to a changing or variable environment. Although sexual reproduction is costly and somewhat inefficient in that it takes twice as many individuals to produce one set of offspring, the genetic variability that is maintained through sexual reproduction seems to have long-term benefits.

SEXUAL REPRODUCTION

Sexual reproduction is costly to a species in that it requires both a male and a female to produce as many offspring as one asexual organism can produce, but there are also benefits to such an expensive reproductive mode. The method of reproduction is not always an either/or matter, however; some species reproduce asexually during one part of the year and sexually during another, thereby reaping the benefits of both methods. The complex series of physiological and behavioral changes associated with sexual reproduction are described below.

For sexual reproduction to occur, specialized cells from both the male and female come together and unite. Yet merely combining any two cells is not adequate. Rather, certain cells first undergo a peculiar type of cell division called **meiosis**, creating gametes called **germ cells**.

In animals, undifferentiated male germ cells are located in the **testes**. These cells undergo two meiotic divisions, called **meiosis I** and **meiosis II**, creating four **sperm cells**. Undifferentiated at first, these sperm cells, known as **spermatids**, undergo differentiation before becoming mature **spermatozoa**. This process, **spermatogenesis**, is the result of the division and maturation of a single diploid **primary spermatocyte**, producing four spermatozoa. In female animals, all the undifferentiated germ cells are located in the **ovaries**, where **oogenesis** occurs. Oogenesis comprises the series of steps that produce an **egg** from a **primary oocyte**, which is also called an **ovum**.

Figure 4.2 shows the process and products of meiosis and differentiation for both spermatogenesis and oogenesis. The entire process in which gametes (sperm and eggs) are developed through meiotic divisions and subsequent maturation and development is known as **gametogenesis**. In the testes of sexually mature male animals, the cells lining the **seminiferous tubules** are always dividing meiotically,

Figure 4.2 Gametogenesis is illustrated, showing how the process involves meiosis, which, in both male and female, consists of a first and second meiotic division, forming either sperm or an ovum.

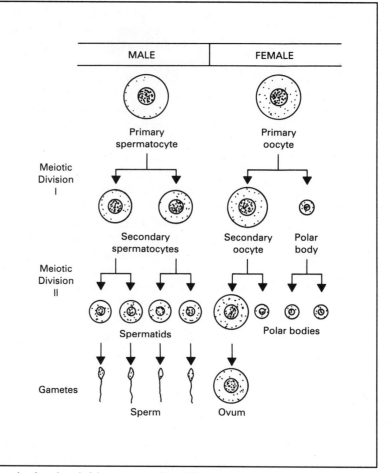

producing haploid sperm cells; this process is termed spermatogenesis.

Gametogenesis in females is known as oogenesis, the process that produces eggs in the ovarian structures called **follicles**. The first meiotic division (meiosis I) produces two daughter cells of unequal size from a **primary oocyte**. The primary oocyte divides into a smaller **first polar body** and a larger **secondary oocyte**, which receives a greater share of the cytoplasm during this meiotic division. The first polar body either disintegrates or divides in the second part of meiosis (meiosis II), creating two **second polar bodies** that disintegrate. During meiosis II, the secondary oocyte divides into two parts unequally; less cytoplasm goes to a third second polar body, and more goes toward the **ootid** that then differentiates into an **ovum**, or **egg**.

In terms of weight, a human egg, through extremely tiny (much smaller than the head of a pin), is approximately 58,000 times heavier than a single sperm cell. In terms of length, a completely differentiated sperm cell is about 1/3 the diameter of a human egg. And if lined up side-by-side, there would be seven completely differentiated human eggs per millimeter. With its whip-like motion, the sperm's tail propels it through the mucosal lining of the vagina toward the ovum.

Only one sperm cell can fertilize each egg. When the sperm cell penetrates the egg, it contributes its **haploid** (sometimes called **monoploid** or **1N**) genetic complement of chromosomal DNA to the haploid (1N) egg, creating a **diploid (2N) zygote**.

While spermatogenesis leads to four equal-sized sperm cells because the cytoplasm is divided equally during each meiotic division, oogensis leads to a single large ovum because of the unequal cytoplasmic divisions. The greater amount of cytoplasm in the egg is used to nourish the embryo. A larger egg may also enhance the chances of being fertilized by a sperm cell.[11]

1. Parthenogenesis is a type of asexual reproduction where an egg can develop into an adult without being fertilized by a sperm cell.
   a. True
   b. False

2. Many plants reproduce _____ , sprouting new plants from leaves or roots or some other part of the parent.
   a. by budding
   b. vegetatively
   c. parthenogenetically
   d. altruistically
   e. parsimoniously

3. Cloning is a form of _____ reproduction.
   a. asexual
   b. sexual

4. Sexual reproduction is costly to a species because _____

   _____

   _____

5. For sexual reproduction to occur, specialized cells from both the male and the female come together and unite, then undergo a peculiar type of cell division called _____.

6. In spermatogenesis, from one primary spermatocyte develop
   a. two secondary spermatocytes.
   b. four secondary spermatocytes.
   c. two spermatids.
   d. four spermatids.
   e. a and d

7. Gametogenesis in females is known as
   a. follicles.
   b. ootid.
   c. oogenesis.
   d. ovum.
   e. c and e

8. Define *haploid* and its function.

   _____

   _____

   _____

   _____

11. *Source:* Steven D. Garber, *Biology: A Self-Teaching Guide.* Wiley, 1989, 65–68.

9. What is the purpose of Figure 4.2?

_____

_____

10. On a separate sheet of paper, compare and contrast asexual and sexual reproduction. What are the benefits and shortcomings of each?

PRACTICE 12

Directions: Read the following technological passage, and answer the questions that follow it in the space provided.[12] You may look back at the passage.

Programming

What Is Programming?

A program is a sequence of instructions written to perform a specific task. **Programming** is the process of defining the sequence of instructions. There are two phases in this process: determining the task that needs doing and expressing the solution in a sequence of instructions.

> **Programming**
> The process of defining the sequence of instructions that make up a program.

The process of programming always begins with a problem. Programs are not written in isolation; they are written to solve problems. Determining what needs to be done means outlining the solution to the problem. This first phase, then, is the **problem-solving phase**.

> **Problem-Solving Phase**
> 1. *Analysis:* Understand (define) the problem.
> 2. *General solution (algorithm):* Develop a logical sequence of steps to be used to solve the problem.
> 3. *Test:* Follow the steps outlined to see if the solution really solves the problem.

The second phase, expressing the solution in a sequence of instructions, is the **implementation phase**. Here, the general solution outlined in the problem-solving phase is converted into a specific solution (a program in a specific language). Testing is part of both phases. The general solution must be shown to be correct before it is translated into a program.

---

12. *Source:* Nell Dale, *Programming in Pascal.* Heath, 1990, 26–28.

> **Implementation Phase**
> 1. *Specific solution (program):* Translate the general solution (algorithm) into statements in a programming language (code the algorithm).
> 2. *Test:* Have the computer follow the instructions. Check the results and make corrections until the answers are correct.
> 3. *Use:* Use the program.

The problem-solving and implementation phases interact with each other as shown in Figure 1–22. The programmer analyzes the problem and develops a general solution called an **algorithm**. Understanding and analyzing a problem take up much more time than the figure suggests. They are the heart of the programming process.

> **Algorithm**
> A step-by-step procedure for solving a problem in a finite amount of time.

We use algorithms every day. They are simply verbal or written descriptions of logical sequences of actions. Recipes and instructions for defrosting a refrigerator are examples of written algorithms.

When you start your car, you go through a step-by-step procedure. The algorithm might look something like this:

1. Insert key.
2. Make sure transmission is in Park (or Neutral).

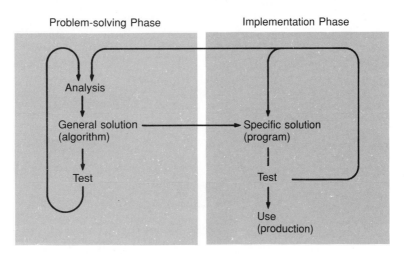

FIGURE 1–22 The programming process

3. Depress the gas pedal.
4. Turn the key to the "start" position.
5. If the engine starts within six seconds, release the key to the "ignition" position.
6. If the engine doesn't start in six seconds, wait ten seconds and repeat Steps 3 through 6 (but no more than five times).
7. If the car doesn't start, call the garage.

Without the phrase "but no more than five times" in Step 6, you could be trying to start the car forever. Why? Because if something is wrong with the car, repeating Steps 3 through 6 over and over again may not start it. This never-ending situation is called an **infinite loop**. If we left "but no more than five times" out of Step 6, our set of steps would not be an algorithm. An algorithm must terminate in a finite amount of time for all possible conditions.

After developing a general solution, we test it, "walking through" the algorithm, performing each step mentally or manually. If the test doesn't produce the correct answers, we repeat the process, analyzing the problem again and coming up with another algorithm. Once we're satisfied with the algorithm, we translate it into a programming language. We use the Pascal programming language in this book. Translating the algorithm into a programming language is called **coding** the algorithm. We test the resulting program by compiling and running it on a computer. If the program fails to produce the results we want, we have to analyze and modify it until it does.

If our definition of a computer program and an algorithm look alike, it's because all programs are algorithms. An algorithm can be in English, but when it is specified in a programming language it is also called a program.

Some students try to take a shortcut in the programming process by going directly from defining the problem to the coding of the program. (See Figure 1–23.) This shortcut is very tempting, and at first it seems to save a lot of time. However, for many reasons that will become obvious to you as you read this book, this approach actually takes more time and effort. By not taking the

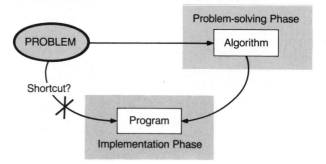

FIGURE 1–23 Programming shortcut?

time initially to think out and polish your algorithm, you will spend a lot of extra time correcting errors (**debugging**) and revising ill-conceived programs. So, think first and code later! The sooner you start coding, the longer it takes to get a correct program.

1. How many terms are defined in this passage?

    _____

    _____

    _____

2. What is the main idea of the passage?

    _____

    _____

    _____

3. What is the point of Figure 1-22?

    _____

    _____

    _____

4. What is the point of Figure 1-23?

    _____

    _____

5. What example is used to explain algorithms?

_____

_____

_____

6. On a separate sheet of paper, write out a problem-solving phase using the design in the passage for calculating the average rainfall over a period of days (*i.e.*):

   Analysis: _____

   General solution (algorithm): _____

   Test: _____

Practices in Reading Imaginative Language

The practices in this section will help you develop the strategies you have learned for reading imaginative language as found in Chapter 11. You may want to keep your dictionary handy while you do these drills.

PRACTICE 1

Directions: Here are some statements that show rather than tell what the author means. In the space at the right of each statement, write a generalized statement that denotatively tells what the author is describing. The first one has been done for you.

Showing connotatively	*Telling denotatively*
1. She wears her clothes as if they were thrown on with a pitchfork. *Jonathan Swift*	<u>She dresses sloppily.</u> _____
2. A sea Harsher than granite. *Ezra Pound*	_____ _____
3. And saw the ruddy moon lean over a hedge Like a red-faced farmer. *T. E. Hulme*	_____ _____
4. You stood at the dresser, put your teeth away, washed your face, smoothed on Oil of Olay. *Mona Van Duyn*	_____ _____
5. He'd cut off his thumbs for her. *C. D. Wright*	_____ _____
6. . . . pleased as a dog with two tails. *Ozark folk expression*	_____ _____
7. A hand like a fat maggot. *Jean-Paul Sartre*	_____ _____

8. No man is an island. . . .
   John Donne

   _____

   _____

9. There is no frigate like a book
   To take us lands away.
   Emily Dickinson

   _____

   _____

10. The pen is mightier than the sword.
    Edward Bulwer-Lytton

    _____

    _____

PRACTICE 2

Directions: Read this paragraph from a short story. Notice how the author's use of words creates sensations of sound, touch, and sight. Then answer the following questions in the space provided.

> By the time the milking was finished, the sow, which had farrowed the past week, was making such a row that the girl spilled a pint of the warm milk down the trough-lead to quiet the animal before taking the pail to the well-house. Then in the quiet she heard a sound of hoofs on the bridge, where the road crossed the creek a hundred yards below the house, and she set the pail down on the ground beside her bare, barn-soiled feet. She picked it up again. She set it down. It was as if she calculated its weight.[1]

1. Identify which of the senses (hearing, touch, sight) the following lines use. Some lines may use more than one sense.
   a. "the sow, which had farrowed the past week, was making such a row"

   _____

   b. "the girl spilled a pint of the warm milk down the trough-lead to quiet the animal."

   _____

   c. "Then in the quiet she heard a sound of hoofs on the bridge."

   _____

   d. "she set the pail down on the ground beside her bare, barn-soiled feet."

   _____

2. Define the following words as they are used in the context of the paragraph.
   a. *farrowed.* _____

   _____

   b. *trough-lead.* _____

1. *Source:* Wilbur Daniel Steele, "How Beautiful with Shoes." Harold Matson Company, Inc.

_____

c. *barn-soiled.* _____

_____

d. *calculated.* _____

_____

3. From the images created, we infer that the story takes place on a

_____

4. Based on the little that is known here, why do you think the girl picked up the pail, then set it down "as if she calculated its weight"?

_____

_____

PRACTICE 3

Directions: Read this short poem, and then answer the questions that follow in the space provided.

The Death of the Ball Turret Gunner
by Randall Jarrell

From my mother's sleep I fell into the State
And I hunched in its belly till my wet fur froze.
Six miles from earth, loosed from its dream of life,
I woke to black flak and the nightmare fighters.
When I died they washed me out of the turret with a hose.[2]

1. In the space provided, write the denotation of each of the following words. Then write the connotative meanings the words suggest as they are used in the poem.

		Denotation	*Connotation*
a.	*mother*	_____	_____
b.	*sleep*	_____	_____
c.	*State*	_____	_____
d.	*belly*	_____	_____
e.	*fur*	_____	_____

2. What images do you see in the following phrases and clauses?

a. "From my mother's sleep I fell into the State"

_____

_____

2. *Source:* Randall Jarrell, *The Complete Poems.* Farrar, 1949.

b.   "hunched in its belly"

_____

_____

c.   "Six miles from earth"

_____

_____

d.   "loosed from its dream of life"

_____

_____

e.   "I woke to black flak"

_____

_____

f.   "the nightmare fighters"

_____

_____

3.   Describe the tone or general feeling of the poem.

_____

_____

_____

PRACTICE 4

Directions: Read this passage from the opening of the novel *Young Lonigan* by James T. Farrell. Then answer the questions that follow in the space provided.

Studs Lonigan, on the verge of fifteen, and wearing his first suit of long trousers, stood in the bathroom with a Sweet Caporal pasted in his mug. His hands were jammed in his trouser pockets, and he sneered. He puffed, drew the fag out of his mouth, inhaled and said to himself:

Well, I'm kissin' the old dump goodbye tonight.

Studs was a small, broad-shouldered lad. His face was wide and planed; his hair was a light brown. His long nose was too large for his other features. His lips were thick and wide, and they did not seem at home on his otherwise frank and boyish face. He was always twisting them into his familiar tough-guy sneers. He had blue eyes; his mother rightly called them baby-blue eyes.

He took another drag and repeated to himself:

Well, I'm kissin' the old dump goodbye.

The old dump was St. Patrick's grammar school; and St. Patrick's meant a number of things to Studs. It meant school, and school was a jailhouse that might just as well have had barred windows. It meant the long, wide, chalk-smelling room of the seventh- and eighth-grade boys, with its forty or fifty squirming kids. It meant the second floor of the tan brick, undistinguished parish building on Sixty-first Street that had swallowed so much of Studs's life for the past eight years. It meant the black-garbed Sisters of Providence, with their rattling beads, their swishing strides, and the funny-looking wooden clappers they used, which made a dry snapping sound and which hurt like anything when a guy got hit over the head with one. It meant Sister Carmel, who used to teach fourth grade, but was dead now; and who used to hit everybody with the edge of a ruler because she knew they all called her the bearded lady. It meant Studs, twisting in his seat, watching the sun come in the windows to show up the dust on the floor, twisting and squirming, and letting his mind fly to all kinds of places that were not like school. It meant Battleaxe Bertha talking and hearing lessons, her thin, sunken-jawed face white as a ghost, and sometimes looking like a corpse. It meant Bertha yelling in that creaky old woman's voice of hers. It meant Bertha trying to pound lessons down your throat, when you weren't interested in them.[3]

1. Explain the following phrases and clauses:

   a. "with a Sweet Caporal pasted in his mug."

   _____

   b. "His hands were jammed in his trouser pockets."

   _____

   c. "Well, I'm kissin' the old dump goodbye."

   _____

   d. "It meant the second floor of the tan brick, undistinguished parish building . . . that had swallowed so much of Studs's life"

   _____

   e. "It meant the black-garbed Sisters of Providence"

   _____

2. Identify the following clauses and phrases by placing in the blank after each *S* for simile, *M* for metaphor, or *N* for neither.
   a. "and school was a jailhouse that might just as well have had barred windows" _____
   b. "hurt like anything" _____
   c. "letting his mind fly to all kinds of places" _____
   d. "her thin, sunken-jawed face white as a ghost" _____

3. *Source:* James T. Farrell, *Young Lonigan.* Vanguard, 1932, 17–18.

   e. "looking like a corpse" _____

   f. "yelling in that creaky old woman's voice" _____

3. State what senses (sight, hearing, touch, and so on) the following phrases and clauses use.

   a. "He puffed, drew the fag out of his mouth, inhaled"

_____

   b. "His lips were thick and wide"

_____

   c. "with their rattling beads, their swishing strides"

_____

   d. "the funny-looking wooden clappers they used, which made a dry snapping sound and which hurt like anything when a guy got hit over the head with one"

_____

4. What impression of Studs Lonigan do you get from this passage?

_____

_____

_____

PRACTICE 5

Directions: Here is an entire chapter on imaginative language from Roger B. Henkle's book *Reading the Novel: An Introduction to the Techniques of Interpreting Fiction.*[4] Apply all the techniques you have learned about reading textbook chapters, making certain you have the time to do it now, marking or taking notes on the key points being made, and using what you know about writing patterns. When you have finished, you will be asked to write about what you learned.

Language: Communication, Confusion, Intensification, Emotive Responses

The medium of fiction is, of course; language. That is well enough understood. Less well understood—or less attended to—is the way that language shapes the experience that we share when reading. Frankly, it is difficult to formulate guidelines that will be useful in interpreting the role of language in telling the story and in communicating the emotive and evaluative content of a novel. The nuances of language are so varied, from book to book and within a book, and the factors so complex—factors such as the denotative (direct explicit meaning or reference) and the connotative (idea suggested by or associated with a word in addition to its direct meaning) aspects of

4. *Source:* Harper, 1977, 118–130.

language, sentence rhythms, unconscious sounds, variations in syntax—that all I am going to presume to do here is to "tune you in" to differences in language, and to suggest how greatly the realization of the author's conception depends upon his language.

The novel, as an art form, has often been thought to favor a language that is *communicative*. That is, the words function largely as a medium for transmitting to the reader experiences or ideas within the fictional world. If the operation of language in a novel is largely communicative, then we do not need to look primarily for the rhythms, patterns, and interactions of words and phrases among themselves. We treat words and phrases as functional; they set forth the thoughts in the character's mind, say, or information about what takes place literally in the novel's world. They transmit information and attitudes and even emotions and values in the dimensions in which these things exist in the novel.

The narrative language in [Saul Bellow's] *Henderson the Rain King* for instance, is primarily communicative—indeed, sometimes desperately so. Here is the opening of Chapter 4:

Is it any wonder I had to go to Africa?

But I have told you there always comes a day of tears and madness.

I had fights. I had trouble with the troopers, I made suicide threats, and then last Xmas my daughter Ricey came home from boarding school. She has some of the family difficulty. To be blunt, I do not want to lose this child in outer space, and I said to Lily "Keep an eye on her, will you?"

The shape of this speech tells us that language is being bent into the rough, solid forms of direct communication. The opening rhetorical question— "Is it any wonder I had to go to Africa?"—is a plain appeal that you understand the speaker's predicament clearly. The expression "to be blunt" is another telltale indication of Henderson's need above all to communicate. His rapid summation, in simple sentences, of his past experiences—"I had fights. I had trouble with the troopers, I made suicide threats, and then last Xmas"—transmits the compulsion of Henderson to explain, to clarify. And he must explain himself in what he hopes will be a logical sequence: "I had fights. I had . . . I made . . . and then. . . ." The rush of such data betrays the immediacy of his emotional distress, and that distress is in itself a fact of the situation that he wants to communicate. Henderson's attempt to be logical and blunt indicates his difficulty (which we noticed before) in piecing together his experiences in a way that makes sense. Here is language being used for a communicative purpose in the most straightforward way.

Yet even within this passage, we can discover occasional uses of language that are not primarily communicative. When Henderson says, vaguely, "I did not want to lose this child in outer space," we understand the emotional situation that he wants to communicate, but our mind also absorbs a new dimension of language. That quick image, of the child lost in outer space, imprints upon our mind, even as we read the passage primarily for information about the character, a kind of unconscious imagery that will subtly shape our assessment of Henderson's plight. The language here is figurative, sending out resonances that we apprehend on another level—on the level of what the imagery suggests to us irrespective of its literal reference. The second sentence in

Henderson's statement, that "there always comes a day of tears and madness," also creates such resonances, and they are of a slightly different kind. Rather than create an image that carries its own special associations in the reader, the choice of the words "tears and madness," preceded by the Biblical phrasing "there always comes a day," evokes the significance of the Biblical accounts themselves of hard times, of endurance, of the inevitability of pain and judgment. We shall have occasion to explore the uncanny operations of these imagistic and associative kinds of language later.

Primarily, the passage that we have examined from *Henderson the Rain King* illustrates the use of language for directly communicative purposes. Our assumption that fictional language will be communicative is so strong that we attune ourselves to stresses in the need to communicate and to failures or insufficiencies of communication. When, as in Henderson's case, those stresses are pronounced—the poor man blurting out all the seamy details of his past—we develop perhaps a certain human caution in responding to him. When, as in Henderson's case, the language appears to be falling short of lucid communication—when he cannot say what he means to say or he says it imperfectly we develop an ironic or comic response to the situation. Irony arises when the author causes the reader to understand the situation differently from the narrator—when the reader is made aware of the narrator's incomprehension or limited insight. As we witness Henderson striving to communicate his situation, and as we gradually perceive that he does not comprehend it well himself, irony governs our response. Modern authors establish ironic relationships of this kind between reader and narrator for a variety of reasons: they give the reader the satisfaction of superior understanding, thus inducing evaluation and criticism; they also seem to speak aptly to the modern condition; and they highlight the problem of fictional communication itself—its difficulty, the insufficiencies of language.

Colloquial language—everyday expressions and phrasing—used by a character narrator like Henderson (or, on occasion, by an omniscient narrator) often produces irony and comedy. It creates potentially comic effects because we know from our own experience that our ordinary conversational speech often falls short of its objectives. Few of us can talk elegantly and dramatically enough to have our spoken words do full justice to what we are trying to convey. We attempt to surmount this by intensifying, by overstating, and there is much of that in Henderson's monologue. The irregular, forced heightening of language to compensate for its imprecision is a frequent source of comedy and sometimes of irony. For how else can we respond to the continued unevenness of control that the rush of colloquial, desperately communicative language betrays?

The potentialities (and limitations) of language influence the choice of narrator. If colloquial self-expression of the kind that Henderson engages in conveys an impression of disjointedness, of confusion, and of variations in control (both of one's language and of the experience one is transmitting), then an author who wants to establish such an impression of a fictional world will choose such a narrator. Because the language of ordinary speech patterns so often sets up irony and comedy, writers of this century who view life ironically or comically lean toward first person character narrations. When Conrad, therefore, wanted to engender confusion and ironic complication about Lord Jim's actions and values, he turned to a narrator, Marlow, whose language, as we have seen, is in form and phrasing philosophical, sometimes flaccid, and meandering. Before that, he used the impersonal authorial narrator, and we can see how different the language of that narrative voice is from Henderson's and Marlow's as we read this description of Jim's companions when he convalesces in an obscure Eastern port from an early injury at sea:

> The majority were men who, like himself, thrown there by some accident, had remained as officers of country ships. They had now a horror of the home service, with its harder conditions, severer view of duty, and the hazard of stormy oceans. They were attuned to the eternal peace of Eastern sky and sea. They loved short passages, good deck-chairs, large native crews, and the distinction of being white. They shuddered at the thought of hard work, and led precariously easy lives, always on the verge of dismissal, always on the verge of engagement, serving Chinamen, Arabs, half-castes — would have served the devil himself had he made it easy enough.

This passage also uses language communicatively. Here the urge to be colloquial or even simple in choice of words, in order to get the message across bluntly, as was Henderson's desire, is not in evidence. The speaker here conveys sure judgments through adroit choices of predicates and adverbs: "attuned," "loved," "shuddered," "precariously." So deft are these cutting insights into the motives of the characters that we can sense the shaping within us, as readers, of the hard instruments of critical dissection. The sentences are grammatically fine. There is a certain coldness in perfect, precise sentence construction, where the words chosen, such as the "distinction of being white" or "always on the verge of engagement," could not be improved upon. The diction is what we call formal, and this, too, compels the reader to react to it as if it were authoritative, for we associate formal diction with someone who is learned and in authority. And the passage is terribly efficient: the sentence, "They had now a horror of the home service, with its harder conditions, severer view of duty, and the hazard of stormy oceans," wraps up all the considerations in succinct parallel phrases which proceed quickly and inexorably one upon the other. Such language, and such phrasing, strikes us as being almost intolerant of people. Crisp and "very British," it seems to contain a sneer of contempt.

Perhaps I am imagining that sneer. But from this illustration, and from the passage in *Henderson the Rain King*, we can observe how readily the mind takes off to erect complementary mental projections from our response to the choice of words and phrasing. At times our responses are almost resonating canyons of memory and emotional reaction — drawing upon our past associations with such language, as well as upon what is being described and talked about. In other cases, the reader's response is almost a quick inhibition, when we put ourselves on guard, say, against formal, authoritative, and too shrewdly judgmental diction, as in the Conrad passage. Ernest Hemingway sought in *The Sun Also Rises* to rid communicative language of its easy tendency to exploit such mental structuring. He wanted to make his prose a transparent, denotative depiction of the thing it described. Writing should, Hemingway contended, transmit "the way it was": the hard truth, without built-in judgments, without clusters of words and ways of speaking that set off long, slow fuses of emotional reaction. When that worked for Hemingway, it produced not only a tough, lean prose but also descriptions that clung tightly to what actually, physically happened, as in this famous description of the movements of Romero the matador in *The Sun Also Rises:*

> Each time he let the bull pass so close that the man and the bull and the cape that filled and pivoted ahead of the bull were all one sharply etched mass. It was all so slow and so controlled. It was as though he were rocking the bull to sleep. He made four veronicas like that, and finished with a half veronica that turned his back on the bull and came away toward the applause, his hand on his hip, his cape on his arm, and the bull watching his back going away.

The language here is purely communicative, and tailored to the rhythm of the action, speeding up to convey the bull's charge: "each time he let the bull pass so close that the man and the bull and the cape that filled and pivoted ahead of the bull. . . . "Then, at the sentence's end, the words are piled up to freeze that movement into a tableau: were all one sharply etched mass." We pause for a second on the word "mass," because of the word's underlying visual picture and also because phonetically the broad *a* and the hissing *s* sound hold on. In the next sentence, the *l*'s and *o*'s drag out our reading, slowing the rhythm of the action, and giving that sentence—"It was all so slow and controlled."—the sensation in itself of the rocking motion that Hemingway says it resembled. Finally the cluster of crisp, summary actions at the close—"his hand on his hip, his cape on his arm"—replicates the hauteur of the bullfighter as he draws himself up in triumph.

Hemingway's concern in the novel about the aridity of the expatriate life in Paris and the importance of clean, graceful action dictated the language he used. But he had another objective: to strip his prose of the sentimentality that highly imagistic, emotive writing seemed to produce. To his mind, the burdening of experience with all manner of subjective, romantic implications was a cause of the fuzzy emotionality that had produced so many illusions for his generation, and which was keeping men from seeing things as they actually were. Paradoxically, Hemingway's novels of this period have come to be thought of as highly sentimental: largely, I suppose, from what we know about Hemingway's life and from the poignancy of Jake's and Brett's situation, but also because it appears that we as readers invest even the sparest of descriptions with our emotional responses. The vacuum is filled up with emotive reverberations even when the language does not induce specific patterns of sentiment.

William Faulkner, on the other hand, draws in emotiveness until the prose becomes absolutely thick with it. The opening of the "Quentin section" of *The Sound and the Fury* is delivered as Quentin's reverie:

> When the shadow of the sash appeared on the curtains it was between seven and eight oclock and then I was in time again, hearing the watch. It was Grandfather's and when Father gave it to me he said, Quentin, I give you the mausoleum of all hope and desire; it's rather excruciatingly apt that you will use it to gain the reducto absurdum of all human experience which can fit your individual needs no better than it fitted his or his father's. I give it to you not that you may remember time, but that you might forget it now and then for a moment and not spend all your breath trying to conquer it. Because no battle is ever won he said. They are not even fought. The field only reveals to man his own folly and despair, and victory is an illusion of philosophers and fools.

To find oneself thus inside a character's mind is almost enough in itself to unleash a swirl of feelings, for we know that this is what occurs in our own minds if we muse about our past, our parents, the significance of a grandfather's watch. But the images caught up in that swirl—"the mausoleum of all hope," "no battle is ever won"—expand with highly charged responses. These particular images take Quentin's situation beyond that of one man's despair to incorporate the grander significance of death and all human despair. Faulkner believes that Quentin's state of being is inextricably tied up with cultural burdens—the decadence of his family, the sickly sweet sensuality of his Southern environment—and with the modern search for identity. Interwoven with all of the character's personal considerations are these larger elements, and Faulkner's prose reflects them. The Faulknerian sentence structures—long, slightly ponderous, built of constructed phrases that roll out one upon the other—further contribute to the effect produced by Quentin's musing upon dark and weighty matters. Language is almost always emotive rather than purely communicative in Faulkner, and *emotive language*, as we have noticed, creates a movement inward to our thoughts and feelings. So, in addition to communicative language, we encounter in fiction *emotive language* which one critic, I. A. Richards, defines as language "used for the sake of the effects in emotion and attitude produced by the reference it occasions."[1]

Another thing worth noting about writers such as Faulkner is that they use language to *intensify* the implications of the material. The references to war, death, time, and the past in Quentin's reverie enhance the importance of his position. His case is made to carry larger significance than that of one depressed Harvard college boy. The combined effect of the prose's emotive quality, which sets off reverberations in our own memories, and of its broader reference to grander concerns, produces in the reader a serious, intensely felt response to the material. The solemn intonations of the prose—"I give you the mausoleum of all hope and desire"—collaborate to this end. Faulkner is a master of the prose that reads darkly, fraught with meanings that seem to reach into all history and all humanity's earthly struggle.

The extra dimension of allusions in a text of this sort establishes an undercurrent of meaning in a novel that can become as integral to our understanding of the book as is the book's overt subject matter. Gradually our attitude is suffused with Faulkner's references to heritage and man's fate so that we perceive all that occurs in *The Sound and the Fury* with those references constantly in mind coloring our vision. We read the novel as one that speaks to such larger issues: it is more than the story of one Southern family.

Within most good fiction one can trace an *internal structure* established solely through the language. Sometimes it is a collection of images (e.g., the "mausoleum"—death images in Faulkner's book); sometimes it is a recurrence of words that denote a specific kind of value judgment (e.g., "distinction" in the Conrad passage, which describes a rather rigorous way of thinking); sometimes it is a pattern of grammatical structures that reappear in particular situations (e.g., the rush of simple sentences breathlessly trying to recapture a number of events in the past in *Henderson*: "I had fights. I had . . ." At times the internal structure I describe is a calculated effect of the writer; more often, I suspect, it is unconscious, a way of thinking. Authors may be only secondarily aware of the imagery and choice of language that they habitually employ. The critic Mark Schorer has suggested the uses we can make of our perception of such a structure. He discovers in a number of nineteenth-century British authors what he calls an "analogic matrix," an inset grid of words and traits of diction which may be "buried or dead metaphors" or aspects of "value assertion."[2] For instance, he finds in Jane Austen's prose consistent use of words whose buried semantic reference is to economics and monetary arrangements: words like "credit," "charge," "value," "gain," "cost." The original reference to economic transactions is "buried" when we use them in other contexts, as when we say, "that act of kindness was to his credit." Jane Austen does not use such words in talking about financial matters, but instead of talk about love and emotional relations. Yet the unconscious choice of such words gives a commercial, bargained quality to human behavior and allows us to intuit the materialistic bent of her fictional world.

A passage in Hawthorne's *The House of the Seven Gables* reveals another matrix or substructure:

> This impalpable claim [by the Pyncheons to a great tract of forest land], therefor, resulted in nothing more solid than to cherish, from generation to generation, an absurd delusion of family importance, which all along characterized the Pyncheons. It caused the poorest member of the race to feel as if he inherited a kind of nobility, and might yet come into the possession of princely wealth to support it. In the better specimens of the breed, this peculiarity threw an ideal grace over the hard material of human life, without stealing away any truly valuable quality. In the baser sort, its effect was to increase the liability to sluggishness and dependence, and induce the victim of a shadowy hope to remit all self-effort, while awaiting the realization of his dreams.

In this excerpt from the novel one finds several words whose semantic origins or secondary meanings seem to be mercantile; for instance, "inherited," "specimens," "increase the liability," "remit." Of course, wealth is in part the subject of the paragraph, but observe that Hawthorne uses some of these words to talk about human "sluggishness and dependence." Combined with the commercial metaphors are words from what one might call medieval aristocratic sources: "cherish," "inherited," "nobility," "princely," and "grace." Other words, such as "shadowy" and "dreams," are to recur all through Hawthorne's prose. We very likely pay scant attention to these terms, whose metaphoric qualities are now so dead that when we use them we do not connect, say, "baser" with base or nonprecious metals. But they operate on us, nonetheless, and in their own particular combination, so that we intuit how crucial to the Pyncheons' story are money, delusions of aristocratic grandeur, and the shadows of false dreams. And, indeed, the choice of words supports what we learn in the nature of the Pyncheons: the undercurrent of language attunes us to the meaning of the action in the novel.

The twentieth-century Irish novelist James Joyce uses imagistic language of this sort to establish an undercurrent of meaning that he then makes serve him in a different way. Where Hawthorne's matrix of analogy very likely was conscious only in the sense that it seemed, as he was writing, the most appropriate choice of words to express his sense of his characters, Joyce, in the semiautobiographical novel *A Portrait of the Artist as a Young Man* consciously establishes, from the beginning of the work, the connotations that certain words shall bear. The novel's protagonist, Stephen Dedalus, is first shown as a boy who is generally repelled by the physical sensations of wetness. We observe this from his vivid recollection of a bed-wetting incident, and when he is thrown into a ditch of stinking, foul water by a bigger boy. Gradually, also, water comes to be associated with death and thus with the dissolution of the stable personality—a classic symbolic meaning of water in its flux and shapelessness. Joyce so painstakingly establishes these meanings for water that it becomes an overt *symbol*: water stands for physical discomfort and psychological dissolution.

As we follow Stephen's story further, however, we become aware that the symbol changes meanings. Water, particularly the water of the sea, begins in later chapters to stand for the possibilities of change (because the sea changes constantly), of travel beyond Ireland, of freedom. The changes in the symbol parallel changes in Stephen's sensibility. As he grows older, comfort and stability become less important than adventure, change, openness. We can, in fact, understand what emotional transformations are occurring in Stephen by tracing the evolution of the water symbolism. The symbol accretes more implications, almost in itself suggesting the growing complexity of Stephen and the growing ambiguity of life for him. So subtly effective is this parallel communication through the symbol that we can understand what is going on within Stephen by looking at the meanings associated with the water symbol. When Stephen's own thoughts or attitudes are not articulated, maybe not even known to him, we gain an insight into them by analyzing what Joyce says that water symbolizes for him at the time. Thus, at a crucial stage in Stephen's growth he is given the opportunity to join the Jesuit order. Before he can sort out his thinking and feelings about the commitment, we can perceive what his real, inner response is, for Stephen talks of spirituality as "dryness," and we know that this contradicts all that the water symbolism has told us he has come to yearn for: change, openness, adventure. Water had always been associated with sensuality in Stephen: as a boy the association was unpleasant, but we have seen that it assumed a more positive association as he matured. We intuit, as readers, that he will not abandon the sensual at this stage in his life for the abstinence of religious duty. Hence the imagery establishes an undercurrent (to continue the water metaphor) of meaning that carries a complex understanding of the character's state of being for us and that at times flows ahead of what the character is able to perceive about personal experience.

Joyce has taken imagery, which we have found embedded in the language of some of the other writers whom we looked at and has abstracted it into a complex set of meanings (and of changing meanings) that we call a literary symbol. The symbol takes on its own life, as it were, and functions openly to shape our reading response. It gathers meanings, as the water symbol in Joyce's novel does, so that whenever we encounter it in the text we think of those meanings. Symbols of this sort are consciously employed in modern fiction to assist us in interpreting the experience of a novel, but those substructures or matrices of imagery and reference and value that we identified in the language of Faulkner and Hawthorne and Jane Austen may function equally powerfully in shaping our response to that experience. Language can thus be made to operate as a continuous or repeated vehicle of interpretation. It can be made to function emotively throughout a novel in several ways: (1) through a suggestive web or matrix established by the choice of words or the phrasing that the author perhaps half-consciously tends to use, as Jane Austen does, in telling the story; (2) through patterns created by the introduction of images or valuative concepts that enhance or intensify the meaning of the book as when Faulkner enlarges the significance of Quentin's situation by references to death, war, and man's spiritual struggles; and (3) through the use of symbols, abstracted concepts that accrue meanings and implications as they reappear in the novel.

To this point we have assumed that language is supportive—that is designed, consciously or not, to amplify or intensify the material it pertains to. The impression that we get from the subject matter of a passage (such as, say, of the clean movements of the bullfighter) are enriched by the prose that describes it. But language can also be used as a contrast to the subject matter. The internal references within the prose may actually cut against the impression we would expect to be given of the character or the action. James Joyce was intrigued with these possibilities, and in his great novel *Ulysses* he frequently plays off the language of his narrative against the content. He experiments with numerous prose styles, many of them parodies of the styles of other well-known authors, to illustrate what occurs when apparently incongruous language is superimposed upon subject matter. In one witty episode, he describes a young woman, Gerty MacDowell, in the prose of women's glamour magazines, with all its exaggeration, trite-ness, and sensuality:

> Why have women such eyes of witchery? Gerty's were of the bluest Irish blue, set off by lustrous lashes and dark expressive brows. Time was when those brows were not so silkily seductive. It was Madame Vera Verity, directress of the Woman Beautiful page of the Princess novelette, who had first advised her to try eyebrowleine which gave that haunting expression to the eyes, so becoming in leaders of fashion, and she had never regretted it. Then there was blushing scientifically cured and how to be tall increase your height and you have a beautiful face but your nose? That would suit Mrs. Dignam because she had a button one. But Gerty's crowning glory was her wealth of wonderful hair. It was dark brown with a natural wave in it. She had cut it that very morning on account of the new moon and it nestled about her pretty head in a profusion of luxuriant clusters and pared her nails too, Thursday for wealth. And just now at Edy's words as a telltale flush, delicate as the faintest rosebloom, crept into her cheeks she looked so lovely in her sweet girlish shyness that of a surety God's fair land of Ireland did not hold her equal.

The "True Romance" manner of this passage can only ridicule the poor character whose way of thinking it purports to represent. Anyone who borrows her ideas from "the Woman Beautiful page of the Princess novelette," and clings desperately to the quick ways to charm and beauty—"blushing scientifically cured and how to be tall"—cannot be very bright. How pathetic the insecurity of a mind like Gerty's, how formulaic all her thinking. And, indeed, Gerty hasn't much more dimension than this, and the setting is a ludicrous moment when the hero of the novel, Leopold Bloom, is leering at Gerty while she pretends not to notice. But the mocking language does not quite demolish the character. In fact, a curious thing happens: as we read, the character of Gerty MacDowell comes alive for us and assumes dimensions. Although the women's confession magazine prose would seem to reduce the humanity of the individual and diminish her into a mushy stereotype, this is not the case. Although we are induced by such prose to make fun of the Gerty MacDowells of life, a poignant affection for them emerges instead. Joyce has performed one of his many tours de force with language. He makes it do things one would never expect: ridicule a character and humanize it at the same time. The reader must hold apparently incongruous responses in suspension, thus making understanding of the person and situation highly complex.

Joyce's experiments demonstrate the creativity of language itself. All good writers seem to find that the meaning of the experience they are trying to record takes its shape—sometimes a different shape from that of its original conception—when put into the plastic materials of the art: language. The twentieth-century British novelist Joyce Cary, in a book called *Art and Reality*,[3] describes the process of converting an "inspiration" or an idea about experience into language: "For the novelist, in fact, there is not only a huge gap between intuition and concept, the first raw statement, but between that statement and its working out in a story. For the truth is that the work of art as completely realised is the result of a long and complex process of exploration, as well as construction." That exploration takes place in the realm of "how one says it"—the language. Invariably, the language modifies the conception: "For the writer has to deal with language which consists of forms which are also contents. That is to say, they are meanings." The novelist "has to ask himself how the manipulation of words, themselves already charged with meaning, will convey the other larger meaning which is to be his content." Cary says it is even more difficult than that. For not only is the artist trying to put a vision into words that have their own references, their own special meanings gained from centuries of use, but those words must also be assembled in grammatical constructions—"sentence by sentence and page by page"—that support the effect of the artistic conception. As we have seen, language is not just words, by syntax and phrasing—arrangements of words that have their own special powers.

Mark Schorer contends that this challenge enriches great novelists. Technique, he says, is a form of discovery. Not only is one forced to evaluate or think through the accuracy of one's conceptions when putting them down on the page (an agonizing reappraisal we have all had to experience), but one discovers new facets of them. "The virtue of the modern novelist—from James and Conrad down—is not only that he pays so much attention to his medium, but that, when he pays most, he discovers through it a new subject matter, and a greater one."[4] The experience expands in significance as it passes through the language in which it must be expressed. Such an expansion into richer meaning is not for the artist only; it is also there for us, as readers, when the language passes on through to us.

1. I. A. Richards, *Principles of Literary Criticism* (New York: Harcourt Brace Jovanovich, 1961), p. 267.
2. Mark Schorer, *The World We Image* (New York: Farrar, Straus & Giroux, 1948), pp. 24–48.
3. Joyce Cary, *Art and Reality: Ways of the Creative Process* (New York: Harper & Row, 1958), rpt. Anchor Books (New York: Doubleday, 1961), pp. 102, 113.
4. *The World We Imagine, op. cit.*, p. 10.

On a separate sheet of paper, write answers to the following questions.

1. Explain the title of the chapter, giving examples of writers to support your explanation.
2. What is the difference between the ways Hemingway and Faulkner used language? Provide some examples.

WHAT DO YOU THINK?

The most significant period of ethical development is early adulthood, between the twenties and thirties, because until that time, people don't have to test their ethics, they don't have to put their money where their mouth is. It's when you first have to decide how important it is for you to keep your job that you decide how much the truth means to you. At that point it's decision-making that's critical, not merely character. Almost everyone wants to be ethical. Everyone I know is capable of being ethical. But whether people are willing to be ethical in a particular decision-making situation depends on a lot of things, including their ability to see the ethical issues, to work out the problems, to anticipate correctly the risks and burdens, and to implement their decision in a way that doesn't cause hazardous and dangerous consequences for themselves.

Michael Josephson, ethicist

3. What does the author mean by *internal structure*? How does language contribute to it?
4. Summarize the points made in this chapter about language use in fiction.

Practices in Reading Expository Writing in the Humanities

The practices in this section, based on what you learned in Chapter 12, will help you read and better understand expository writing as it appears in humanities textbooks.

PRACTICE 1

Directions: Read this paragraph and answer the questions that follow it in the space provided.

> Specifically, philosophy means and includes five fields of study and discourse: logic, esthetics, ethics, politics, and metaphysics. *Logic* is the study of ideal method in thought and research: observation and introspection, deduction and induction, hypothesis and experiment, analysis and synthesis—such are the forms of human activity which logic tries to understand and guide; it is a dull study for most of us, and yet the great events in the history of thought are the improvements men have made in their methods of thinking and research. *Esthetics* is the study of ideal form, or beauty; it is the philosophy of art. *Ethics* is the study of ideal conduct; the highest knowledge, said Socrates, is the knowledge of good and evil, the knowledge of the wisdom of life. *Politics* is the study of ideal social organization (it is not, as one might suppose, the art and science of capturing and keeping office); monarchy, aristocracy, democracy, socialism, anarchism, feminism—these are the **dramatis personae** of political philosophy. And lastly, *metaphysics* (which gets into so much trouble because it is not, like the other forms of philosophy, an attempt to coordinate the real in the light of the ideal) is the study of the "ultimate reality" of all things: of the real and final nature of "matter," of "mind," and of the interrelationship of "mind" and "matter" in the processes of perception and knowledge.[1]

1. What is the main idea of the paragraph?

   _____

   _____

1. *Source:* Will Durant, *The Story of Philosophy.* Simon, 1961, xxvii–xxviii.

2. What primary writing pattern is used to develop the main idea?

_____

_____

3. What terms are defined, and what do they represent as a whole?

_____

_____

PRACTICE 2

Directions: Read this paragraph and answer the questions that follow it in the space provided.

There are two schemes whereby harmony is achieved in the history of Western music. One, which is called polyphony or counterpoint, implies the use of two or more simultaneously sounded melodic lines, a scheme which deals with the musical materials in a linear fashion. The other, which we will call homophony, deals with the musical materials in a chordal-harmonic or vertical-block fashion. Both achieve the result of having tones of different pitch sounded simultaneously, a phenomenon which was described in Chapter 11 as harmony, under the basic elements of music.[2]

1. What is the main idea of the paragraph?

_____

_____

2. What two writing patterns are used to support the idea?

_____

_____

PRACTICE 3

Directions: Read this passage from an art textbook. Look for the main idea of the entire passage, using writing patterns to help you distinguish between main ideas and supporting details. Then answer the questions that follow it in the space provided.

Style

There are styles of music, styles of dress, styles of interior design, even styles of speaking and walking. When an automobile manufacturer changes the way its cars look from year to year, we speak of the "new

2. *Source:* Milo Wold and Edmund Cykler, *Introduction to Music and Art in the Western World,* Brown, 1985, 93.

style." If a person we know always wears jeans and cowboy boots, or always wears long flowing dresses and flowered prints, we identify that person with his or her particular style of dress. Furthermore, we may say of someone, "She really has style!" Or we might describe the decor of a particular home as "stylish." In the latter two cases, we mean the person or place shows a *desirable* style, one we admire, because everybody and everything has *some* style or other. But what exactly is style?

Above all, *style* is a characteristic or group of characteristics that we can identify as constant, recurring, or coherent. For instance, suppose you have a friend who has very long hair and always wears it in braids; then your friend gets a short haircut. You would call this a sudden change of style. Or perhaps you know a family whose home is entirely decorated with antiques, except for one very modern chair and table in the living room. You would recognize a mix of styles—not necessarily bad, but obvious.

In the visual arts, just as in any other area of life, style indicates a series of choices an artist has made. *Artistic style* is the sum of constant, recurring, or coherent traits identified with a certain individual or group. In painting, for example, a particular style could be composed of many elements—the materials used, the type of brush strokes, the colors, the way forms are handled, the choice of subject matter, the degree of resemblance to the natural world (representational vs. abstract style), and so on.

Style may be associated with a whole artistic culture (the Song dynasty style in China); with a particular time and place (the early Renaissance style in Rome); with a group of artists whose work shows similar characteristics (the Abstract Expressionist style); with one artist (Van Gogh's style); or with one artist at a certain time (Picasso's Blue Period style). In all these instances there are common elements—constant, recurring, coherent—that we can learn to recognize. Once you become familiar with Van Gogh's mature style, with its licking, flamelike brush strokes and vivid color, you will probably be able to identify other paintings by Van Gogh, even if you have never seen them before. Some artists develop a style and stick to it; others work in several styles, simultaneously or sequentially.

One way to think of style is to consider it an artist's personal "handwriting." You know that if you give ten people identical pieces of paper and identical pens and tell them to write the same sentence, you'll get ten very different results, because no two people have the same handwriting. Penmanship styles are interesting. Each is absolutely unique, yet there are characteristics we can identify, even if we don't know the person who did the writing. If you study handwriting at all, a given sample should be able to tell you if the writer is male or female, old or young, American or European, and so forth. Much the same is true of artistic styles. Every one is individual, but we may find similarities among artists of a particular time, place, or group.

To get a sense of style variations in art, let us consider three paintings (59, 60, 61) with similar subject matter. Each depicts a woman in profile, from the waist up, but the paintings are very different. Even someone who knows practically nothing about art would observe differences in style, although he or she might not be able to articulate those differences. The first, by Alesso Baldovinetti, was painted in Italy in the 15th century (59). It shows the woman in sharp outline, against a plain blue background, almost as flat as a silhouette. The drawing is lifelike but probably idealized, made to look more beautiful than the

left: **59.** Alesso Baldovinetti. *Portrait of a Lady in Yellow.* c. 1463. Wood panel, 24¾ x 16". National Gallery, London (reproduced by courtesy of the Trustees).

below left: **60.** *Lady with a Bird*, from Hyderabad, India. c. 1730. Gouache on paper, 13 x 8½". Victoria & Albert Museum, London.

below: **61.** Joshua Reynolds. *Mrs. Mary Robinson* (*Perdita*), 1784. Oil on canvas, 30½ x 25". Wallace Collection, London (reproduced by permission of the Trustees).

subject actually was. All is elegance, from the pure features to the long neck to the prominent leaf pattern on the sleeve.

The second painting was made in India in the 18th century. Again the outline is sharp against a plain background, but the subject's pose is even more rigid, almost ritually frozen. The woman holds a bird in one hand and, presumably, the bird's treat in the other, but these are really ornaments for the carefully used hands. She does not look at the bird but instead stares off into an unseen distance. Following the artistic style of that culture, the artist has bared the woman's breasts and exaggerated her enormous, almond-shaped eyes. Our third example (61), painted at almost the same time as the Indian picture, is by the great English portraitist Sir Joshua Reynolds. Here we see no flat background, but rather the illusion of deep space—a vale and romantic seascape toward which the woman seems to be gazing. Unlike the first two artists, Reynolds invites us into the sitter's mind. She is pensive, perhaps a little sad, perhaps daydreaming or remembering. Her pose is more relaxed than either of the previous two, more dramatic, even a bit theatrical. Colors are softer, the forms slightly blurred.

Three lovely portraits, each by a skilled artist, but markedly different from one another—that is the nature of style. In every case the artist's style will be influenced by choices related to time, place, and the artist's expressive needs. We said at the beginning of this chapter that many periods in the history of art have been marked by a cohesive style, common to much or all of the art produced then. Such cohesion may occur whenever artists are strongly influenced by their societies or when they work closely together. An extreme example of style similarity occurred in the early part of this century. From 1908 to about 1912 the artists Pablo Picasso and Georges Braque worked virtually side by side in developing the style that would come to be called *Cubism* (Chapter 17). So harmonious were their efforts that, in some cases, only experts can definitely tell their paintings apart. Later, the styles of Picasso and Braque diverged, but for a short time they painted almost as one.[3]

1. What is the purpose or main idea of the passage?

     _____

     _____

2. What writing patterns are used to support the main idea?

     _____

     _____

3. What aids do the authors use to help you understand the passage?

     _____

     _____

3. *Source:* Rita Gilbert and William McCarter, *Living with Art.* Knopf, 1988, 55–57.

4. What is *artistic style*?

5. What artists are used as examples to help define *style*?

PRACTICE 4

Directions: Read this passage from a humanities textbook, applying all the skills you have learned. Then answer the questions that follow it in the space provided.

The Humanities Today

What, it may well be asked, can the study of the humanities do for a student in the final years of the twentieth century? We are no longer certain, as the Renaissance humanists were, that the study of the humanities will make one a better or "more human" person. Yet most of today's humanists do still believe that the study of the humanities involves a process of individual growth and self-knowledge that is as valid today as it was hundreds of years ago. True involvement with the humanities means stretching and expanding one's capacity for thought, sensitivity, and creativity. It means searching for the answers to fundamental questions, such as: What is good and evil? What is the nature of God? What constitutes the good life and the just society? What is beauty? What is love?

The study of the humanities will not provide ready-made answers to these or other questions, but it will provide contact with great minds and imaginations that have pondered them, and it should help students to prune away sloppiness and superficiality from their thinking. Understanding developed through work in the humanities may, it is hoped, change lives as well as ideas.

The Interdisciplinary Humanities

In this introductory text we cannot pretend to deal with all of the fields mentioned in the definition above. Our focus will be on literature, art history, cultural history, and music, with some attention to philosophy, dance and theater arts, and film. The interdisciplinary method of approaching the humanities stresses their relationships but at the same time makes clear the limits and boundaries of each discipline.

What justifies studying a poem or story, a building, a statue, a dance, a musical composition, and a work of philosophy together? One reason often given is enriched understanding of a particular human culture: the study of the masks, dances, poetry, music, and religion of the Yoruba people will give more insight into their culture than will the study of their poetry alone. Another reason lies in the fact that the comparative method enables one art form to shed light on another. A third, more general, reason is that all of these enable us to understand more about the human spirit and its creative capacity.

The various disciplines in the humanities are all concerned with human values, beliefs, and emotions and with the way in which these are expressed through human creations. Philosophy and religion embody more or less systematically organized values and beliefs, whereas works of art (in literature, painting, music, or other) embody the creative expression of these values and beliefs. But these distinctions are not hard and fast. A philosophical tract may also be artistic, and a play or a statue may open up new dimensions in philosophy. The study of cultural history—of values and beliefs prevalent at certain times and places—helps to bind the humanities together, even if a work of genius may *oppose* prevailing values and systems.

What do the arts have in common? Let us suppose that for the creation of a work of art, basically two elements are needed: some kind of raw material and a creative mind. Some examples from the Western tradition come to mind: Michelangelo and a block of marble, Shakespeare and the English language, Beethoven and the tones of the scale and instruments of the orchestra. The artist works on the raw material, giving it shape and form. The finished product then bears the imprint of the artist's individual genius, but it also shows the influence of the cultural tradition and the era from which it comes. The combination of these will constitute its style. The work of art will also have a certain subject matter, structure, and theme that will be composed of the "fundamentals" of the art form used. All of these can be analyzed, step by step. A technical analysis of a work of art, though a necessary and useful step in the process of understanding, is still only a means to an end. The end can be called "aesthetic awareness"—the expansion of one's capacity to perceive meaning in art and react to it.

The artist gives shape, power, and expression to stone, words, or notes; and you, the humanities student, through some technical or historical knowledge and a willingness to expand your creative awareness, prepare yourself to receive a personal impact from the work of art. Of course, you can choose not to expand but rather to judge, through the limits and prejudices of your present experience, deciding immediately that you simply "like" or "dislike" or "agree with" or "don't agree with" certain works or ideas. In that case, you will not be receiving an education in the humanities. A humanistic education presupposes a willingness to open the mind and senses to the unfamiliar and to judge only after attempting to understand. And the interdisciplinary method invites speculation and comparisons that transcend traditional boundaries.[4]

1. What can studying the humanities do for a student today?

_____

_____

2. What is meant by *Interdisciplinary Humanities*?

_____

_____

4. *Source:* Mary Ann Frese Witt et al. *The Humanities*, vol. 1, 3rd ed. Heath, 1989, 4–5.

3. With what are all the disciplines in the humanities concerned?

_____

_____

4. What do all the arts have in common?

_____

5. What is meant by *aesthetic awareness*?

_____

_____

6. Do you care whether or not you expand your creative awareness? Explain.

_____

_____

PRACTICE 5

Directions: Is, as Confucius said, a picture worth ten thousand words? Read this passage[5] and see what the author thinks. Then answer the questions that follow it by circling the letter of the correct answer or filling in the blank as appropriate.

*T*he best advertising is a combination of words that make pictures in the mind and pictures that make words in the mind . . . usually strong, simple words and arresting, obvious art combined in a fresh and surprising manner.[1]

The Headline

The headline is generally considered to be the most important part of any ad. Since advertising folklore claims that the average ad is looked at for about eight seconds, it becomes vital for any headline to grab the reader's attention quickly. Studies reported by Ogilvy & Mather show that five times as many people read the headline as read any other part of the ad; therefore, the headline is the hook that must catch the reader. A poor headline means the reader will be gone to the next page, and anything of value in the ad will be lost. An eminently noncompelling headline is shown in Figure 9.2. Developed for the U. S. Postal Service and nine-digit zip codes, it actually doesn't say anything. "We're taking off into the future." So what? Goodbye. Have a nice trip. "Zip + 4." Another floor wax? With four new chemicals? Nice sun and clouds. What's on the next page? All the benefits are buried in the copy—nine-digit zips are supposedly faster and cheaper,

Illustration

Along with the headline, the element most likely to stop the reader is the illustration. Although it has been said by many (including Confucius) that a picture is worth ten-thousand words, in advertising the visual component rarely accomplishes the communications task without verbal assistance. During the years that advertising has been a major force in U. S. culture (most of the twentieth century), there has been a gradual shift from almost totally verbal print advertising to highly visual print advertising with less verbal content.

5. *Source:* M.L. Rothschild, *Advertising: From Fundamentals to Strategies.* Heath, 1987, 259, 288–295.

This shift probably reflects changes in viewpoint on how consumers absorb and use advertising. As practitioners became more aware that consumers pay little attention to most advertising, there also was more awareness of a need for grabbing attention, conveying information quickly, and generating some emotion. Illustrations in advertising do these tasks well.

Given the above, the first task of the illustration is to *attract attention to the headline* and to a lesser degree, to the body copy. This may be too broad a task, though. Naked ladies and gorillas in tutus attract attention (especially in the same picture), but the attention must be relevant in terms of target market and benefit. Spurious attention generally has little value in relation to the firm's objectives; it is therefore to be avoided. The best illustrations share the ideas of the headline and the strategy in such a way as to convey the message creatively while gaining attention. Just as with borrowed interest, the elements of the ad must contribute to the selling strategy.

This brings up the second task. The illustration should *convey the main ideas or benefits* of the brand. For food, this may be appetite appeal (appearance), for liquor it may be a good time, or for cologne it may be finding oneself in a sensuous setting. Visually demonstrating a benefit can be challenging. "Is it live or is it Memorex?" makes a fine headline or slogan; showing the taped sound breaking glass makes it more memorable. The illustration must convey the main idea or benefit.

The ad shown in Plates 1 and 2 is a combination of a creative ad and creative media. By showing both the front and back of the television monitor on opposite sides of the same sheet of a magazine, the ad first attracts attention ("What's going on here?"), then shows the benefits of the product, and ultimately leads the reader into the copy. The unique two-page format grabs attention.

The third task adds even more specificity; the ad must attract attention through relevant benefits but must do so in a creative way to *generate feeling and emotion* as well. It is difficult to convey feelings in words; this is a task well suited to the visual part of the ad. This is especially the case when the message must be short. A ten-word headline can't convey feelings well, but the supporting illustration can. If a picture is worth ten-thousand words, it is in this context—that is, in adding feeling and emotion to a specific benefit—that the picture is most valuable.

Related to this is the task of *telling a story*. In this way the benefit becomes more memorable to the reader and shows how the product helps solve a problem. This task puts quite a burden on the illustration, and many never make it, but in creating advertising that will sell, the creative department must strive to meet these goals.

In Figure 10.5 the illustration does several things well: it shows feeling, tells a story, attracts attention, and ties well to the headline. It also shows the product and package, and even presents a coupon. This ad works hard; no part of it is wasted.

As stated above, the illustration should

1. Attract attention
2. Tie to the headline
3. Show the benefit
4. Convey feelings and emotions
5. Convey a story

Figure 10.5 *An illustration that tells a story*

Given these tasks, what guidelines can be used to achieve them? A recent McGraw-Hill study of readers of business publications showed the value of illustrations. The survey showed that, for all dependent variables, ads with illustrations led to a greater level of response. Table 10.1 shows these data in a format that gives scores of 100 for ads with no illustrations and gives the illustrated ads a value in relation to the score of 100.

Table 10.1 Advertisements with illustrations achieve better results

	No illustration	*Illustration*
"When you first looked through this issue, did you see this ad?"	100	132
Ability of ad to alert readers to something not previously known	100	105
Ability of ad to cause reader to plan or take some action	100	126
"Did this ad intensify a positive feeling you already had for this brand?"	100	122
Reinforce a reader's perceptions about company	100	109

Source: McGraw-Hill Research, LAP Report 3170.1.

1. *Photographs seem to work better than other art forms.* Although this is a guideline and not an absolute rule, the realism of photography shows the product or the situation as it really is. In most cases, art cannot improve the reality of an appetizing dish of food or a new automobile, or the emotion of a smile.

There are exceptions. Photography, especially color, reproduces poorly in newspapers, so many art directors turn to line drawings in the latter medium. Another exception is the case of an imaginary character acting as spokesperson for the product. Third, there are concepts that just don't translate well into a photograph. Figure 9.8, which showed a man committing suicide with a gas pump, would lose much of its impact if it were a photograph. Generally, though, photography produces the strongest illustrations for print advertising.

2. *Color works better than black and white.* Despite the truth of this statement, color may not be cost effective. A four-color ad costs 33% more to print than a black and white one and returns slightly above 20% more readership (i.e., the ad was noted during magazine reading). This makes the use of color a creative decision; if it enhances the benefit (e.g., appetite appeal), use it. If the color has no intrinsic merit toward the benefit, then save the money and buy more repetition of the ad. Functional color, which works toward the goals of the message, is good investment; color for its own sake isn't.

3. *Action illustrations enhance readership.* A pure product shot, one of a person standing next to the product, or one of a person holding onto the product does not seem to generate as much attention as an action shot. Generally, an illustration showing the product in use or solving a problem is more likely to involve the reader. Before and after, or problem–solution setups also work well. On the left, Ms. Smith is shown when she weighed 847 pounds. Then on the right, she is shown two weeks later weighing $91\frac{1}{2}$ pounds.

A product shot with a dynamic background also helps. This allows the product and its benefits to be shown simultaneously as in Figure 10.6.

4. *Size and arrangement of illustrations are important.* An alternative is to consider a series of small illustrations. These can show several facets of the product and can tie nicely to the body copy. Often, small illustrations end up as a cluttered page when they don't each have a specific purpose. The danger of this format is that it requires work on the part of the consumer to go through the copy and pictures. Unless there is involvement or outstanding illustration, it may simply be too easy to turn the page. For this reason, one large illustration is generally felt to have a greater impact and is therefore a safer format selection. Figure 10.7 shows a series of small illustrations that tie well to the copy and emphasize the benefits.

Given a set of tasks and guidelines, the art director can next consider what to use in the illustration. The following list, like other lists in this text, is incomplete, but it does include the major possible subjects:

1. *The product and/or the package alone* In the absence of the type of creativity shown in Figure 10.5, this is the least attention-getting illustration.

2. *Product in use, with or without people* These are more interesting than a straight product shot. Adding people adds interest. Readers can relate better to an ad with people. Figures 10.8 through 10.10 show ads for the same product class—floor covering. The first is product alone, the second shows the product in use in a home, and the third adds people. Which seems to hold interest the best?

Figure 10.6   *Product in action*   **Figure 10.7**   *Use of a series of small illustrations*

3. *Benefits of using or costs of not using the product*   This illustration can show the result of product use (boy wins heart of girl), or the problems associated with not using the product (boy loses, then wins, heart of girl). The first probably works best in print; the second, with its temporal development, is best suited for radio or television.

4. *Dramatization of product features*   This can be done by showing the brand features alone or in a comparison shot with other brands. Our ketchup drips more slowly than the competitor's. Our paper diaper absorbs more than the competitor's.

5. *Developing a mood, feeling, or emotion*   This is a common illustration that may or may not include the product or people. It is commonly used for products that try to enhance the self-image of the reader. Common themes include sunsets, nature scenes, fireplaces, or a variety of objects shot with a soft focus.

Other illustrative themes include

6. *Cartoon characters*
7. *Trade spokespersons*
8. *Charts and/or diagrams*
9. *Abstractions*
10. *Testimonials*[1]

Figure 10.8   *Floor coverings—product shot*

Figure 10.9   *Floor coverings—product in use*

Figure 10.10 *Floor coverings—product being used by real people*

Although the choice of illustration is quite broad, in reality it may be limited by what is being shown in television commercials. Often the print advertising is a spinoff from television and will use one of its scenes. This leads to continuity across the campaign and is to be encouraged.

And a final suggestion on illustrations comes from the renowned art director, Anonymous:

> *When the client moans and sighs,*
> *Make his logo twice the size.*
> *If he still should prove refractory,*
> *Show a picture of his factory.*
> *Only in the gravest cases,*
> *Should you show the clients' faces.*

Design

Some principles of design

Several characteristics of design need to be considered if the ad is to be visually pleasing, inviting to the eye, and easy to read. These principles should guide the design of the layout in the same way that grammar guides the writer.

Nelson has written that the advertising designer "tries to achieve both order and beauty. The *order* which the designer creates out of a chaos of pictures, copy blocks, headlines and white space makes it easy for the reader to read and understand the ad. The *beauty* makes him glad he's there."[2]

***Plates 1 and 2   Combination of creative layout
and creative media placement***

1. What is the most important part of any ad?

   _____

2. The first task in the use of an illustration in advertising is to attract attention to the
   a. written headline copy.
   b. product.
   c. illustration.
   d. all of the above
   e. none of the above

3. The second task of using illustration in advertising is to convey the main ideas or benefits of the brand being advertised.
   a. True
   b. False, because _____

4. The third task of using illustration in advertising is to
   a. generate interest in the brand.
   b. generate emotion.
   c. generate emotion and feeling.
   d. avoid using print.
   e. all of the above

5. Related to the third task is the task of

   _____

6. Advertisements with illustrations achieve better results.
   a. True
   b. False, because _____

7. Which of the following is true regarding the use of illustrations in ad copy?
   a. Photographs seem to work better than other art forms.
   b. Black and white works better than color.
   c. Action illustrations increase readership.
   d. Size and arrangement of illustrations are not as important as clever written copy.

8. Based on the information provided, explain which of the three ads for floor coverings (Figures 10.8 through 10.10) hold interest the best.

   _____

   _____

   _____

9. Compare and contrast the benefits of using or not using the product in an illustrated ad.

   _____

   _____

10. Why is an illustration that develops a mood, feeling, or emotion commonly used? What is its intent?

_____

_____

_____

PRACTICE 6

Directions: Look at the advertisement[6] on page 414. On a separate sheet of paper, using the information in the reading in Practice 5, (a) explain how many of the recommended guidelines the ad follows; and (b) write a statement regarding your personal reaction to the ad.

6. *Source:* The Nature Conservancy.

NOW DISAPPEARING AT A LOCATION NEAR YOU.

©Art Wolfe

This baby trumpeter swan will require wetland acres in the Pacific Northwest all the way to Alaska to complete the migration its species has depended upon for eons.

But soon these beautiful birds may be extinct because their wetlands are vanishing.

Since 1951, The Nature Conservancy has protected millions of acres of wildlife habitat in the U.S. alone. And we've done it by using a novel approach—we've bought it.

Our philosophy is to use the money we receive to protect rare plants and animals by buying the lands they need to survive.

But we can't do it alone, so join us. Help us save this living legacy. Write The Nature Conservancy, Adirondack Chapter, P.O. Box 188, Elizabethtown, NY 12932. Or call 518-873-2610.

Conservation Through Private Action

Original concept courtesy of Lewis & Partners, San Francisco

Practices in Reading Fiction

The practices in this section will help you develop the strategies you learned in Chapter 13 for study-reading novels and short stories.

PRACTICE 1

Directions: Here is the opening from Mark Twain's *The Adventures of Huckleberry Finn.* There is not enough space to reprint the entire book, but read this passage and answer the questions that follow it in the space provided.

The Adventures of Huckleberry Finn
by Mark Twain

You don't know about me without you have read a book by the name of *The Adventures of Tom Sawyer;* but that ain't no matter. That book was made by Mr. Mark Twain, and he told the truth, mainly. There was things which he stretched, but mainly he told the truth. That is nothing. I never seen anybody but lied one time or another, without it was Aunt Polly, or the widow, or maybe Mary. Aunt Polly—Tom's Aunt Polly, she is—and Mary, and the Widow Douglas is all told about in that book, which is mostly a true book, with some stretchers, as I said before.

Now the way that the book winds up is this: Tom and me found the money that the robbers hid in the cave, and it made us rich. We got six thousand dollars apiece—all gold. It was an awful sight of money when it was piled up. Well, Judge Thatcher he took it and put it out at interest, and it fetched us a dollar a day apiece all the year round—more than a body could tell what to do with. The Widow Douglas she took me for her son, and allowed she would sivilize me; but it was rough living in the house all the time, considering how dismal regular and decent the widow was in all her ways; and so when I couldn't stand it no longer I lit out. I got into my old rags and my sugar-hogs-head again, and was free and satisfied. But Tom Sawyer he hunted me up and said he was going to start a band of robbers, and I might join if I would go back to the widow and be respectable. So I went back.

The widow she cried over me, and called me a poor lost lamb, and she called me a lot of other names, too, but she never meant no harm by it. She put me in them new clothes again, and I couldn't do nothing but sweat and sweat, and feel all cramped up. Well, then, the old thing commenced again. The widow rung a bell for supper, and you had to come to time. When you got to the table you couldn't go right to eating, but you had to wait for the widow to tuck down her head and grumble a little over the victuals, though there warn't really anything the matter with them—that is, nothing, only everything was cooked by itself. In a barrel of odds and ends it is different; things get mixed up, and the juice kind of swaps around, and the things go better.

After supper she got out her book and learned me about Moses and the Bulrushers, and I was in a sweat to find out all about him; but by-and-by she let it out that Moses had been dead a considerable long time; so then I didn't care no more about him, because I don't take no stock in dead people.

Pretty soon I wanted to smoke, and asked the widow to let me. But she wouldn't. She said it was a mean practice and wasn't clean, and I must try to not do it any more. That is just the way with some people. They get down on a thing when they don't know nothing about it. Here she was a-bothering about Moses, which was no kin to her, and no use to anybody, being gone, you see, yet finding a power of fault with me for doing a thing that had some good in it. And she took snuff, too; of course that was all right, because she done it herself.

Her sister, Miss Watson, a tolerable slim old maid, with goggles on, had just come to live with her, and took a set at me now with a spelling-book. She worked me middling hard for about an hour, and then the widow made her ease up. I couldn't stood it much longer. Then for an hour it was deadly dull, and I was fidgety. Miss Watson would say, "Don't put your feet up there, Huckleberry"; and "Don't scrunch up like that, Huckleberry—set up straight"; and pretty soon she would say "Don't gap and stretch like that, Huckleberry—why don't you try to behave?" Then she told me all about the bad place, and I said I wished I was there. She got mad then, but I didn't mean no harm. All I wanted was to go somewheres; all I wanted was a change, I warn't particular.

1. Who is the main character? What other characters are important?

   _____

   _____

2. Where and when is everything happening? How do you know?

   _____

   _____

3. What is happening?

   _____

   _____

4. Through whose eyes do we learn what is happening?

   _____

   _____

5. What kinds of words or language does the author use and why?

   _____

6. What does the author seem to be showing or telling us at this point?

    _____

    _____

7. What do you think will happen next?

    _____

    _____

PRACTICE 2

Directions: Here is the opening from the novel *Anna Karenina* by Leo Tolstoy. Read it, then answer the questions that follow it in the space provided.

Anna Karenina
by Leo Tolstoy

Happy families are all alike; every unhappy family is unhappy in its own way. Everything was in confusion in the Oblonskys' house. The wife had discovered that the husband was carrying on an intrigue with a French girl, who had been a governess in their family, and she had announced to her husband that she could not go on living in the same house with him. This position of affairs had now lasted three days, and not only the husband and wife themselves, but all the members of their family and household, were painfully conscious of it. Every person in the house felt that there was no sense in their living together, and that the stray people brought together by chance in any inn had more in common with one another than they, the members of the family and household of the Oblonskys. The wife did not leave her own room, the husband had not been at home for three days. The children ran wild all over the house; the English governess quarreled with the housekeeper, and wrote to a friend asking her to look out for a new situation for her; the man-cook had walked off the day before just at dinner-time; the kitchen-maid, and the coachman had given warning.

Three days after the quarrel, Prince Stepan Arkadyevitch Oblonsky—Stiva, as he was called in the fashionable world—woke up at his usual hour, that is, at eight o'clock in the morning, not in his wife's bedroom, but on the leather-covered sofa in his study. He turned over his stout, well-cared-for person on the springy sofa as though he would sink into a long sleep again; he vigorously embraced the pillow on the other side and buried his face in it; but all at once he jumped up, sat up on the sofa, and opened his eyes . . .

. . . he cheerfully dropped his feet over the edge of the sofa, and felt about with them for his slippers, a present on his last birthday, worked for him by his wife on gold-colored morocco. And, as he had done every day for the last nine years, he stretched out his hand, without getting up, towards the place where his dressing gown always hung in his bedroom. And thereupon he suddenly remembered that he was not sleeping in his wife's room, but in his study, and why: the smile vanished from his face, he knitted his brows.

"Ah, ah, ah! Oo! . . ." he muttered, recalling everything that had happened. And again every detail of his quarrel with his wife was present to his imagination, all the hopelessness of his position, and worst of all, his own fault.

"Yes, she won't forgive me, and she can't forgive me. And the most awful thing about it is that it's all my fault—all my fault, though I'm not to blame. That's the point of the whole situation," he reflected. "Oh, oh, oh!" he kept repeating in despair, as he remembered the acutely painful sensations caused him by this quarrel.

Most unpleasant of all was the first minute when, on coming, happy and goodhumored, from the theater, with a huge pear in his hand for his wife, he had not found his wife in the drawing-room, to his surprise had not found her in the study either, and saw her at last in her bedroom with the unlucky letter that revealed everything in her hand.

She, his Dolly, forever fussing and worrying over household details, and limited in her ideas, as he considered, was sitting perfectly still with the letter in her hand, looking at him with an expression of horror, despair, and indignation.

"What's this? this?" she asked, pointing to the letter.

And at this recollection, Stepan Arkadyevitch, as is so often the case, was not so much annoyed at the fact itself as at the way in which he had met his wife's words.

There happened to him at that instant what does happen to people when they are unexpectedly caught in something very disgraceful. He did not succeed in adapting his face to the position in which he was placed towards his wife by the discovery of his fault. Instead of being hurt, denying, defending himself, begging forgiveness, instead of remaining indifferent even—anything would have been better than what he did do—his face utterly involuntarily (reflex spinal action, reflected Stepan Arkadyevitch, who was fond of physiology) utterly involuntarily assumed its habitual, good-humored, and therefore idiotic smile.

This idiotic smile he could not forgive himself. Catching sight of that smile, Dolly shuddered as though at physical pain, broke out with her characteristic heat into a flood of cruel words, and rushed out of the room. Since then she had refused to see her husband.

"It's that idiotic smile that's to blame for it all," thought Stepan Arkadyevitch.

"But what's to be done? What's to be done?" he said to himself in despair, and found no answer.

1. Who is the main character? What other characters are important?

_____

_____

2. Where and when is everything happening? How do you know?

_____

_____

3. What is happening?

_____

4. Through whose eyes do we learn what is happening?

_____

_____

5. What kinds of words or language does the author use and why?

_____

_____

6. What does the author seem to be showing or telling us at this point?

_____

_____

7. What do you think will happen next?

_____

_____

PRACTICE 3

Directions: Here is the opening to Ernest Hemingway's novel *A Farewell to Arms.* Read it, then answer the questions that follow it in the space provided.

A Farewell to Arms
by Ernest Hemingway

In the late summer of that year we lived in a house in a village that looked across the river and the plain to the mountains. In the bed of the river there were pebbles and boulders, dry and white in the sun, and the water was clear and swiftly moving and blue in the channels. Troops went by the house and down the road and the dust they raised powdered the leaves of the trees. The trunks of the trees too were dusty and the leaves fell early that year and we saw the troops marching along the road and the dust rising and leaves, stirred by the breeze, falling and the soldiers marching and afterward the road bare and white except for the leaves.

The plain was rich with crops; there were many orchards of fruit trees and beyond the plain the mountains were brown and bare. There was fighting in the mountains and at night we could see the flashes from the artillery. In the dark it was like summer lightning, but the nights were cool and there was not the feeling of a storm coming.

Sometimes in the dark we heard the troops marching under the window and guns going past pulled by motor-tractors. There was much traffic at night and many mules on the roads with boxes of ammunition on each side of their pack-saddles and gray motor-trucks that carried men, and other trucks with loads covered with canvas that moved slower in the traffic. There were big guns too that passed in the day drawn by tractors, the long barrels of the guns covered with green branches and green leafy branches and vines laid over the tractors. To the north we could look across a valley and see a forest of chestnut trees and behind it another mountain on this side of the river. There was fighting for that mountain too, but it was not successful, and in the fall when the rains came the leaves all fell from the chestnut trees and the branches were bare and the trunks black with rain. The vineyards were thin and bare-branched too and all the country wet and brown and dead with the autumn. There were mists over the river and clouds on the mountain and the trucks splashed mud on the road and the troops were muddy and wet in their capes; their rifles were wet and under their capes the two leather cartridge-boxes bulged.

There were small gray motor-cars that passed going very fast; usually there was an officer on the seat with the driver and more officers in the back seat. They splashed more mud than the camions even and if one of the officers in the back was very small and sitting between two generals, he himself so small that you could not see his face but only the top of his cap and his narrow back, and if the car went especially fast it was probably the King. He lived in Udine and came out in this way nearly every day to see how things were going, and things went very badly.

At the start of the winter came the permanent rain and with the rain came the cholera. But it was checked and in the end only seven thousand died of it in the army.[1]

1. Who is the main character? What other characters are important?

_____

_____

2. Where and when is everything happening? How do you know?

_____

_____

3. What is happening?

_____

_____

4. Through whose eyes do we learn what is happening?

_____

_____

1. *Source:* Ernest Hemingway, *A Farewell to Arms.* Scribner's, 1929.

5. What kinds of words or language does the author use and why?

_____

_____

6. What does the author seem to be showing or telling us at this point?

_____

_____

7. What do you think will happen next?

_____

_____

PRACTICE 4

Directions: Here is the opening to a short story. Read it, then answer the questions that follow it in the space provided.

No One's a Mystery
by Elizabeth Tallent

For my eighteenth birthday Jack gave me a five-year diary with a latch and a little key, light as a dime. I was sitting beside him scratching at the lock, which didn't seem to want to work, when he thought he saw his wife's Cadillac in the distance, coming toward us. He pushed me down onto the dirty floor of the pickup and kept one hand on my head while I inhaled the musk of his cigarettes in the dashboard ashtray and sang along with Rosanne Cash on the tape deck. We'd been drinking tequila and the bottle was between his legs, resting up against his crotch, where the seam of his Levi's was bleached linen-white, though the Levi's were nearly new. I don't know why his Levi's always bleached like that, along the seams and at the knees. In a curve of cloth his zipper glinted, gold.

"It's her," he said. "She keeps the lights on in the daytime. I can't think of a single habit in a woman that irritates me more than that." When he saw that I was going to stay still he took his hand from my head and ran it through his own dark hair.

"Why does she?" I said.

"She thinks it's safer. Why does she need to be safer? She's driving exactly fifty-five miles an hour. She believes in those signs: 'Speed Monitored by Aircraft.' It doesn't matter that you can look up and see that the sky is empty."

"She'll see your lips move, Jack. She'll know you're talking to someone."

"She'll think I'm singing along with the radio."

He didn't lift his hand, just raised the fingers in salute while the pressure of his palm steadied the wheel, and I heard the Cadillac honk twice, musically; he was driving easily eighty miles an hour. I studied his boots. The elk heads stitched into the leather were bearded with frayed thread, the toes were scuffed, and there was a compact wedge of muddy manure between the heel and the sole—the same boots he'd been wearing for the two years I'd known him.[2]

1. Who is the main character? What other characters are important?

   _____

   _____

2. Where and when is everything happening? How do you know?

   _____

   _____

3. What is happening?

   _____

   _____

4. Through whose eyes do we learn what is happening?

   _____

   _____

5. What kinds of words or language does the author use and why?

   _____

   _____

6. What does the author seem to be showing or telling us at this point?

   _____

   _____

7. What do you think will happen next?

   _____

   _____

8. Why would you or would you not want to read the rest of the story?

   _____

   _____

2. *Source:* Elizabeth Tallent, *Harper's*, August 1985, and reprinted in *The Available Press/PEN Short Story Collection*, Ballantine, 1985.

PRACTICE 5

Directions: Read this short story. Then answer the questions that follow it on a separate sheet of paper.

Charles
by Shirley Jackson

The day my son Laurie started kindergarten he renounced corduroy overalls with bibs and began wearing blue jeans with a belt; I watched him go off the first morning with the older girl next door, seeing clearly that an era of my life was ended, my sweet-voiced nursery-school tot replaced by a long-trousered, swaggering character who forgot to stop at the corner and wave good-bye to me.

He came home the same way, the front door slamming open, his cap on the Boor, and the voice suddenly become raucous shouting, "Isn't anybody here?"

At lunch he spoke insolently to his father, spilled his baby sister's milk, and remarked that his teacher said we were not to take the name of the Lord in vain.

"How *was* school today?" I asked, elaborately casual.

"All right," he said.

"Did you learn anything?" his father asked.

Laurie regarded his father coldly. "I didn't learn nothing," he said.

"Anything," I said. "Didn't learn anything."

"The teacher spanked a boy, though," Laurie said, addressing his bread and butter. "For being fresh," he added, with his mouth full.

"What did he do?" I asked. "Who was it?"

Laurie thought. "It was Charles," he said. "He was fresh. The teacher spanked him and made him stand in a corner. He was awfully fresh."

"What did he do?" I asked again, but Laurie slid off his chair, took a cookie, and left, while his father was still saying, "See here, young man."

The next day Laurie remarked at lunch, as soon as he sat down, "Well, Charles was bad again today." He grinned enormously and said, "Today Charles hit the teacher."

"Good heavens," I said, mindful of the Lord's name, "I suppose he got spanked again?"

"He sure did," Laurie said. "Look up," he said to his father.

"What?" his father said, looking up.

"Look down," Laurie said. "Look at my thumb. Gee, you're dumb." He began to laugh insanely.

"Why did Charles hit the teacher?" I asked quickly.

"Because she tried to make him color with red crayons," Laurie said. "Charles wanted to color with green crayons so he hit the teacher and she spanked him and said nobody play with Charles but everybody did."

The third day—it was Wednesday of the first week—Charles bounced a see-saw on to the head of a little girl and made her bleed, and the teacher made him stay inside all during recess. Thursday Charles had to stand in a corner during story-time because he kept pounding his feet on the floor. Friday Charles was deprived of blackboard privileges because he threw chalk.

On Saturday ı remarked to my husband, "Do you think kindergarten is too unsettling for Laurie? All this toughness, and bad grammar, and this Charles boy sounds like such a bad influence."

"It'll be all right," my husband said reassuringly. "Bound to be people like Charles in the world. Might as well meet them now as later."

On Monday Laurie came home late, full of news. "Charles," he shouted as he came up the hill; I was waiting anxiously on the front steps. "Charles," Laurie yelled all the way up the hill, "Charles was bad again."

"Come right in," I said, as soon as he came close enough. "Lunch is waiting."

"You know what Charles did?" he demanded, following me through the door. "Charles yelled so in school they sent a boy in from first grade to tell the teacher she had to make Charles keep quiet, and so Charles had to stay after school. And so all the children stayed to watch him."

"What did he do?" I asked.

"He just sat there," Laurie said, climbing into his chair at the table. "Hi, Pop, y'old dust mop."

"Charles had to stay after school today," I told my husband. "Everyone stayed with him."

"What does this Charles look like?" my husband asked Laurie. "What's his other name?"

"He's bigger than me," Laurie said. "And he doesn't have any rubbers and he doesn't ever wear a jacket."

Monday night was the first Parent-Teachers meeting, and only the fact that the baby had a cold kept me from going; I wanted passionately to meet Charles's mother. On Tuesday Laurie remarked suddenly, "Our teacher had a friend come to see her in school today."

"Charles's mother?" my husband and I asked simultaneously.

"Naaah," Laurie said scornfully. "It was a man who came and made us do exercises, we had to touch our toes. Look." He climbed down from his chair and squatted down and touched his toes. "Like this," he said. He got solemnly back into his chair and said, picking up his fork, "Charles didn't even *do* exercises."

"That's fine," I said heartily. "Didn't Charles want to do exercises?" "Naaah," Laurie said. "Charles was so fresh to the teacher's friend he wasn't *let* do exercises.

"Fresh again?" I said.

"He kicked the teacher's friend," Laurie said. "The teacher's friend told Charles to touch his toes like I just did and Charles kicked him."

"What are they going to do about Charles, do you suppose?" Laurie's father asked him.

Laurie shrugged elaborately. "Throw him out of school, I guess," he said.

Wednesday and Thursday were routine; Charles yelled during story hour and hit a boy in the stomach and made him cry. On Friday Charles stayed after school again and so did all the other children.

With the third week of kindergarten Charles was an institution in our family; the baby was being a Charles when she cried all afternoon; Laurie did a Charles when he filled his wagon full of mud and pulled it through the kitchen; even my husband, when he caught his elbow in the telephone cord and pulled telephone, ashtray, and a bowl of flowers off the table, said, after the first minute, "Looks like Charles."

During the third and fourth weeks it looked like a reformation in Charles; Laurie reported grimly at lunch on Thursday of the third week, "Charles was so good today the teacher gave him an apple."

"What?" I said, and my husband added warily, "You mean Charles?"

"Charles," Laurie said. "He gave the crayons around and he picked up the books afterward and the teacher said he was her helper."

"What happened?" I asked incredulously.

"He was her helper, that's all," Laurie said, and shrugged.

"Can this be true, about Charles?" I asked my husband that night. "Can something like this happen?"

"Wait and see," my husband said cynically. "When you've got a Charles to deal with, this may mean he's only plotting."

He seemed to be wrong. For over a week Charles was the teacher's helper; each day he handed things out and he picked things up; no one had to stay after school.

"The P.T.A. meeting's next week again," I told my husband one evening. "I'm going to find Charles's mother there."

"Ask her what happened to Charles," my husband said. "I'd like to know."

"I'd like to know myself," I said.

On Friday of that week things were back to normal. "You know what Charles did today?" Laurie demanded at the lunch table, in a voice slightly awed. "He told a little girl to say a word and she said it and the teacher washed her mouth out with soap and Charles laughed."

"What word?" his father asked unwisely, and Laurie said, "I'll have to whisper it to you, it's so bad." He got down off his chair and went around to his father. His father bent his head down and Laurie whispered joyfully. His father's eyes widened.

"Did Charles tell the little girl to say *that*?" he asked respectfully.

"She said it twice," Laurie said. "Charles told her to say it *twice*."

"What happened to Charles?" my husband asked.

"Nothing," Laurie said. "He was passing out the crayons."

Monday morning Charles abandoned the little girl and said the evil word himself three or four times, getting his mouth washed out with soap each time. He also threw chalk.

My husband came to the door with me that evening as I set out for the P.T.A. meeting. "Invite her over for a cup of tea after the meeting," he said. "I want to get a look at her."

"If only she's there," I said prayerfully.

"She'll be there," my husband said. "I don't see how they could hold a P.T.A. meeting without Charles's mother."

At the meeting I sat restlessly, scanning each comfortable matronly face, trying to determine which one hid the secret of Charles. None of them looked to me haggard enough. No one stood up in the meeting and apologized for the way her son had been acting. No one mentioned Charles.

After the meeting I identified and sought out Laurie's kindergarten teacher. She had a plate with a cup of tea and a piece of chocolate cake; I had a plate with a cup of tea and a piece of marshmallow cake. We maneuvered up to one another cautiously, and smiled.

"I've been so anxious to meet you," I said. "I'm Laurie's mother."

"We're all so interested in Laurie," she said.

"Well, he certainly likes kindergarten," I said. "He talks about it all the time."

"We had a little trouble adjusting, the first week or so," she said primly, "but now he's a fine little helper. With occasional lapses, of course."

"Laurie usually adjusts very quickly," I said. "I suppose this time it's Charles's influence."

"Charles?"

"Yes," I said, laughing, "you must have your hands full in that kindergarten, with Charles."

"Charles?" she said. "We don't have any Charles in the kindergarten."[3]

Literal comprehension questions	1. Who is the main character? What is she or he like? 2. What other characters are important? 3. Where and when is everything happening? 4. What is happening? 5. Through whose mind or eyes do we learn what is happening?
Interpretive comprehension questions	6. What is the point (theme) of the story? 7. How does the author use events, scenes, or characters to develop her theme? 8. How is the title related to the theme? 9. How effective is the ending?
Affective comprehension questions	10. What feelings do you have for the main character? 11. What passages do you feel are well written? Why do they seem effective? 12. Why do you (or do you not) like the story?

PRACTICE 6

Directions: If you have not been assigned or have not selected a novel to read, you may wish to choose one from this very incomplete list of good reading. Look over the titles, select three or four that sound interesting, and locate them in your library or bookstore. Decide on one. Then read it, applying the comprehension questions presented in Chapter 13.

Margaret Atwood, *Cat's Eye*
Saul Bellow, *Henderson the Rain King*
Ray Bradbury, *Fahrenheit 451*
Walter Van Tilburg Clark, *The Ox-Bow Incident*
Stephen Crane, *The Red Badge of Courage*
Ralph Ellison, *Invisible Man*
Louise Erdrich, *Love Medicine*
James T. Farrell, *Young Lonigan*
William Faulkner, *The Bear* or *The Sound and the Fury*
F. Scott Fitzgerald, *The Great Gatsby*
William Golding, *Lord of the Flies*
Joseph Heller, *Catch-22*
Ernest Hemingway, *A Farewell to Arms* or *The Sun Also Rises*
James Joyce, *A Portrait of the Artist as a Young Man*
Harper Lee, *To Kill a Mockingbird*
Sinclair Lewis, *Babbitt*

3. *Source:* Shirley Jackson, *The Lottery*. Farrar, 1949.

Jack London, *Martin Eden*
Bernard Malamud, *The Natural*
Larry McMurtry, *Lonesome Dove*
Warren Miller, *The Cool World*
Toni Morrison, *Beloved* or *Tar Baby*
Tim O'Brien, *Going After Cacciato*
George Orwell, *1984*
Walker Percy, *The Moviegoer*
Katherine Anne Porter, *Noon Wine*
J. D. Salinger, *The Catcher in the Rye*
Irwin Shaw, *The Young Lions*
Nevil Shute, *On the Beach*
John Steinbeck, *The Grapes of Wrath*
Lawrence Thornton, *Imagining Argentina*
Dalton Trumbo, *Johnny Got His Gun*
Mark Twain, *The Adventures of Huckleberry Finn*
John Updike, *Rabbit, Run* (the first in a series of four novels about the main character)
Kurt Vonnegut, Jr., *God Bless You, Mr. Rosewater*
Alice Walker, *The Color Purple*
Nathanael West, *The Day of the Locust*
Herman Wouk, *The Caine Mutiny*
Richard Wright, *Native Son*

Practices in Reading Poetry

The practices in this section will help you become familiar with study-reading and analyzing poetry. Apply what you learned in Chapter 14 when you do them.

PRACTICE 1

Directions: Here is a passage from Laurence Perrine's *Sound and Sense: An Introduction to Poetry.* Read it, then answer the questions that follow it in the space provided.

<u>Chapter nine</u>

Meaning and Idea

LITTLE JACK HORNER

Little Jack Horner
Sat in a corner
Eating a Christmas pie.
He stuck in his thumb
And pulled out a plum
And said, "What a good boy am I!"

Anonymous

The meaning of a poem is the experience it expresses—nothing less. But readers who, baffled by a particular poem, ask perplexedly, "What does it mean?" are usually after something more specific than this. They want something they can grasp entirely with their minds. We may therefore find it useful to distinguish the total meaning of a poem—the experience it communicates (and which can be communicated in no other way) from its prose meaning—the ingredient that can be separated out in the form of a prose paraphrase. If we make this distinction, however, we must be careful not to confuse the two kinds of meaning. The prose meaning is no more the poem than a plum is a pie or than a prune is a plum.

The prose meaning will not necessarily or perhaps even usually be an idea. It may be a story, it may be a description, it may be a statement of emotion, it may be a presentation of human character, or it may be some combination of these. "The Mill" tells a story; "The Eagle" and "A Hummingbird" are primarily descriptive; "Bereft" and "Those Winter Sundays" are expressions of emotion; "A Study of Reading Habits" and "My Last Duchess" are accounts of human character. None of these poems is directly concerned with ideas. Message hunters will be baffled and disappointed by poetry of this kind, for they will not find what they are looking for, and they may attempt to read some idea into the poem that is really not there. Yet ideas are also part of human experience, and therefore many poems are concerned, at least partially, with representing ideas. But with these poems message-hunting is an even more dangerous activity, for the message hunters are likely to think that the whole object of reading the poem is to find the message—that the idea is really the only important thing in it. Like Little Jack Horner, they will reach in and pluck out the idea and say, "What a good boy am I!" as if the pie existed for the plum.

The idea in a poem is only part of the total experience that it communicates. The value and worth of the poem are determined by the value of the total experience, not by the truth or the nobility of the idea itself. This is not to say that the truth of the idea is unimportant, or that its validity should not be examined and appraised. But a good idea alone will not make a good poem, nor need an idea with which the reader does not agree ruin one. Good readers of poetry are receptive to all kinds of experience. They are able to make that "willing suspension of disbelief" that Coleridge characterized as constituting poetic faith. When one attends a performance of Hamlet, one is willing to forget for the time being that such a person as Hamlet never existed and that the events on the stage are fictions. The reader of poetry should also be willing to entertain imaginatively, for the time being, ideas he objectively regards as untrue. It is one way of understanding these ideas better and of enlarging the reader's own experience. The person who believes in God should be able to enjoy a good poem expressing atheistic ideas, just as the atheist should be able to appreciate a good poem in praise of God. The optimist should be able to find pleasure in pessimistic poetry, and the pessimist in optimistic poetry. The teetotaler should be able to enjoy "The Rubaiyat of Omar Khayyam," and the winebibber a good poem in praise of austerity. The primary value of a poem depends not so much on the truth of the idea presented as on the power with which it is communicated and on its being made a convincing part of a meaningful total experience. We must feel that the idea has been truly and deeply felt by the poet, and that the poet is doing something more than merely moralizing. The plum must be made part of a pie. If the plum is properly combined with other ingredients and if the pie is well baked, it should be enjoyable even for persons who do not care for the brand of plums from which it is made. Consider, for instance, the following two poems.

BARTER

Life has loveliness to sell,
All beautiful and splendid things,
Blue waves whitened on a cliff,
Soaring fire that sways and sings,
And Children's faces looking up,
Holding wonder like a cup.

Life has loveliness to sell,
Music like a curve of gold,
Scent of pine trees in the rain,
Eyes that love you, arms that hold,
And for your spirit's still delight,
Holy thoughts that star the night.

Spend all you have for loveliness,
Buy it and never count the cost;
For one white singing hour of peace
Count many a year of strife well lost,

And for a breath of ecstasy
Give all you have been, or could be.

Sara Teasdale (1884–1933)

STOPPING BY WOODS ON A SNOWY EVENING

Whose woods these are I think I know.
His house is in the village though;
He will not see me stopping here
To watch his woods fill up with snow.

My little horse must think it queer
To stop without a farmhouse near
Between the woods and frozen lake
The darkest evening of the year.

He gives his harness bells a shake
To ask if there is some mistake.
The only other sound's the sweep
Of easy wind and downy flake.

The woods are lovely, dark and deep,
But I have promises to keep,
And miles to go before I sleep,
And miles to go before I sleep.

Robert Frost (1874–1963)

QUESTIONS

1. How do these two poems differ in idea?
2. What contrasts are suggested between the speaker in the second poem and (a) his horse and (b) the owner of the woods?

Both of these poems present ideas, the first more or less explicitly, the second symbolically. Perhaps the best way to get at the idea of the second poem is to ask two questions. First, why does the speaker stop? Second, why does he go on? He stops, we answer, to watch the woods fill up with snow—to observe a scene of natural beauty. He goes on, we answer, because he has "promises to keep"—that is, he has obligations to fulfill. He is momentarily torn between his love of beauty and these other various and complex claims that life has upon him. The small conflict in the poem is symbolic of a larger conflict in life. One part of the sensitive thinking person would like to give up his life to the enjoyment of beauty and art. But another part is aware of larger duties and responsibilities—responsibilities owed, at least in part, to other human beings. The speaker in the poem would like to satisfy both impulses. But when the two conflict, he seems to suggest, the "promises" must be given precedence.

The first poem also presents a philosophy but an opposed one. For this poet, beauty is of such supreme value that any conflicting demand should be sacrificed to it. "Spend all you have for loveliness, / Buy it and never count the cost . . . And for a breath of ecstasy / Give all you have been, or could be." Thoughtful readers will have to choose between these two philosophies—to commit themselves to one or the other—but this commitment should not destroy for them their enjoyment of either poem. If it does, they are reading for plums and not for pies.

Nothing so far said in this chapter should be construed as meaning that the truth or falsity of the idea in a poem is a matter of no importance. Other things being equal, good readers naturally will, and properly should, value more highly the poem whose idea they feel to be more mature and nearer to the heart of human experience. Some ideas, moreover, may seem so vicious or so foolish or so beyond the pale of normal human decency as to discredit by themselves the poems in which they are found. A rotten plum may spoil a pie. But good readers strive for intellectual flexibility and tolerance, and are able to entertain sympathetically ideas other than their own. They will often like a poem whose idea they disagree with better than one with an idea they accept. And, above all, they will not confuse the prose meaning of any poem with its total meaning. They will not mistake plums for pies.[1]

1. What does the author mean when he says, "The meaning of a poem is the experience it expresses — nothing less"?

   _____

   _____

   _____

2. What is the difference between the *total meaning* of a poem and its *prose meaning*?

   _____

   _____

   _____

3. Why does the author say that "message hunting" is dangerous when reading poetry?

   _____

   _____

   _____

4. How do the ideas in the Teasdale and Frost poems differ?

   _____

   _____

   _____

5. Do you agree or disagree with the author's position on meaning and idea in poetry? Explain.

   _____

1. *Source:* Laurence Perrine, *Sound and Sense*, 7th ed. Harcourt, 1987, 129–133.

_____

_____

_____

PRACTICE 2

Directions: Read this poem, applying what you learned in Chapter 14. Then answer the questions that follow it in the space provided.

The World Is Too Much with Us
by William Wordsworth

The world is too much with us; late and soon,
Getting and spending, we lay waste our powers;
Little we see in Nature that is ours;
We have given our hearts away, a sordid boon!
This Sea that bares her bosom to the moon;
The winds that will be howling at all hours,
And are up-gathered now like sleeping flowers,
For this, for everything, we are out of tune;
It moves us not. — Great God! I'd rather be
A Pagan suckled in a creed outworn;
So might I, standing on this pleasant lea,
Have glimpses that would make me less forlorn;
Have sight of Proteus rising from the sea;
Or hear old Triton blow his wreathéd horn.

1. Define the following words that are used in the poem. You may consult your dictionary.
   a. *boon*

   _____

   b. *creed*

   _____

   c. *lea*

   _____

   d. *Proteus*

   _____

   e. *Triton*

   _____

2. What two relevant denotations does *wreathéd* have?

   _____

   _____

3. Why do you think the poet chose his wording rather than these alternatives:
    a. *earth* for "world"

    _____

    b. *selling and buying* for "getting and spending"

    _____

    c. *exposes* for "bares"; *stomach* for "bosom"

    _____

    d. *dozing* for "sleeping"

    _____

    e. *nourished* for "suckled"

    _____

4. State the theme (central idea) of the poem in a sentence.

    _____

    _____

PRACTICE 3

Directions: Read this poem, and then answer the questions that follow it on a separate sheet of paper.

Richard Cory
by Edwin Arlington Robinson

Whenever Richard Cory went down town,
We people on the pavement looked at him:
He was a gentleman from sole to crown,
Clean favored, and imperially slim.

And he was always quietly arrayed,
And he was always human when he talked;
But still he fluttered pulses when he said,
"Good-morning," and he glittered when he walked.

And he was rich—yes, richer than a king—
And admirably schooled in every grace:
In fine, we thought that he was everything
To make us wish that we were in his place.

So on we worked, and waited for the light,
And went without the meat, and cursed the bread;
And Richard Cory, one calm summer night,
Went home and put a bullet through his head.[2]

2. *Source:* Edwin Arlington Robinson, *The Children of the Night,* Scribner's.

Literal comprehension questions

1. What is going on in the poem?
2. Who is the speaker?
3. List some key words in the poem, and define them at both the denotative and the connotative level. Make three columns, with headings as follows:

Words from the poem	Denotative meanings	Connotative meanings

4. What are some of the figures of speech (similes and metaphors) used in the poem to create particular images or emotions?

Interpretive comprehension questions

5. What do some of the images imply or suggest to you?
6. What do all the images in the poem suggest as a whole; that is, how are they related?
7. What is the point of the poem?

Affective comprehension questions

8. What mood does the poem create in you?
9. Which lines are particularly effective for you? Which are ineffective?
10. What is your reaction to the poem?

Practices in Reading Drama

The practices in this section will help you develop the strategies you have learned for study-reading drama. Apply what you learned in Chapter 15.

PRACTICE 1

Directions: Here is the opening to Arthur Miller's play *Death of a Salesman*. Read it, applying what you have learned about study-reading drama. Then answer the questions that follow it in the space provided.

Death of a Salesman
by Arthur Miller

Certain Private Conversations in Two Acts and a Requiem

The action takes place in Willy Loman's house and yard and in various places he visits in the New York and Boston of today.

Throughout the play, the stage directions left and right mean stage left and stage right.

ACT I

A melody is heard played upon a flute. It is small and fine, telling of grass and trees and the horizon. The curtain rises.

Before us is the Salesman's house. We are aware of towering, angular shapes behind it, surrounding it on all sides. Only the blue light of the sky falls upon the house and forestage; the surrounding area shows an angry glow of orange. As more light appears, we see a solid vault of apartment houses around the small, fragile-seeming home. An air of the dream clings to the place, a dream rising out of reality. The kitchen at center seems actual enough, for there is a kitchen table with three chairs, and a refrigerator. But no other fixtures are seen. At the back of the kitchen there is a draped entrance, which leads to the livingroom. To the right of the kitchen, on a level raised two feet, is a bedroom furnished only with a brass bedstead and a straight chair. On a shelf over the bed a silver athletic trophy stands. A window opens onto the apartment house at the side.

Behind the kitchen, on a level raised six and a half feet, is the boys' bedroom, at present barely visible. Two beds are dimly seen, and at the back of the room a dormer window. (This bedroom is above the unseen livingroom.) At the left a stairway curves up to it from the kitchen.

The entire setting is wholly or, in some places, partially transparent. The roof-line of the house is one-dimensional; under and over it we see the apartment buildings. Before the house lies an apron, curving beyond the forestage into the orchestra. This forward area serves as the back yard as well as the locale of all Willy's imaginings and of his city scenes. Whenever the action is in the present the actors observe the imaginary wall-lines, entering the house only through the door at the left. But in the scenes of the past these boundaries are broken, and characters enter or leave a room by stepping "through" a wall onto the forestage.

From the right, Willy Loman, the Salesman, enters, carrying two large sample cases. The flute plays on. He hears but is not aware of it. He is past sixty years of age, dressed quietly. Even as he crosses the stage to the doorway of the house, his exhaustion is apparent. He unlocks the door, comes into the kitchen, and thankfully lets his burden down, feeling the soreness of his palms. A word-sigh escapes his lips.

It might be "Oh, boy, oh, boy." He closes the door, then carries his cases out into the livingroom, through the draped kitchen doorway.

Linda, his wife, has stirred in her bed at the right. She gets out and puts on a robe, listening. Most often jovial, she has developed an iron repression of her exceptions to Willy's behavior — she more than loves him, she admires him, as though his mercurial nature, his temper, his massive dreams and little cruelties, served her only as sharp reminders of the turbulent longings within him, longings which she shares but lacks the temperament to utter and follow to their end.

Linda (hearing Willy outside the bedroom, calls with some trepidation): Willy!

Willy: It's all right. I came back.

Linda: Why? What happened? (*slight pause*) Did something happen, Willy?

Willy: No, nothing happened.

Linda: You didn't smash the car, did you?

Willy (with casual irritation): I said nothing happened. Didn't you hear me?

Linda: Don't you feel well?

Willy: I am tired to the death. (*The flute has faded away. He sits on the bed beside her, a little numb.*) I couldn't make it. I just couldn't make it, Linda.

Linda (very carefully, delicately): Where were you all day? You look terrible.

Willy: I got as far as a little above Yonkers. I stopped for a cup of coffee. Maybe it was the coffee.

Linda: What?

Willy (after a pause): I suddenly couldn't drive any more. The car kept going onto the shoulder, y'know?

Linda (helpfully): Oh. Maybe it was the steering again. I don't think Angelo knows the Studebaker.

Willy: No, it's me, it's me. Suddenly I realize I'm goin' sixty miles an hour and I don't remember the last five minutes. I'm—I can't seem to—keep my mind to it.

Linda: Maybe it's your glasses. You never went for your new glasses.

Willy: No, I see everything. I came back ten miles an hour. It took me nearly four hours from Yonkers.

Linda (resigned): Well, you'll just have to take a rest, Willy, you can't continue this way.

Willy: I just got back from Florida.

Linda: But you didn't rest your mind. Your mind is overactive, and the mind is what counts, dear.

Willy: I'll start out in the morning. Maybe I'll feel better in the morning. (*She is taking off his shoes.*) These goddam arch supports are killing me.

Linda: Take an aspirin. Should I get you an aspirin? It'll soothe you.

Willy (with wonder): I was driving along, you understand? And I was fine. I was even observing the scenery. You can imagine, me looking at scenery, on the road every week of my life. But it's so beautiful up there, Linda, the trees are so thick, and the sun is warm. I opened the windshield and just let the warm air bathe over me. And then all of a sudden I'm goin' off the road! I'm tellin' ya, I absolutely forgot I was driving. If I'd've gone the other way over the white line I might've killed somebody. So I went on again — and five minutes later I'm dreamin' again, and I nearly — (*He presses two fingers against his eyes.*) I have such thoughts, I have such strange thoughts.

Linda: Willy, dear. Talk to them again. There's no reason why you can't work in New York.

Willy: They don't need me in New York. I'm the New England man. I'm vital in New England.

Linda: But you're sixty years old. They can't expect you to keep traveling every week.

Willy: I'll have to send a wire to Portland. I'm supposed to see Brown and Morrison tomorrow morning at ten o'clock to show the line. Goddammit, I could sell them! (*He starts putting on his jacket.*)

Linda (taking the jacket from him): Why don't you go down to the place tomorrow and tell Howard you've simply got to work in New York? You're too accommodating, dear.

Willy: If old man Wagner was alive I'd a been in charge of New York now! That man was a prince, he was a masterful man. But that boy of his, that Howard, he don't appreciate. When I went north the first time, the Wagner Company didn't know where New England was!

Linda: Why don't you tell those things to Howard, dear?

Willy (encouraged): I will, I definitely will. Is there any cheese?

Linda: I'll make you a sandwich.

Willy: No, go to sleep. I'll take some milk. I'll be up right away. The boys in?

Linda: They're sleeping. Happy took Biff on a date tonight.

Willy (interested): That so?

Linda: It was so nice to see them shaving together, one behind the other, in the bathroom. And going out together. You notice? The whole house smells of shaving lotion.

Willy: Figure it out. Work a lifetime to pay off a house. You finally own it, and there's nobody to live in it.

Linda: Well, dear, life is a casting off. It's always that way.

Willy: No, no, some people — some people accomplish something. Did Biff say anything after I went this morning?[1]

1. How does the information regarding the stage setting let us know that the play will cover both the past and the present?

---

1. *Source:* Arthur Miller, *Death of a Salesman.* Viking, 1949.

_____

2. What do we know about the characters Willy and Linda before the play begins?

_____

_____

3. What do we learn about Willy and Linda from the dialogue?

_____

_____

4. What problem or conflict is established in these opening lines?

_____

_____

5. What other characters will probably come onstage next?

_____

_____

6. What purpose do you think the flute music serves?

_____

_____

7. Explain why you would or would not like to read more of this play or see a production of it.

_____

_____

PRACTICE 2

Directions: Read this one-act play. Then on a separate sheet of paper answer the questions that follow.

Trifles
by Susan Glaspell

CHARACTERS

George Henderson, county attorney
Henry Peters, sheriff
Lewis Hale, a neighboring farmer
Mrs. Peters
Mrs. Hale

SCENE. *The kitchen in the now abandoned farmhouse of John Wright, a gloomy kitchen, and left without having been put in order—unwashed pans under the sink, a loaf of bread outside the breadbox, a dish towel on the table—other signs of incompleted work. At the rear the outer door opens and the Sheriff comes in followed by the County Attorney and Hale. The Sheriff and Hale are men in middle life, the County Attorney is a young man, all are much bundled up and go at once to the stove. They are followed by two women—the Sheriff's wife first; she is a slight wiry woman, a thin nervous face. Mrs. Hale is larger and would ordinarily be called more comfortable looking, but she is disturbed now and looks fearfully about as she enters. The women have come in slowly, and stand close together near the door.*

County Attorney (rubbing his hands): This feels good. Come up to the fire, ladies.

Mrs. Peters (after taking a step forward): I'm not—cold.

Sheriff (unbuttoning his overcoat and stepping away from the stove as if to mark the beginning of official business): Now, Mr. Hale, before we move things about, you explain to Mr. Henderson just what you saw when you came here yesterday morning.

County Attorney: By the way, has anything been moved? Are things just as you left them yesterday?

Sheriff (looking about): It's just the same. When it dropped below zero last night I thought I'd better send Frank out this morning to make a fire for us—no use getting pneumonia with a big case on, but I told him not to touch anything except the stove—and you know Frank.

County Attorney: Somebody should have been left here yesterday.

Sheriff: Oh—yesterday. When I had to send Frank to Morris Center for that man who went crazy—I want you to know I had my hands full yesterday. I knew you could get back from Omaha by today and as long as I went over everything here myself—

County Attorney: Well, Mr. Hale, tell just what happened when you came here yesterday morning.

Hale: Harry and I had started to town with a load of potatoes. We came along the road from my place and as I got here I said, "I'm going to see if I can't get John Wright to go in with me on a party telephone." I spoke to Wright about it once before and he put me off, saying folks talked too much anyway, and all he asked was peace and quiet—I guess you know about how much he talked himself; but I thought maybe if I went to the house and talked about it before his wife, though I said to Harry that I didn't know as what his wife wanted made much difference to John.

County Attorney: Let's talk about that later, Mr. Hale. I do want to talk about that, but tell now just what happened when you got to the house.

Hale: I didn't hear or see anything; I knocked at the door, and still it was all quiet inside. I knew they must be up, it was past eight o'clock. So I knocked again, and I thought I heard somebody say, "Come in." I wasn't sure, I'm not sure yet, but I opened the door—this door (*indicating the door by which the two women are still standing*) and there in that rocker—(*pointing to it*) sat Mrs. Wright.

(They all look at the rocker.)

County Attorney: What—was she doing?

Hale: She was rockin' back and forth. She had her apron in her hand and was kind of—pleating it.

County Attorney: And how did she—look?

Hale: Well, she looked queer.

County Attorney: How do you mean—queer?

Hale: Well, as if she didn't know what she was going to do next. And kind of done up.

County Attorney: How did she seem to feel about your coming?

Hale: Why, I don't think she minded—one way or other. She didn't pay much attention. I said, "How do, Mrs. Wright, it's cold, ain't it?" And she said, "Is it?"—and went on kind of pleating at her apron. Well, I was surprised; she didn't ask me to come up to the stove, or to set down, but just sat there, not even looking at me, so I said, "I want to see John." And then she—laughed. I guess you would call it a laugh. I thought of Harry and the team outside, so I said a little sharp: "Can't I see John?" "No," she says, kind o' dull like. "Ain't he home?" says I. "Yes," says she, "he's home." "Then why can't I see him?" I asked her, out of patience. "'Cause he's dead," says she. *"Dead?"* says I. She just nodded her head, not getting a bit excited, but rockin' back and forth. "Why—where is he?" says I, not knowing what to say. She just pointed upstairs—like that (*himself pointing to the room above*). I got up, with the idea of going up there. I walked from there to here—then I says, "Why, what did he die of?" "He died of a rope round his neck," says she, and just went on pleatin' at her apron. Well, I went out and called Harry. I thought I might—need help. We went upstairs and there he was lyin'—

County Attorney: I think I'd rather have you go into that upstairs, where you can point it all out. Just go on now with the rest of the story.

Hale: Well, my first thought was to get that rope off. It looked (*stops, his face twitches*) but Harry, he went up to him, and he said, "No, he's dead all right, and we'd better not touch anything." So we went back downstairs. She was still sitting that same way. "Has anybody been notified?" I asked. "No," says she, unconcerned. "Who did this, Mrs. Wright?" said Harry. He said it businesslike—and she stopped pleatin' of her apron. "I don't know," she says. "You don't *know*?" says Harry. "No," says she. "Weren't you sleepin' in the bed with him?" says Harry. "Yes," says she, "but I was on the inside." "Somebody slipped a rope round his neck and strangled him and you didn't wake up?" says Harry. "I didn't wake up," she said after him. We must 'a looked as if we didn't see how that could be, for after a minute she said, "I sleep sound." Harry was going to ask her more questions but I said maybe we ought to let her tell her story first to the coroner, or the sheriff, so Harry went fast as he could to Rivers' place, where there's a telephone.

County Attorney: And what did Mrs. Wright do when she knew that you had gone for the coroner?

Hale: She moved from that chair to this one over here (*pointing to a small chair in the corner*) and just sat there with her hands held together and looking down. I got a feeling that I ought to make some conversation, so I said I had come in to see if John wanted to put in a telephone, and at that she started to laugh, and then she stopped and looked at me—scared. (*The County Attorney, who has had his notebook out, makes a note.*) I dunno, maybe it wasn't scared. I wouldn't like to say it was. Soon Harry got back, and then Dr. Lloyd came, and you, Mr. Peters, and so I guess that's all I know that you don't.

County Attorney (*looking around*): I guess we'll go upstairs first—and then out to the barn and around there. (*To the Sheriff.*) You're convinced that there was nothing important here—nothing that would point to any motive.

Sheriff: Nothing here but kitchen things.

(*The County Attorney, after again looking around the kitchen, opens the door of a cupboard closet. He gets up on a chair and looks on a shelf. Pulls his hand away, sticky.*)

County Attorney: Here's a nice mess.

(*The women draw nearer.*)

Mrs. Peters (*to the other woman*): Oh, her fruit; it did freeze. (*To the County Attorney.*) She worried about that when it turned so cold. She said the fire'd go out and her jars would break.

Sheriff: Well, can you beat the woman! Held for murder and worryin' about her preserves.

County Attorney: I guess before we're through she may have something more serious than preserves to worry about.

Hale: Well, women are used to worrying over trifles.

(*The two women move a little closer together.*)

County Attorney (*with the gallantry of a young politician*): And yet, for all their worries, what would we do without the ladies? (*The women do not unbend. He goes to the sink, takes a dipperful of water from the pail and pouring it into a basin, washes his hands. Starts to wipe them on the roller towel, turns it for a cleaner place.*) Dirty towels! (*Kicks his foot against the pans under the sink.*) Not much of a housekeeper, would you say, ladies?

Mrs. Hale (*stiffly*): There's a great deal of work to be done on a farm.

County Attorney: To be sure. And yet (*with a little bow to her*) I know there are some Dickson county farmhouses which do not have such roller towels.

(*He gives it a pull to expose its full length again.*)

Mrs. Hale: Those towels get dirty awful quick. Men's hands aren't always as clean as they might be.

County Attorney: Ah, loyal to your sex, I see. But you and Mrs. Wright were neighbors. I suppose you were friends, too

Mrs. Hale (*shaking her head*): I've not seen much of her of late years. I've not been in this house—it's more than a year.

County Attorney: And why was that? You didn't like her?

Mrs. Hale: I liked her all well enough. Farmers' wives have their hands full, Mr. Henderson. And then—

County Attorney: Yes—?

Mrs. Hale (*looking about*): It never seemed a very cheerful place.

County Attorney: No—it's not cheerful. I shouldn't say she had the homemaking instinct.

Mrs. Hale: Well, I don't know as Wright had, either.

County Attorney: You mean that they didn't get on very well?

Mrs. Hale: No, I don't mean anything. But I don't think a place'd be any cheerfuller for John Wright's being in it.

County Attorney: I'd like to talk more of that a little later. I want to get the lay of things upstairs now.

(*He goes to the left, where three steps lead to a stair door.*)

Sheriff: I suppose anything Mrs. Peters does'll be all right. She was to take in some clothes for her, you know, and a few little things. We left in such a hurry yesterday.

County Attorney: Yes, but I would like to see what you take, Mrs. Peters, and keep an eye out for anything that might be of use to us.

Mrs. Peters: Yes, Mr. Henderson.

(*The women listen to the men's steps on the stairs, then look about the kitchen.*)

Mrs. Hale: I'd hate to have men coming into my kitchen, snooping around and criticizing.

(*She arranges the pans under the sink which the County Attorney had shoved out of place.*)

Mrs. Peters: Of course it's no more than their duty.

Mrs. Hale: Duty's all right, but I guess that deputy sheriff that came out to make the fire might have got a little of this on. (*Gives the roller towel a pull.*) Wish I'd thought of that sooner. Seems mean to talk about her for not having things slicked up when she had to come away in such a hurry.

Mrs. Peters (*who has gone to a small table in the left rear corner of the room and lifted one end of a towel that covers a pan.*) She had bread set.

(*Stands still.*)

Mrs. Hale (*eyes fixed on a loaf of bread beside the breadbox, which is on a low shelf at the other side of the room. Moves slowly toward it.*): She was going to put this in there. (*Picks up loaf then abruptly drops it. In a manner of returning to familiar things*) It's a shame about her fruit. I wonder if it's all gone. (*Gets up on the chair and looks.*) I think there's some here that's all right, Mrs. Peters. Yes—here; (*holding it toward the window*) this is cherries, too. (*Looking again.*) I declare I believe that's the only one. (*Gets down, bottle in her hand. Goes to the sink and wipes it off on the outside.*) She'll feel awful bad after all her hard work in the hot weather. I remember the afternoon I put up my cherries last summer.

(*She puts the bottle on the big kitchen table, center of the room. With a sigh, is about to sit down in the rocking-chair. Before she is seated realizes what chair it is; with a slow look at it, steps back. The chair which she has touched rocks back and forth.*)

Mrs. Peters: Well, I must get those things from the front room closet. (*She goes to the door at the right, but after looking into the other room, steps back.*) You coming with me, Mrs. Hale? You could help me carry them.

(*They go in the other room; reappear, Mrs. Peters carrying a dress and skirt, Mrs. Hale following with a pair of shoes.*)

Mrs. Peters: My, it's cold in there.

(*She puts the clothes on the big table, and hurries to the stove.*)

Mrs. Hale (examining her skirt): Wright was close. I think maybe that's why she kept so much to herself. She didn't even belong to the Ladies Aid. I suppose she felt she couldn't do her part, and then you don't enjoy things when you feel shabby. She used to wear pretty clothes and be lively, when she was Minnie Foster, one of the town girls singing in the choir. But that—oh, that was thirty years ago. This all you was to take in?

Mrs. Peters: She said she wanted an apron. Funny thing to want, for there isn't much to get you dirty in jail, goodness knows. But I suppose just to make her feel more natural. She said they was in the top drawer in this cupboard. Yes, here. And then her little shawl that always hung behind the door. (*Opens stair doors and looks.*) Yes, here it is.

(*Quickly shuts door leading upstairs.*)

Mrs. Hale (abruptly moving toward her): Mrs. Peters?

Mrs. Peters: Yes, Mrs. Hale?

Mrs. Hale: Do you think she did it?

Mrs. Peters (in a frightened voice): Oh, I don't know.

Mrs. Hale: Well, I don't think she did. Asking for an apron and her little shawl. Worrying about her fruit.

Mrs. Peters (starts to speak, glances up, where footsteps are heard in the room above. In a low voice): Mr. Peters says it looks bad for her. Mr. Henderson is awful sarcastic in a speech and he'll make fun of her sayin' she didn't wake up.

Mrs. Hale: Well, I guess John Wright didn't wake when they was slipping that rope under his neck.

Mrs. Peters: No, it's strange. It must have been done awful crafty and still. They say it was such a—funny way to kill a man, rigging it all up like that.

Mrs. Hale: That's just what Mr. Hale said. There was a gun in the house. He says that's what he can't understand.

Mrs. Peters: Mr. Henderson said coming out that what was needed for the case was a motive; something to show anger, or—sudden feeling.

Mrs. Hale (who is standing by the table): Well, I don't see any signs of anger around here. (*She puts her hand on the dish towel which lies on the table, stands looking down at the table, one half of which is clean, the other half messy.*) It's wiped to here. (*Makes a move as if to finish work, then turns and looks at loaf of bread outside the breadbox. Drops towel. In that voice of coming back to familiar things*) Wonder how they are finding things upstairs. I hope she had it a little more red-up up there. You know, it seems kind of *sneaking*. Locking her up in town and then coming out here and trying to get her own house to turn against her!

Mrs. Peters: But Mrs. Hale, the law is the law.

Mrs. Hale: I s'pose 'tis. (*Unbuttoning her coat.*) Better loosen up your things, Mrs. Peters. You won't feel them when you go out.

(*Mrs. Peters takes off her fur tippet, goes to hang it on hook at back of room, stands looking at the under part of the small corner table.*)

Mrs. Peters: She was piecing a quilt.

(She brings the large sewing basket and they look at the bright pieces.)

Mrs. Hale: It's log cabin pattern. Pretty, isn't it? I wonder if she was goin' to quilt it or just knot it?

(Footsteps have been heard coming down the stairs. The Sheriff enters followed by Hale and the County Attorney.)

Sheriff: They wonder if she was going to quilt it or just knot it!

(The men laugh; the women look abashed.)

County Attorney (rubbing his hands over the stove): Frank's fire didn't do much up there, did it? Well, let's go out to the barn and get that cleared up.

(The men go outside.)

Mrs. Hale (resentfully): I don't know as there's anything so strange, our takin' up our time with little things while we're waiting for them to get the evidence. *(She sits down at the big table smoothing out a block with decision.)* I don't see as it's anything to laugh about.
Mrs. Peters (apologetically): Of course they've got awful important things on their minds.

(Pulls up a chair and joins Mrs. Hale at the table.)

Mrs. Hale (examining another block): Mrs. Peters, look at this one. Here, this is the one she was working on, and look at the sewing! All the rest of it has been so nice and even. And look at this! It's all over the place! Why, it looks as if she didn't know what she was about!

(After she has said this they look at each other, then start to glance back at the door. After an instant Mrs. Hale has pulled at a knot and ripped the sewing.)

Mrs. Peters: Oh, what are you doing, Mrs. Hale?
Mrs. Hale (mildly): Just pulling out a stitch or two that's not sewed very good. *(Threading a needle.)* Bad sewing always made me fidgety.
Mrs. Peters (nervously): I don't think we ought to touch things.
Mrs. Hale: I'll just finish up this end. *(Suddenly stopping and leaning forward.)* Mrs. Peters?
Mrs. Peters: Yes, Mrs. Hale?
Mrs. Hale: What do you suppose she was so nervous about?
Mrs. Peters: Oh—I don't know. I don't know as she was nervous. I sometimes sew awful queer when I'm just tired. *(Mrs. Hale starts to say something, looks at Mrs. Peters, then goes on sewing.)* Well, I must get these things wrapped up. They may be through sooner than we think. *(Putting apron and other things together.)* I wonder where I can find a piece of paper, and string.
Mrs. Hale: In that cupboard, maybe.
Mrs. Peters (Looking in cupboard.): Why, here's a birdcage. *(Holds it up.)* Did she have a bird, Mrs. Hale?
Mrs. Hale: Why, I don't know whether she did or not—I've not been here for so long. There was a man around last year selling canaries cheap, but I don't know as she took one; maybe she did. She used to sing real pretty herself.

Mrs. Peters (glancing around): Seems funny to think of a bird here. But she must have had one, or why would she have a cage? I wonder what happened to it.

Mrs. Hale: I s'pose maybe the cat got it.

Mrs. Peters: No, she didn't have a cat. She's got that feeling some people have about cats—being afraid of them. My cat got in her room and she was real upset and asked me to take it out.

Mrs. Hale: My sister Bessie was like that. Queer, ain't it?

Mrs. Peters (examining the cage): Why, look at this door. It's broke. One hinge is pulled apart.

Mrs. Hale (looking too): Looks as if someone must have been rough with it.

Mrs. Peters: Why, yes.

(*She brings the cage forward and puts it on the table.*)

Mrs. Hale: I wish if they're going to find any evidence they'd be about it. I don't like this place.

Mrs. Peters: But I'm awful glad you came with me, Mrs. Hale. It would be lonesome for me sitting here alone.

Mrs. Hale: It would, wouldn't it? (*Dropping her sewing.*) But I tell you what I do wish, Mrs. Peters. I wish I had come over sometimes when *she* was here. I—(*looking around the room*)—wish I had.

Mrs. Peters: But of course you were awful busy, Mrs. Hale—your house and your children.

Mrs. Hale: I could've come. I stayed away because it weren't cheerful—and that's why I ought to have come. I—I've never liked this place. Maybe because it's down in a hollow and you don't see the road. I dunno what it is but it's a lonesome place and always was. I wish I had come over to see Minnie Foster sometimes. I can see now—

(*Shakes her head.*)

Mrs. Peters: Well, you mustn't reproach yourself, Mrs. Hale. Somehow we just don't see how it is with other folks until—something comes up.

Mrs. Hale: Not having children makes less work—but it makes a quiet house, and Wright out to work all day, and no company when he did come in. Did you know John Wright, Mrs. Peters?

Mrs. Peters: Not to know him; I've seen him in town. They say he was a good man.

Mrs. Hale: Yes—good; he didn't drink, and kept his word as well as most, I guess, and paid his debts. But he was a hard man, Mrs. Peters. Just to pass the time of day with him—(*Shivers.*) Like a raw wind that gets to the bone. (*Pauses her eye falling on the cage.*) I should think she would 'a wanted a bird. But what do you suppose went with it?

Mrs. Peters: I don't know, unless it got sick and died.

(*She reaches over and swings the broken door, swings it again. Both women watch it.*)

Mrs. Hale: You weren't raised round here, were you? (*Mrs. Peters shakes her head.*) You didn't know—her?

Mrs. Peters: Not till they brought her yesterday.

Mrs. Hale: She—come to think of it, she was kind of like a bird herself—real sweet and pretty, but kind of timid and—fluttery. How—she—did—change. (*Silence; then as if struck by a happy thought and relieved to get back to everyday things)* Tell you what, Mrs. Peters, why don't you take the quilt in with you? It might take up her mind.

Mrs. Peters: Why, I think that's a real nice idea, Mrs. Hale. There couldn't possibly be any objection to it, could there? Now, just what would I take? I wonder if her patches are in here—and her things.

(They look in the sewing basket.)

Mrs. Hale: Here's some red. I expect this has got sewing things in it. *(Brings out a fancy box.)* What a pretty box. Looks like something somebody would give you. Maybe her scissors are in here. *(Opens box. Suddenly puts her hand to her nose.)* Why *(Mrs. Peters bends nearer, then turns her face away.)* there's something wrapped up in this piece of silk.

Mrs. Peters: Why, this isn't her scissors.

Mrs. Hale (lifting the silk): Oh, Mrs. Peters—it's—

(Mrs. Peters bends closer.)

Mrs. Peters: It's the bird.

Mrs. Hale (jumping up): But, Mrs. Peters—look at it! Its neck! Look at its neck! It's all—other side to.

Mrs. Peters: Somebody—wrung—its—neck.

(Their eyes meet. A look of growing comprehension, of horror. Steps are heard outside. Mrs. Hale slips box under quilt pieces, and sinks into her chair. Enter Sheriff and County Attorney. Mrs. Peters rises.)

County Attorney (as one turning from serious things to little pleasantries): Well, ladies, have you decided whether she was going to quilt it or knot it?

Mrs. Peters: We think she was going to—knot it.

County Attorney: Well, that's interesting, I'm sure. *(Seeing the bird-cage.)* Has the bird flown?

Mrs. Hale (putting more quilt pieces over the box): We think the—cat got it.

County Attorney (preoccupied): Is there a cat?

(Mrs. Hale glances in a quick covert way at Mrs. Peters.)

Mrs. Peters: Well, not now. They're superstitious, you know. They leave.

County Attorney (to Sheriff Peters, continuing an interrupted conversation): No sign at all of anyone having come from the outside. Their own rope. Now let's go up again and go over it piece by piece. *(They start upstairs.)* It would have to have been someone who knew just the—

(Mrs. Peters sits down. The two women sit there not looking at one another, but as if peering into something and at the same time holding back. When they talk now it is in the manner of feeling their way over strange ground, as if afraid of what they are saying, but as if they can not help saying it.)

Mrs. Hale: She liked the bird. She was going to bury it in that pretty box.

Mrs. Peters (in a whisper): When I was a girl—my kitten—there was a boy took a hatchet, and before my eyes—and before I could get there—*(Covers her face an instant.)* If they hadn't held me back I would have—*(Catches herself, looks upstairs where steps are heard, falters weakly)*—hurt him.

Mrs. Hale (with a slow look around her): I wonder how it would seem never to have had any children around. (*Pause.*) No, Wright wouldn't like the bird—a thing that sang. She used to sing. He killed that, too.

Mrs. Peters (moving uneasily): We don't know who killed the bird.

Mrs. Hale: I knew John Wright.

Mrs. Peters: It was an awful thing was done in this house that night, Mrs. Hale. Killing a man while he slept, slipping a rope around his neck that choked the life out of him.

Mrs. Hale: His neck. Choked the life out of him.

(*Her hand goes out and rests on the birdcage.*)

Mrs. Peters (with rising voice): We don't know who killed him. We don't know.

Mrs. Hale (her own feeling not interrupted): If there'd been years and years of nothing, then a bird to sing to you, it would be awful—still, after the bird was still.

Mrs. Peters (something within her speaking): I know what stillness is. When we homesteaded in Dakota, and my first baby died—after he was two years old, and me with no other then—

Mrs. Hale (moving): How soon do you suppose they'll be through, looking for the evidence?

Mrs. Peters: I know what stillness is. (*Pulling herself back.*) The law has got to punish crime, Mrs. Hale.

Mrs. Hale (not as if answering that): I wish you'd seen Minnie Foster when she wore a white dress with blue ribbons and stood up there in the choir and sang. (*A look around the room.*) Oh, I *wish* I'd come over here once in a while! That was a crime! That was a crime! Who's going to punish that?

Mrs. Peters (looking upstairs): We mustn't—take on.

Mrs. Hale: I might have known she needed help! I know how things can be—for women. I tell you, it's queer, Mrs. Peters. We live close together and we live far apart. We all go through the same things—it's all just a different kind of the same thing. (*Brushes her eyes; noticing the bottle of fruit, reaches out for it.*) If I was you I wouldn't tell her her fruit was gone. Tell her it *ain't.* Tell her it's all right. Take this in to prove it to her. She—she may never know whether it was broke or not.

Mrs. Peters (takes the bottle, looks about for something to wrap it in: takes petticoat from the clothes brought from the other room, very nervously begins winding this around the bottle. In a false voice): My, it's a good thing the men couldn't hear us. Wouldn't they just laugh! Getting all stirred up over a little thing like a—dead canary. As if that could have anything to do with—with—wouldn't they *laugh!*

(*The men are heard coming downstairs.*)

Mrs. Hale (under her breath): Maybe they would—maybe they wouldn't.

County Attorney: No, Peters, it's all perfectly clear except a reason for doing it. But you know juries when it comes to women. If there was some definite thing. Something to show—something to make a story about—a thing that would connect up with this strange way of doing it—

(*The women's eyes meet for an instant. Enter Hale from outer door.*)

Hale: Well, I've got the team around. Pretty cold out there.

County Attorney: I'm going to stay here a while by myself. (*To the Sheriff.*) You can send Frank out for me, can't you? I want to go over everything. I'm not satisfied that we can't do better.

Sheriff: Do you want to see what Mrs. Peters is going to take in?

(*The County Attorney goes to the table, picks up the apron, laughs.*)

County Attorney: Oh, I guess they're not very dangerous things the ladies have picked out. (*Moves a few things about, disturbing the quilt pieces which cover the box. Steps back.*) No, Mrs. Peters doesn't need supervising. For that matter, a sheriff's wife is married to the law. Ever think of it that way, Mrs. Peters?

Mrs. Peters: Not—just that way.

Sheriff (chuckling): Married to the law. (*Moves toward the other room.*) I just want you to come in here a minute, George. We ought to take a look at these windows.

County Attorney (scoffingly): Oh, windows!

Sheriff: We'll be right out, Mr. Hale.

(*Hale goes outside. The Sheriff follows the County Attorney into the other room. Then Mrs. Hale rises, hands tight together, looking intensely at Mrs. Peters, whose eyes make a slow turn, finally meeting Mrs. Hale's. A moment Mrs. Hale holds her, then her own eyes point the way to where the box is concealed. Suddenly Mrs. Peters throws back quilt pieces and tries to put the box in the bag she is wearing. It is too big. She opens box, starts to take bird out, cannot touch it, goes to pieces, stands there helpless. Sound of a knob turning in the other room. Mrs. Hale snatches the box and puts it in the pocket of her big coat. Enter County Attorney and Sheriff.*)

County Attorney (facetiously): Well, Henry, at least we found out that she was not going to quilt it. She was going to—what is it you call it, ladies?

Mrs. Hale (her hand against her pocket): We call it—knot it, Mr. Henderson.[2]

CURTAIN

Literal comprehension questions

1. Who is the main character? What is he or she like? What values does he or she hold? Are there one or more other main characters? What are they like? What values do they hold?
2. What other characters are important in the play?
3. Where and when is everything happening? (setting)
4. What action (plot) is taking place?

Interpretive comprehension questions

5. How does the playwright use events, characters, or dialogue to develop the play's conflict?
6. What is the theme or message of the play?
7. How is the title related to the theme?
8. What effect does the ending have?

2. *Source:* Susan Glaspell, *Plays.* Dodd, 1920.

Affective comprehension questions

9. What feeling do you have for the main character? the other characters?
10. What passages do you find well written?
11. Why do you like or not like the play?

WHAT DO YOU THINK?

The most important thing we face is a rediscovery of community. We're a very individually oriented country, and I love that. I'd rather be more individually oriented than community oriented like the Soviets or the Chinese. But somewhere along the line we've gotten a peculiar idea of what an individual is, what individual pleasure is, what individual purpose is. We see everything in terms of personal autonomy—in terms not only of my rights under law, but also in terms of pleasure, in terms of privilege. I think we've trained a whole generation of people to think in terms of the isolated "I." But anyone like myself, trained in biology, knows that the human being is not like an amoeba, it's not a thing. We're much more like coral, we're interconnected. We cannot survive without each other. . . . The people who are living in Harlem, who cannot go out to shop at night because of the crack addicts, are in prison, and we've helped create the prison by ignoring what community means in this country.

Willard Gaylin, bioethicist

APPENDIX
PROCEDURE FOR DOING A RESEARCH PAPER

Some of the basic steps in writing a research paper are listed below.[1]

1. Select a subject. In making the choice of a topic, consider the following factors:
   a. Is this a subject of sufficient interest to you that you can make it interesting to your readers?
   b. Can you study it seriously in the length of time allotted for writing the paper?
   c. Can you cover it adequately in the number of words prescribed by your instructor?
   d. Is it likely that you will find sufficient material on it to write a paper, or is it too new, too highly specialized, or too limited in appeal to have received coverage in books, newspapers, magazines, or other sources?

2. Restrict your subject if the topic you have chosen is too broad or too general for the assigned paper.
   a. Look in the library catalog under your subject and read the subject headings immediately following to see how that subject is subdivided. Notice the subject headings listed at the bottom of each card to find further subdivisions and related headings. For example, if you are looking for material on the general topic "music," you may find in the catalog:

Music	Music, National
Music, American	Music, Popular (songs, etc.)
Music, American—Discography	Musical fiction
Music as a profession	Musical instruments,
See Music—Vocational guidance	Electronic
Music festivals	
Music, Gipsy	
See Folk Music—Gipsy	

   b. Find the subject in a periodical index; notice subdivisions; e.g.:

Music	Musical performance
Music, Black	*See* Music—Performance
See Black music	Musicians
Music festivals	*See also*
Music in advertising	Orchestras
Musical instruments	Rock Musicians
Musical instruments, Electronic	

---

1. *Source:* Jean K. Gates, *Guide to the Use of Libraries and Information Sources,* 6th ed. McGraw, 1989, 308–316.

    c. See how a general encyclopedia index subdivides your subject.

Music	Music box
Acoustics	Music festivals
Band	Music history
Computers	Musical comedy
Dance	Musical Instruments: Types
Folk	Musical theater
Jazz	
Rhythm	

    d. You may restrict your topic according to a period of time or geographical location or according to historical, social, cultural, or political significance; for example:

Music in Colonial America
The Contribution of Music to Media Production
Military Marches
Music in Television Commercials
The Influence of the Computer on Music

    e. In the following list of subjects, notice the progression from general to specific:

Music
National Music
National music—United States
Music for national holidays
Music for the Fourth of July
Yankee Doodle Dandy

3. Choose the phase of your subject that you wish to investigate.
4. Determine the chronological period in which your subject falls.
5. Decide upon the purpose of your paper.
    a. Is it to inform?
    b. Is it to show progress?
    c. Is it to analyze an event, a situation, or a period?
    d. Is it to persuade and recommend?
6. Make a tentative statement of your thesis or purpose—that is, the proposition you will attempt to defend, clarify, or develop. For example, "Monasticism was of major importance in the preservation and development of literature during the Middle Ages," or "The printing press hastened the era of discovery and exploration."
    a. Analyze your thesis as to the subject areas it includes or touches: geography, sociology, economics, history, literature, politics.
    b. Decide what kinds of sources will provide the information you will need to write your paper.
        (1) Primary sources[2]—interviews, questionnaires, letters, diaries, manuscripts, memoirs
        (2) Secondary sources—books, journals, encyclopedias, other reference books, and nonbook materials.
7. Begin your preliminary search for material. . . . Since subject headings are the key to the library catalog, the indexes, and most reference books, it is necessary, before using any of these sources, to determine the headings under which your subject may be listed.

---

2. Primary sources are those materials which have not been interpreted by another person. Secondary sources are materials which have been reported, analyzed, or interpreted by other persons.

a. Consult the library catalogs and indexes to find the books and other materials in your library in which your subject, or any relevant phase of it, is discussed. Read the entire card or citation carefully to see what the source covers, the amount and kind of illustrative material it includes, the bibliographical references provided, the number of topics treated, and the topic which is given the greatest emphasis. Study the subject headings and *see* references as indications of other subjects which will lead to material. For example, if your subject is "folk music," some of the headings under which you will find material are:

Folk music
See also
    Folk dance music
    Folk-songs
    Folk dancing
    Folk-lore
Folk music, American
    See also Country music
Folk music, French
Folk music, Gipsy

Country music
See also
    Bluegrass music
    Fiddle tunes
    Gospel music
    Guitar—Methods (country)
    Country and Western music
Country musicians

b. Take the class number or numbers, and browse in these sections of the stacks, looking at the tables of contents and the indexes of books which may be helpful.

c. Consult a printed bibliography or guide to find material on your subject which may not be listed in the library catalog, such as parts of books, pamphlets, and reports.

d. Use a general dictionary for general definitions; use a subject dictionary for specialized definitions and terminology.

e. Find an overview of your topic in a general encyclopedia, and then consult a subject encyclopedia for technical and specialized information. Consult the bibliography at the end of the article for additional readings and the index volume for other headings under which to look; remember than an encyclopedia is *only* the starting point.

f. Use general and subject indexes to find recent material in periodicals and to find selections in collected works.

g. Consult a handbook for statistical information or for identification of allusions to persons, events, dates, and legendary or mythological figures.

h. Look up important persons connected with your subject in a biographical dictionary.

i. Establish geographical locations and facts with the aid of an atlas or a gazetteer.

j. Consult nonbook sources—microforms and visual and audiovisual materials—for information on your subject; you may want to use pictures, slides, or other forms to illustrate, clarify, or support points you wish to make in your paper.

k. Look for current information and statistics in government publications, especially on topics in the social sciences, history, education, and the sciences.

l. Use primary sources whenever possible.

It is essential that you use a variety of sources in order to obtain a broad view of your subject; to see its various aspects; to discover the factors which influenced or contributed to it; to know the individuals, groups, or organizations associated with it; to become acquainted with current thinking as well as with past opinion regarding it; and to have some understanding of the terminology of the field in question.

8. Begin preliminary reading.
   a. Read a background or overview article in a textbook or in a history of the subject.
   b. Examine a general article in an encyclopedia.
   c. Read a popular article in a periodical.
   d. Skim through the material at first.
   e. Make brief notes of references for later serious reading, giving adequate information for finding these references easily.
9. As you examine material, make a tentative bibliography of the materials which you think you will use. (See Figure 25.1.)
   a. Make the bibliography on cards.
      (1) Use cards of uniform size.
      (2) Use a separate card for each bibliographical reference.
   b. Give basic information for each reference.
      (1) Author
      (2) Title
      (3) Facts of publication
      (4) Page or pages on which the information you are using can be found
   c. Include a brief descriptive statement of each work, indicating the content and its usefulness for your subject.
10. Make a tentative outline of the major divisions of your paper. A possible outline of the major topics in a paper on "The Music Festival in the United States" is as follows:

    I. Definition and origin of the music festival
    II. Beginnings in the United States
       A. Nineteenth century
       B. Early twentieth century
    III. Development in the United States since the 1960s
       A. Sponsors
       B. Themes
       C. Artists, performers
       D. Seasons
    IV. Popularity
       A. Number
       B. Locations
       C. Attendance
    V. Contribution to the cultural life in the United States

11. Begin serious reading.
12. Take notes. (See Figure 25.2.)
    a. The kinds of notes you may take include:
       (1) A restatement, in your own words, of the thought or thoughts of an author. It is important that in your paraphrase you do not lose the meaning of the original statement when you take it out of context.
       (2) A direct quotation, copied exactly, including punctuation. Any omission must be indicated by an ellipsis (. . .); any interpolation must be indicated by brackets ([ ]). Credit for a quotation must be given in a footnote.[3]
       (3) A critical or evaluative comment about a book or a person.
    b. Use cards for your notes.
       (1) Use cards of uniform size throughout.

---

3. A footnote gives credit for—or explains—a specific part of the text. Failure to give the source for a quotation or a paraphrase in which the language, thoughts, or ideas of another person are used as one's own is plagiarism.

```
Ref
ML     New Oxford History of Music.   Vol. X:
160         The Modern Age 1890-1960.   London:
N4          Oxford University Press, 1974.

            The background of music in the United
       States during the period 1918-1960 is
       discussed on pp. 569-574.
```

```
       Vinton, John.   "Change of Mind."
            Music Review, XXXV (November, 1974),
            301-318.

            Discusses changes in music in the
       19th and 20th centuries.
```

```
       Ref
       ML      Fuld, James J. The Book of World-
       113          Famous Music--Classical, Popular
       F8           and Folk.   Revised and enlarged edition.
                    New York:  Crown Publishers, 1971.

                    Gives information about many hundreds of
            the best known musical compositions.
```

FIGURE 25.1
Sample bibliography cards.

```
Ref
ML     Thompson, Oscar (ed.).  The International
100        Cyclopaedia of Music and Musicians.
T47        10th ed.  Edited by Bruce Bohle.  New
           York: Dodd, Mead & Company, 1975.

           Before primitive man could speak
       intelligibly, he expressed feelings of
       joy, grief, and fear in bodily movements
       accompanied by rhythmic noises.  (p. 990)
```

```
Ref
N      Encyclopedia of World Art.  New York:
31         McGraw-Hill Book Company, 1959-
E533       1968. 15 vols.

           "Among the most important factors
       that influence the evolution of musical
       instruments are...the prevailing style
       of the period and...the status of
       technology."  (Vol. X, p. 431)
```

```
Ref
ML     Fink, Robert, and Ricci, Robert.  The
100        Language of Twentieth Century Music:
F55        A Dictionary of Terms.  New York:
           Schirmer Books, A Division of Macmillan,
           1975.

           Useful for brief definitions of terms
       used in contemporary music.
```

FIGURE 25.2
Sample note cards: (top) restatement or paraphrase; (center) quotation; (bottom) evaluative comment.

  (2) Give complete bibliographical information on the first card for each reference:
   (a) Author's full name
   (b) Complete title
   (c) Imprint: place of publication, publisher, date
   (d) Pages and volume
   (e) Month, day, year, volume, and pages of periodical articles
   (f) Month, day, year, and pages of newspaper articles
 c. Use one card for each reference. If more than one card is required to complete a note, number all cards and put the author's last name on all cards after the first.
 d. Leave space at the top of the card for the subject headings, which will be the subdivisions of your outline.

13. Formulate your thesis.
 a. State it simply, expressing the basic idea that you will develop.
 b. Restrict it to one approach to the subject.
 c. Avoid using ambiguous words or phrases.
14. Study your notes in order to restrict your subject further.
15. Make a preliminary detailed outline, either topical or in sentence form. Whatever form you choose, use it throughout your outline.
 a. Make sure that your outline is organized in a logical manner, that each division and subdivision receives proper emphasis, and that each part of the outline is in the appropriate relationship to other parts of the outline.
 b. Fill in the gaps in your outline by additional reading and note taking.
 c. Discard irrelevant material.
16. Remake your outline.
17. Write the first draft of your paper.
18. Use footnotes or endnotes when necessary.
 a. Give the source of a direct quotation.
 b. Acknowledge the source of an opinion or a discussion which you have paraphrased or of any specific material which cannot be considered common knowledge.
 c. Give credit for statistical information, graphs, and charts you have used.
 d. Suggest additional reading on a particular point.
 e. Add an explanation to clarify or expand a statement in the text of your paper.
 f. Make cross references to other parts of your paper.
19. Make a bibliography.
 a. Give sources of materials you have used in writing the paper.
 b. Suggest additional reading materials.
 c. Include an entry for each work mentioned in a footnote.
20. Revise your paper.
21. Evaluate the entire paper, as to clarity of purpose, proper emphasis of important ideas and divisions, elimination of gaps and irrelevant material, accuracy in presenting or in interpreting facts, appropriateness of the choice of words, correctness of grammatical structure and form, unity and coherence in writing, adequacy of documentation, and consistency of bibliographical and footnote form.
22. Write the final draft of your paper.

Acknowledgments

Text Credits

Woody Allen. "Death Knocks" from *Getting Even* by Woody Allen, Copyright © 1971 by Woody Allen. Reprinted by permission of Random House Inc.

American Museum of Natural History. "Galloping Wild Boar" is reproduced by Courtesy Department of Library Services, American Museum of Natural History.

Thomas A. Bailey and David M. Kennedy. From *The American Pageant* Eighth Edition, Copyright © 1987 by D. C. Heath and Company. Reprinted by permission.

Jules R. Benjamin. Copyright © 1975 by Jules R. Benjamin from the book *A Student's Guide to History* and reprinted with permission from St. Martin's Press, Inc. NY, NY.

John M. Blum. Excerpts from *The National Experience*, Seventh edition by John M. Blum et al, copyright © 1989 by Harcourt Brace Jovanovich, Inc., reprinted by permission of the publisher.

Joseph Campbell. From *Myths to Live By* by Joseph Campbell. Copyright © 1972 by Joseph Campbell. Used by permission of Viking Penguin, a division of Penguin Books USA Inc.

Robert A. Dahl. *Modern Political Analysis*, 4e, © 1984. Reprinted by permission of Prentice Hall, Englewood Cliffs, New Jersey.

Nell Dale. From *Programming in Pascal*, Copyright © 1989 by D. C. Heath and Company. Reprinted by permission.

Lawrence Ferlinghetti. "The World Is a Beautiful Place" from *A Coney Island of the Mind*. Copyright © 1958 by Lawrence Ferlinghetti. Reprinted by permission of New Directions Publishing Corporation.

Robert Frost. "Stopping by Woods on a Snowy Evening" from *The Poetry of Robert Frost* edited by Edward Connery Lathem. Copyright 1923, © 1969 by Holt, Rinehart and Winston. Copyright 1951 by Robert Frost. Reprinted by permission of Henry Holt and Company, Inc.

Steven D. Garber. From *Biology: A Self-Teaching Guide*, Copyright © 1989. Reprinted by permission of John Wiley & Sons, Inc.

John A. Garraty. Excerpts from *The American Nation, A History of the United States to 1877*, Volumes I and II, 4th ed. By John A. Garraty. Copyright © 1966, 1971, 1975, 1979 by John A. Garraty. Reprinted by permission of HarperCollins Publishers.

Jean Key Gates. Excerpts from *Guide to the Use of Libraries and Information Sources*, Sixth Edition, copyright © 1989. Reprinted by permission of McGraw-Hill Publishing Company.

Susan Glaspell. "Trifles" from *Plays* by Susan Glaspell, Dodd, Mead, 1920.

Morris Hein. From *Foundations of College Chemistry*, 7th Edition, by Morris Hein. Copyright © 1990 by Wadsworth Inc. Reprinted by permission of Brooks/Cole Publishing Company, Pacific Grove, CA 93950.

Ernest Hemmingway. Reprinted with permission of Charles Scribner's Sons, an imprint of Macmillan Publishing Company, from *A Farewell to Arms* by Ernest Hemingway. Copyright 1929 by Charles Scribner's Sons, renewed 1957 by Ernest Hemingway.

Roger B. Henkle. Excerpts from *Reading the Novel* by Roger B. Henkle. Copyright © 1977 by Roger B. Henkle. Reprinted by permission of HarperCollins Publishers.

Morris K. Holland. From *Introductory Psychology*, Copyright © 1981 by D. C. Heath and Company. Reprinted by permission.

Langston Hughes. "Mother to Son" from *Selected Poems* by Langston Hughes, Copyright 1926 by Alfred A. Knopf, Inc. and renewed 1954 by Langston Hughes. Reprinted by permission of the publisher.

Rodney Stark. From *Sociology*, 2/e by Rodney Stark © 1987 by Wadsworth, Inc. Reprinted by permission of the publisher.

Cecie Starr and Ralph Taggart. From *Biology: The Unity and Diversity of Life*, 5/e by Cecie Starr and Ralph Taggart © 1989 by Wadsworth, Inc. Reprinted by permission of the publisher.

Savatore Tocci. From *Biology Projects for Young Scientists* by Savatore Tocci, copyright © 1987. Reprinted by permission of Franklin Watts, Inc.

Joseph F. Trimmer. "Telling Stories About Stories," from Teaching English in the Two-Year College, October, 1990. Copyright 1990 by the National Council of Teachers of English. Reprinted with permission.

Mary Ann Frese Witt, et al. From *The Humanities*, Vol. I and Vol. II, Second Edition, Copyright © 1985 by D. C. Heath and Company. Reprinted by permission.

Wold and Cykler. From *Introduction to Music and Art in the Western World*, Copyright © 1985. Reprinted by permission of William C. Brown.

Edward F. Zeigler and Matia Finn-Stevenson. From *Children*, Copyright © 1987 by D. C. Heath and Company. Reprinted by permission.

Photo Credits

p. **28,** *Duffy* by Bruce Hammond © 1985, Universal Press Syndicate. Reprinted with permission. All rights reserved; p. **188,** Neg. #317635, Courtesy Department of Library Services, American Museum of Natural History; p. **289,** Richard Chase; p. **367** (a) *top left,* Photo Researchers, © Charles M. Falco; p. **367** (b) *top right,* Fundamental Photographs, © Paul Silverman; p. **367** (c) *bottom,* Fundamental Photographs; p. **400,** *top,* Reproduced by courtesy of the Trustees, The National Gallery, London; p. **400,** *left foot,* Courtesy of the Trustees of the Victoria and Albert Museum, London; p. **400,** *right foot,* Wallace Collection, London; p. **406,** The Pillsbury Company and Leo Burnett Advertising; p. **408,** *left,* Courtesy of AT&T; p. **408,** *right,* Samsonite Corporation, Denver, CO; p. **409,** *top,* Armstrong World Industries, Inc; p. **409,** *foot,* Mannington Mills, Inc., Salem, NJ; p. **410,** Courtesy of Congoleum Corporation, Resilient Flooring, Kearney, NJ; p. **411,** Courtesy RCA/Consumer Electronics Division.

Index